AVID

READER

PRESS

The

Encyclopedia

of

New York

BY THE EDITORS
OF

SIMON & SCHUSTER

NEW YORK | LONDON | TORONTO | SYDNEY | NEW DELHI

AVID READER PRESS
An Imprint of Simon & Schuster, Inc.
1230 Avenue of the Americas
New York, NY 10020

First Avid Reader Press hardcover
edition October 2020

AVID READER PRESS and
colophon are trademarks of
Simon & Schuster, Inc.

For information about special
discounts for bulk purchases,
please contact
Simon & Schuster Special Sales at
1-866-506-1949 or
business@simonandschuster.com.

The Simon & Schuster Speakers
Bureau can bring authors to your
live event. For more information
or to book an event contact the
Simon & Schuster Speakers
Bureau at 1-866-248-3049 or
visit our website at
www.simonspeakers.com.

Manufactured in the United
States of America

10 9 8 7 6 5 4 3 2 1

Library of Congress Cataloging-
in-Publication Data

ISBN 978-1-5011-6695-2
ISBN 978-1-5011-6696-9 (ebook)

Contents

The first sketch of the I ♥ NY logo,
made on the back of an envelope during
a New York City taxicab ride.
DRAWING BY MILTON GLASER, 1976

Introduction

EVERY CITY HAS A FOUNDATION STORY, and a lot of those stories foretell the future. Romulus slew his brother, Remus, and subsequently founded Rome upon the latter's burial place, framing the imperial rapaciousness and bloodshed to come. Chicago's earliest speculators bet on its future as a transit hub, and two centuries later, we still all change planes at O'Hare. A mobster built Las Vegas out of thin desert air, aided by a huge federal subsidy in the form of Hoover Dam, to separate people from their paychecks while letting them think they'd had a great time: a con made manifest.

And New York? From its beginnings as part of New Netherland, it was fundamentally mercantile, effectively an arm of the Dutch West India Company. Even before that, when in 1609 Henry Hudson came up the river that now bears his name, he made landfall, met a few native Lenape people, and headed back to England with a small cargo of furs. Indigenous New Yorkers had encountered a European for the first time, and already they'd made an export deal.

At first, the city's product came mostly from the land—beaver pelts, lumber—but within a few generations, New Amsterdam, and then New York, established itself as a manufacturing town. Take a walk downtown, and you can still see that physical city. Those little brick buildings in the South Street Seaport? To modern eyes they may look like townhouses, but in fact many were warehouses for dry goods and chandlery, feeding the eighteenth century's global trade. The cast-iron buildings of Soho were once factories; before the widespread use of electricity, their high ceilings and huge windows admitted more light for the underwear-makers and Linotypers working within. Even those buildings' façades were themselves made here, in foundries nearby. Until the 1960s, nearly every piece of store-bought clothing in America came from New York's cutting tables and sergers. Early in the twentieth century, there was a car factory in Times Square.

As the scale of the world's appetites grew, most of that kind of heavy manufacturing shifted to places that fronted on highways instead of narrow streets, with big truck bays instead of cramped elevators, where the real estate wasn't so precious and the rents didn't eat up everyone's margins. (The last heavy industry in Times Square—the basement pressroom of the New York *Times*—closed in 1997.) As the sewing machines stopped whirring and the forges cooled, another and even larger export came to dominate: intellectual property. In parallel with the decline of the manufacturing city grew an equally robust production line for movements and ideas. "Manhattan as laboratory," as the architect-philosopher Rem Koolhaas called it, is "a factory of man-made experience." Even if an idea does not strictly start here, New York is, disproportionately often, the place where it is dropped off, trimmed to size, matted and framed, and displayed to everyone with an explanatory wall text.

As the nineteenth century gave way to the twentieth, authors and academics came here to live and write, more than ever before. Even those who didn't still published through New York. So had the music business. So had the art galleries, the fashion houses. (Sometimes this creative work took place in the very same loft buildings, spiffed up, that had housed the underwear factories.) Those products were marketed through New York ad agencies, which invented new tricks and wrote jingles and taglines to sell the toothpaste and cars manufactured elsewhere. If we were no longer makers of everything, we could become those makers' amplification system, and that was a giant business. The ads in turn supported the national media—magazines, then radio, then television, now digital—that were and are nearly all based here, and their stories shaped everyone's understanding of everything.

All those businesses are undergirded by loans and investors, and the money comes from here too. From the eighteenth century, New York established itself as the financial hub of the United States, and as the country became a superpower, its banking center became the world's. Aside from the fact that New York had the money itself—the Fed, the stock exchange, a gold reserve, dealmaking propinquity—it had a lot of people who wanted to make more of it. In the 1960s, when the stock exchange grew to the point where its paper-based methods were overwhelmed, people figured out how to build computerized trading systems. When, a few years after that, traders craved more and more data, Michael Bloomberg devised and rented them terminals bursting with information and made himself $60 billion or so. When the hedge fund became a way of managing wealth, the administrators' fees—typically 2 percent of each trade and 20 percent of profit—made billionaires of them too. Riding the market up made money; so did shorting it. Wall Street always finds innovative ways to skim a little off.

Why did this majestic confluence of creativity appear here? Some of the explanation can be put to New York's sheer size: Big ideas are magnetic, and in a big town rather than a small one, you can gather enough Trotsky-ites or avant-garde poets at an event to make waves. Certainly, the presence of Columbia University, New York University, and CUNY in one tight cluster gave various movements a boost—proximity to great research universities fosters innovation, as Stanford and Berkeley, adjacent to Silicon Valley, continue to show. There's a self-fulfillingness to these things too: Self-confidence begets self-confidence, and centrality draws people who want to be at the center, which makes the center bigger. It's worth mentioning that concentrations of talent also work off the clock. Artists sitting around a bar deep into the night, taking stock and one-upping and arguing—Pollock and Rothko at the Cedar Tavern, Basquiat and Haring at some dive in the East Village, name your scene of choice—feed off each other's brains and creativity, not to mention competitiveness. Having investors and media nearby to support them helps as well.

Certain types are drawn to a place like this. They tend to be young. They tend to be smart and ambitious. Definitionally, they are dissatisfied with their hometowns, whether they are coming from Utah or the Pale of Settlement or Fujian. (Otherwise, why leave?) Immigration, certainly, feeds the New York innovation machine more than almost any other force. During the first huge wave of arrivals, in the nineteenth century, much of the contribution by new Americans was sheer labor—laying brick, making neckties, slicing fish. The next surge, starting in the 1960s, brought a different mix, with graduate-student engineers and biochemists among the table-bussers and floor-moppers. All their kids were born American, and a lot of them tended toward entrepreneurship and the creative industries. They are, in short, strivers, and although plenty of them do indeed want to get rich—and some do—what they're striving for is not always wealth. New York City pays in a variety of currencies, including fame, proximity to fame, and acceptance.

It is, of course, not a place for everyone. The speed and grit and crowding and relentlessness of New York life tend to cause a weeding out. It's an expensive place to live if you're not making progress, and it's inhospitable if you're one of those freaks who need to sit in the woods to think. People come here to try to shoot the moon. If it doesn't work out, a lot of them go back to where they came from, or sometimes to New Jersey. Those who hang on are a self-selected subset, intent on making something never before seen.

And the things they have made are big and small, broad and narrow. Baseball—that ostensibly pastoral American sport—was first called "the New York game." One of the first recorded matches was played not in a Kansas wheat field but at East 34th Street and Lexington Avenue. Four and a half blocks to the west is the spot where Thomas Edison unveiled the Vitascope, effectively the first movie projector. A two-minute walk away, on West 36th Street, Leo Gerstenzang wrapped bits of cotton around sticks and thus created the Q-tip. Four blocks up on West 40th, in the newsroom of the New York *Herald Tribune,* a sportswriter popularized the term *Ivy League* for the ancient colleges of the Northeast. In that same room a generation later, the New Journalism took root beneath the glinting cuff links of Tom Wolfe as he typed. All that, and we're still not out of a six-block radius.

You can hardly go a day without encountering something that started here. Neoconservatism was born in the City College cafeteria. The nightclub was created on East 11th Street. The American ideal of Christmas—Santa, gifts, eight tiny reindeer—came from Washington Irving's pen and Clement Clarke Moore's. TV comedy found its legs in 30 Rockefeller Plaza's Studio 6B, where Milton Berle went on the air in 1948, and down the street on Sid Caesar and Imogene Coca's show. The rabbit-ears antenna that received their programs came from Queens. The pastrami sandwich, General Tso's chicken, the Oreo—all ours. The puffer coat, the wrap dress, designer jeans—all ours. The list is, you might say, encyclopedic.

Which brings us to the contents of this book.

The Encyclopedia of New York is, we hope, a useful A-to-Z reference. But it's not a book that just celebrates the Empire State Building and Lombardi's pizza, although they're noted here. We've instead made it a history of New York's core idea—innovation—and of the ways in which one city exports the ideas that shape everyone's everyday existence.

We set ground rules as we made our list. Everything had to come from today's five boroughs—which is to say, if it was made in the City of Brooklyn before it merged with the City of New York in 1898, that was okay. You will not find entries for individual people—Alain Locke or Dominique Ansel or Alexander Hamilton or DJ Larry Tee, or even Robert Moses, who is all over this book as both creator and antagonist. Instead, you'll see celebrations of their most influential ideas, whether corporeal or intangible: the idea of Harlem, the Cronut, federalism, electroclash, the elevated highway. At the tops of these pages you'll see addenda that we hope will get you out of your reading chair. When you read about the Automat, you'll learn how to make its mac and cheese. When you read about Abstract Expressionism, *New York's* art critic, Jerry Saltz, will recommend paintings you should seek out when you visit the Museum of Modern Art and the Whitney. A timeline (see pages x through xv) will help place any entry you're reading in its historical context.

Even figuring out what belonged in this book made us realize what an innovation engine New York City has been. Take the bagel, for example. It's from Poland (probably). No historian worth a shmear would argue that it originated with us. But is it a New York *creation?* We as a city refined it to its ultimate form; we preserved it as it vanished from its homeland; now it's everywhere, identified worldwide with our city (plus a little side action in Montreal). Of course it's ours, and of course it's on these pages. So is the skyline, Chicago's claim on the form notwithstanding. So are unions, invented in Britain but inescapably bound up with New York labor. So is Central Park, different in scope and texture from any other urban park in the world—except Brooklyn's Prospect Park, of course.

There has been, these past few years, some talk around New York that its great days of creativity are over, that it chases away people with ideas because the taxes are heavy and the rent is too damn high. That chatter grew louder in 2020 (just as this book was going to press), as the COVID-19 pandemic all but paralyzed the city, closing cultural institutions, restaurants, workplaces, and most parts of an efficient and pleasant cosmopolitan life. During the shutdown, huge protests erupted against police abuse, followed by crackdowns. Rumors swirled of mass departures, of housing prices about to plummet.

The thing is, people have been saying "New York is finished" for quite some time now. When the city was hours from declaring bankruptcy, in 1975, an apartment on a nice street in Manhattan was still more expensive than it would have been in any other American city. We invented our way out of that crisis with new financial instruments and a reimagining of the city's economy. This time, some of the basic problems are different—among other things, parts of the city are now arguably too rich rather than too poor—but the effort to preserve the city's cultural, economic, and physical vibrancy is not. New Yorkers are, despite appearances, a pragmatic breed. Brainy strivers look at problems and attack and solve them.

And anyway, you have *always* been a little too late to get started here, in good times or bad. One of our *New York* Magazine colleagues remembers a moment in 1996—as he considered buying a one-bedroom in midtown for $68,000—when a friend sneered, "Nice job calling the top of the market." (It would sell for ten or twelve times that price now.) In the 1970s, people talked about cities as anachronisms whose time had passed. A decade before *that*, in 1968, *New York* ran a cover story about finding a place to live in "the year of the great apartment squeeze." You can find published references to the ridiculous costs of housing in 1944, in 1924, in 1904. Greenwich Village has been declared "over" uncountable times. We as a city got through yellow-fever epidemics and typhoid and Spanish flu, and so it will go, at great cost, with COVID-19. It was always a terrible, great idea to move here and shoot your shot, and it still is. The apartment next door to you may be cramped, but the ideas that will shape everyone's life a few years hence may lie within. And the same will likely be true a century from now, when another new arrival lives in that same room, eating a bagel and creating something that couldn't be made anywhere else.

THE HALVE MAEN

121 Milestones in the Life of a City

DUTCH CAPTAIN PETER STUYVESANT

1600 — NEW NETHERLAND

● **September 11, 1609**
On the island of Manaháhtaan—"the place where we get wood for bows"—indigenous Lenape scouts spot a ship: **the Dutch East India Company's** *Halve Maen* **("Half Moon"), captained by Henry Hudson.**

★ **1612–1613**
Adrian Block and Hans Christiansen open the city's first brewery, inaugurating the town's long and complicated relationship with booze.

● **August 1647**
Peter Stuyvesant sets foot (and peg leg) on the New Netherland shore as director-general. He turns the ragged outpost into a proper port town, sets up an operational government, and **authorizes the building of a wall against possible ground attack. Wall Street follows its location today.**

THE CAPITAL OF THE U.S.

1794 ●
The city leases the charming Belle Vue Farms estate, three miles north of the city, for use as a **quarantine site for yellow-fever patients.** It later becomes Bellevue Hospital.

May 17, 1792 ■
After one of America's first financial panics is narrowly averted, twenty-four stockbrokers meet on Wall Street—by legend, under a buttonwood tree—to hammer out the protocols of securities trading. **The Buttonwood Agreement is the basis of the New York Stock Exchange.**

WASHINGTON'S HOUSE

April 23, 1789 ●
A week before his inauguration, **George Washington moves into a mansion on Cherry Street** (near today's South Street Seaport) with his wife, Martha; two grandchildren; and at least seven enslaved people from Mount Vernon.

1800

● **January 2, 1800**
After a woman named Elma Sands is found dead, **Aaron Burr and Alexander Hamilton are hired to defend Levi Weeks,** accused of her murder. Weeks would be acquitted. Four years later, Burr kills Hamilton in a duel.

★ **1801**
Dr. David Hosack opens the Elgin Botanic Garden, a repository of exotic medicinal plants, on the site of the future Rockefeller Center.

★ **1807**
Trinity Church, a major landlord, develops **New York's first upscale neighborhood** around St. John's Park in today's Tribeca. It's eventually demolished after the rich head uptown.

● **June 1808**
Despite lawsuits from farmers as he goes, **John Randel Jr. begins surveying Manhattan.** His work becomes the basis of the Commissioners' Plan of 1811, carving the island into orderly numbered streets.

★ **December 6, 1809**
Washington Irving publishes a satirical history of New York attributed to the (fictitious) Diedrich Knickerbocker. In 1946, Ned Irish names the city's new pro basketball team for him.

"NEVERMORE!"

January 29, 1845 ★
The New York *Evening Mirror* publishes **"The Raven," by Edgar Allan Poe,** written in part at a house on the Upper West Side. The next year, Poe and his wife move to the village of Fordham (in today's Bronx).

July 1844 ◆
Governor DeWitt Clinton, who died in 1828, is reinterred at **Green-Wood Cemetery in Brooklyn.** New York's elite rush to bury their families nearby, turning Green-Wood into Brooklyn's first public park.

October 14, 1842 ●
New Yorkers gather to watch **fifty feet of water spout from City Hall's new fountain.** Thanks to the new Croton Aqueduct system, millions of gallons from Westchester County feed the city.

1839 ■
Daniel Richards begins transforming **forty acres of marshy Red Hook** into a dock and warehouse complex called Atlantic Basin, transforming the waterfront and helping to turn independent Brooklyn into one of the largest cities in America.

THE GREAT IMMIGRATION WAVE BEGINS

★ **October 10, 1847**
Henry Ward Beecher begins preaching at Plymouth Church in Brooklyn and becomes a huge national celebrity. Five years later, his sister Harriet Beecher Stowe publishes *Uncle Tom's Cabin.*

▲ **May 10, 1849**
A rivalry between actors Edwin Forrest and William Macready sparks **a violent riot outside an Astor Place opera house.** When militia fire indiscriminately into the crowd, bleeding civilians flee in terror.

● **1852**
The western Long Island town of **Williamsburgh** becomes a chartered city of New York State and loses its *h.* Three years later, it is absorbed into the ever-expanding metropolis of Brooklyn.

● **September 1, 1858**
Fearful and claiming self-defense, **angry Staten Island residents burn a quarantine hospital** on the eastern shore. This act of terror works; future facilities are moved to two small nearby islands.

★ **February 27, 1860**
Abraham Lincoln poses for his portrait in Mathew Brady's photo studio at 785 Broadway, then gives a speech at Cooper Union **that will help make him president.** He also stops at McSorley's for a drink.

KEY

● = Government and the Physical City
■ = Business, Finance, and Technology
▲ = Activism and Social Change
★ = Arts, Culture, Food, and Religion
◆ = Only in New York

KING'S COLLEGE

1700 — **BRITISH COLONIAL PERIOD**

● **September 8, 1664**
New Amsterdam becomes New York as the English forces peacefully take the town from the Dutch. A disgruntled Peter Stuyvesant spends the rest of his life on his Manhattan farm in today's East Village.

■ **December 13, 1711**
A market for the sale of enslaved people opens on Wall Street at the East River, ensuring the importance of the British colony of New York as a **key destination in the transatlantic slave trade.**

★ **April 8, 1730**
Congregation Shearith Israel—made up of Sephardic families with New Amsterdam roots—establishes **New York's first synagogue** on Mill Street (now South William Street).

▲ **November 17, 1734**
New York *Weekly Journal* printer John Peter Zenger is jailed for publishing **"seditious libel" against Governor William Cosby.** Zenger's case, exonerating him, establishes American freedom of the press.

★ **October 31, 1754**
In competition with the College of New Jersey (a.k.a. Princeton), the New York colony **founds King's College** in a schoolhouse next to Trinity Church. Today it's called Columbia University.

REVOLUTION

ARSDALE, WITH POLE

◆ **November 25, 1783**
As British troops cede New York Harbor (and America), they affix a Union Jack to a greased flagpole at Fort George. John Van Arsdale, a veteran of Washington's Continental Army, **manages to climb the slippery pole and remove the flag.** For decades, New York's annual Evacuation Day celebrations feature a greased-pole-climbing contest.

▲ **July 9, 1776**
Following General George Washington's reading of the Declaration of Independence, a crowd storms down to Bowling Green and **dismantles an equestrian statue of King George III.**

▲ **August 23, 1775**
King's College students and rebels (including Alexander Hamilton) **steal guns from the Battery.** In response, the Royal Navy's HMS *Asia* fires upon New York, smashing the roof of Samuel Fraunces's tavern.

STEADY GROWTH

● **1808–1811**
Fearing a return appearance of the British during the War of 1812, New Yorkers build **a fort just off lower Manhattan.** It's still there (now on the expanded mainland), having served as the Castle Garden concert venue, an immigration station, and then the home of the New York Aquarium.

★ **August 9, 1819**
The city **bans velocipedes** from lower Manhattan just months after the proto-bicycle first appears on the streets, terrorizing pedestrians and horses.

THE ALL-POWERFUL VELOCIPEDE

▲ **September 27, 1825**
Shortly before abolition in New York, Andrew Williams buys a plot of land in what becomes **Seneca Village, an enclave for Black New Yorkers** including newly freed slaves. It is later wiped off the map by Central Park.

FREDERICK DOUGLASS

▲ **September 1838**
The African-American writer-bookseller David Ruggles, an abolitionist operator of the Underground Railroad through New York, **shelters an escaped slave who later takes the name Frederick Douglass.**

● **December 16, 1835**
A devastating blaze **destroys hundreds of buildings in lower Manhattan,** its menacing amber glow reportedly seen upon the night sky as far away as Philadelphia.

● **1828**
The city buys a narrow outcrop in the East River called Blackwell's Island—later Welfare Island, now Roosevelt Island—and **builds an asylum, a smallpox hospital, a workhouse, and a prison.**

★ **December 13, 1827**
The brothers Delmonico open a **pastry shop on William Street.** A decade later, they expand into a much grander dining space they call Delmonico's and introduce fine dining to New York.

CIVIL WAR

● **January 7, 1861**
Mayor Fernando Wood suggests in a speech to the Common Council that New York City, financially reliant on southern businesses, **secede along with the Confederacy.** (It doesn't.)

◆ **February 10, 1863**
Charles Stratton (a.k.a. General Tom Thumb) marries fellow little person Lavinia Warren at Grace Church—a **coup for their boss, P. T. Barnum,** cementing his role as America's great purveyor of "humbug."

▲ **July 13, 1863**
The **Draft Riots** start at a marshal's office on Third Avenue at 47th Street when white volunteer firemen, angry over conscription and fearful of Black freedom, attack the building and burn it down.

★ **November 25, 1864**
Edwin Booth performs *Julius Caesar* at the Winter Garden Theatre with his brothers Junius Brutus Booth and John Wilkes Booth. It's a fundraiser for a Shakespeare statue in Central Park—one that still stands on Literary Walk.

THE BROOKLYN BRIDGE, BUILT BY JOHN, WASHINGTON, AND EMILY ROEBLING

★ **September 12, 1866**
The Black Crook, the **first Broadway musical,** debuts at the 3,200-seat Niblo's Garden. It's **five and a half hours long**— and it's a hit anyway.

● **July 22, 1869**
John A. Roebling, **designer of the Brooklyn Bridge,** dies after an accident while surveying the site. The project passes to his son Washington, then to Washington's wife, Emily, before it's finished in 1883.

● **May 31, 1871**
Mary Amelia Tweed, daughter of political boss William Tweed, **is married near Madison Square Park.** The wedding is so opulent that Tweed's hugely corrupt organization finally comes under investigation.

● **December 5, 1876**
A blaze at the Brooklyn Theatre, near Brooklyn City Hall, breaks out during a production of the play *The Two Orphans,* killing nearly 300 people—the worst disaster in Brooklyn's history.

★ **January 22, 1881**
Cleopatra's Needle, **an obelisk from the ancient Egyptian city of Heliopolis,** is erected in Central Park with a bizarre Masonic ceremony behind the brand-new redbrick Metropolitan Museum of Art.

October 27, 1904 ●
On opening day of the subway, Mayor George McClellan Jr. **refuses to relinquish control of the train he is ceremonially piloting,** running it most of the way from City Hall to 145th Street.

June 15, 1904 ▲
Philip Payton charters **the Afro-American Realty Company,** buying property in Harlem, until then a mostly white area. It's a step toward the eventual creation of a new American Black identity and culture.

June 15, 1904 ★
The *General Slocum,* a steamship on a church-sponsored day trip, **catches fire and sinks** in the East River, killing more than 1,000 people. It's the deadliest day in New York City until 9/11.

May 14, 1904 ●
Dreamland opens on Coney Island, one of three amusement parks that will delight millions with the Shoot-the-Chute ride, a nightly re-creation of the fall of Pompeii, and a display of preemie babies in incubators.

April 30, 1903 ★
The New York Highlanders baseball team opens its new Hilltop Park field against the Washington Senators. When they move to the Polo Grounds a few years later, they're renamed the Yankees.

★ **June 25, 1906**
Stanford White, **architect and standard-bearer of Gilded Age style,** is shot and killed by a former lover's husband in the roof garden of Madison Square Garden, **a building he designed.**

▲ **April 17, 1907**
Ellis Island has its busiest day ever, **processing more than 11,000 newly arrived immigrants.** Most are from Russia, Italy, and Eastern Europe.

★ **December 31, 1907**
A ball covered in one hundred lightbulbs **is dropped at midnight to mark the New Year** atop the New York *Times* offices at the south end of the square recently renamed in honor of the paper.

▲ **November 24, 1909**
Over 20,000 workers, mostly women and girls employed in shirtwaist factories, go on strike, **the first of several major protests within New York City's thriving garment industry.**

THE UNION LABEL

EMPIRE STATE BUILDING: TALLER!

CHRYSLER BUILDING: TALL!

October 24–29, 1929 ■
Days after the Chrysler Building tops out, the exuberance of the Jazz Age evaporates when the stock market starts to crash, losing a third of its value. **The Great Depression has begun.**

October 23, 1929 ●
A silver Art Deco spire, a design element from architect William Van Alen, is secretly hoisted to the top of the Chrysler Building and bolted in place, abruptly making it **the tallest in the world.**

June 4, 1929 ●
The Casino restaurant in Central Park becomes a "night office" for **the dashing, corrupt mayor Jimmy Walker.** But the good times are fading: Prohibition agents raid the Casino in 1930.

April 20, 1927 ▲
Mae West, the star, writer, and producer of the bawdy Broadway comedy *Sex,* is sent to the workhouse on Welfare (now Roosevelt) Island on **obscenity charges.** Upon her release, she founds the Mae West Memorial Library there.

● **May 1, 1931**
Eighteen months later, **the even taller Empire State Building opens**—and sits half-empty for a decade.

★ **December 24, 1931**
Workers put up a twenty-foot balsam fir at the Rockefeller Center building site, decorating it with spent blasting caps from the excavation, and **the Christmas-tree tradition there begins.**

● **September 1, 1932**
Mayor Jimmy Walker resigns after a commission led by Judge Samuel Seabury exposes deep corruption throughout the city's legal system and police force. It's also the beginning of the end for the Tammany Hall Democratic political machine.

★ **December 27, 1932**
Opening night at Radio City Music Hall! And it bombs. The program is a **bloated, ill-conceived, exhausting six-hour extravaganza** with dozens of acts, from vaudeville performers to Martha Graham.

YOUNG GRIFFO

■ September 4, 1882
Let there be light! America's first power plant, **Thomas Edison's Pearl Street Station,** begins illuminating homes and shops in lower Manhattan.

★ December 3, 1883
The poem **"The New Colossus," by Emma Lazarus,** is first read at a fund-raiser to build a pedestal for the Statue of Liberty. A gift from the French, the statue sits in crates for months awaiting the pedestal's construction. It finally goes up in 1886.

● June 15, 1894
America's first bike lane opens **along Ocean Parkway in Brooklyn.** Owing to fears that it will tempt riders to race, the speed limit is set at twelve miles per hour.

★ May 4, 1895
Brother filmmakers Otway and Gray Latham shoot the first movie made in New York City, showing **a boxing match between "Battling" Charles Barnett and Young Griffo** filmed on the roof of the old Madison Square Garden.

◄ 1900

THE FIRST FATAL CAR CRASH

September 13, 1899 ●
Real-estate broker Henry H. Bliss is struck and **killed by an electric taxicab** at West 74th Street and Central Park West. He is the first person in the U.S. to die in an automobile crash.

January 1, 1898 ●
Consolidation! Four civic entities **merge to form Greater New York,** an enormous new metropolis of five boroughs. In Brooklyn, those who fought the epic merge mourn what they call "the Great Mistake."

1897 ★
The Port Arthur and Chinese Tuxedo **open in Chinatown:** two grand eating establishments that compete with uptown's best restaurants and establish New Yorkers' deep love of Chinese food.

September 13, 1896 ■
Chicago retailer Siegel-Cooper opens **the world's biggest department store**—and the first in a steel-framed building on the Sixth Avenue shopping district known as Ladies' Mile.

WORLD WAR I

● August 9, 1910
Mayor William Jay Gaynor is shot in the throat by an angry dockworker. Gaynor **survives with the bullet lodged in his neck for more than three years** but dies before his term is up.

★ February 17, 1913
The avant-garde International Exhibition of Modern Art, a.k.a. the Armory Show, opens, **giving New Yorkers conniptions** over Marcel Duchamp's *Nude Descending a Staircase, No. 2.*

● July 25, 1916
Fearing a city of deep shadows, the Board of Estimate passes a **zoning rule requiring tall buildings to be built with setbacks.** The "wedding cake" style dominates a whole era's tapered towers.

★ April 1918
Dorothy Parker's first theater review runs in *Vanity Fair.* While there, she befriends columnist Robert Benchley and film critic Robert Sherwood. By 1920, they've begun gallivanting at the Algonquin Hotel.

▲ February 17, 1919
The African-American 369th Infantry Regiment, a.k.a. **the Harlem Hellfighters,** returns from war and marches up Fifth Avenue to cheers after serving in segregated U.S. forces overseas.

BOOM AND PROHIBITION

AT THE SAVOY BALLROOM

March 12, 1926 ★
The cavernous Savoy Ballroom opens on Lenox Avenue in Harlem, **launching several dance crazes and musical talents** into the American consciousness. Unlike whites-only nightclubs like the Cotton Club, the Savoy's floor is integrated, and many drag balls are held there as well.

November 27, 1924 ★
The first Macy's Thanksgiving Day Parade stars actual animals borrowed from the zoo. They scare small children, and a few years later, **enormous helium balloons replace them.**

September 16, 1920 ■
A bomb explodes at lunch hour on Wall Street, killing thirty-eight people and injuring hundreds. It's widely blamed on anarchists, but the bombers are never caught. You can still see shrapnel scars on the stonework of the J.P. Morgan building.

● January 18, 1934
The ambitious politician **Robert Moses becomes New York City Parks commissioner.** It's the latest in a list of many government jobs held (simultaneously) by Moses, a ruthless power-wielder who funds hundreds of local projects using federal funds.

● June 28, 1934
The elevated West Side Freight Line opens in Chelsea, its railroad tracks twisting through factories and warehouses. Largely abandoned by the 1980s, the railbed is eventually, in stages, **transformed into the elevated park known as the High Line.**

◆ November 1934
In a publicity stunt, **Mayor Fiorello La Guardia refuses to exit a TWA flight at Newark Metropolitan Airport,** the region's largest, because his ticket lists "New York" as the destination. Five years later, New York's own airport opens—and it's named for him.

FOUND IN THE SEWER: NOT A MYTH!

KEY

● = Government and the Physical City

■ = Business, Finance, and Technology

▲ = Activism and Social Change

★ = Arts, Culture, Food, and Religion

◆ = Only in New York

WORLD WAR II

◆ February 9, 1935
Three East Harlem teens find **a full-grown eight-foot alligator in the sewer,** setting up one of New York's enduring urban legends.

★ March 1939
Billie Holiday steps up to the mic at the integrated Greenwich Village nightclub Café Society and first **performs "Strange Fruit,"** a protest song vividly describing a lynching.

■ April 30, 1939
A speech by President Franklin D. Roosevelt **opening the 1939 World's Fair in Queens** is broadcast live by NBC to a handful of New Yorkers watching on experimental black-and-white televisions throughout the city.

FDR AT THE WORLD'S FAIR

● March 21, 1947
Police discover Homer Collyer dead in his Harlem brownstone **surrounded by tons of hoarded trash:** car parts, piles of newspapers, a canoe. On April 9, the rat-eaten corpse of his brother, Langley, turns up in a booby trap he'd set himself.

FISCAL CRISIS AND CRIME WAVE

June 28, 1969 ▲
The Stonewall uprising: Gays, lesbians, and transfolk, many of them people of color, say they've had enough. A year later, a march from Sheridan Square to Central Park is the city's first Pride parade.

June 3, 1968 ★
Believing that Andy Warhol has been stealing her work, **Valerie Solanas shoots him** (and critic Mario Amaya) at his studio off Union Square. Warhol spends two months in and out of hospitals.

November 28, 1966 ◆
Truman Capote hosts the **Black and White Ball at the Plaza Hotel,** ostensibly in honor of Washington *Post* publisher Katharine Graham but mostly an excuse to make the best guest list ever.

June 30, 1966 ●
After it's decommissioned by the Department of Defense, **the Brooklyn Navy Yard closes.** Once one of America's greatest shipyards, it falls into the hands of corrupt managers, recovering only in the next century.

November 9–10, 1965 ●
A blackout plunges most of the Northeast into darkness at evening rush hour. **Relatively little crime is reported.** Power resumes in New York approximately fourteen hours later.

★ August 11, 1973
Clive Campbell, a.k.a. DJ Kool Herc, throws one of his house parties in a **rec room at 1520 Sedgwick Avenue in the Bronx,** spinning and mixing LPs on two turntables. Hip-hop is born.

◆ August 7, 1974
Sixteen months after the opening of the **World Trade Center,** French acrobat Philippe Petit sneaks a tightrope across the tops of the Twin Towers and **nimbly walks across it.**

PHILIPPE PETIT

● February 27, 1975
An East Village fire wrecks New York Telephone's switching center and **severs phone service** to thousands of people. Several firefighters later die of cancers likely caused by fumes from burning cables.

● September 9, 1975
As the city faces bankruptcy, New York State takes over the finances and hands oversight to the **Emergency Financial Control Board,** a new committee of government and private interests. It manages the city's money until 1986.

2000

ECONOMIC RECOVERY

February 4, 1999 ▲
A Guinean immigrant named Amadou Diallo is **killed in a shower of 41 bullets fired** outside his Bronx home when police officers believe he is reaching for a gun. (It is his wallet.)

June 22, 1992 ★
New York runs a cover story, "The New Bohemia," identifying **the migration of young, mostly white artists** to Williamsburg, a neighborhood of Puerto Rican and Hasidic residents.

August 19, 1991 ●
Hasidic and Black residents in Crown Heights clash in **three days of violence** after a car driven by Yosef Lifsh strikes and kills a **7-year-old child of Guyanese immigrants.** Mayor David Dinkins is perceived as having lost control and is voted out two years later.

December 1990 ●
The annual murder rate, driven by crack, job loss, and bad policy, **peaks at 2,245.**

● September 11, 2001
New York is forever changed when two jetliners, hijacked by Al Qaeda terrorists, **crash into the towers of the World Trade Center.** Within two hours, both buildings collapse, leaving nearly 3,000 dead. The ensuing wars last two decades.

★ October 15, 2006
The legendary punk venue CBGB, at 315 Bowery, closes with a **bittersweet** performance by **Patti Smith.** Too symbolically, the store becomes a John Varvatos clothing boutique.

■ September 15, 2008
Lehman Brothers falls apart owing to a huge bet on subprime mortgages, and **the world's financial markets follow it down the tubes.** A giant federal bailout prevents total financial collapse.

▲ September 17, 2011
Shouting "We are the 99 percent!" protesters angered by class inequality and the bank bailouts **begin gathering in Zuccotti Park,** launching the Occupy Wall Street movement.

● October 29, 2012
Hurricane Sandy **devastates Greater New York,** wrecking buildings, knocking out power, and flooding subways and tunnels. A large part of Breezy Point, Queens, is ruined by fire.

JACKIE ROBINSON

FRESH KILLS LANDFILL

▲ April 15, 1947
Jackie Robinson makes his **Major League debut with the Brooklyn Dodgers** at Ebbets Field. More than half the spectators in the stands are African-American.

▲ August 1, 1947
The first tenants move into **Stuyvesant Town,** a massive East Side housing complex aimed at middle-class World War II veterans. But it's all white; tenants (who want to integrate) fight management for years thereafter.

● April 16, 1948
Fresh Kills landfill in Staten Island receives its first barge of city waste. Within a decade, **it becomes the world's largest landfill.** Closed on March 22, 2001, it is temporarily reopened after 9/11 as a debris sorting ground.

■ November 5, 1955
Robert Moses's **Cross Bronx Expressway** opens, slashing through working-class neighborhoods and displacing thousands of residents. Activists do manage to stop another plan: two highways cutting across lower and midtown Manhattan.

April 22, 1964 ★
The World's Fair of 1964 opens in Flushing Meadows. The first day, rain-soaked visitors arrive to find construction incomplete. Activists protest a speech by President Lyndon B. Johnson and a minstrel-show revival called *America, Be Seated!*

August 2, 1962 ★
Jane Jacobs, Philip Johnson, and other concerned preservationists picket to **protest the destruction of Pennsylvania Station,** the 1910 Beaux-Arts monument designed by McKim, Mead & White. They don't succeed; demolition begins on October 28, 1963.

December 16, 1960 ●
Two airplanes—one heading to Idlewild (now JFK), the other to La Guardia—**collide over New York.** One crashes at the intersection of Seventh Avenue and Sterling Place in Park Slope, Brooklyn. All passengers are killed instantly except for an 11-year-old boy who dies the following day at Methodist Hospital.

June 29, 1956 ◆
After two years at a Lower East Side theater, Joe Papp takes his Shakespeare troupe to an outdoor venue **in East River Park.** The series moves uptown and—after a tussle with Robert Moses—becomes Shakespeare in the Park.

BIANCA JAGGER

◆ May 2, 1977
Bianca Jagger celebrates her birthday on a white horse. **On the dance floor. At Studio 54.**

● July 13–14, 1977
After lightning hits a substation, **another blackout darkens most of New York City.** Crime and looting are said to cause hundreds of millions of dollars in damage, although there are hints that this is overreported. Power resumes to the entire city 25 hours later.

● November 8, 1977
Ed Koch is elected mayor on a public-safety platform, positioning himself—in opposition to his predecessors John Lindsay and Abe Beame—as a **"liberal with sanity."**

April 19, 1989 ●
The rape of a Central Park jogger leads to the arrest and imprisonment of several purportedly "wilding" Black and Latino teenagers. The convictions of the "Central Park Five" are overturned in 2002.

October 19, 1987 ■
The Dow falls 22.6 percent, still the largest one-day drop ever. "Everyone agrees," writes John Taylor in *New York* a few months later, "that the eighties are over."

December 22, 1984 ●
Bernhard Goetz shoots four young Black men on the No. 2 train as (depending on whom you believe) they are either panhandling or robbing him. The "Subway Vigilante" similarly splits opinion: racist overreaction or self-defense?

January 4, 1982 ▲
Larry Kramer and five other activists form **Gay Men's Health Crisis** at Kramer's Manhattan apartment in response to news of a "gay cancer" that the CDC would later call AIDS.

September 25, 1980 ■
The Commodore Hotel reopens as the Grand Hyatt, its brick façade wrapped in a charcoal glass sheath. It's the first big project of Donald Trump, son of Queens real-estate developer Fred Trump.

★ February 17, 2015
Inwood resident Lin-Manuel Miranda, fresh off the success of his musical *In The Heights*, finds inspiration in the story of another former upper-Manhattan resident—Alexander Hamilton—and **opens *Hamilton*** at the Public Theater.

■ January 16, 2019
New York's official tourist marketing agency reports that **65.1 million tourists visited in 2018,** the most in its history. Among the hottest attractions is the One World Observatory at the rebuilt World Trade Center.

● March 1, 2020
The first confirmed case of **COVID-19** in New York, in a 39-year-old woman returning from Iran, is reported. By July, more than 200,000 people in the city have become sick, and more than 17,000 are dead.

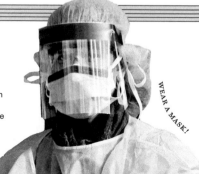

WEAR A MASK!

From

ABSTRACT EXPRESSIONISM

to

**AUTOMATED
TELLER MACHINE**

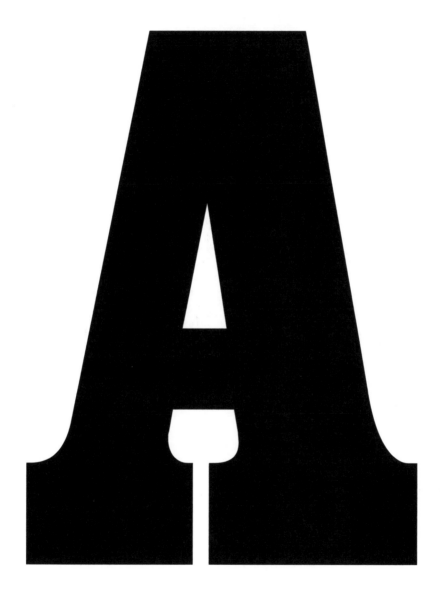

*Abstract Expressionism was the first American art
movement to have worldwide influence.*

MARK ROTHKO, *UNTITLED (VIOLET, BLACK, ORANGE,
YELLOW ON WHITE AND RED)*, 1949

① **The Essential Abstract Expressionist Paintings in New York Museums**

Chosen by New York's *art critic,* Jerry Saltz

1.

2.

Abstract Expressionism [1]

The first American art movement to have worldwide influence came into being in New York City, and its gestation was fraught. It began during the Great Depression, as scores of European artists immigrated to the United States from strife-torn Europe, then grew during and after World War II as humanity attempted to come to terms with tens of millions dead, mass atrocities, and the explosion of two atomic bombs. Before this moment, American art had always played second fiddle, or worse, to European art. By the 1940s, these two immense historical-psychic forces crashed together; the thunder came, and the rest is history.

After years of destitution, of being ignored and laughed at, a generation of New York artists—Jackson Pollock, Willem de Kooning, Mark Rothko, Barnett Newman, and Franz Kline, among others—broke through the stultifying supremacy of European art history and overcame decades of feeling overawed and intimidated by Cubism, Picasso, and all the rest. These artists, many living in and around Greenwich Village, met one another and commiserated in bars, at loft parties, and in Washington Square in the middle of dark winter nights. They scraped together their numerous influences (including premodern, archaic art and so-called primitive art) while scrapping many others. In the late 1940s, they began to shatter ideas of pictorial composition, skill, mark-making, scale, surface, subject matter, line, and tools. Newman said they'd started "from scratch, to paint as if painting never existed before." De Kooning said they had to "destroy painting" and "see how far one could go."

The term *Abstract Expressionism* was coined by the critic Robert Coates in New York in 1946. (Various other appellations have been applied to the movement's styles, notably action painting, gestural abstraction, and color-field painting.) The Abstract Expressionist idea was to eliminate hierarchies of composition in favor of "all-overness," meaning the entire surface of an artwork should be taken in at once, with no part ever more or less conceptually or visually important than any other. This notion had never existed in painting before. Furthermore, all forms of illusionistic space and perspective were to be eliminated so a work existed always on its surface alone.

Pollock created monumental, pulsating canvases by deploying only drips of paint, never touching tool to canvas (his technique almost arcing back to the origin of the medium, the cave-painting strategy of blowing liquid pigment from the mouth over extended fingers to create negative handprints). He fused drawing and painting, creating symphonic fields of skeins that all but destroyed the category of what a painting is. (De Kooning generously said Pollock "broke the ice.") Rothko turned down the optical rheostat to create glowing fields of geometric, biomorphic forms and energies that produce silence, static, and disintegration—something almost spiritual. He wanted his work to have "the impact of the unequivocal" to evoke the "tragic and timeless." De Kooning went a different route by employing discernible figures (Pollock accused him of betraying abstraction) to explore the primacy and voluptuousness of oil paint while devising a new kind of ugly beauty and a non-illusionistic fusion of subject matter, surface, gesture, and line. "Flesh is the reason oil paint was invented," he said. Meanwhile, Newman's huge, monochromatic fields of intense color presented visual nothingness, compositional totality, enveloping optical effects, and intellectual conundrums (his work set the stage for Minimalism and other genres; *see also* CONCEPTUAL ART). Alas, this was an all-white boys' club. Only much later did the female New York artists of the time receive their full due, especially Helen Frankenthaler, Lee Krasner, Janet Sobel, Hedda Sterne, and Louise Bourgeois.

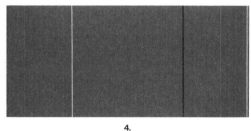

3.	4.

Abstract Expressionism discovered optical solutions that changed the language of painting and simultaneously created total visual access to a work as well as producing an otherness. The work of which Newman said "We were making it out of ourselves" became the bedrock of this momentous new American art style, one that remained in force until the very late 1950s, when it was displaced by a brand-new vision (*see also* POP ART).

Acrylic Paint

In 1932, Leonard Bocour opened Bocour Hand Ground Artist Colors, a shop at 2 West 15th Street that supplied oil-based paint to many Greenwich Village artists. A few years later, his nephew Sam Golden joined the business, and the store's clientele eventually grew to include the Abstract Expressionists Mark Rothko, Willem de Kooning, Helen Frankenthaler, and Jackson Pollock. At the request of one of his clients in the 1940s, Bocour began work on a new formula in which pigment was suspended in plastic resin rather than in oil. Introduced under the name Magna, it had brilliance, gloss, and good adherence properties and dried much more quickly than oil paint. For most of his career, Roy Lichtenstein used Magna in his works to evoke the high, bright sheen of pop culture and advertising. Marketed by Bocour as "the First New Painting Medium in 500 Years," acrylic paints (including those made by Bocour's descendant company, Golden) are today ubiquitous, available in any art-supply store and used by students and pros alike.

ACT UP [2]

By 1987, the AIDS epidemic had claimed almost half a million lives worldwide and over 6,500 in New York City, where gay men bore the brunt of the losses. Early that year, the playwright Larry Kramer, a co-founder of the volunteer group Gay Men's Health Crisis, spoke at the LGBTQ Community Center on West 13th Street and told a roomful of primarily gay men that two-thirds of them would be dead in a few years if they did not take radical new steps to fight for treatment and care. "That night not only was a terrifying wake-up call but a kick in the ass to take to the streets," said longtime HIV/AIDS activist Eric Sawyer, who was diagnosed with HIV in 1985.

Two nights later, about two dozen people met at Kramer's Greenwich Village apartment and launched what would soon be named ACT UP (for AIDS Coalition to Unleash Power), a nonhierarchical activist collective that went on to score some of the biggest gains against the epidemic before an effective treatment emerged in 1996. With its unapologetically queer rhetoric and aesthetic—loud, angry masses of (mostly) gay men and lesbians in combat boots and sleeveless white T-shirts emblazoned with the group's logo chanting, "We're here! We're queer! Get used to it!" and "How many more have to die?"—ACT UP effectively defined what it meant to be LGBTQ and political in the U.S. in the late 1980s and early 1990s. Its pink triangle (which the Nazis had used to tag gay people) and powerful "Silence = Death" slogan became shorthand for militant gay activism in the Reagan-Bush era.

The group targeted, infiltrated, and occupied realms of power for dragging their feet on the epidemic. In September 1989, ACT UP took over the NYC stock-market floor to successfully pressure a drop in the (then-astronomical) $8,000 annual price of AZT, the only FDA-approved AIDS drug at the time. Bearing bold, graphic posters and banners, the group descended on and temporarily shut down the headquarters of the FDA to demand an acceleration in testing and approval of scores of medicines that could combat HIV, the virus

(2) AIDS-Activism Artifacts to See at the New York Public Library

Chosen by Jason Baumann, coordinator of the library's Humanities and LGBTQ collections

The library's **Manuscripts and Archives Division** holds the records of ACT UP New York and more than 300 hours of taped interviews with members; the archives of the People With AIDS Coalition and Gay Men's Health Crisis; and diaries of activists and everyday people who lived through the epidemic.

SOME HIGHLIGHTS:
➤ Documentary video of ACT UP demonstrations and meetings, including DIVA TV (Damned Interfering Video Activist Television)
➤ Pioneering safer-sex instruction materials produced by Gay Men's Health Crisis
➤ Rare magazines, including *Diseased Pariah News*

➤ Original posters and designs by AIDS-activist artists' collective Gran Fury
➤ Documentation of early needle-exchange programs and AIDS activism by people in prison
➤ Oral histories from members of ACT UP and Gay Men's Health Crisis

---

that causes AIDS. The women of ACT UP also spearheaded protests that eventually got the U.S. government to expand its crucial federal definition of AIDS to include symptoms experienced only by women. In ensuing years, these protests led to government agencies opening their doors to activists and revising their clinical trials and approval methods to get more drugs more quickly to more people with HIV/AIDS.

As AIDS mortality rates rose dramatically into the mid-1990s, ACT UP was split between those focused on treatment advances and those focused on broader social issues related to AIDS: homelessness, intravenous-drug addiction, racism, sexism, and homophobia. The group's wing of activists that had gained ad hoc expertise in the science founded Treatment Action Group, a think tank that worked closely with federal health bureaucrats and drugmakers to usher in the new wave of protease medications in 1996 that began to change HIV from a death sentence to a manageable chronic illness.

Most of the ACT UP chapters that had sprung up in dozens of other cities waned and folded in the years that followed. "The advent of effective drugs sucked a lot of the rage and urgency out of the group's energy," said Sawyer, and many turned their attention to treatment access on a global scale. The New York and Philadelphia branches played a large role in forcing down the price of AIDS drugs worldwide, with some members founding a new group, Health GAP, for that specific purpose. In recent years, those chapters have partnered with other groups fighting to maintain health-care protections against the policies of the Trump administration (*see also* TRUMPISM) and the Republican-led Congress.

Perhaps more than any movement since the civil-rights era, AIDS activism proved the power of street-based direct action and civil disobedience in both fighting government policies and swaying public opinion. "We proved that when regular people band together and speak truth to power," said Sawyer, "they can change the world."

Advertising *see* MADISON AVENUE

Air-Conditioning

In 1902, Willis Carrier, a year out of Cornell with an engineering degree, figured out that controlling the humidity of air is the key to cooling it. Although he set up shop in Buffalo, his first client—and the world's first installation of what can definitively be called air-conditioning—was in Bushwick, Brooklyn, in the printing plant of the Sackett-Wilhelms Lithographing & Publishing Company. (It was meant not for employees' comfort but to solve summertime quality-control problems.) The next year, Carrier's rival, a cooling engineer named Alfred Wolff, custom-built an elaborate, madly expensive system to chill the air at the New York Stock Exchange, and an industry was born.

Owing to its early expense, AC took twenty or so years to become commonplace in public spaces like movie theaters and another generation to become ubiquitous in homes. Since then, it has changed the face of the planet by creating Abu Dhabi and other desert metropolises out of sand and thin air; making cities like Miami and Phoenix tolerable for retirees year-round; nearly destroying the atmospheric ozone layer through its use of CFCs (since regulated, allowing the ozone's recovery); and vastly increasing global electricity consumption, putting the future of life on Earth at risk.

Algonquin Round Table

The Algonquin Hotel, at 59 West 44th Street, was a nice, if unremarkable, place to stay in midtown until one afternoon in June 1919. Although the origin story has been told a few ways, most agree that a handful of theater- and newspaper-world friends met in the hotel's Oak Room to welcome their frenemy Alexander

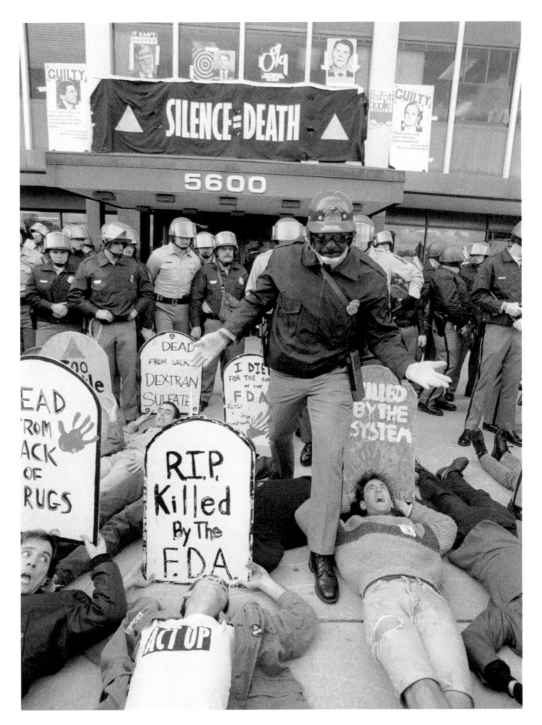

*In October 1988, ACT UP protesters
stage a die-in at the headquarters
of the Food and Drug Administration.*
PHOTOGRAPH BY J. SCOTT APPLEWHITE

Woollcott back from his stint as a war correspondent in Europe. After a couple of hours of jokes and ripostes, someone said, "We should do this all the time," and a version of the group continued to convene at the Algonquin daily for the next ten years. The regular list grew to include, among others, the *Vanity Fair* contributors Dorothy Parker and Robert Benchley; Harold Ross, founder of *The New Yorker*; the columnists and writers George S. Kaufman, James Thurber, Franklin P. Adams, Robert Sherwood, Donald Ogden Stewart, Heywood Broun, and Edna Ferber; Harpo Marx and, occasionally, his brother Groucho; and the early feminists Ruth Hale and Jane Grant. The group was celebrated for its quick, slashing wit and big-city sophistication, qualities that soon came to define *The New Yorker*'s voice as well as *Vanity Fair*'s. The journalist and politician Clare Boothe Luce, a sometime visitor, reported that the scene was self-perpetuating: "You couldn't say 'pass the salt' without somebody trying to turn it into a pun or trying to top it." Kaufman later called the group "a motley and nondescript bunch of people who wanted to eat lunch, and that's about all."

Ultimately, the legend of the Round Table came to overwhelm its members. Several of them (Parker, the Marxes, Kaufman, Ross, Thurber) made lasting contributions to the culture, but others are remembered for little besides those few bons mots over lunch. Parker, whose reputation for spoken virtuosity overshadowed her fine short stories and wry light verse, grew weary of the myth. Asked about the Round Table in 1965, two years before her death, she said, "It's difficult to get terribly interested in food I digested 45 years ago." The Algonquin, now owned by Marriott, disagrees: Each hotel guest to this day receives a copy of *The New Yorker*, and although the Oak Room has been renovated out of existence, the restaurant in more or less the same spot is now called the Round Table Restaurant. Yet the myth of the great, bantering table of funny people is more durable than ever. It's reflected in the popular image of the sitcom writers' room, where, at brainstorming sessions and table readings, stiletto wit and one-upmanship rule and (as at the Algonquin) far more men than women are allowed entrance.

Alt-Weekly[3]

In the mid-1950s, no fewer than seven general-interest dailies were covering New York City, along with a vast array of ethnic and specialty papers such as the *Jewish Daily Forward*, the *Amsterdam News*, and the *Daily Worker*. What did not yet exist, however, was a paper aimed at an emerging urban-bohemian-leftist sensibility. In 1955, the novelist Norman Mailer and the journalists Ed Fancher and Dan Wolf co-founded *The Village Voice*, a newspaper for that particular audience. Although it took years to turn a profit—and was a squabbly, sometimes journalistically uneven product—it hit its readers square between the eyes.

The *Voice* gained wider attention with the addition of satirical cartoonist Jules Feiffer and built momentum when the rest of the city's papers went on strike in 1962; the left's developing antiwar consensus and the counterculture's booming arts scene gradually made it a necessary read, and it soon grew thick with advertising despite an editorial ethos that openly disdained moneymaking. Its great strengths over the next three decades were investigative reporting in the muckraking tradition (notably from Wayne Barrett and Tom Robbins), opinion and advocacy journalism (Nat Hentoff), and deep coverage of the emerging cultural and civil-rights revolutions. J. Hoberman and Andrew Sarris wrote memorably about film, and Robert Christgau and Ellen Willis on popular music; the theater critic Jerry Tallmer created the Obie Awards; and the all-lowercase jill johnston contributed free-form essays about dance that were a vehicle for her sexual awakening and coming-out.

By the 1980s, every major city in America had an "alternative weekly," as the form became known. Most of these were cheap to run, paying writers little and editing them lightly in exchange for exposure and space to riff and ramble. The *Voice*, by this time part of the media Establishment, was in some circles perceived to have lost its edge and, in 1988, gained a serious competitor: *New York Press*, a free paper that skewed toward personal essays and conservative-libertarian politics.

For a time, the two duked it out, and the *Voice* eliminated its cover price in response, doubling its circulation but perhaps diminishing its status.

In the late 1990s, the mainstay of the alt-weekly business—classified advertising—was siphoned away by Craigslist and various other digital outlets, and over the next decade most papers saw their impact on their communities decline. (After going through three owners in its final decade, *The Village Voice* quit printing in September 2017 and closed its online operations a year later; plans for a digital archive have been announced.) Today's online-only readers, however, would find much that is familiar in the pages of the alt-weeklies, most notably the self-reflection and personal perspective that inform their news stories and memoir pieces alike, forecasting the autobiographical mode we're now used to in the blogosphere. Their unabashed contentiousness, meanwhile, helped pave the way for Twitter's discourse of open outrage.

Amazon.com

A few years out of Princeton in 1990, Jeff Bezos was living in New York, working for Bankers Trust. Looking to move into tech, he took a job at the two-year-old firm D. E. Shaw, one of the first quantitative hedge funds—that is, a company that used large amounts of algorithmic and computing power to gain trading advantages (*see also* QUANT). (In its early days, it was headquartered in a loftlike rental upstairs from Revolution Books, a communist bookstore on 16th Street.) Just around the time Bezos joined Shaw, the World Wide Web became the new portal to the internet, and his job centered on research into the business opportunities it created.

By 1994, he had determined that the future lay in online shopping, and made a list of products that could be sold that way. Books seemed a promising start, because they were easy to warehouse and ship. Bezos

The Village Voice, *vol. 1, no. 1.*

offered the idea to D. E. Shaw, which declined; he then made the unorthodox decision to leave the firm midyear without waiting for his bonus. He and his then-wife drove across the country as Bezos made revenue projections in the passenger seat, and he incorporated the new firm, Amazon, in a Bellevue, Washington, garage. As of early 2020, he was the richest person on the planet, with a net worth (depending on Amazon's stock price) around $150 billion; owing in part to the online-commerce boom during the COVID-19 pandemic (*see also* QUARANTINE), that figure was projected to reach $1 trillion in the next few years. Statistically, the odds are better than not that you bought this book from him.

American Museum of Natural History

see TYRANNOSAURUS REX

Anchorman

The institution of the network anchor persists even as perennial eulogies are written for it, even as the broadcast networks give way to the individualized narrowcasting of social networks. As Andrew Heyward, the former president of CBS News, describes the atavistic absurdity of the franchise, the very concept that an anchor could "organize the world in a coherent way" is now a non sequitur. But, like the cockroach, the anchorman (and -woman) has outlasted countless changes in the ecosystem.

Even the provenance of the term *anchorman* has been retouched for public consumption. For years it was said to have first gained currency in 1952, when it turned up in a CBS press release to characterize Walter Cronkite's role at the political conventions. It turns out that the term was first used on television in 1948 at NBC to describe the permanent member of a rotating panel of celebrities on the quiz show *Who Said That?*—a program that, tidily enough, was among the first to blur the roles of press and entertainment, as it

was hosted by the newsman-pitchman John Cameron Swayze.

Cronkite ascended to the anchor chair of the *CBS Evening News* in 1962. By the time he retired prematurely in 1981, the identity of the network anchor as the voice-of-God arbiter of American civic virtue had been indelibly fixed in his image. Not without reason. He was a first-class reporter and an enforcer of standards, and he didn't take himself as seriously as his idolaters did. He is generally canonized for three career highlights in his tenure as CBS anchor: welling up while delivering the bulletin of President Kennedy's death on the day of the assassination; being declared "the most trusted man in America" in a poll (which turned out to be somewhat skewed); and traveling to Vietnam in the wake of the Tet Offensive in 1968, at which point he declared the war unwinnable, prompting President Johnson's announcement weeks later that he would not seek reelection (again, likely a connection that was drawn after the fact).

In the early 1980s, the anchor business entered a twenty-year period of stable respectability, with the ascent of Peter Jennings (ABC), Tom Brokaw (NBC), and Dan Rather (CBS). All three stayed in their jobs until the end of 2004, leaving in the space of four months (two retirements, one death). Until Katie Couric and Diane Sawyer in the early 2000s, there were no solo women anchors in the weekday job, and no solo African-American ones until Lester Holt in 2015. As *60 Minutes* in particular has demonstrated, the most impressive, and bravest, practitioners of television news have rarely been anchors—many cite the show's Bob Simon, who was held hostage for 40 days in an Iraqi jail during the first Gulf War and did not spend his authority at an anchor desk. Today, as the half-hour 6:30 p.m. newscast is viewed by fewer and fewer (and older and older) Americans, much of the anchoring energy has shifted, with the hosts of the network morning shows now commanding more viewers, more national clout, and higher salaries than their evening-news peers. After dinner, straight-news cable anchors and commentators dominate, with the hourlong broadcasts of Sean Hannity and Rachel Maddow usually the highest-rated shows on, respectively, the right and the left. But even they have just 3 million viewers on a big day, perhaps one-tenth of Cronkite's old audience. Most Americans are just checking their phones instead.

The Anthora cup, once a Greek diner staple, now rarely encountered.

Anthora Cup

It is usually known as "the Greek diner cup," but it has a name. The Anthora was introduced in the mid-1960s by a small manufacturer called Sherri Cup, when the company's director of marketing, an Auschwitz survivor named Leslie Buck, wanted a product that would appeal to the Greeks who dominated the coffee-shop business. His design had a blue-and-white color scheme to match the Greek flag, a meander pattern around the top and bottom, stylized amphorae up the side, and two panels of quasi-Hellenic lettering that read, WE ARE HAPPY TO SERVE YOU. It became the mainstay of those takeout shops, with variants available from other cup manufacturers (the discus thrower, IT'S OUR PLEASURE TO SERVE YOU, etc.). The Anthora design was produced in massive numbers, hundreds of millions per year, in the pre-Starbucks era. Today it is semiretired, as Dart (the company that absorbed Sherri Cup) produces the Anthora only upon request. As a pop-culture icon, however, it has taken on a second life as, among other things, a ceramic collectible, a print on T-shirts and bags, and a New York signifier in movies and TV shows.

Athlete As Celebrity

There were prominent athletes in the nineteenth century, especially boxing champs like "Gentleman" Jim Corbett, but the appearance of the celebrity athlete can be traced to three near-simultaneous events: the rise of commercial sports radio, beginning with the New York Giants in the 1921 World Series, which aired on WJZ out of Newark (*see also* RADIO BROADCASTING; SPORTS TALK RADIO); the creation of the tabloid press, starting with the New York *Daily News* in 1919 (*see also* TABLOID); and the arrival of Babe Ruth in New York, also in 1919, after the Red Sox sold him to the Yankees. The media went crazy for Ruth. His appetite for hot dogs and beer and pretty girls made for great copy, and if he wrecked a few fast cars along the way, well, his roguishness just made the stories better. When a reporter remarked to him in 1930 that he had drawn a higher salary than President Hoover, he wisecracked, "Well, I had a better year." New York, a city full of business and nightlife opportunities, was the perfect stage for him. Only the fighter Jack Dempsey, another New Yorker, came close to rivaling Ruth in the public sphere.

Many athletes did not enjoy the limelight the way Ruth and Dempsey did, and some had uneasy relationships with fame. Joe DiMaggio was known for being distant and clipped with reporters (even after his retirement from baseball, the circus surrounding his marriage to Marilyn Monroe didn't change things much). Ted Williams, up in Boston, was actively hostile to the press, and the press returned the favor. But others wore it better. Mickey Mantle's good-ol'-boy-in-the-big-city persona went over well enough that, adhering to the conventions of the day, the press was willing to ignore the fact that, despite being an open and friendly guy, he cheated on his wife relentlessly and could be a mean drunk. A few years later, Joe Namath's late-night carousing went over better, probably because the 1970s were the perfect time for it, and because he, like Ruth, wore the role of the ebullient rogue so lightly. The same went for the early-1970s Knicks, fronted by the

Broadway Joe in off-duty uniform, 1971.

breathtakingly dandyish Walt "Clyde" Frazier, and the 1986 Mets, whose late-night partying habits left a couple of players in the much less charming realm of addiction and rehab. Indeed, many athlete celebrities lost control of their behavior after their playing days ended: Namath has been open about his drinking problem, Mantle ended up needing a liver transplant, and Ruth's heavy consumption of cigars and booze probably led to the nasopharyngeal cancer that killed him at 53.

The Yankees' Reggie Jackson was perhaps the first of the next generation of celebrity athletes, and it wasn't for his late-night shenanigans; it was for his media savvy. "I'm the straw that stirs the drink," he memorably said, irritating the rest of the teammates in that cocktail, not to mention his manager, Billy Martin, and his team's owner, George Steinbrenner. But in the fame game, he was outhitting everyone. His successors are the superstar athletes of our time—Derek Jeter, Alex Rodriguez, Aaron Judge, Lebron James, Tom Brady—who, although they may date supermodels and hit the clubs, seem a little denatured, distant, and managed, more like CEOs than Broadway Joes.

Atomic Bomb

When the Italian physicist Enrico Fermi arrived in the United States in 1939, he took a position on the faculty of Columbia University. There he began experiments in nuclear fission, hiring the school's football players to handle the large, heavy volume of graphite and uranium required to build his experimental apparatus, called an "atomic pile." In a matter of weeks—in the basement of Pupin Hall on January 25, 1939—he had split a uranium atom for the first time in this country, reproducing and advancing upon earlier work done in Germany.

Within the year, Albert Einstein signed a letter to President Roosevelt suggesting the United States begin looking into the use of atomic energy for defense, after which the Navy issued Columbia a $6,000 research grant. That work continued in multiple locations, notably the secret, sprawling camp at Los Alamos, New Mexico, but its administrative center was at 270 Broadway in what is now Tribeca—and for that reason, it became known as the Manhattan Project.

Much of its business was conducted through a front company headquartered nearby in the Woolworth Building, at 233 Broadway, and tons of uranium were stored in a warehouse on West 20th Street, among what are now Chelsea's galleries. J. Robert Oppenheimer, a native New Yorker—he grew up on Riverside Drive near 88th Street and attended the Ethical Culture School—was the project's scientist-in-chief. The work led to the Trinity test outside Alamogordo, New Mexico, on July 16, 1945, the first nuclear detonation, which was hot enough to melt the desert sand of the test site into a field of green glass. Hiroshima and Nagasaki were obliterated three weeks later, raising the prospect, ever more present in later years, of New York's own mortality. "The city, for the first time in its long history," E. B. White wrote in 1948, "is destructible. A single flight of planes no bigger than a wedge of geese can quickly end this island fantasy, burn the towers, crumble the bridges, turn the underground passages into lethal chambers, cremate the millions."

Auteur Theory

NOTE: *Brooklyn-born Andrew Sarris, one of the most influential film critics in history, is best known as the chief proponent of the auteur ("author") theory in the United States. Although he didn't invent the concept—it was first discussed in the seminal French film journal* Cahiers du Cinéma *in the mid-1950s—he codified and broadly promoted this new way of thinking about a director as not simply a hired hand but as a film's primary, personal creator. Here, the film critic and author*

(4) **How to Make Horn & Hardart's Macaroni and Cheese**
According to a recipe rediscovered by the New York Public Library.

¼ pound elbow macaroni	2 tablespoons light cream
1½ tablespoons flour	1 cup cheddar cheese, shredded
1½ tablespoons butter	
½ teaspoon salt	½ cup canned tomatoes, diced
Dash white pepper	
Dash red pepper	½ teaspoon sugar
1½ cups milk	

1. Cook macaroni according to package directions. Preheat oven to 400 degrees.
2. Melt butter in the top of a double boiler. Gradually blend in flour, salt, and both peppers. When mixture is smooth, add milk and cream, stirring constantly. Cook for a few minutes until it thickens.

3. Add cheese, and continue to heat until it melts and the sauce looks smooth. Remove from heat. Add the cooked macaroni to the sauce. Mix the sugar with the tomatoes, and add.
4. Pour mixture into a buttered baking dish, and bake until the surface browns.

Molly Haskell (who is also Sarris's widow) recounts the story of its development.

I was working for the French film office when I met Andrew Sarris. I saw him on a panel. I had been reading his film reviews in *The Village Voice*, and I was enraptured by him and his writing. We started going out. He was like my graduate school—he was my mentor and everything else. He actually gave me the chance to write my first review, in the *Voice*. Our relationship was completely intertwined with movies and always would be. It's hard to know where one thing left off and the other began.

Andrew was really taking issue with the kind of film criticism that existed then in America. It was often about socially important films, or if certain films were canonical, and there was no sense of director or style whatsoever. It started with a piece he did in *Film Culture* in 1962, "Notes on the Auteur Theory," in which he laid out the ground rules for reexamining cinema. Film studies were coming into vogue in the academy, but there were no principles like Aristotle's *Poetics*. There needed to be something, and this was a first step. It was open-minded. I mean, it was provocative, and it was presumptuous in a way—here he was, creating categories and listing directors—but on the other hand, it was done in all modesty, inviting controversy and comment.

He realized that directorial style was something very mysterious. He had to train himself, because, he said, American audiences are much more attuned to the ear than the eye. Everybody was so focused on the what: What was the story, what was the reality that was being dealt with. He was talking about how it was, and how different directors approached the same thing. There were certain genres that were beneath respect, like the woman's film and the Western and even the gangster film. He showed how genre was actually a freeing thing, because you had this basic formula, a template, and you worked these variations on it, which were very different according to each director. It was a way of seeing films.

You don't want to use the word *author* because it's too literary. The one thing we're not talking about is the script. He would always say that other factors are important, but the director is the one who puts his imprint on the film, and the great directors more than the lesser directors. The lesser directors are practically interchangeable, but the great directors are personal. I mean, the compositions of John Ford, or the kinetic back-and-forth between actors in a Howard Hawks film, all contain a wealth of psychological perception, of attitude. It has to be a little bit open-ended, because it's something you deduce as you watch film after film. It's a process of discovery, of making connections—and getting that much more from a film in so doing.

I've talked with people who are a little younger than me, people who were in college at the time and who loved movies. It was like a bible to them. They tried to catch up on the movies he wrote about. So it really did guide, even spawn, a whole generation of movie lovers.

Automat [4]

The Horn & Hardart Automat was, after a fashion, a restaurant built as a giant vending machine. You walked in with a pocketful of change and faced a wall of small, windowed compartments. Drop a coin in the slot next to any one, and the door would be unlocked; behind each door lay a food item: a burger, a plate of mashed potatoes, or a slice of pie. It seemed modern and mechanical to diners of the 1920s—never mind that, behind the wall, toiled more or less the same kitchen staff as in any restaurant. Eating at the Automat was the urban fast-food experience of its time, created to be clean, sanitary, and quick, with no anxiety about tipping. The macaroni-and-cheese recipe was, by most accounts, excellent; the pies were famous.

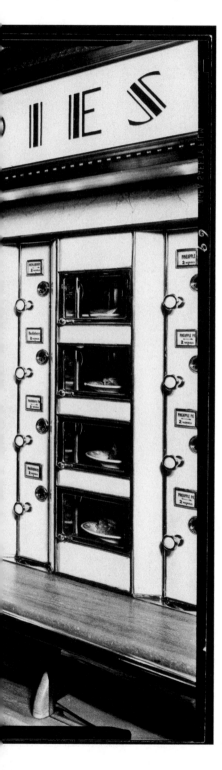

The Automat at Eighth Avenue and 57th Street, February 1936.
PHOTOGRAPH BY BERENICE ABBOTT

The first Automat opened in Philadelphia in 1902, but the most famous ones, by far, appeared over the next few decades all over New York City. Many were inside showy Art Deco buildings with nickel or porcelain fittings, and they always featured a huge central coffee urn with a dolphin-shaped spigot that never went dry. Some locations were open all night. They were integrated deeply into the fabric of city life, in part because they served all classes: Secretaries and telephone operators ate there, and so did their banker and chief-executive bosses.

In the 1960s—as dining tastes changed, McDonald's came east, and car culture came to dominate America—the Automats began disappearing, but it took a while. The world's last Horn & Hardart, on East 42nd Street, closed in 1991. A distant descendant called Bamn!, serving Japanese food from similar little compartments, operated briefly on St. Marks Place in the mid-aughts but met the same fate, as did, in 2017, the city's two branches of Eatsa, a San Francisco–based chain whose midtown office-worker clientele retrieved their grain bowls from small windows after ordering on iPads.

Automated Teller Machine

The Armenian-American immigrant Luther George Simjian wasn't trained as an engineer, but he managed to accumulate 200 patents in his lifetime, many of them relating to optics. In 1939, while living in New York City, Simjian began developing a device called the Bankograph that could accept deposits for checks and cash and keep a record as it did so. First National City Bank—now Citigroup—eventually installed one, in 1960, but it failed to catch on. At the time, people's banking habits were ingrained, and apparently the only customers interested in retrieving or depositing cash at odd hours were gamblers and prostitutes. Nine years later, Chemical Bank (long since absorbed into JPMorgan Chase) tried again, this time with digitally linked machines made by a Dallas company called Docutel. The first one was in Rockville Centre; others quickly followed in Penn Station, LeFrak City, and a few other New York locales. In 1972, *New York* Magazine included the new gadget in its "And Now the Good News" issue under the headline "How Do You Rob a Robot?"

From

BAGEL

to

BYSTANDER EFFECT

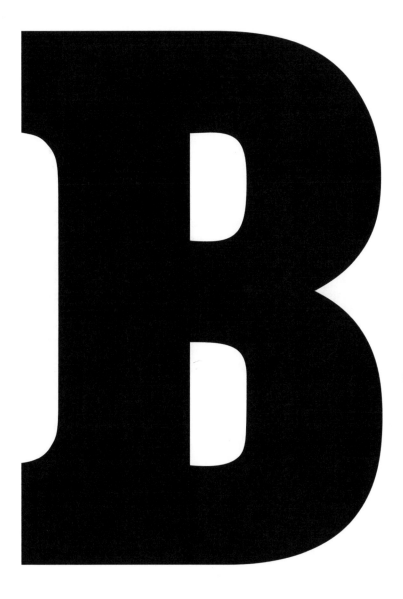

Burlesque dancer Bubbles Darlene,
who advertised her act with the
tagline "World's Most Exciting Body," 1955.

① **The Key to a Perfect Baked Alaska**

From Delmonico's executive chef Billy Oliva

"The true hallmark of a perfect Baked Alaska is **an inner gelato core that's just soft enough to cut through with a spoon.** Each spoonful should yield a medley of each component—gelato, golden meringue, apricot compote, and brioche—in one bite."

Bagel

The definitive New York breakfast bread, a ring of dough that has been boiled before baking to produce a hard, shiny crust, came from Eastern Europe. That much we know, or think we do—familiar-seeming breads are mentioned in records from fourteenth-century Poland. Unless the bagel was derived from the Italian tarallo, another boiled-and-baked (though yeastless) ring-shaped treat? Or the steamed-then-baked *girde*, of Muslim northwestern China? Or, vaguely, the pretzel? The name apparently comes from a German baker named Shlomo Beigel, although even that attribution is questionable. In short, the bagel—in its early days in the U.S. often spelled "beigel"—is the quintessential American item, a mash-up of multiple cultures that was funneled through Ellis Island, became established as a local staple in Jewish New York, and eventually, after some denaturing, caught mainstream acceptance across the country and the rest of the world.

One incontestable fact is that, by the end of the nineteenth century, you could buy bagels in Jewish enclaves in New York. They contained no dairy, unlike some breads, and thus were pareve: People who kept kosher could eat them with anything. The bakeries were hard on their workers—brutally hot, infested with vermin, demanding long hours for low pay—and, starting in the 1880s, the bagel bakers began to unionize. Within a generation, their union was among the most powerful in New York City, with members receiving notably high wages. Which they absolutely earned for this difficult work, not least because the dough was notoriously stiff and exhausting to knead. Consequently, their product was tough to chew and crunchy to the bite. The standard analogy was to a "cement doughnut." A day-old bagel was widely known to be an effective teething ring for babies.

Even while it vanished from its homeland, as the Jews of Poland were murdered en masse, the bagel embedded itself ever more deeply into the Jewish culture of New York, becoming a distinctive regional ethnic item. (A smaller bagel culture sprang up, paralleling New York's, in Montreal.) In 1954, however, that niche status began to change when a New Haven, Connecticut, baker named Harry Lender started storing his products in the freezer. He and his sons made them by machine, which required a slightly softer dough that yielded a somewhat squishier bagel, and bagged them up, six at a time, for supermarket distribution. The Lenders were widely criticized among traditionalists—and wildly popular among everyone else. (The firm's other innovations include the cinnamon-raisin bagel. Another *shandeh*.)

By the end of the 1960s, Lender's bagels were widespread in the East; a decade later, they were national, and Murray Lender, one of Harry's sons, was appearing in TV commercials and on Johnny Carson's *Tonight Show*. An item that a generation earlier had been exotic enough to New York *Times* readers that it required a pronunciation guide ("baygle") was becoming as all-American as pizza or General Tso's chicken. The softer variety even spread to the majority of bagel shops in New York City, and it has since become difficult to find the old cement-doughnut style. Today, you can get a fairly characterless, un-chewy bagel at a Dunkin' Donuts virtually anywhere in America. You can also, owing to several new bakeries, once again find a bagel in Krakow.

Baked Alaska [1]

As is true of the bagel, the prehistory of this dessert—a walnut sponge cake topped with apricot compote and a layer of banana ice cream, the whole thing encased in a blanket of meringue that is then lightly browned—is somewhat hard to pin down. It has been traced to

The neo-original:
Delmonico's Baked Alaska.

related desserts created by French and Chinese chefs, but the definitive version, most accounts agree, was created at Delmonico's, the legendary Gilded Age restaurant in lower Manhattan. Chef Charles Ranhofer, probably in 1867, named his new dish "Alaska, Florida" to celebrate both its hot-cold nature and the recent American purchase of the Alaska territory. (It was an extremely expensive dish to make and serve in the days before commercial refrigeration and cheap fruit imports.) By the 1890s, when it appeared in Fannie Farmer's cookbook, it had acquired its familiar name, and by the 1950s, it had become broadly popular—after which it entered a long, unfashionable twilight. Like many such bits of Americana, it has been rediscovered in the past two decades because it is both showy and delicious.

Ballet

Ballet has been around since the French kings and the courts of the Italian Renaissance—once people figured out that dancing legs looked great in tights, the cat jetéd out of the bag. In the years since, classical ballet style solidified through tradition and training: the steps and orientation of the carriage, a rotation at the hips to achieve the "turned-out" position, and the vocabulary of weightlessness created through extension, pointe work, and a flowing port de bras (movement of the arms).

In the early twentieth century, Sergei Diaghilev's Ballets Russes began to experiment, investigating craft for its own sake and de-emphasizing story. The basis for a dance could be as slight as a mood (Mikhail Fokine's "Les Sylphides") or a vernacular movement (Vaslav Nijinsky's version of a tennis match, "Jeux"). The last of the Ballets Russes' great choreographers, George Balanchine, refined this art of subtraction to the sharp point of neoclassical ballet, a "purified," nonnarrative form that used the impersonality of modernism to put the focus on steps as steps, rather than references to something else.

In 1933, at the invitation of the impresario Lincoln Kirstein, Balanchine came to New York, and the ballet took a monumental evolutionary leap forward. The two men established the School of American Ballet, and the choreographer began to build both the works and the performers that would change the world of dance. This was ballet for the American century: His (trademarked) Balanchine technique exaggerates and elongates the classical form, pushing an energetic tension through all those floating limbs—he told dancers to "reach for diamonds" when they were in arabesque so their hands wouldn't look too relaxed. His techniques prioritized speed and space. Watch Balanchine-trained dancers and you'll see that they inhabit more volume, somehow, than other dancers of the same size.

In the 1940s, Kirstein and Balanchine started the subscription-based Ballet Society to perform Balanchine works like *The Four Temperaments*; this group became the New York City Ballet after it was invited to take root at City Center. In the following decades in New York, Balanchine choreographed hundreds of dances, including the abstract masterpiece *Agon*, the evening-length storyless ballet *Jewels*, and a whole series of works made to the music of Igor Stravinsky, his longtime friend and musical kindred spirit. Balanchine also worked in the movies and fought for Broadway shows to include a choreography credit; he paved the way for our current notion of the star dance-maker, all while putting that sweeping "American" movement at the core of what had been a European form. And his invention hasn't been undone: This fusion of modernism and classicism still defines contemporary ballet. His school and NYCB still exist and continue to disseminate his methods. Twyla Tharp once called him God—and verily, his word goes forth.

Barbicide

As a teenager, Maurice King loathed barbershops. He was disgusted that barbers simply used water to clean their combs. And so, in 1947, after earning a graduate degree in chemical engineering, King found himself mixing the first batches of his now-ubiquitous chemical concoction in the bathroom of his Brooklyn apartment. The key to his invention was a new kind of disinfectant, an ammonium compound found in the mud used to drill oil wells. He dyed the poisonous mixture electric blue to signal a natural purity, leaving a permanent stain on his bathtub, and packaged the elixir in tall jars that contained a lift-out comb holder. He then began making trips to state capitals to lobby for a law requiring the use of disinfectants in barbershops. The states bit, and many wrote legislation requiring the product by its name, Barbicide—which, King liked to joke, means "kill the barber," a nod to his teenage distaste. Until 2006, the stuff was made on 12th Street in Brooklyn, right next to the similarly radioactive-looking Gowanus Canal. Now it comes from Wisconsin.

Baseball [2]

For all the efforts to slap a pastoral gloss on the sport, baseball as we know it is an urban game. More precisely, it is "the New York game." That is what modern baseball was first called, and where it was first played. It was here that baseball's rules were perfected and where we first kept score, where the curveball, changeup, and bunt were devised and the home run came into its own. New York was where spectators first paid admission, where the idea of a sports league was invented, and where the first "world championship" was held.

It was in New York, too, where the game's color line was finally broken, the reserve clause was made law, a players' league was conceived and died, and the first modern free agent was signed; where the first modern baseball stadiums were built, sportswriting was revolutionized, the first great radio broadcasters plied their trade, and the first game was televised. The only perfect game in World Series history was pitched here (in 1956), an expansion team won a World Series for the first time here (1969), and the World Series was fixed by gamblers here (1919). Baseball grew up inextricably linked to the pace, customs, and demands of New York, shaped by all the city had to offer—its inventiveness and ambition, its grandiosity and corruption.

A prohibition against Sunday ball-playing in New Amsterdam dates to 1656, but by 1805 two clubs from Columbia College, the Gymnastics and the Sons of Diagoras, were playing ball next to Tyler's "pleasure garden," and by at least 1823, "the manly athletic game of 'base ball'" was being played regularly at the Jones' Retreat tavern. The question is, just what were they playing? The New York game had two main competitors: Philadelphia "town ball" and "the Massachusetts game." The Philly version was a sort of exaggerated cricket with rules that were never conclusively decided. The Massachusetts game was barely organized anarchy in which runners were retired by "soaking," or being hit with a light rubber ball, on a playing field with no fixed baselines or foul territory; batters could turn and hit the ball *behind* them and run anywhere they wanted to get to the next base.

But a game with an endless playing field makes it hard to put up a grandstand near the action, and those rubber balls couldn't be thrown more than 200 feet. Both problems would be resolved under what came to be known as "the Knickerbocker Rules." Founded in 1845, the Knickerbockers were not the first New York baseball club, but they were adept at revising the rules and improving the conditions others had been playing

William Beebe
in his bathysphere,
ca. 1930.

under. The first clubs were composed of just the sorts of individuals only a major city could provide—"merchants, lawyers, Union Bank clerks, insurance clerks and others who were at liberty after 3 o'clock in the afternoon," as the sport's first shortstop, Dr. Daniel Lucius Adams, would recall. (In an early daguerreotype, they look like a conclave of sporty Mennonites.) They preferred to play among themselves, hence many games took place near taverns, hotel dining rooms, and pleasure gardens (*pleasure* being a euphemism for "beer").

By the 1840s, clubs began to spread all over the growing city, wherever empty lots and fields could still be found. The equipment began to change, too, thanks to "Dock" Adams, who was in charge of making equipment for the Manhattan clubs. Tired of having to run out to gather all the light rubber balls his teammates couldn't throw back to the infield, Adams found a "Scotch saddler" who showed him how to put together "three or four ounces of rubber cuttings, wound with yarn and then covered with the leather [horsehide]." This was much softer than a modern baseball but not a ball you could easily soak a runner with, not without risking serious injury or a brawl. And it was the death knell for the running-fielding Massachusetts game in favor of the pitcher-hitter game we know today. Adams and his Scotch saddler also brought the whiff of death into the sport—something else that would come to pass on a New York ball field. They had invented a weapon that could be hurled or batted toward a player's head with truly lethal force. Only true athletes would be able to throw it, field it, hit it, *dodge* it. As a bloodsport, baseball would prove more popular than ever.

By the start of the Civil War, the New York game had annihilated its northeastern competitors, and the war spread the city's version around the country. There were an estimated 50 clubs in New York and Brooklyn alone, along with another 60 youth or "feeder" clubs. They now dressed in elaborate uniforms modeled after militia companies and were filled with men from all classes, colors, ethnicities, and professions. There were the Manhattans, a club made up entirely of policemen; the Phantoms, who were bartenders; and the Pocahontas Club (milkmen), the Metropolitans (schoolteachers), and the Aesculapeans of Brooklyn (physicians).

Over the ensuing 35 years or so, the Knickerbocker Rules would be honed again and again, settling on three

strikes and four balls to a batter, nine innings to a game, fair and foul territories, eliminating outs for balls caught on one bounce, allowing overhand and sidearm pitching, and, most important, those seemingly magical distances of ninety feet between each base and sixty feet, six inches, from the pitcher's mound to the plate. Major League teams would come and go, playing in every borough of the consolidated city, even Staten Island. But what we play today is still the New York game.

Basketball *see* HOOPS

Bathysphere

The New York naturalist William Beebe, the story goes, was conversing with Theodore Roosevelt about ocean exploration when the president sketched a ball-shaped miniature submarine on a napkin. After many years of development and quite a few technological problems, with funding from the New York Zoological Society, the sketch became a thick-walled steel sphere attached to a long cable. After a few test dives off the Bahamas, on June 10, 1930, Beebe and his colleague Otis Barton smashed every diving record, descending a quarter-mile beneath the waves of the Atlantic, roughly three times farther down than any living human had been. For the first time, they saw the inky darkness of the sea past the level at which sunlight can penetrate and observed some of the strange phosphorescent creatures that live there. (Many of their observations were initially doubted by other scientists but were confirmed by later submersibles.) Beebe and Barton made more than 30 dives altogether, the deepest one to 3,028 feet, and the pair became more well known after they wrote about their trips, notably for *National Geographic*. NBC radio covered at least one of their dives with a live shipboard broadcast.

New, safer, more maneuverable submersibles eventually superseded the bathysphere, and the little sub was variously exhibited, forgotten, and (eventually) dumped in a storage yard under the Coney Island Cyclone, where it sat for a couple of decades. In 2005, the New York Zoological Society—now called the Wildlife Conservation Society—reclaimed it, restored it, and put it on display at the New York Aquarium. "Beebe's Bathysphere" also surfaces in Stephen Sondheim's 1971

(3) **The Essential Beats Reading List**

Chosen by Oliver Harris, president of the European Beat Studies Network

» **"Howl,"** by Allen Ginsberg (1956)
» **On the Road,** by Jack Kerouac (1957)
» **Naked Lunch,** by William S. Burroughs (1959)
» **Go,** by John Clellon Holmes (1952)

» **Minor Characters,** by Joyce Johnson (1983)
» **The Beard,** by Michael McClure (1965)
» **Revolutionary Letters,** by Diane di Prima (1971)
» **Turtle Island,** by Gary Snyder (1974)

» **Fast Speaking Woman,** by Anne Waldman (1975)
» **The works published by Lawrence Ferlinghetti's City Lights Books** (beginning in 1953)

song "I'm Still Here," in which a tough-old-babe singer recalls all the mid-century culture she's outlasted.

Bearer Bonds

How did a 1980s action villain stuff half a billion dollars into just a couple of suitcases? Bearer bonds, dating from the highly unregulated mid-nineteenth century, did the trick. These bonds, designed to circulate like banknotes, were created by Alexander Bryan Johnson—grandson-in-law of John Adams—who split his time and his banking business between New York City and Utica. These securities were unregistered: Whoever physically held the piece of paper was the legal owner. After the Civil War, the bonds took off in popularity, being convenient in the absence of a centralized banking system. But because of that anonymity—and because they allowed for transport of a ton of money with just a few pieces of paper—they became a useful currency for criminals. Corporations stopped issuing them in the mid-1960s, and in 1982, the U.S. Treasury got out of the game, too, preferring to know who owns its debt. (Though largely out of use, the bearer bond lives on in spirit; whoever holds the private key to a bitcoin is effectively its owner.)

At this point, the bonds took off as plot devices in the golden era of big-budget action films. In *Beverly Hills Cop,* the rogue detective played by Eddie Murphy finds out who murdered his friend for his stash of bearer bonds, and *Heat* starts off with Robert De Niro and his crew stealing $1.6 million in the currency to the chagrin of an especially yelly Al Pacino. But their high point in pop culture came with *Die Hard* in 1988, when Alan Rickman's Hans Gruber takes over the Nakatomi Building and demands its $640 million stash of bearer bonds in his implacable accent. That amount in cash, weighing one gram per note, would total over 6.6 tons, roughly the weight of two Ford F-250 trucks; in *Die Hard,* the pile of crisp bearer bonds can be handled by one person.

Beats, The [3]

The writers now generally referred to as the Beats—centering on the poet Allen Ginsberg and the novelists Jack Kerouac and William S. Burroughs—cohered in the bars and coffeehouses around Columbia University and Greenwich Village in the late 1940s and early '50s. They were of the generation shaped by the Second World War and, immediately thereafter, the first looming dread of nuclear annihilation. As most Americans leaned toward domesticity and consumerism, they went the opposite way, dropping out, living unconventionally, forgoing most sexual and family norms, and making expressive and (in some cases) good, lasting art.

The name was reportedly coined by a friend of theirs, the poet and grifter Herbert Huncke, from whom Kerouac picked it up, and was soon popularized by another friend, John Clellon Holmes, in a *New York Times Magazine* story published in November 1952. "The origins of the word 'beat' are obscure, but the meaning is only too clear to most Americans," Holmes wrote of his cohort. "More than a mere weariness, it implies the feeling of having been used, of being raw. It involves a sort of nakedness of mind, and, ultimately, of soul; a feeling of being reduced to the bedrock of consciousness. In short, it means being undramatically pushed up against the wall of oneself. A man is beat whenever he goes for broke and wagers the sum of his resources on a single number; and the young generation has done that continually from early youth."

Certainly the most familiar image of the Beats comes from Kerouac's 1957 novel *On the Road,* based on his cross-country drive with his friend Neal Cassady, and while San Francisco had its own contingent of Beats in and around North Beach (Ginsberg's *Howl* made its debut there at City Lights Books in 1956), most of their time and artistic output can be traced back to New York. Ginsberg and Kerouac met through their mutual friend Lucien Carr while at Columbia. (That was before

Miles Davis plays the Village Vanguard, 1958.

Ginsberg was ejected, Kerouac quit, and Carr went to prison for manslaughter.) The San Remo Cafe, at the corner of Bleecker and Macdougal Streets, was perhaps their hangout of choice, although really any dive would do. Beat culture defined downtown New York for the next two decades, segueing into the coffeehouse-folksinger scene of the early '60s, the Soho-loft artist scene that came after, and (ultimately) the national mainstreaming of the counterculture in the early 1970s. By then, Kerouac was gone—he drank himself to death in 1969—but Ginsberg remained primarily a New Yorker till his death in 1997, long enough to become the accessible elder statesman of bohemianism. A trip to meet him in his apartment at 12th Street and Avenue A became a sort of merit badge among arty young New Yorkers.

Bebop

Minton's Playhouse, a club in a Harlem hotel, was a hothouse for jazz innovation in the 1930s and '40s. The house band itself was a phenomenon—Thelonious Monk on piano, Kenny Clarke on drums—but the star

most nights was the guitarist Charlie Christian, who would come in after his gigs with the Benny Goodman Sextet. These musicians stripped popular songs down to their barest elements and took endless turns improvising over the chords. Christian's solos were jarring to everyone; he'd play against the dominant rhythm, halt in the middle of phrases, and run circuitous paths through the chord changes.

Christian died young in 1942, but the saxophonist Charlie Parker and the trumpeter Dizzy Gillespie picked up where he left off. They performed at Minton's night after night, often until 4 a.m., trying out harmonic devices that had never been used in popular music. The next generation of jazz greats, including Miles Davis, Dexter Gordon, and Art Blakey (though not John Coltrane) came mainly out of the Minton's scene.

By some accounts, the term *bebop* was originally the nickname of a scale interval these performers favored, the flatted fifth (in terms of do-re-mi, it fits between "fa" and "sol"). Others say it came from scat singing or it's supposed to mimic the staccato rhythms of the music. "We wouldn't call it anything, really, just music," Clarke later said.

The Beats at their peak: from left, Allen Ginsberg, Jack Kerouac, and Gregory Corso in Greenwich Village, 1957.

PHOTOGRAPH BY
BRUCE DAVIDSON

4 The New York Cycle Club's Favorite Bike Route in New York

A sixteen-mile trip for moderately experienced cyclists along the historic Ocean Parkway bike path.

Start in **Chinatown** on Canal Street and head over the Manhattan Bridge. Bike south through **Clinton Hill, Grand Army Plaza,** and **Prospect Park.** From there, pick up the historic **Ocean Parkway** and follow it all the way to **Coney Island.** Tour the **Riegelmann Boardwalk,** enjoy lunch at Nathan's Famous, buy some Russian delicacies at New York Bread, and picnic in **Kaiser Park** overlooking Gravesend Bay. Have pizza and beers at Totonno's, then take the subway back.

"'Bebop' was a label that certain journalists later gave it." In the '50s, Davis and Coltrane moved on to other styles, and bebop faded from the forefront of musical invention, giving way to other forms like free jazz. Now it mainly lives at universities. But it still dominates the nightly fare at local New York clubs like Smalls, the Blue Note, the Village Vanguard, and the renovated Minton's.

Beefsteak

The gluttonous all-you-can-eat banquet known as a beefsteak had gained a foothold in New York by 1870. Working-class groups would celebrate at clubhouses or taverns or even just in a basement with vast amounts of charcoal-grilled beef and beer. Cutlery and napkins were disallowed; diners were issued aprons on which they'd wipe their hands. Most such events in the early days admitted only men, although the twentieth century eventually brought female diners (and a few refinements, like side dishes) into the scene. *The New Yorker's* Joseph Mitchell wrote in 1943 that in the halcyon days of the beefsteak, individual diners were routinely known to put away six pounds of meat and thirty glasses of beer.

By the 1960s, the beefsteak had begun to fade in popularity as dining habits changed and meat prices rose, although it never entirely disappeared from working-class enclaves of northern New Jersey. It has recently undergone a small-scale revival, resurrected among Brooklyn and Manhattan food enthusiasts. Forks are still eschewed, but the beef at these neobeefsteaks sometimes comes from high-quality artisanal farms, and the beer is typically microbrewed.

Belgian Waffles

Aren't they from Belgium? Of course they are. But the presence of Belgian waffles on your local coffee-shop menu can be traced precisely to April 22, 1964, when the New York World's Fair opened in Queens's Flushing Meadows. There, a café constructed as part of an ersatz Flemish village introduced to the United States a variant known as the Brussels waffle, which was lighter and tastier than the usual American breakfast version. The Vermersch family, operators of the restaurant, added strawberries, powdered sugar, and whipped cream to cater to the American sweet tooth, and a diner classic was born. "From the moment we opened, there was a line," Mariepaul Vermersch recalled in a radio interview 50 years later, adding that she and her parents, Maurice and Rose, were soon selling 2,500 waffles a day. Their recipe, still a family secret, is used at (and only at) the New York State Fair each summer in Syracuse.

Bike Lane [4]

Brooklyn's Ocean Parkway was conceived by the landscape architects Frederick Law Olmsted and Calvert Vaux in 1866, after they completed their plan for Prospect Park, to connect their new greensward with the upscale seaside resort at Coney Island. It would be a broad boulevard with a walkway cutting along its grassy median. Nearly 20 years later, as the national craze for bicycling reached its zenith, that pedestrian lane was divided and half its space given over to what was called the Ocean Parkway Cycle Path, which opened on June 15, 1894. It was so popular that its crushed-stone surface had to be replenished a month later, and a return path was built on the other side of the parkway in 1896.

In 2014, as bike lanes returned to New York City in a big way under the administration of Mayor Michael Bloomberg, the oldest one in the world was refurbished, and still sees significant use. It no longer reaches all the way north to Prospect Park, though; the first half-mile of Ocean Parkway (and its bike path) was demolished for the construction of the all-automobile Prospect Expressway in 1950.

Birth-Control Clinic

For ten days in October 1916, a storefront at 46 Amboy Street in Brownsville, Brooklyn, was open to women. The neighborhood was littered with fliers printed in English, Italian, and Yiddish, asking, "Mothers! Can you afford to have a large family? Do you want any more children? If not, why do you have them? Do not kill, Do not take life, but Prevent. Safe, Harmless Information can be obtained of trained Nurses … All Mothers Welcome." Pamphlets entitled "What Every Girl Should Know" were for sale for ten cents; included in the cost were a brief lecture on the female reproductive system and information about the most modern forms of contraception. These were illegal under section 1142 of the New York State Penal Code in an echo of the federal Comstock Laws, a set of prohibitions issued in the late nineteenth century that had forbidden the circulation of "obscene literature and articles of immoral use"—which included any information about what had only recently come to be called "birth control." On the first day it was open, more than a hundred women, many of them pushing baby carriages, availed themselves of the Brownsville clinic and the pessaries, rubber condoms, vaginal suppositories, and salt-and-vinegar douches it promoted, with over 400 more visiting in the days that followed.

Ten days after the opening, undercover police officers raided the place and arrested its proprietors: the nurse, activist, and sex educator Margaret Sanger; her sister and a registered nurse, Ethel Byrne; and a Russian Yiddish interpreter named Fania Mindell.

Once she got out of jail, Sanger attempted to reopen the Brownsville location but was shut down by police again and again. Byrne began a hunger strike during her thirty-day jail sentence; as Sanger described her sister's motivations, "Mrs. Byrne feels that one more death laid at the door of the government of this state is of little consequence," given the fact that other "unfortunate women go to their graves unnoticed and their agonies and deaths unknown." (Sanger's outreach to immigrant women sometimes uncomfortably overlapped with the drive of eugenicists who also wanted to see lower birthrates among them, but for different reasons.)

Sanger herself would be offered a suspended sentence as long as she agreed not to violate more obscenity laws. She refused the deal. "With me it is not a question of personal imprisonment or personal disadvantage," Sanger said at the time. "I am today and have always been more concerned with changing the law … regardless of what I have to undergo to have it done." Sanger would go on to found the American Birth Control League in 1921 and, in 1923, the Birth Control Clinical Research Bureau—the first legal birth-control clinic in the United States, which was headed up by Dr. Hannah Stone. In 1939, the two organizations would merge, forming the Birth Control Federation of America, which soon would become known as the Planned Parenthood Federation of America.

As Sanger recalled about those first days in Brownsville, "The women came in pairs, with friends, married daughters, some with nursing babies clasped in their arms. Women from the far end of Long Island … from Connecticut, Massachusetts, Pennsylvania, New Jersey. They came to learn the 'secret' which was possessed by the rich and denied the poor."

Blockbuster Museum Show

 The "Treasures of Tutankhamun" exhibit, which landed at the Metropolitan Museum of Art in 1978 at the end of a six-city American tour, abounded in riches of every kind. But the most impressive feature of the "King Tut" show was the mile-long line to get in. The first blockbuster museum exhibit to be so labeled, one that brought in 8 million visitors nationwide and

filled Egypt's coffers with gift-shop profits, was unprecedented. It was a display of ancient art that was also a pop-culture moment, fodder for—among other modern artifacts—Steve Martin's *Saturday Night Live* sketch and million-selling single named for the boy pharaoh ("He gave his life for tourism!"). The enormous attendance shocked the museums that hosted it into revamping their entry systems, but over the long term, it set museums on an irreversible path to an era ruled by populism, commercialism, and fierce competition for treasures and visitors.

No one did more to bring Tut to the States, or indeed to bring museums into the larger world of marketing and commerce, than the Metropolitan Museum's then-director, Thomas P. F. Hoving. It was Hoving who worked his way through Egypt's labyrinthine bureaucracy and shaky infrastructure to secure those precious objects, paying off functionaries, electricians, and even an Egyptian critic along the way. Hoving had taken over the Met in 1967, when the museum was sleepy and (after nearly a century) still half built. The institution chartered to advance "popular instruction and recreations" had become a warren of "incredibly dusty, static exhibits," as curator Morrison Heckscher remembered. "You'd come in during the week and there'd never be anyone in the gallery. The place was empty, and the labels were incomprehensible."

Dropped into that sleepy environment, Hoving acted fast and systematically. Fresh off a colorful year as New York's Parks commissioner, with a Ph.D. in art and a father who ran Tiffany & Co., Hoving was a politician with the instincts of a scholar (or perhaps the other way around). At his first meeting with the curators, he asked to see the special-exhibit schedule—there was none—and then to meet with the exhibition committee, which didn't exist. He soon decided to turn the Met's 1970 centennial into an 18-month cavalcade of exhibitions and concerts: Nina Simone! "Harlem on My Mind"! Original fanfares by Bernstein and Copland!

Eight years later, more than a million King Tut visitors poured into a museum Hoving had utterly transformed. First there was the show itself, a feat of storytelling; objects were arranged in order of their excavation to give a sense of the archaeologists' own discovery and were accompanied by contemporaneous photographs and crisp wall text. Some exhibit windows opened onto the brand-new Sackler Wing, a hangar-size jewel box built to house the newly installed Temple of Dendur.

By the time Tut himself came to town, however, Hoving was gone from the Met. After ten years, he'd resigned under growing pressure from the board. The pace of his changes, disruptive in every sense, had turned out to be unsustainable, and he couldn't go on steamrolling his internal critics indefinitely. "He alienated a great many of the curators by storming through a lot of his decisions," his long-serving successor, Philippe de Montebello, said, and that had long-term effects. "I used to say, 'You see these banners on the façade? It's not the glow of health but the flush of fever.'"

As in any other field—publishing, moviemaking—blockbusters don't always earn out. "Once you're on that treadmill, in terms of budgetary matters and visitorship, it's extremely difficult to pull back," said de Montebello. "But in the end, I think what he did was a very good thing for the museum world." After Tut, Hoving's once-revolutionary populist ethos rapidly became dominant. Carrie Barratt, a deputy director at the Met who worked on its 150th anniversary, put it like this: "When you ask people, 'What's the principal reason you go to museums,' the number one reason is 'to have fun,'" she said. "That's what makes people come back."

Bloomberg Terminal

"Michael R. Bloomberg was a partner at Salomon Brothers, the securities firm, until last September," reported the New York *Times* in May 1982. "His new company, Innovative Market Systems, which opened for business in February, is developing computer software systems for financial analysts." He had offered his idea—a dedicated, customized computer terminal that delivered then-unprecedented amounts of data to finance professionals at a steep subscription fee—to Salomon, which had declined. IMS soon became Bloomberg L.P., and the dedicated terminal eventually gave way to software that could run on any standard PC. The data are displayed in a distinctive visual format, densely and without much adornment, on a black background that makes the screen instantly recognizable to insiders, even from across the room.

Today, a Bloomberg terminal costs its user about $25,000 a year, and the company holds about a 30 percent share of the financial-services data market. The company remains privately held, mostly by Bloomberg himself, and it has made him the wealthiest person in New York City and one of the richest people on Earth, with a net worth of roughly $60 billion. He was elected mayor of New York in November 2001 and put management of the company into a trust during his twelve years in office, returning as its CEO in 2014. He also became a major philanthropist, giving hugely to his alma mater, Johns Hopkins University, and donating billions of dollars for a variety of causes, notably gun control, the environment, and public-health concerns. In part to spotlight these issues, he made a brief run for president in 2020.

Bodega

The small, street-corner grocery in New York City has a distinctive flavor profile—something involving egg sandwiches on kaiser rolls, cheap cigars, gray-market Duracell batteries, rampantly marked-up pints of Häagen-Dazs, beer sold with a tiny brown bag to disguise the can for outdoor drinking, seltzer in every possible flavor, light-and-sweet coffee, Tropical Fantasy fruit-flavored sodas, Snapple, Boar's Head cold cuts, and a scattering of Latin American or Asian specialty ingredients. The two terms many New Yorkers use for these places are *bodega* (which, in Spanish-speaking parts of the world, variously means "wine shop" or "grocery store") and *Korean greengrocer*, which has less to do with the clientele or offerings than with the immigrant owners, at least historically. (Many of the operators nowadays are not Korean but Chinese.) The Latin American bodega's visual signature is the awning, which is almost always red and yellow with blocky lettering, once hand-painted, now usually a decal.

These small stores serve multiple complicated social functions in their neighborhoods, extending well beyond their classic wares. In a city of tiny apartments with little or no storage space, they act as a collective pantry and freezer for the block. Most are open 24 hours a day, thus supplying the round-the-clock street-corner lighting and incidental surveillance that helps to keep streets safer (*see also* "EYES ON THE STREET"). A lot of bodega owners befriend their regulars, and once you know yours, they'll often hold a key for your arriving visitor or accept a

package delivered when you're not around. You can, in a pinch, make a pretty decent dinner out of the stuff your corner bodega sells; maybe you wouldn't want to eat every meal from there, but you wouldn't be miserable if you had to do so for a couple of weeks. As businesses, they can also serve as boosts into the middle class for the Korean or Dominican or Chinese or Yemeni families that run them. A lot of underprivileged kids have gone to college because their parents scrimped and saved the slim profits they retained after selling thousands of turkey-and-Swiss sandwiches. In 2017, when President Donald Trump put in place a ban on immigration from majority-Muslim countries, the Yemeni bodega owners of New York went on a daylong strike and received an outpouring of local support.

Book Party

Presumably Lady Murasaki poured out a little plum wine for her friends upon the completion of *The Tale of Genji*, possibly the world's first novel, in early-eleventh-century Kyoto. Certainly most authors and editors need no excuse to have a couple of drinks. As a codified type of event, however, the book party was honed, perfected, and raised to an art form by George Plimpton, co-founder of *The Paris Review* in 1953 and its proprietor for the next fifty years. Plimpton was affluent enough to have his own big apartment in a townhouse on East 72nd Street, from which the magazine was published in its early days, and it was a great, roomy place but the slightest bit worn, so guests would be at ease if they got a little sloppy. Plimpton was gregariously casual and patrician-charming enough to be a superb host. He was also notoriously cheap, and therein lay a secret of his book parties: He'd supply the room, and the book's publisher would pay for the food and drink. If you turned up at one of these events as a young editorial assistant, you could perhaps be hit on by Terry Southern, smiled at by Jackie Onassis, sized up by Gay Talese, or punched by Norman Mailer, or (far more likely) you could fill up on canapés, toss back a few drinks, and maybe go home with another editorial assistant. A perfect night in publishing, right up through Plimpton's death in 2003. (In 2018, his widow gave a "Last Call" party for *The Paris Review*'s 65th birthday, then sold the apartment and moved to Santa Fe.) Unfortunately, this ritual is on the

endangered list: Today's budget-conscious publishers hold big book parties only for their top-tier authors, and sometimes at those parties, the book being celebrated isn't handed out to guests but *sold* to them.

Bowery, The

A *bouwerij* is a farm, and Peter Stuyvesant, the Dutch governor of New Amsterdam, had one about a mile north of lower Manhattan, to which a main thoroughfare was carved out of the forest by Manaháhtaan natives and enslaved African-Americans. The name, anglicized, stuck to the street as the city grew northward and enveloped the Stuyvesant farm; by the early nineteenth century, the street known as the Bowery Lane, effectively the southern extension of Third Avenue, had become a broad boulevard with affluent residents, comparable to Fifth Avenue. At its northern end, the prestigious Cooper Union for the Advancement of Science and Art began operating in 1859. But the Bowery—the name changed officially in 1813—was also becoming a commercial strip, a center of eating, drinking, and entertainment; over the subsequent decades, that part of its street life came to dominate. By the late nineteenth century, the rich folk had fled, and the Bowery was the city's central honky-tonk, with a namesake gang (the Bowery Boys) and cheap nickel theaters, sideshows, and taverns on every block.

From there, it progressed from mild notoriety to infamy as its slide down the socioeconomic ladder accelerated. As the theaters got shabbier and the new Third Avenue Elevated train line threw the street into grimy shadow, the Bowery soon, and definitionally, became the place where the down-and-out went to get drunk and go to sleep. It was a grim stretch, by far the biggest skid row in America (much more populous than the district actually called Skid Row in Los Angeles), and had become a street most New Yorkers avoided, although the hopeless residents of its flophouses and

missions were more often pathetic than dangerous. In 1930, roughly 14,000 men (these places were all-male) lived in them and out on the sidewalks. The Depression did nothing to improve their situation. By the mid-'30s, the Bowery so thoroughly represented lost souls in the national consciousness that a well-hyped saloon called Sammy's Bowery Follies became a tourist attraction where uptown swells could go slumming with the riffraff. Buses full of out-of-towners began to drop off and pick up patrons there.

The Third Avenue El was demolished in 1955, but sunlight did not do much, at first, to elevate the men of the Bowery. As the Lower East Side's overall fabric was decaying, the area's buildings got older and dirtier, its residents more desperate and drug addled. The only people who seemed to be there by choice—during the day, at least—were sellers of restaurant and lighting fixtures, who operated most of the unfancy storefronts. At night, however, another crowd began to appear: young musicians and artists, who appreciated the district's cheapness and lack of glossy consumer culture. In 1973, Hilly Kristal opened a music club at 313 Bowery, intending to showcase American music, and called it CBGB & OMFUG, for "country, bluegrass, and blues, and other music for uplifting gourmandizers," but it was very soon co-opted as the principal venue of the rapidly cohering punk movement.

Over the next three decades, the Bowery lagged but generally followed the city's trend: gradually rising property values despite increasing levels of crime, then skyrocketing rents once the murder rate fell. By the end of the 1990s, instead of being a place where people washed up when they had no choice, it was becoming a place where people chose to be. CBGB closed in 2006, becoming a John Varvatos menswear store. The next year, the New Museum moved to a rather aggressively designed new building at 235 Bowery. The restaurant-supply houses have also begun to disappear, replaced by the

(6) How to Do a Headspin

From break-dancer Steve Stylez of Dance Stylez Entertainment

1. **"Use a headspin hat that has a pad in it to protect your head."** You don't want a permanent bald spot or bump on your head—I know a few friends with that."

2. **"Get into a headstand position with your legs wide open,** standing on the middle of your head. Make sure your back is straight (tripod position). Try to hold this position for fifteen to thirty seconds. Lean a little toward your arms, so you won't fall."

3. **"Twist your hips and follow with your upper body,** using your hands to catch and keep your balance."

4. **"With two hands, take small steps in the direction you want to spin,** then let your body rotate. You can use your fingertips or flat hands. Turn, then tap, then turn, then tap, and repeat. Go slow. When you start picking up speed, creating rotation, let go."

5. **"Take breaks and rehydrate.** Breaking is intense."

---

upscale restaurants they formerly stocked. In 2014, the Salvation Army mission at 223 Bowery shut down, and the building turned into luxury condominiums. Its departure left the Bowery Mission, in operation next door since 1879, the last such place on the street.

Brassiere [5]

In 1913, Mary Phelps Jacob, a 21-year-old New York debutante, was dressing for a dance. Repeatedly frustrated with the corset that was, at the time, the literal foundation of a well-dressed woman's attire, Jacob asked her maid to bring her two silk handkerchiefs, a ribbon, and a needle and thread. The garment she assembled, she later said, "was delicious. I could move more freely, a nearly naked feeling, and in the glass I saw that I was flat and proper." A few months later, she applied for a U.S. patent, which was granted on November 3, 1914. Although a variety of similar garments predate hers, she is generally credited with the invention of the modern bra.

After her underwear breakthrough, Jacob led a continually fascinating life. She moved to Paris for a while; co-founded the Black Sun Press, publishing early work by Ezra Pound and Ernest Hemingway; married three times; changed her name to Caresse Crosby; worked as an antiwar activist; dabbled with opium-smoking in North Africa; owned a dog named Clytoris; opened an art gallery in Washington and launched an arts magazine called *Portfolio*; and died in 1970 at the age of 78, not far from the castle she owned in Rome.

Break-Dancing [6]

Hip-hop was a revolution on several fronts (*see also* HIP-HOP). The first generation of its luminaries figured out in short order new approaches to music, slang, fashion, visual art, and dance. When hip-hop broke nationwide in the early '80s, it was thanks in no small part to b-boys, whose fluid, acrobatic moves captivated audiences across the country. Hollywood quickly took notice. Many of the early motion-picture portrayals of the new youth culture percolating in the Bronx—*Wild Style, Beat Street, Body Rock, Breakin' and Enterin', Flashdance, Rappin', Breakin', Style Wars,* and *Breakin' 2: Electric Boogaloo*—focused on dancers as much as (in some cases, more than) DJs and MCs. Legends like Crazy Legs and Frosty Freeze of the Bronx's Rock Steady Crew hooked audiences with moves that seemed to defy gravity.

Breaking brought dance back to its essentials. You didn't need formal training in a prestigious school to excel at it. The tools of the trade were a stretch of cardboard, comfortable clothing, limber joints, and an active imagination. Early arbiters took inspiration from around the world; you can see elements of ballet and twentieth-century African-American social dance, a healthy serving of the whirring intensity of gymnastics, and the speed and fancy footwork on loan from martial-arts films screening at the movie theaters peppering 42nd Street. Breakers looped kicks, twists, hops, flips, and headspins into alluring combo sequences. Crews engaged in battles for respect.

When DJ Kool Herc started isolating loops in funk records at parties in the South Bronx, he did it for dancers. Breaking is thus as crucial to the development of hip-hop music as rappers, producers, DJs, and graffiti artists, and dancers continue to carry the culture out into new territories at competitions and showcases worldwide.

Brill Building

The Art Deco building at 1619 Broadway looks like any other midtown office tower of its era. Between the 1930s and the 1970s, however, it did not *sound* like any other, because the Brill Building—named for the Brill Bros. clothing store that once occupied its ground floor—was stuffed with popular-music songwriters, arrangers,

The Rock Steady Crew, break-dancing in Harlem, 1983.

PHOTOGRAPH BY
JANETTE BECKMAN

copyists, and publishers. It was, broadly speaking, a song factory, one that fed lyrics and music to the artists, attempting to manufacture pop music as a product rather than letting it evolve organically out of nightclubs and basements. In the early days, its composers and lyricists supplied songs and arrangements to the likes of the Benny Goodman Orchestra.

More specifically, though, in the late 1950s and early 1960s, a particular style emanating from its offices and hallways came to dominate American pop music. It was characterized by teenage love-song longing, of course—most pop is—but it included a certain sass and snap that was new and a rhythmic bounce that borrowed from rhythm and blues. It was also unusually female, heavily dependent on the ensembles commonly referred to as girl groups.

Al Nevins and his partner, Don Kirshner, the so-called Man With the Golden Ear, ran their publishing company, Aldon Music, across the street, and held under contract a number of the most successful songwriters of the day. In their Brill Building cubbyholes, Carole King and Gerry Goffin wrote "Will You Love Me Tomorrow" (for the Shirelles), "The Loco-Motion" (recorded by Little Eva), "One Fine Day" (the Chiffons), and many, many others. Ellie Greenwich co-wrote "Da Doo Ron Ron," "Be My Baby," and "Leader of the Pack." Neil Sedaka co-wrote and recorded "Breaking Up Is Hard to Do." Burt Bacharach and Hal David met there. Phil Spector found songs to produce there. The Brill Building became so well-known for its concentration of music businesses that doo-wop groups began just hanging out in the hallways, hoping to catch somebody's ear and get a record deal.

The Brill Building style of hitmaking—like most styles of pop—took off fast and burned out quickly. The Beatles' explosive success in 1964 and the British Invasion that followed pushed homegrown stars off the charts, and rock and roll's newfound self-seriousness in the Vietnam War years favored the more authentic-seeming singer-songwriter over the factory model. But the songs of that era are covered and replayed endlessly (Goffin and King's seem especially durable), and at least two Broadway jukebox musicals have been constructed out of them: *Leader of the Pack*, about Greenwich herself, and *Beautiful*, about King. The building still has some showbiz-related tenants, including Lorne Michaels's Broadway Video and Paul Simon.

Today, the assembly-line Brill Building songwriting method has, with a new generation of pop stars, come roaring back. Teams of songwriters supply performers like Ariana Grande and Katy Perry with lyrics, work-shopped by producers and artists through countless rewrites. It's not uncommon to see six or eight writers credited on a three-minute pop single. Beyoncé's "Hold Up" had fifteen.

Broadway

The street itself has been around since long before European colonizers showed up in New York Harbor—slicing south to north up Manhattan island, it follows the Wickquasgeck trail, a Native American path named after a Delaware-speaking tribe from the Lower Hudson. The Dutch paved it and then the English rechristened it Broadway, in honor of the way ... it was broad. These days, the term *Broadway* has a technical, contractual definition that encompasses forty-one professional theaters, each with five hundred or more seats, located from 40th Street to 54th Street between Sixth and Eighth Avenues (plus Lincoln Center up on 65th Street). But when a non-union-rep actually uses the word, it generally refers to the cream of American commercial theater as represented by the shows staged in the Theater District of New York.

Even though we know serious dramas can happen there, Broadway makes the average American think of the high-gloss razzle-dazzle of musical comedy, the area's most successful export. In reality, Broadway theater is a hurly-burly, full of the brilliant and the terrible, with Shakespearean tragedies and revivals of Eugene O'Neill jostling against imported British productions and new American playwriting, and with jukebox musicals and their paper-thin books nestling cheek-to-cheek with golden-age standards and new masterpieces like *Hamilton*. In its very broadness, Broadway can also be a metonym for our theater world as a whole, for New York herself, and even for these United States: "Give my regards to Broadway," sang George M. Cohan, and every patriotic American got a twinge in the tear duct.

The center of the commercial-theater district wasn't always where it is today. (Because this is a New York story, it is also a real-estate story.) In the early nineteenth century, Americans of all stripes attended a wild mix of entertainments: medicine shows, Wild West shows, minstrel shows, vaudeville shows, melodramas, operas, performing-animal shows, classic tragedies, and European operettas—all often programmed onto the same large stages. (Many of these were indeed still along Broadway, like Niblo's Garden, way downtown at the intersection with Prince Street.) In 1847, though, the process of categorizing American theatricals into "elite" and "popular" got a boost when the New York aristocracy, eager to separate itself from the rabble, built the Astor Place Opera House near the corner of Broadway and 8th Street in the Village. It was meant to attract a "better class" of patron; there was a dress code, seats were more expensive, and the operas weren't performed in English.

This anti-populist hostility led, unsurprisingly, to conflict. In 1849, roiling class antagonism, sparked by hooligans harassing a visiting British actor trying to play Macbeth, turned to several days of riots in front of the Opera House. When the police fired into the crowd, around two dozen people were killed and 150 injured. The building was torn down (a Starbucks sits there now), but the process of segregating high-class art from democratic entertainments had begun. There was also an increasingly firm geography to the division: Highbrow opera people started going uptown to the Metropolitan Opera House at 39th Street, while the popular shows kept on in the variety houses downtown. What constituted "uptown" changed throughout the century. As promoters and producers looked for cheap land, the popular entertainment district also moved gradually north, starting near Union Square at 14th Street in the 1870s and crawling upward over the next fifty years, square by square, until it reached the 42nd Street area. The elite stuff was pushed north ahead of it, so the Metropolitan Opera House is now up on 65th Street.

In the late 1890s, theaters were wired with electric light, which also made possible the attention-getting, flashing commercial signs, brilliantly illuminated with the sheer force of AC/DC capitalism, along the midtown stretch of Broadway (hence its nickname, the Great White Way). By the turn of the century, the bow tie formed by 42nd Street, Seventh Avenue, and Broadway had become a commercial hot zone first known as Longacre Square and then by the name of the newspaper headquartered there (*see also* TIMES SQUARE). In the years around World War I, a large

number of theaters were built in the district, many of which are still in operation. Over the next two decades, it became the place where most dramatic artists—playwrights, actors, directors—aspired to work and where the big American statements by the likes of Tennessee Williams, Eugene O'Neill, and Arthur Miller were made. Simultaneously, its larger houses cultivated the American musical, a distinct form that combined elements of opera, operetta, song cycle, and dramatic play (*see also* MUSICAL THEATER). Broadway theatergoing occupied a much larger place in the culture before talking pictures cut into its viewership, and even after that; only in the era when television really started keeping a large part of the audience at home, which coincided with increasing ticket prices and the rise of crime in and around Times Square, did the Theater District see attendance really shrink. By the early 1980s, Broadway was considered an industry on life support, with many theaters dark for portions of the year. Quite a few were sold off or demolished, and most big hits of that decade were imports from London, like *Cats* and *Phantom of the Opera.*

That all changed in the late 1990s, when the district received a massive state and city reconstruction and big entertainment companies, led by Disney, began to realize that a Broadway musical could launch a lucrative business in other places and in other media. The new crop of shows—led in 1997 by *The Lion King*, staged in the restored New Amsterdam Theatre—were aimed not at adult New York theater regulars but at day trippers, tourists, and families with kids, and because their audience was perpetually being replenished, they could run forever. *Phantom* has now run well past the 30-year mark, while the mid-1990s productions of *Chicago* and *The Lion King* are approaching 25 years each. Yet they coexist with new theater, often cultivated Off Broadway and transferred uptown, that is genuinely inventive: the blockbuster that is *Hamilton*, the intimate monologues of *What the Constitution Means to Me*, the quiet charm of an unexpected hit like *The Band's Visit.*

Today, Broadway is at the heart of New York's tourism economy, bringing in nearly $2 billion a year and supporting the hub of gift shops, bars, restaurants, guys standing around in Elmo costumes ready to take a picture with your child, and assorted New York chutzpah in the neighborhood. (Or did, anyway, until the abrupt and dire closure of theaters in 2020; *see also* QUARAN-TINE.) The economics are nonsensical—only about 20 percent of shows recoup their investment—and the snoots are always grumbling that the good stuff is actually Off Broadway, which is often true. But if you can make it there, you can make it anywhere. Probably by touring.

"Broken Windows" Policing

In an article published in *The Atlantic Monthly* in March 1982, the scholars George Kelling and James Q. Wilson observed that visible policing—foot patrols in at-risk neighborhoods, mostly—didn't necessarily decrease crime but did tend to maintain order. It inherently improved those neighborhoods' quality of life, they found, because the officers doing it were able to distinguish between minor infractions the community could accept and bad trends that were actually disruptive. Deviations from the norm, Kelling and Wilson maintained, had to be nipped in the bud. "Disorder and crime are usually inextricably linked," they wrote. "Social psychologists and police officers tend to agree that if a window in a building is broken and is left unrepaired, all the rest of the windows will soon be broken. This is as true in nice neighborhoods as in run-down ones ... one unrepaired broken window is a signal that no one cares, and so breaking more windows costs nothing."

As New York City grappled with a crime rate that continued to rise through the 1970s and 1980s, this idea was seized upon by the NYPD, in particular by William Bratton, whom Mayor Rudolph Giuliani hired as police commissioner in 1994. "Broken-windows policing" became shorthand for an elevated level of attention given to small crimes that contributed to a perception of lawlessness. The implementation of that policy, paired with improved crime tracking and trendspotting provided by the NYPD (*see also* COMPSTAT), coincided with an astounding drop in the crime rate: 70 percent in nine years and well more than that over the following decade. In that time, the misdemeanor arrest rate rose roughly 70 percent. The numerical results, at least, make for a stunning contrast. There were 2,245 homicides in New York in 1990; in 2018 the number was 289. Similar statistics apply to other violent crimes, from rape to robbery, not to mention everyday indignities like auto theft, which have gone from epidemic to relatively rare.

The question people began to ask, of course, was whether the relationship between better policing and fewer crimes was causal. Bratton, who returned for a second stint as police commissioner under Mayor Bill de Blasio from 2014 to 2016, absolutely thinks so. He called the policy the single most important reason for falling crime rates. Other observers, some academic, some journalistic, put much of the responsibility elsewhere: on the increasing wealth in the city, on demographic shifts, on the end of the crack boom, on the removal of lead from gasoline and paint (because violent behavior has been tied to childhood lead poisoning), and even on the legalization of abortion.

Most of all, there is increasing recognition that higher-intensity policing has damaged communities whose relations with law enforcement are troubled. In theory, it should cause officers to engage with citizens more consistently, without escalation. In practice, it offered vast new opportunities for harassment and police abuse. The related policy known as stop and frisk (before its curtailment in 2013) became a severe risk to young people of color, particularly young Black men, who too often faced regular law-enforcement encounters that their white counterparts did not—and thus ended up with criminal records (or worse) that were vastly more formidable than their lives merited.

"Brooklyn"

Not as the name of a real-life borough but as an idea, the word *Brooklyn* has come to represent a certain type of bourgeois-bohemian village-in-the-city life. Certainly it owes a lot to past incarnations of Greenwich Village or San Francisco's North Beach, but its particular mix of vigor and tweeness, of work and leisure, of aesthetics and rank mercantilism, are very much of our time.

Its roots can be seen in an essay Pete Hamill wrote for *New York* in 1969 titled "Brooklyn: The Sane Alternative." Hamill had grown up in Park Slope, when the neighborhood was a mostly Irish slum. The borough back then had been a national punch line: If a wartime

Michael and Rick Mast,
Brooklyn chocolatiers.
PHOTOGRAPH BY TARA DONNE

entertainer like Bob Hope asked a crowd of soldiers where they were from, and someone said Brooklyn, that was enough to get a big laugh. (Today's equivalent is New Jersey.) Returning a generation later, after the Dodgers had left for L.A. and much of the borough's middle class had moved to the suburbs, Hamill was surprised by what he saw: Young families, increasingly white, were buying seedy old brownstone rowhouses for comparatively little money, restoring their architectural details, and raising families there. In another essay a few years later, John McPhee made reference to "the neobohemians, out of the money and into the arts." Similar activity began to take place in Carroll Gardens, Boerum Hill, and other neighborhoods with short subway rides to Manhattan and good-quality housing.

This new Brooklyn remained largely a bedroom community for Manhattan until the 1990s, when "the city" began to grow too expensive for anyone who didn't have a straight job, and people of all incomes began to see Brooklyn as a deal. That was also when Williamsburg—a district along the waterfront, formerly devoted to heavy industry, whose thinning population was mostly Polish dockworkers, Puerto Ricans, and Hasidic Jews—began to attract artsy young residents in large numbers. (A 1992 cover story in *New York* called it "The New Bohemia.") Different, this time, was that these new Brooklynites had increasingly not oriented their lives toward Manhattan, either for leisure or even for work. Some stayed in Brooklyn all the time, where it was quiet and they could do their thing. Occasionally, one of their Manhattan friends could be coaxed across the river, with difficulty; it was impossible to hail a cab back. They had, in their midst, one early avatar of the world to come. Brooklyn Brewery, established in 1987 by Steve Hindy and Tom Potter to produce high-quality beer in contravention of every direction the brewing industry seemed to be taking, was flourishing to great acclaim. (Never mind that the beer was mostly made under contract in Utica.)

If anything cemented this new community, it was a newfound type of small-scale entrepreneurship, most often centered on food. Driven in part by the prohibitive cost of running a small business in Manhattan, entrepreneurial men and women—most of them veterans of ambitious Manhattan kitchens—sought more affordable rents in the various recently or soon-to-be gentrified northwestern and north Brooklyn neighborhoods, gradually spreading to Red Hook and Bushwick. This idealistic movement was defined by a professed dedication to local, organic, sustainably farmed ingredients, and the notion of seasonality and market sensitivity was paramount. (In this, it owed much to the California cooking of Alice Waters and others, not to mention several hundred years of French and Italian country folk.) This wasn't always feasible for obvious logistical, financial, and gustatory reasons, as evidenced by the disclaimer "organic and local whenever possible" that became an increasingly conspicuous tagline on so-called locavore menus.

In 2006, *New York*'s Robin Raisfeld and Rob Patronite gave this particular idiom a name: "the New Brooklyn Cuisine." New Brooklyn restaurants were small in size and mom-and-pop in fact or feeling, built on low or moderate budgets without the benefit of marketing departments, PR firms, or a media-savvy celebrity chef in the kitchen. The aesthetic was rustic, homespun, or stripped-down, and a hands-on DIY approach to everything from the construction of the restaurant spaces to the checking of coats was standard practice. In this sense, these spots marked a return to the make-it-from-scratch, family-run Brooklyn restaurants of another era.

The movement was not just about restaurants, of course. This New Brooklyn made and sold all sorts of stuff, and promulgated a very particular aesthetic. Boutiques up and down Bedford Avenue in Williamsburg carried carefully selected vintage clothes and a mix of early-twentieth-century and mid-century goods. Barbershops that offered straight-razor shaves sprung up cheek-by-jowl

(7) **How to Maintain a Brownstone**

Tips from brownstone architect Elizabeth Roberts

➡ **Stay ahead of rust.** "The historic iron railings that line many stoops are extremely valuable and very difficult and expensive to replace. Keeping them painted helps avoid rust."

➡ **Clean the gutters.** "The brownstone on the façade of many townhouses is actually just a thin layer of stone that covers brick. If that layer becomes saturated with water and then freezes, the frozen water will cause the layer to crack and possibly even fail. Repairing the brownstone façades is very expensive and time consuming."

➡ **Watch the cornices.** "Many of the intricate cornices that line the tops of the façades are unique, hand-carved wood. Best to keep them painted. And if they do seem to be failing, it's very important to install a sidewalk scaffold to prevent broken cornice parts from falling on passersby."

---

with tattoo parlors, often serving the same customers. Brooklyn Brewery's products were soon served alongside hundreds of other India pale ales, ciders, porters, stouts, and really anything beer-related that wasn't a Budweiser. (Paradoxically, this lineup included cans of Pabst Blue Ribbon, the reverse-snob's beer of choice; *see also* HIPSTER.) Mast Brothers promulgated its bean-to-bar manufacture of artisanal chocolate in Williamsburg, the pedigree of which eventually turned out to be somewhat iffy. (The brothers at one point tried to distribute it via sailing ship, an indelible if ridiculous bit of ecobranding.) On rooftops, little farming operations appeared, producing salad greens; down at street level, small-batch distillers of gins, bourbons, and ryes flourished.

Many new companies got going at the Brooklyn Flea, a market opened in 2008 mainly as a furniture bazaar and crafts fair that turned into an accidental handcrafted-foods incubator. Soon New Brooklyn brands began to draw the attention of national retailers like Whole Foods, and their products spread to other American cities as well as to Europe and Japan. An aesthetic of nineteenth-century-style typography, rough-hewn lumber, and industrial cast iron tied it all together, and the word *curated* became ubiquitous.

The influence of the New Brooklyn aesthetic on restaurant culture in New York and beyond has been tremendous. In the late aughts, in a kind of boomerang effect, Manhattan restaurants began showing symptoms of New Brooklynism. But as the New Brooklyn movement gained global momentum and businesses founded on the ideals of old-fashioned, small-batch sustainability faced the modern-day challenge of scaling up or fading away, the inevitable backlash occurred. Critics derided the movement as a fantasy of white privilege oblivious to economic realities and the effects of the gentrification it had itself ushered into the neighborhoods where it took root. Brooklyn had become a brand, a commodity whose target audience was tourists

(many of them Manhattanites); one of the worst things you could do to an innocent neighborhood, some said, was to "Brooklynize" it. Nonetheless, every big city seems now to have a smaller district nearby that's known for its youth, vigor, and excitingly rough-finished restaurant tables. Logan Square is the Brooklyn of Chicago, Spenard is the Brooklyn of Anchorage, Oakland is absolutely fed up with being called the Brooklyn of San Francisco, and Montreuil is the Brooklyn of Paris—where, these days, anything in this vein is described as *"très Brooklyn."*

Brooklyn Bridge *see* SUSPENSION BRIDGE

Brownstone Rowhouse [7]

Neither the brownstone nor the rowhouse comes from New York. Iron-rich, earth-colored sandstone was quarried in Connecticut, and the serried line of virtually identical homes standing shoulder to shoulder originated on the streets of Europe. But the practice of facing rowhouses with a brownstone veneer allowed New York to grow nimbly in the nineteenth century and put homeownership within reach for the rapidly expanding bourgeoisie. As lots narrowed from 25 feet to 20 to 18 and even an emaciated 14, houses looked taller and skinnier, an effect accentuated by the traditional brick fronts. Brownstone, which could be cut in large sheets and fitted together with the most inconspicuous of seams, glossed over the awkward proportions and produced a monumental streetscape worthy of a Romantic painting: a rocky cliff of domesticity on either side of a riverlike thoroughfare.

⑧ **Where to See Real Burlesque**

From entertainer Agent Wednesday

➽ **The Slipper Room**
(167 Orchard St.)
"The heart of New York's current burlesque era, it exclusively features variety acts with every kind of burlesque: classic, nerdy, neo, you name it!"
➽ **Duane Park**
(308 Bowery)
"Great for the old-school, classic style. Dancers perform to a live band while the audience enjoys a full-course meal in a beautiful club. Dress code is mandatory. That's how fancy it is."
➽ **BURLESK! at Birdland**
(315 W. 44th St.)
"A fairly new production at the descendant of the oldest venue, one whose past performers include Ella Fitzgerald, Billie Holiday, and Duke Ellington."
➽ **House of Yes**
(2 Wyckoff Ave.)
"Brooklyn's home for a night of exciting performances and dancing."
➽ **Club Cumming**
(505 E. 6th St.)
"Owned by actor Alan Cumming, this cozy East Village venue is

---

Cheap, soft, and plentiful, brownstone was considered the apex of elegance in the mid–nineteenth century. "Brown sandstone houses are the rage among the new rich men," one reporter noted in 1860, an observation that would remain true for the rest of the century. One reason for the stone's popularity was its workability. As block after block of Brooklyn and the Upper East and West Sides filled in with new residences, masons unfurled ribbons of carved scrolls, banisters, stoops, lintels, and sills. The material's color and ubiquity offended the novelist Edith Wharton, who described the city of her childhood in the 1860s as "this little low-studded rectangular New York, cursed with its universal chocolate-colored coating of the most hideous stone ever quarried."

Wharton was correct in her use of the word *coating*. Brownstone isn't tough enough to carry structural loads. Its softness makes it brittle, particularly when cut and laid with the grain, and it weathers to a dark mush. Repairs became challenging after the quarry in Portland, Connecticut, flooded in the 1930s and shut down. Today's homeowners on leafy side streets restore their façades with a look-alike mixture of stucco and concrete.

By the 1920s, tall apartment buildings were popping up all over Manhattan, making townhouses seem dark, old, and cramped—in a word, unmodern. The Depression revealed an unsuspected virtue, however: They were easily chopped up into small units, which made them ideal for conversion to rooming houses, the lowest form of residential real estate above the flophouse. Brownstones remained staunchly out of fashion for decades. The postwar popularity of suburban ranch houses, open-plan kitchens, and sleek penthouses all made staircases seem strenuous and practically primitive. Townhouses were demolished en masse to make way for towers; many more fell into not-so-genteel shabbiness.

When the historical-preservation movement took hold in the mid-1960s, brownstone blocks began to seem charming rather than seedy—but only for those who could afford to have a whole townhouse (or at least half of one) to themselves. As upper-middle-class parents rediscovered the notion of bringing up kids in the city, walk-up warrens of studios and one-bedrooms were cleared out and reconverted for family use, ready for jogging strollers to be parked in the hallway. On many blocks, the population dropped, prices rose, the demographics grew more homogeneous, and *voilà*: Brownstone Brooklyn.

Burlesque, American Style[8]

The essence of American burlesque is that it dumbed down the Victorian-era burlesque that had once parodied the operas of Mozart and Bizet for educated Britons, sexed it up, and made the whole business much funnier. The transatlantic adaptation can be attributed to Michael B. Leavitt, a blackface minstrel performer turned entrepreneur; after being introduced to the form in New York in the 1860s by the English dancer Lydia Thompson and her troupe, the British Blondes, he saw an opportunity to meld it with the comedy of vaudeville, the songs and dances of minstrel performers, and the skimpy costumes popular in so-called leg shows. Leavitt staged his first production, which was billed as Mme. Rentz's Female Minstrels, in 1870. He soon took his show on the road and inspired a scantily clad revolution that didn't come to an end until Mayor Fiorello La Guardia, under pressure from the well-financed League of New York Theatres and Producers, was persuaded to ban burlesque in 1937. Burlesque was revived in the late twentieth century as retro-facing hipsters in New York and elsewhere reclaimed the genre with tongue-in-cheek themes (Dungeons & Dragons, monster movies) and tattooed performers.

almost always packed with mostly locals hanging out to have a drink and be surprised by whoever drops in."
» **The Box**
(189 Chrystie St.)
"Known for outrageous performances, and it doesn't allow photography. The only way to learn about certain acts is by word of mouth."

... AND THE RULES OF BURLESQUE ETIQUETTE:
» **"Consent!** We're here to entertain an audience, not a private client. Don't touch us unless we explicitly say you may. Don't get angry if we decline your invite to dinner."
» **"You like something? Say something!** Cheer and scream! We performers

feed off your energy."
» **"Tip us!** It means a lot. Almost all of us have Venmo, too—just ask for our handle."

Bystander Effect

On March 13, 1964, Kitty Genovese was murdered in Queens and the bystander effect was born. Genovese was a 28-year-old bar manager in Kew Gardens, and the well-known story of her killing goes like this: A serial killer attacked her outside her apartment, stabbing her repeatedly with a hunting knife; thirty-eight people, according to newspaper reports, witnessed the crime, yet no one intervened. No one ran to her assistance, no one called the police, and the death of Genovese was thus blamed not only on the acts of the killer but on her neighbors' inaction. As one of the witnesses said to a New York *Times* reporter, "I didn't want to get involved."

The incident went as viral as possible in those days and within a decade had generated a new area of interest among social scientists. In 1968, psychologists Bibb Latané and John Darley were the first to empirically test the so-called bystander effect, and their results seemed to confirm the behavior: People—even otherwise helpful people—tend not to help in an emergency if others are present. Over the years, it has become one of social psychology's most robust findings, standing up to replication attempts and meta-analyses; in 2015, researchers in Germany and the U.K. found that even young children are susceptible to the bystander effect. Though five-year-olds were eager to help an experimenter mop up a spill when they were alone, they were less likely to help if other kids were present.

But the Genovese story is more complicated than its popular narrative relates. In truth, only about 5 or 6 neighbors could plausibly testify during trial, not 38. Two of these witnesses called the police, and one screamed out his window at the murderer, causing him to stop his attack and run away, albeit only briefly. A woman named Sophia Farrar even risked her own life to help Genovese, rushing out of her apartment to hold her dying neighbor in her arms. Some people *did* help, in

other words. The Genovese case turns out to be an unconvincing example of the very concept it helped create.

In recent years, psychologists have argued that the misunderstanding of the Genovese story has resulted in misguided research around the bystander effect. The role individuals' personalities play in their responses, for instance, has hardly been touched upon, perhaps partly because the bystander effect has been understood as a universal phenomenon—a product of a situation, not a disposition. Evolutionary instinct has largely been ignored, too. But in 2018, a team of researchers suggested that perhaps we hold back in such situations because we feel on some instinctive level that it's best if only the "fittest individual" offers help, to ensure "efficient help that maximizes individual survival."

From
CAFÉ SOCIETY
to
CROSSWORD PUZZLE

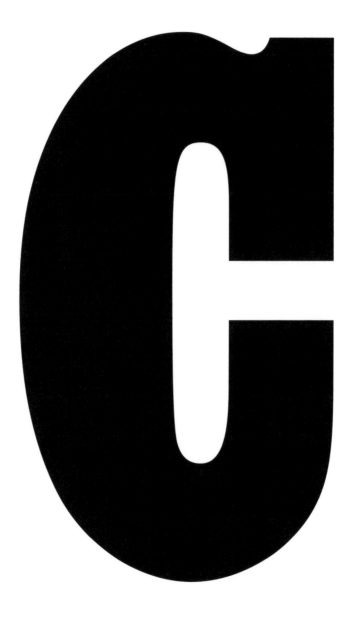

Superman makes his debut on the cover of
Action Comics *No. 1, 1938.*
© DC COMICS

At the Stork Club, 1949.
PHOTOGRAPH BY
STANLEY KUBRICK

(1) **How to Make a Stork Club Cocktail**

According to The Stork Club Bar Book *(1946), by Lucius Beebe, rediscovered by historian Philip Greene*

1. Combine:
Dash of lime juice
Juice of half an orange
Dash of triple sec
1 ½ oz. gin
Dash of Angostura bitters
2. Shake well with ice and strain into a chilled 4 oz. glass.

Café Society [1]

Socializing, in the world known as Society, once occurred principally in the homes of wealthy people. (It helped to have your own ballroom.) In the 1920s, though, young Society men and women began to break with this tradition, going out to nightclubs and speakeasies where they could dance and drink and otherwise misbehave (*see also* NIGHTCLUB). A gossip columnist, Maury Paul of the New York *Evening Journal*, named this crowd "Café Society," and soon enough the term was taken up everywhere. (His rival columnist Lucius Beebe referred to their world as "Chromium Mist," which is perhaps more vivid but also sounds like a paint color.) In 1925, the young socialite Ellin Mackay scandalized her set with an insider's account of Café Society, titled "Why We Go to Cabarets: A Post-Debutante Explains," which was picked up by Harold Ross's brand-new magazine *The New Yorker*, becoming its first newsstand hit and saving the flat-broke publication from closing.

The term became widespread in the 1930s and lent its name to one of the great Greenwich Village clubs of the era, and more broadly came to describe the scene at places like the Stork Club, El Morocco, and the '21' Club. Although it eventually drifted into disuse, the social whirl it described has yet to end. In the 1950s, Igor Cassini, Paul's gossip-page successor, coined the term *jet set*, which still gets an occasional airing even though jet travel is no longer elite.

Canyon of Heroes *see* TICKER-TAPE PARADE

Capital of the United States [2]

The capital of the United Kingdom is London. France's is Paris. Surely the United States of America ought to be run from its most influential city? Indeed it was, briefly,

(2) **How to Visit the Original Capital of the United States**

Federal Hall, at 26 Wall Street in the Financial District, is open to visitors for solo or park-ranger-guided tours during the week. The George Washington Inaugural Gallery contains pieces of the original building, and the **Bible on which Washington was sworn into office** is occasionally on view.

at the beginning. As the Sixth Congress of the Confederation met in 1785 to continue the work of establishing a new country, its members did so in lower Manhattan at the no longer British City Hall on Wall Street. Several subsequent meetings there, held in parallel with the Constitutional Convention in Philadelphia, set down the U.S. form of government, and on April 30, 1789, George Washington took the oath of office on the second-floor balcony of that same building, which had been renovated to suit the legislature and renamed Federal Hall. The first U.S. Congress met there that day and later created the departments now called State, Defense, and Treasury. Debates and sessions continued in the building for a year, while President Washington lived a short walk away, over at Pearl and Cherry Streets (now Pearl and Dover).

But over the course of the Revolutionary War, the northern colonies in particular had accumulated millions of dollars in debt and pressured the new federal government to pay off the banks. The representatives of the southern states did not want to permit this; they also wanted a capital closer to home and disliked New York City's cosmopolitanism and emphasis on commerce. Thomas Jefferson and James Madison of Virginia and Alexander Hamilton of New York worked out a compromise and persuaded their respective states to agree, and on July 10, 1790, Congress passed the Residence Act, transferring the capital temporarily to Philadelphia and then permanently to a swampy dump on the Potomac, soon to be called Washington.

Cast-Iron Building[3]

First produced in large quantities by British foundries in the late eighteenth century, cast iron offered some key advantages over the brick and stone that builders had been using for thousands of years. Although brittle, it was very strong in compression, and because it could be poured into molds, it could be mass-produced to look like carved masonry without the need for skilled stonecutters. A few early buildings and bridges in England and Bermuda predate its use in New York, but far and away its most prominent and widespread employment began in the downtown neighborhood we now call Soho. There, in the late 1840s, a builder named James Bogardus began casting and selling building parts that could be assembled from a catalogue. His structures made excellent factories because the iron façades, being pound-for-pound stronger than brick, allowed for larger windows, which, in turn, permitted larger factory floors in the days before electric lighting. Some Bogardus buildings went a step further and were completely constructed from this new material. His and others' catalogues supplied the parts for hundreds of structures, mostly in Manhattan, through the beginning of the twentieth century, when steel and concrete took over.

By the 1960s, these century-old buildings were mostly obsolete, as manufacturing moved to even larger factory floors with cheaper labor in the South and West and then overseas. Lower Manhattan's cast-iron architecture was declared "worthless" in one study ordered by planning czar Robert Moses; his plan for the Lower Manhattan Expressway called for a large swath of Soho's cast-iron buildings to be demolished. Meanwhile, many of their floors had been colonized by artists, who found their large windows and open spaces as appealing for art-making as they had been for manufacturing. The efforts of community activists, notably Jane Jacobs, led to not only the cancellation of the highway but the preservation of the Soho Cast Iron Historic District, which subsequently became an arts district and has since turned into one of the most expensive retail and residential neighborhoods in the U.S.

Four Bogardus buildings survive in New York City. The story of a lost fifth one, built for the Edgar H. Laing company in 1849, is unique. In the 1960s, the new Landmarks Preservation Commission (*see also* LANDMARKS

(3) **Cast-Iron Gems Worth Stopping to Look At**

From the New York Preservation Archive Project's Anthony W. Robins

➠ TRIBECA
Cary Building, 105–107 Chambers St. and 89–91 Reade St. (1856–57): A fancy-goods firm ordered a cast-iron façade imitating stone for the Chambers Street front and, since cast iron was prefabricated, an identical façade for the Reade Street side.

➠ SOHO
E. V. Haughwout Building, 488–492 Broadway, at Broome St. (1857): J. P. Gaynor modeled his design on the Library of St. Mark in Venice.

➠ LADIES' MILE
B. Altman, 615–629 Sixth Ave., at 19th St. (1876–77): The oldest of the big department stores here is covered in detailed, geometric neo-Grec ornament.

➠ WILLIAMSBURG
183–195 Broadway, at Driggs Ave., Brooklyn (1882–83): Williamsburg has the city's only sizable collection of cast-iron façades outside Manhattan. This one has enormous cast-iron calla lilies on the second story.

LAW) agreed to allow its demolition with the proviso that its cast-iron parts be disassembled and stored toward a later reconstruction. But in 1974, three men were caught removing a large piece of it from a storage yard. It became clear that, over the preceding months, two-thirds of the façade had been taken and sold for scrap. (A few pieces were recovered from a Bronx junkyard, but most had presumably been melted down.) Beverly Moss Spatt, chair of the Landmarks Preservation Commission, announced the news by darting into the press room at City Hall and shouting, "Someone has stolen one of my buildings!"

Cel-Ray Soda

Soda in the nineteenth century was not typically a bright, fruity beverage. Often flavored with roots, barks, seeds, and various other pungent botanical ingredients, it was treated as a health tonic and sold at drugstore pharmacy counters. A few of those flavors and their manmade analogs are still in use, including kola nut (in, of course, Coca-Cola and Pepsi), sassafras bark (root beer), birch sap (birch beer), gentian root (Moxie), and celery seed, in the form of Dr. Brown's Cel-Ray soda.

There was, it appears, an actual Dr. Henry E. Brown, a pharmacist who in 1867 invented a syrup of sugar and crushed celery seeds and mixed it with carbonated water to settle stomachs on the Lower East Side and in Williamsburg. Within a couple of years, a celery tonic bearing his name was being produced by the firm of Schoneberger & Noble on Water Street. The Cel-Ray name was trademarked in 1947 (along with a logo showing two crossed celery stalks), and "Jewish Champagne" was its nickname; it sold well in delicatessens, not least because it complements a fatty, meaty meal, like a pastrami sandwich. The word *tonic* left the label in the 1950s when the FDA began to object to its hint of medical efficacy.

As tastes changed and Jewish delis began to disappear in the 1970s and 1980s, Dr. Brown's became more of a specialty item sold mostly in New York markets and scattered gourmet shops around the country. In 1982, the brand was sold to Canada Dry, which continues to bottle it. Part of an old Schoneberger & Noble plant in Williamsburg is now occupied by Brooklyn Brewery (*see also* "BROOKLYN").

Central Bank *see* FEDERAL RESERVE SYSTEM

Central Park

The 843 acres at the center of Manhattan look like a nature preserve with added footpaths and bridges. They are anything but. Every bit of what you see in Central Park, save for the outcrops of Manhattan schist bedrock, is an artful human construct, specified by the landscape architects Frederick Law Olmsted and Calvert Vaux or their successors. The streams were dug by hand before the bridges went over them, all but a few of those trees were placed and planted, and the meadows were graded and sited as thoroughly as a baseball infield might be. Low-lying areas were deliberately flooded into ponds and a reservoir.

A competition in 1857 led to Olmsted and Vaux's hiring, and the first round of construction ended in 1858, when the park opened to visitors. But it was hardly finished. Trees had been planted as saplings, spaced according to their projected appearance in the far future, when they would coalesce into an arched grove or a deep thicket. A bridge or outbuilding might initially look slightly overscale and ornate when surrounded by nothing, but a generation later it would be enclosed by undergrowth and settled in. (Olmsted and Vaux both lived long enough to see the park largely mature.)

The genius of Central Park's design takes multiple

*The myriad
functions of Central
Park on view, 1992.*
PHOTOGRAPH BY
BRUCE DAVIDSON

forms, and its eerily unnatural naturalism is only one. So is the incorporation, new for its time, of active recreation sites like play areas and ball fields. The transverse drives, set below ground level and thus barely disruptive to the parkgoer's eye, are another—one that seems especially visionary given that they were specified a half-century before the automobile age. In fact, the distinction among drives, footpaths, and bridle paths (which still see a few horses, though not many) remains a significant hierarchy within the park, one that was reinforced in 2018, when—after years of argument, pushback, and lobbying—the shared pedestrian-and-traffic paths were closed to cars for good.

Which is not to say that the park has been preserved in amber as Olmsted and Vaux envisioned it. Over the years, it has seen heavy adaptation. A onetime reservoir has long since been filled in to form the Great Lawn. The Metropolitan Museum of Art has encroached. A little bandstand gazebo gave way to the larger Naumburg Bandshell. The highly ornamented building known as the Dairy fell apart and has been restored. The Ramble—from the beginning the most densely planted, seemingly wild portion of the park—became overgrown and tangled, and for a while gained a reputation as a place for sex. Much of the remainder of the park was for a couple of decades known as a dangerous place to be at night, not a place to take a nice walk after dinner but one where you'd be beaten and robbed, or worse. (The rape of a jogger in 1989 near 102nd Street cemented this reputation, and the erroneous conviction and imprisonment of five Black and Latino teenagers for the crime remains a blot on the city's history.)

For much of its life, the park was undermaintained and drifted into disrepair; only since the 1980 creation of the Central Park Conservancy, a public-private partnership, has the money flowed in and the repairs and maintenance been brought back up to snuff. Today, the park is in far better shape than it has been for a century. It is also, according to officials, suffering from a new problem: overuse. Garbage cans fill up too quickly to be emptied, and lawns wear out under the pressure of too many feet. As in so many other aspects of New York life, many people have come to prefer spending time in Brooklyn—and thus find themselves in Prospect Park, the subsequent project of Olmsted and Vaux. There the designers applied the lessons they'd learned in

Manhattan, and in the end they came to believe they'd done a better job the second time out.

Chabad Judaism

Excuse me, are you Jewish? It's a question posed on street corners to all non-blonds by adherents of the Chabad sect of Judaism, especially on certain Jewish holidays and in the Friday-afternoon hours before the sabbath. Most of those who are accosted mumble out a reply in the negative or keep walking. But if you say yes, you'll be cheerfully guided in a little exploration of Jewish ritual: perhaps wrapping your arms in tefillin, waving a palm frond on the holiday of Sukkot, or lighting sabbath candles. For you, the experience may be a curiosity; for Chabad believers, it's a dire obligation, handed down by a now-dead leader whom many adherents regard as the Messiah. Such obligations have motivated Chabad to become one of the most dynamic, proactive forces in Jewish history, taking off from a Brooklyn launching pad and arriving in the four corners of the earth.

Chabad did not originate in New York but came into flower here. The name is an acronym for three Hebrew words—*chochmah* ("wisdom"), *binah* ("understanding"), and *da'at* ("knowledge")—though it is also known as Lubavitch, after the Russian town where the sect was once based. It's a strand of the Hasidic movement, which began in eighteenth-century Eastern Europe and in which Jews were encouraged to develop an ecstatic, deeply personal relationship with the Divine. Chabad emerged in 1775 and has been directed by a succession of supreme spiritual leaders known as the rebbes. For well over a century and a half, Chabad was largely a European entity. Then came the Bolsheviks and the Nazis.

The person responsible for the group's rise in the city was the sixth rebbe, Yosef Yitzchak Schneerson. He had faced tremendous persecution for his beliefs at the hands of the Soviets and sought refuge in Poland, only to find himself once again under threat after the German invasion of September 1939. The U.S. was still neutral in the war, and American Jewish leaders pressed for his rescue. In a truly bizarre turn of events, the German government agreed to send Nazi soldiers from Jewish backgrounds (yes, there were such people) to extract him. In March 1940, Schneerson arrived in Manhattan and permanently moved the center of

Chabad life to this country. He saw a unique mission before him: to take the increasingly secular Jewish diaspora in America and make its people believe again.

Schneerson shifted his base of operations to 770 Eastern Parkway in Crown Heights, an area provocatively close to more liberal Jewish populations. (Chabad receives a great deal of criticism from some Jewish communities for its hard-line stances on Israeli security and the strict, traditional rules that govern its adherents, particularly regarding gender roles.) From Brooklyn, he began his program of sending out *shlichim* (roughly, "emissaries") in 1950. Chabadniks believe it's a commandment of the highest order to assist other Jews in being more Jewish, and the sixth rebbe sent out rabbis and their wives to act as spiritual guides for Jews worldwide. His successor and son-in-law, Menachem Mendel Schneerson, took over in 1951 and expanded the *shlichim* to an extent his predecessor could not have imagined. Chabad outposts now operate in one hundred countries and all fifty states.

Menachem Mendel became the greatest of all the rebbes (two decades after his death, he's simply known as "the Rebbe" among his followers). After settling here, he almost never left Crown Heights, traveling only occasionally to visit his father-in-law's grave in Queens. Instead, he held court with visitors ranging from New York mayors to Israeli prime ministers. His operation became a fund-raising dynamo, buoyed by celebrity endorsers like Bob Dylan and frequent Chabad telethon host Jon Voight, and he received commendations from every U.S. president from Nixon onward. Until his death in 1994, he was purported by some to have supernatural abilities and be the long-foretold Messiah. He did not name a successor.

Chemex Coffeepot

The idea of dripping hot water through coffee grounds held in a paper filter originated with Amalie Liebscher (known by her middle name, Melitta) in Dresden, Germany, in 1908. It reached its aesthetic peak in 1939, when an extremely eccentric inventor in New York, Peter Schlumbohm, developed a borosilicate-glass brewer in the form of a carafe, its wasp waist wrapped in hardwood and a leather tie. It was a Bauhaus-esque product that was affordable and friendly, one that

looked like a particularly sleek piece of lab equipment, thus inspiring its name: Chemex.

During the Second World War, when production of metal consumer goods was highly restricted, the glass construction gave Chemex a leg up. In 1942, it made the cover of a Museum of Modern Art publication devoted to superior wartime design and soon entered the museum's permanent collection. Schlumbohm also created a handsome companion product to boil water called the Fahrenheitor Kettle. Most of his other products, which included the Fahrenheitor Minnehaha aerating pitcher, the Fahrenheitor Bottle Cooler, the Fahrenheitor Ice Vault, and the Cinderella trash bucket—all emanating from his workroom on Murray Street—are long gone.

Although it bobbed up regularly over the years, notably in Mary Tyler Moore's sitcom kitchen, the Chemex, too, slowly faded from widespread use. Then, in the early 2000s, coffee enthusiasts began to fetishize the so-called pour-over, in which coffee is made, painstakingly, by slowly drizzling freshly boiled water through the grounds off the heat. As it happens, the Chemex brewing method is precisely that, and the pot's looks jibe with the tech-gadget pour-over aesthetic. The surge in visibility and enthusiasm that the device has recently received may be because, as Schlumbohm put it in 1946, "with the Chemex, even a moron can make good coffee." Now a family-run operation based in Massachusetts, Chemex continues to produce the kettle and the coffeepot, the latter in multiple sizes and variations, including a mouth-blown version for the uncompromising aesthete.

Chicken and Waffles

Fried chicken and biscuits: inescapably a southern thing. Stewed chicken in gravy poured over a waffle: a Pennsylvania Dutch thing. But deep-fried crispy chicken perched on a couple of waffles—well, entities all over the country have tried to claim it, but the most persuasive ones bind it to Harlem. Certainly it could be found there by the mid-1930s; a spirited Bunny Berigan tune called "Chicken and Waffles" was recorded in New York in 1935. Inarguably, the dish's alpha and omega was Wells Supper Club, which opened on Seventh Avenue (now Adam Clayton Powell Jr. Boulevard) near 132nd Street in 1938. Elizabeth and Joseph Wells's little restaurant served chicken and waffles from the get-go, and grew

④ Five Museums Made for Kids

» **Children's Museum of the Arts** (103 Charlton St.) offers classes and studio activities including animation, sound design, and a "clay bar," where kids can sculpt.
» **New York Hall of Science** (47-01 111th St., Corona, Queens), which made its debut at the 1964 World's Fair, helps children learn about space, explore

animated worlds, or just play mini-golf outside.
» **DiMenna Children's History Museum** (170 Central Park West) provides a full immersion into 350 years of New York and American history with live reenactments on weekends.
» **National Museum of Mathematics** (11 E. 26th St.), also called MoMath, features

interactive exhibits and a tessellation station.
» **Children's Museum of Manhattan** (212 W. 83rd St.) is a 40,000-square-foot, five-story complex where kids can engage in imaginative play and art and water activities while exploring dozens of interactive installations.

---

famous on it, eventually expanding from a few counter stools to a hopping 250 seats. The Wells was open very late, and as a result it caught the post-nightclub crowd—the dinner rush, dissolving into the early breakfast rush, came at 2 a.m. The dining room was integrated, too, often half Black and half white. By the 1950s, it was prominent enough that Frank Sinatra and Sammy Davis Jr. would show up for a bite after an evening out.

What makes chicken and waffles work as a combination? Some of its deliciousness derives from the texture: two different crispinesses, two similar but not identical batters. The maple syrup ties them together nicely (some diners add jam to the mix, too, or melted butter). It's also, these days, something you have to seek out. Waffle House, the chain that's everywhere in the Deep South, doesn't do fried chicken; fast-food places like Popeyes and KFC don't sell waffles; and Wells Supper Club is gone, closed in 1982. But you can find it on a good scattering of New York City restaurant menus or any day at the celebrated Los Angeles mini-chain Roscoe's House of Chicken and Waffles. Barack Obama dropped by there, unscheduled, for a bite in 2011, and the presidential order—the menu's No. 9—is now called Obama's Special.

Children's Museum [4]

Although all museums are in a sense children's museums, the world's first devoted entirely to kids and their interests is the Brooklyn Children's Museum, opened in 1899 on the grounds of Bedford Park (now Brower Park) in Crown Heights. Its exhibits, in its earliest days, included natural-history artifacts—shells, minerals, stuffed birds—that city children might not otherwise encounter, and over time came to include jigsaw puzzles and other hands-on items. That interactivity-and-play aspect has come to dominate the children's-museum experience, especially at halls of science like the

Exploratorium in San Francisco, opened in 1969, and its East Coast counterpart the New York Hall of Science, created for the 1964–65 World's Fair. The Brooklyn Children's Museum continues to operate in its now expanded building in Brower Park.

Children's Programming

A surprising amount of early TV history dates to one crucial event: the 1939 World's Fair in Queens, which early television entrepreneurs used as a platform to introduce the nascent technology to a wider public. (RCA introduced its first line of television sets there too.) W2XBS, the experimental broadcast station that would later be renamed NBC, began regular transmissions during the first week of the Fair that April, bringing about several important TV milestones: the first televised presidential speech (FDR, at the opening ceremony), the first televised jugglers, and, on May 3, 1939, the first televised Walt Disney cartoon, a short called "Donald's Cousin Gus" (in which Gus Goose comes to visit and eats all of Donald's food).

Recurring commercial TV shows for kids didn't begin until several years later, when the DuMont network began airing *Small Fry Club* (originally titled *Movies for Small Fry*) on March 11, 1947. It featured stand-alone cartoons, puppet segments, and other short stories meant to entertain while promoting good behavior. In one early sketch, *Small Fry*'s narrator, "Big Brother" (played by Bob Emery), tells viewers to send postcards to a post-office box at Grand Central Station with details of any vacations they'd been on. The program lasted only four years but became one model for children's programming, offering a combination of interactive appeals, variety-show-style short segments, and a mix of songs, puppets, cartoons, and live-action material. The similarly structured *Howdy Doody Show* premiered later in 1947 and became an enormous hit, making the format a standard for decades.

Big Bird, originated by Caroll Spinney.

PHOTOGRAPH BY
VICTOR LLORENTE

That formula was upended in 1969 with the arrival of *Sesame Street,* which grew out of the newish educational-television movement that prioritized learning as well as entertainment. The show, created by Joan Ganz Cooney, was also intended to span divides of class and wealth; its setting was not a white-picket-fence scene out of Mark Twain but a sooty-looking city street with brownstone stoops, a small grocery store on the corner, and a grouch living in the beat-up trash can out front. In its early days, it fell short of achieving its goals of representation—among other things, the original Muppet characters were almost all male, and there was no Spanish-speaking presence, although both those problems were eventually addressed—but its performers were absolutely real, its instincts urban, and its songs reminiscent of street jump-rope chants. Parallel versions have included productions in Russian, Hebrew, and Pashto. If you measure by pop-culture stickiness after 50 years, *Sesame Street* is arguably the most far-reaching television series ever. Its worldwide audience today is said to be at least 156 million children. A plurality of TV-watching adults today grew up with Big Bird and Oscar or their international cousins.

Chinatown *see* IMMIGRATION

Christian Realism

When Reinhold Niebuhr came to New York in 1928, he considered himself a radical pacifist and socialist. But the rise of Hitler in the 1930s, while Niebuhr was teaching at Union Theological Seminary uptown, changed his mind. In a series of books, starting with *Moral Man and Immoral Society* in 1932, he began arguing that liberal Protestantism, which regarded history as an endless march of progress toward utopia, was dangerously naïve. It failed to account for the fallenness of human nature, for the evil that people are prone to commit. Christian moral duty, he wrote, sometimes demands military action.

Niebuhr wasn't making a plug for American exceptionalism. Just as dangerous, he thought, was the notion of America acting as God's envoy, trying to set history on the right course. In his 1952 masterpiece, *The Irony of American History,* he uses the word *irony* in the dramatic sense: the condition that applies when the audience understands more about what's happening onstage than a character does. America, he suggested, is the character that doesn't know where history is headed. It's difficult for humans to accept that "the whole drama of history is enacted in a frame of meaning too large for human comprehension or management."

All of this explains why U.S. politicians, both hawks and doves, love to cite him as an influence. He's easy to invoke but hard to reckon with, and applying Christian realism to real life is harder still. "At best, Niebuhr's counsel serves as the equivalent of a flashing traffic light at a busy intersection," wrote the historian and former Army officer Andrew Bacevich. "Go, says the light, but proceed very, very carefully. As to the really crucial judgments—Go when? How fast? How far? In which direction?—well, you're on your own."

Christmas

Twenty centuries ago, during the reign of Caesar Augustus, two young Brooklyn residents named Joseph and Mary made their way to a hotel in lower Manhattan, where they were denied a room for the night and instead lay down in a nearby parking garage . . .

All right, fine. New York City can claim a lot, but not the arrival of the Christian Messiah. But your idea, your image, your very concept of an American Christmas was utterly shaped by New York's celebrations and creations. The Puritans, arriving in Massachusetts in 1620, had outlawed Christmas, disdaining its pagan winter-solstice roots. Elsewhere in the colonies and then the United States, it was banned to cut back on the carousing it encouraged—though not in New Netherland, where Dutch holiday gift-giving traditions persisted. In 1809, the widely read New York writer Washington Irving published his delightful if only half-true *A History of New York,* in which he spuriously claimed that the Dutch ship that carried the first scouting party to land in New Amsterdam carried before it the image of St. Nicholas. Ten years later, in another best seller, *The Sketch Book of Geoffrey Crayon, Gent.,* he laid out images of Christmases past in England: "The old halls of castles and manor-houses resounded with the harp and the Christmas carol, and their ample boards groaned under the weight of hospitality. Even the poorest cottage welcomed the festive season with green decorations of bay and holly—the cheerful fire glanced its rays through the lattice, inviting the passenger to raise the latch, and join the gossip knot huddled round the hearth, beguiling the long evening with legendary jokes and oft-told Christmas tales." Irving described Christmas Eve celebrations, candles, mistletoe, and gifts for children. Americans over the next couple of generations bought it all and gradually blew up a version of this imagined Britain to larger-than-life size.

In 1821, another New York writer, Arthur J. Stansbury, put St. Nick, who had heretofore traveled by horse and carriage, into a sleigh drawn by reindeer. Two years later, Clement Clarke Moore, living in a house on West 22nd Street, published the poem "A Visit from St. Nicholas." Better known by its first words, "'Twas the night before Christmas," it cemented the eight-tiny-reindeer-on-the-roof story forevermore. Santa's physical appearance became codified during the Civil War, when the New York political cartoonist Thomas Nast began drawing him in *Harper's Weekly* as a round figure with a big beard (and identifying him with the North rather than the South; the politicization of Christmas is apparently nothing new). Within a few years, Macy's started dolling up its Yuletide displays (*see also* DEPARTMENT-STORE HOLIDAY WINDOW DISPLAY) and eventually created another kind of spectacle to kick off the shopping season (*see also* MACY'S THANKSGIVING DAY PARADE). The quintessential Christmas movie even name-checks a New York thoroughfare in its very title, *Miracle on 34th Street*. And where is the country's collective public Christmas tree? Yes, there's one on the White House lawn, but the crowds all gather at Rockefeller Center.

Christmas Lights

The lit candles traditionally decorating a Christmas tree were certainly a lovely thing to see—and also a spectacular fire hazard. In 1882, mere weeks after the Edison Electric Light Company began to send power to its downtown customers (*see also* ELECTRICAL GRID), an Edison executive named Edward H. Johnson tried something new. He wired 108 little handmade lightbulbs into strings and, hoping to get some attention for the new company, invited reporters to see them draped around a pine tree and across the ceiling in his home on West 12th Street. The tree was mounted on a little wooden box with a motor, so it spun. By 1894, the White House had Christmas lights on its tree, and by 1903, General Electric (descended from Edison's company) was selling them in sets. Today, the U.S. imports half a billion dollars' worth of Christmas-tree lights each year.

Chrysler Building *see* SKYLINE

Club Kids

The term *club kids* precisely describes a subculture of nightclubgoers who came to prominence in the downtown New York scene of the late 1980s. Some were middle class, others affluent, but all were teenagers or in their early twenties who were fantastically, raucously stylish (or aspired to be). In the preceding few years, the disco scene had largely given way to more sedate venues populated by relatively conservative customers—but then came this new bunch of much younger people dressed in insane ensembles showing up at outré clubs like Tunnel in far-west Chelsea. They were relatively straight-edge when it came to drug use (at least at first). According to Michael Alig, who was among the earliest club kids, the new threat of AIDS meant "it was now all going out and looking very freaky so that nobody would have sex with you."

The "club kids" moniker first appeared in the March 14, 1988, issue of *New York,* headlining a cover story about the scene by Amy Virshup. The kids subsequently gained national visibility on the daytime-talk-show circuit, most memorably in a 1993 episode of *The Joan Rivers Show.* Hosting, as she called them, "five simple people with a dream and a wardrobe from hell," Rivers chatted with Alig, Amanda Lepore, James St. James, Ernie Glam, and the soon-to-be-legendary London-based performance artist and club manager Leigh Bowery, whose *faux* bosom Rivers envied. As she grilled them about trends and moneymaking and repeatedly called them "adorable," her cheerful, supportive tone was infectious. "They're not hurtin' nobody" was the prevailing viewpoint from the crowd.

When *New York* asked Virshup to revisit her club-kid subjects thirty years later, Alig (who by then had served 17 years in prison for manslaughter in the death of another club kid, Andre "Angel" Melendez) asked her where she'd picked up that phrase. Said Alig, "We didn't call ourselves that." Virshup suggested she might have made it up, and Alig responded, "When it was on the cover, we were like, *Oh my God, that's what we are.*"

Club Sandwich

Finding America's Ur–club sandwich is a tall order, kind of like the towering dish itself. Two origin stories, both New York–based, compete for authenticity: One traces the sandwich to the club cars of trains departing the city at the turn of the century (perhaps its layers— bread, meat, bread, meat, bread—mimicked the two-decker passenger cars popular in Europe at the time); another claims the name is short for the "clubhouse sandwich," which appeared around the same time in men's social clubs. The earliest published recipes date to 1889. The New York *Sun* described the ingredients for the Union Club's sandwich as heretofore "a mystery to the outside world" and promptly revealed all ... three of them: two slices of wheat toast, ham, and either chicken or turkey, served warm. "It differs essentially from any other sandwich made in the town," the paper told readers, calling it the go-to dish "of club men who like a good thing after the theater or just before their final nightcap."

The *Sun*'s editors wouldn't recognize today's club, not so much because the modern version, served everywhere from Hong Kong to Barcelona, adds lettuce, tomato, and mayo and jabs a frilly toothpick into each stack, but more because it gained that middle slice, likely in the early 1900s. That extra piece chafed purists and was bemoaned

over the years by such authorities as *Town & Country* food editor James Villas and James Beard himself. Beard warned in 1972 that it had "bastardized" the sandwich. "Whoever started that horror," he wrote, "should be forced to eat three-deckers three times a day the rest of his life." (Critics might retort that Beard's preference goes by a different name: the chicken BLT.)

Three slices have become the club's hallmark, at any rate. Enough that the term has been expanded to describe various multilayered inedible things as well: Jupiter's moon Ganymede, which may contain several alternating layers of ice and water, is a "club-sandwich moon." Meanwhile, *club-sandwich generation* refers to the unlucky adults who support their elderly parents, their grown-up children, and their grandkids, all at once.

College Entrance Exam

In November 1900, the deans and presidents of fifteen elite American schools met at Columbia University to lay down a plan for standardized admissions tests. The group voted to call itself the College Entrance Examination Board, and their planned exam was quite different from today's: a little bit of English-literature analysis; grammar in Latin, Greek, and French; and some (relatively primitive) physics, chemistry, zoology, botany, and mathematics. It did indeed screen students for college— or rather for the elite education of the era, a high-minded certification for a few thousand sons and daughters of the well-off.

During World War I, the United States began intelligence-testing Army recruits, and after the armistice, the College Board, working with a Princeton psychology professor named Carl Campbell Brigham, began to experiment along similar lines. The result, in 1926, was the creation of the Scholastic Aptitude Test, a standardized exam of vocabulary exercises, number puzzles, and analogies. As a measure of intelligence, the

(5) **Tips for Becoming a Stand-up**

From comedian Charlie Bardey

➻ **Focus on getting actually good, not on building your career.** "Think about what you think is funny and how you can share that with other people."

➻ **Find a job you can actually stand.** "Like, be a museum educator or something."

➻ **Make friends and champion their work.** "A rising tide lifts all boats."

➻ **Develop a skill that's not stand-up.** "So when you don't feel like stand-up is going well, you can still have a sense of self-worth."

➻ **Prepare to be humbled.** "You will spend $14 on a car to a show where you will bomb in the back room of an overpriced *faux* dive bar for three people, one of whom is your mom."

original SAT seems rudimentary, naïve, and just plain odd today, with questions like

Of the five things following, four are alike in a certain way. Which is the one not like these four?
(1) **tar** (2) **snow** (3) **soot** (4) **ebony** (5) **coal**

and

A tree always has
(1) **leaves** (2) **fruit** (3) **buds** (4) **roots** (5) **a shadow**

But even this improved on what had come before. James Bryant Conant, the president of Harvard University, championed the SAT as a democratizing admissions tool, a meritocratic counterbalance to the my-prep-school-headmaster-called-the-admissions-office method. And indeed, Harvard in Conant's era achieved a (limited) new measure of openness.

By the 1960s, a more sophisticated and nuanced SAT had been adopted by virtually all American colleges, even as it became evident that it was full of inherent biases against nonwhite and nonaffluent students. Since then, the test has been reworked again and again, with major changes put in place every decade or so; the scoring system has been adjusted numerous times. The old name, "Scholastic Aptitude Test," gave way to the less loaded "Scholastic Assessment Test" and then to the officially rootless initialism SAT. Some elite schools now treat the exam (and its competitor, the ACT) as optional, and many more consider it a modest part of their admissions decision. But will they still take notice of a kid who scores a perfect 1600? The answer is almost surely (a) yes.

Comedy Club [5]

Stand-up comedy, a definitively American and particularly New York art form, took decades to assert that it deserved to be the centerpiece of a night of entertainment. To paraphrase one of its great practitioners: It got

no respect. In its earliest days, stand-up was performed in burlesque and vaudeville theaters (*see also* BURLESQUE, AMERICAN STYLE; VAUDEVILLE) on mixed bills with singing and dancing. In the early 1950s, the action moved to (often mob-run) Vegas nightclubs or (often mob-run) Vegas-style nightclubs. Then the shift began, as the likes of Lenny Bruce, Mort Sahl, Jonathan Winters, Joan Rivers, and Shelley Berman began making stand-up more personal and cerebral, at jazz clubs, Beatnik bars, coffee shops, and small downtown theaters. By the 1960s, with Attorney General Robert Kennedy cracking down on the Mafia, it was clear comedians deserved a space of their own.

George Schultz, a failed comic with such a sense of talent that comedians called him "the Ear," gave them the first one. In 1962, in Sheepshead Bay, Brooklyn, he opened Pips (named for his dog and his favorite Dickens character), a club that showcased up-and-coming singers and comedians. Despite its being inconvenient to Manhattan, Pips attracted enough attention over the years to host talent like Rivers, George Carlin, Andy Kaufman, and Billy Crystal, among many others. It launched the careers of Rodney Dangerfield and David Brenner. And despite the neighborhood's rough edges (morning DJ "Goumba Johnny" Sialiano called it a place where "you could get heckled by the bartender"), the New York *Times* later labeled it "an Algonquin Round Table for a generation of comedians."

In 1963, aspiring Broadway producer Budd Friedman opened the folk-music venue the Improvisation in Hell's Kitchen, where he kept a redbrick wall behind the stage because he couldn't afford to drywall, inadvertently creating the much-copied stand-up backdrop. Comedy's increasing popularity made these two clubs into showcases exclusively for stand-up, ascribing new value to the form and changing it nearly overnight. No longer were audiences just looking for a nice evening out—they were expecting to laugh. Comedians had to

⑥ **The City's Best Comic-Book Stores**

Chosen by comic-book artist Fred Van Lente

➤ **Desert Island Comics**
(540 Metropolitan Ave., Williamsburg)
"Like an old '60s head shop that would have sold R. Crumb's *Zap Comix*."

➤ **Bulletproof Comics**
(2178 Nostrand Ave., Flatbush)
"Right around the corner from Brooklyn College, it has been around since the '90s.

The owner, Hank Kwon, has stayed successful by knowing his customers."

➤ **Midtown Comics Downtown**
(64 Fulton St.)
"The best signings in the city. The staff is super-knowledgeable."

➤ **Mysterious Time Machine**
(418 Sixth Ave.)
"Basically a basement room

down concrete stairs, it's filled with boxes upon boxes of old comics—but they have this week's latest titles, too."

➤ **Forbidden Planet**
(832 Broadway, near 13th St.)
"Probably the best overall comics store in the city—big, clean, and you're not constantly tripping over other people."

---

be faster, funnier, and always writing new material. In 1975, Friedman opened a second Improv in Los Angeles, joining the already popular Comedy Store, owned by Mitzi Shore. On the West Coast, the rooms were bigger and filled with talent scouts (in part because Johnny Carson had moved *The Tonight Show* to Burbank). From then, the stereotypes of the New York and L.A. comedy scenes were set: New York is where you go to get good, and L.A. is where you go to get noticed. By the 1980s, however, the road was where stand-ups went to get paid, and Friedman opened Improvs all over the country, soon joined by Chuckle Huts and Ha-Has and a plethora of stupidly named clubs. The Comedy Boom was on, and it was promptly followed by a comedy bust, owing to an oversupply of venues undersupplied with real talent.

Partly out of a desire to move past the joke-after-joke demands of the clubs, and partly because most of those clubs had closed (Pips, after a long twilight, shuttered for good in the mid-aughts, and the New York Improv went bankrupt in 1992 and subsequently closed, although there are more than twenty locations in other cities), stand-ups in the 1990s began to look for whatever venues they could find to develop their craft, in the process creating what would become known as alternative comedy. By the early aughts, some of its practitioners (Eugene Mirman, Janeane Garofalo, Amy Poehler) had found permanent New York homes without all the trappings of a comedy club (no drink minimum, fewer hacks) in places like Luna Lounge on the Lower East Side, Rififi in the East Village, and the Upright Citizens Brigade Theatre in Chelsea. They created a second comedy boom, one that was somewhat more accepting of brainy, unconventional talent. More recently, the Comedy Cellar in Greenwich Village has established itself as the national standard-bearer, the comic's hangout of choice. But a lot of stand-up is taking place in hybrid performance spaces,

like Union Hall and Littlefield, venues within blocks of each other near the Gowanus Canal. On most nights today, the best comedy in America is once again happening in Brooklyn.

Comic Book [6]

The American comic book was built on a foundation of iniquity. Its not-so-reputable parents, publications known as "nudies" and "smooshes," were two genres of the so-called pulp magazines of the 1920s. Pulps got their name from their low-grade paper stock, and their contents were as degraded as the material they were printed on. Smooshes were primarily about sex and danger, whereas nudies depicted, as one might expect, women wearing just enough to keep the publisher out of jail. (Even if he did get a slap on the wrist, he could easily pay off someone at City Hall and escape.) Wasps in the established literary houses had no interest in publishing such things, but a smattering of Jews from immigrant families picked up what others wouldn't touch.

Those publishers made comic books popular, but volumes of comic strips had been being compiled since at least the 1840s, and an 1897 book of the New York *World*'s "The Yellow Kid" strips (*see also* YELLOW JOURNALISM) seems, on its back cover, to have first used the term *comic book*. But these publications looked very little like a modern comic book. Only in 1929 was that kind of object produced, when publisher George T. Delacorte Jr. released *The Funnies*, an insert for tabloid newspapers that was filled with strips that hadn't been picked up by the syndicates that ruled the industry.

It was a flop on the newsstands and canceled in the autumn of 1930. But all was not lost. Maxwell Charles Gaines, a necktie salesman and ex-teacher who was looking to score big in the depths of the Great Depression, linked up with a Connecticut publisher called the

Eastern Color Printing Company and worked out a deal to repackage its hit newspaper strips in a new booklet called *Funnies on Parade*. It was released in 1933 as a coupon giveaway from Procter & Gamble and did well, leading to a follow-up called *Famous Funnies*, which can unreservedly be called a comic book, given that it was sold on its own and had a wraparound cover. A different publisher, Malcolm Wheeler-Nicholson, went even further a year later, when he put together National Allied Publications and, in 1935, released *New Fun*, the first comic book to feature new material.

When Harry Donenfeld, who'd established himself as a pornography publisher, got involved, the pulps started to soar. He was a Romanian Jewish immigrant from the Lower East Side who was allegedly so mobbed up that he'd helped Frank Costello smuggle liquor from Canada in boxes intended to hold paper. In the mid-1930s, New York's mayor, Fiorello H. La Guardia, decided to crack down on vice, wrecking the business of nudies and smooshes. Jack Liebowitz, Donenfeld's business manager, connected with Wheeler-Nicholson, and the men all went into business together. Store owners were always uptight about selling girlie rags, and Liebowitz and Donenfeld could sweeten deals if they threw in some clean fun for the kids.

They struck gold with a series of runaway hits. Other low-rent publishers got onboard, turning comics into a nationwide fad. The contents typically hewed close to the sci-fi, crime, and adventure stories in the era's other youth magazines. But only when Donenfeld and Liebowitz kicked Wheeler-Nicholson out of National and one of their employees found an intriguing slush-pile submission did things really get going. The lead character in the story was the brainchild of two Jewish kids from Cleveland, Jerry Siegel and Joe Shuster, and he was called Superman. The hero made his debut in National's *Action Comics* No. 1, whereupon the comic-book business finally took flight.

CompStat

No New York invention has arguably saved more lives in the past 26 years than CompStat, the computer system introduced by the NYPD in 1994. It has helped drive down the city's crime rates to historic lows and revolutionized policing around the world. Los Angeles, London, and Paris use a form of CompStat, while Baltimore has CitiStat, and New Orleans has BlightStat. Its basic practices lie in the massing and sorting of data to find spots where a lot of crime is taking place, allowing police to focus on those locations.

It all started in a much different city from today's New York. Jack Maple was a 41-year-old former "cave cop," a veteran of the then-separate Transit Police Department who had developed an off-duty taste for homburg hats, bow ties, spectator shoes, and the Oak Bar at the Plaza. While patrolling the decaying subway of the '70s and early '80s, Maple had assembled what he called "Charts of the Future," paper maps into which he stuck color-coded pins to track crime. It sounds simple and fairly obvious, but no one in New York's police departments had done it until Maple, who soon was locking up dozens of gang members and getting promoted to lieutenant. At night, he parked himself at his table at Elaine's and watched closely as the owner, Elaine Kaufman, monitored every waiter and bar tab. Maple wrote four goals on a napkin: accurate, timely intelligence; rapid deployment; effective tactics; relentless follow-up and assessment (*see also* "BROKEN WINDOWS" POLICING). After Maple became the NYPD's top anti-crime strategist under the incoming police commissioner Bill Bratton in 1993, those principles, called CompStat, began to be disseminated through weekly meetings at police headquarters. Within weeks, crime rates started to plunge, and they have never really stopped.

That's the beloved, mostly true myth, anyway. Maple's friends admit that "the Jackster," who died in

Virgin Warrior—Two Hearts, *a 2006 conceptual piece that*
Marina Abramovic described as a reflection on "the power of female energy."
PERFORMANCE BY MARINA ABRAMOVIC WITH JAN FABRE

2001, may have embellished a bit of the CompStat origin story. Bratton is quick to say that he was using wall charts to identify crime hot spots as a young sergeant in Boston in 1976. Later, hired as New York's transit-police chief under Mayor David Dinkins, Bratton recognized a like-minded ally in Maple, and when Bratton returned to the city as police commissioner for new mayor Rudy Giuliani, Maple was one of his first hires. "Maple's concepts met Bratton's systems, and that's what this is actually all about," said John Miller, Bratton's press spokesman in 1994 and today the NYPD's deputy commissioner for intelligence and counterterrorism.

CompStat has plenty of detractors, who say it helped fuel the stop-and-frisk harassment of hundreds of thousands of Black and brown New Yorkers. There is also debate about just how much credit CompStat, and the NYPD, deserves for the crime decline. Cities including Houston and Phoenix saw similar drops and attribute them mostly to economic development and community policing. Others place some credit on private security, like business-improvement districts and anti-theft systems like LoJack. "Two decades of an expanding economy, and mass incarceration, have contributed the most to the crime drop," said Rick Rosenfeld, a professor of criminology at the University of Missouri, St. Louis. "Smarter policing, informed by digitized crime data, has contributed in a number of places, including New York City. But we don't know how much." We do, however, know what happened. In 1991, the city had more than 2,000 murders for the second year in a row. In 2017, the total dipped under 300, the lowest it had been since 1951.

Conceptual Art

By the late 1960s, something had to blow in the stupendously speeded-up molecule that was the New York art world. What came to be known as Conceptual Art was the Krakatoa super-eruption from which art is still feeling the aftereffects.

In the postwar years, the work fashioned by a group of straggling New York painters (*see also* ABSTRACT EXPRESSIONISM) had grown into the first American art movement with international repercussions, but it was soon eclipsed by Jasper Johns, Robert Rauschenberg, and the new mega art market that was burgeoning in the city; this was followed by Pop Art (*see also* POP ART),

which almost instantly mutated into Minimalism. In the span of just 15 years, one world was born, died, was reborn, and then kept mutating. Conceptual Art was delineated in 1969 at the School of Visual Arts by one of its early proponents, the artist Joseph Kosuth, who wrote that "all art after [Marcel] Duchamp [the creator in 1913 of the first readymade, a bicycle wheel mounted on a stool] is conceptual in nature because art only exists conceptually"—meaning that art, while acknowledging the importance of all the styles that came before it, could now be reduced to what seemed to be its philosophical essence, its idea.

In New York, Vito Acconci masturbated under the floor of a gallery and called it art; Sol LeWitt wrote out instructions for other people to execute his drawings on walls, and collectors purchased the instructions; Mel Bochner measured art galleries; Hans Haacke documented the right-wing ties of museum board members; and William Wegman made comedic videos of himself and his Weimaraner, Man Ray. In California, Chris Burden had a friend shoot him in the arm with a .22 rifle, and Bruce Nauman videotaped himself doing funny walks in his studio. Marina Abramovic traded places with a prostitute for a night during the run of her show in Amsterdam, and Robert Smithson built the great earthwork called *Spiral Jetty* in the Great Salt Lake. Conceptual Art encompassed almost anything, including earth art, performance, video, dance, filmmaking, and simply speaking, all the while, and most important, using photography and text. This triggered a reconfiguration of more than a hundred years of photography, from a fine art judged like painting to a tool used by anyone who chose to, creating whole new criteria for art and giving rise to other New York artists like Cindy Sherman, Barbara Kruger, Jenny Holzer, Richard Prince, and Robert Gober.

By the 1970s, money had left the art world, and cities began to fall into disrepair. All over the world, artists started living together cheaply in clusters functioning almost like tribes, their hive minds working on thousands of shared and sharpened Post-Minimalist issues. For better and worse (worse being that only the artists and their cadres had any idea what certain work was about), art withdrew from the wider world of commerce. Criticism totally changed. New art theories blossomed everywhere and became part of social movements like Black Power, feminism, gay liberation, the antiwar protests,

⑦ **Classic Forms of Resisting Consciousness**

Excerpted from Kathie Sarachild's Outline for Consciousness-Raising *(1970)*

"OR, HOW TO AVOID FACING THE AWFUL TRUTH:

Anti-womanism

Glorification of the Oppressor

Excusing or Feeling Sorry for the Oppressor

Romantic Fantasies

'An Adequate Personal Solution'

Self-cultivation, Rugged Individualism

Self-blame

Ultra-militancy, etc."

---

and scores of other radical thrusts at Establishment values around the world. This reshaped the art world as well as art itself. Art school was now the rule, rather than the exception; everyone knew the codes, meanings, and secret handshakes, what felt "real" and what felt like a past that had to be questioned or moved on from. The art world began to grow exponentially with the idea that anyone could be an artist. It was art liberation.

Consciousness-Raising [7]

In 1968, Kathie Sarachild, an early member of a feminist group called New York Radical Women (*see also* RAPE, MODERN VIEW OF), wrote an essay titled "A Program for Feminist Consciousness Raising." "In our groups," it read, "let's share our feelings and pool them. Let's let ourselves go and see where our feelings lead us." New York women soon began gathering in apartments to discuss, often for the first time in their lives, the circumstances of their gender—from their husbands' unwillingness to wash the dishes or change diapers to stories about backroom abortions or the "myth of the vaginal orgasm" (as the title of Anne Koedt's pioneering essay phrased it). These meetings were often a thrilling, heady experience. As the activist Chude Pamela Allen recalled to *New York* for a story on NYRW's fiftieth anniversary, "Somebody was commenting about her boyfriend saying something to her, and everybody in the room went: 'Oh my God. That's *exactly* what mine says to me.'" Robin Morgan, another participant, remembered, "I admitted that on occasion in my marriage I had faked an orgasm. I was convinced that I was the only person in the world sick and perverse enough to have done this. Every woman in the room said, 'Oh, you too?' It was an amazing moment."

By the mid-'70s, consciousness-raising had found its way into pop culture. In the 1975 social-satire horror film *The Stepford Wives*, Joanna and her friend Bobbie (newly resettled in the Connecticut suburbs, they confide that

they were involved in "women's lib" in the city) attempt to organize a consciousness-raising group for the women of Stepford after noticing their submissiveness. Turns out they're more interested in sharing home-cleaning tips because they've been murdered and replaced with sub-servient fembots.

For some real-life practitioners, consciousness-raising, once seen as radical, began to feel more like a drawn-out group-therapy session, as the original idea that it would ignite widespread activism hadn't panned out. By the 1980s, the practice as such had mostly withered. Nevertheless, it's hard not to see all that sharing as a forebear of everything from the 44,000 Lean In Circles across the world to Me Too.

Consensus Theory of History

Richard Hofstadter's landmark book *The American Political Tradition*, released in 1948, details how a number of presidents—including Jackson and Lincoln—seemed to improvise their political philosophy as they went along. Despite this, the historian argues that there's a through line to their behavior: a bourgeois capitalist ethos, an attachment to private property and individualism.

Hofstadter, a Columbia professor, was responding to the left-wing historians who had dominated the field during his own education, particularly Charles Beard, who saw American history as the history of class conflict. Hofstadter was arguing the opposite: that deep down, everyone had always agreed, or at least everyone who wielded much power.

This concept resonated with other historians of his generation, and in books like *The Genius of American Politics* and *The Liberal Tradition in America*, they praised the consensus as a mark of America's greatness. But for Hofstadter, the consensus was a cause for shame. "I hate capitalism and everything that goes with it," he once told a friend.

John Lennon and Yoko Ono,
noted co-op apartment shareholders,
at the Dakota in November 1980.

Cooking Show

Like children's programming, commercial-television cookery originated during the first week of W2XBS broadcasting during the New York World's Fair at the end of April 1939, with one fifteen-minute segment hosted by a man named Tex O'Rourke. Network internal records list it with the title "How to Roast a Suckling Pig."

When regular TV broadcasting began in 1946, one of the first half-dozen series to make it into rotation was James Beard's *I Love to Eat*, which debuted as part of a program called *Radio City Matinee* and was broken out into its own time slot later that year. As a live-broadcast cooking show, *I Love to Eat* (sponsored by Borden Dairy's Elsie the Cow) presented some challenges. "Jim would perspire a great deal," remembered producer E. Roger Muir several decades later. "We would be concerned about keeping him presentable. But at the end of the shows, the crew ate pretty good food." Beard was only moderately successful, because he was not entirely comfortable on-camera and was slightly too early to the medium—in 1946, a lot of TVs were still in bars, and the audience there was mostly men who were not inclined to go home and immediately roast a chicken. A few years later, in 1962, Julia Child, who had become good friends with Beard, stepped behind a counter on a soundstage in Boston to tape her first show. She turned out to have the broadcasting secret sauce that Beard had lacked, and American food has never looked back.

Cooperative Apartment Building

Co-ops, in which groups of people pool their resources to live communally and thus less expensively, seem to have originated in the U.K. As the financial structure for residents of an apartment building, however, the co-op is almost entirely identified with New York. (A few co-ops exist in Washington, D.C., and other cities, but nothing like the number here.) In a co-op, residents buy shares of ownership in a building rather than actual cubic footage. They designate a board to manage finances and maintenance and pay monthly fees to cover the costs of services, upgrades and repairs, and staff.

For decades, co-ops appealed to the rich and/or famous, because there was no deed for their purchase and therefore no public record of what they'd paid. (The law changed, making co-op purchases public, in 2004.) Most of all, co-ops allow exclusivity because potential residents are screened both financially and in person by members of the board before they are approved. Although it's never been proven, elite co-ops were always known to reject people—and a few are still said to—on the basis of race and religion. After all, a buyer can be turned down for any reason, without explanation. An ugly necktie at the interview is reason enough, although most turndowns relate to money.

As for the first co-op, the architectural historian Christopher Gray has made a strong case for the Rembrandt, erected in 1881 at 152 West 57th Street next to the Carnegie Hall site. Although the Rembrandt's corporation failed—the building went rental within its first twenty years—others followed, and the idea boomed again in the 1920s and crashed during the Depression.

A few buildings turned to co-op ownership in the postwar decades. The residents of the Dakota Apartments, arguably the most famous luxury apartment house in New York, adopted co-op ownership in 1961, shortly after the building was sold and the new owner hinted that he might tear it down. But the real momentum for the co-op movement began in the 1970s, under a unique set of circumstances. Oil prices (and thus operating costs) had risen, while regulated rents (set by the city) had not. Landlords wanted out, and residents wanted control over their homes. Tax laws also slightly favored the co-op. Between 1978 and 1988, more than 3,000 rental buildings converted to cooperative ownership. Today, that fervor has faded slightly, as most new buildings are constructed as condominiums instead. But co-ops remain, and will continue to be, a huge piece of the New York market, numbering about 380,000 apartments in 7,200 buildings.

Crayon

Although French artists had been using Conté crayons for a century, credit for the schoolchild's brightly colored wax drawing tool belongs to Crayola. Its founders, Joseph and Edwin Binney and C. Harold Smith, set up shop in New York City in 1880, building on the Binneys' earlier business making black pigments upstate. At first, the company made slate drawing pencils; in 1903, responding to schools' need for inexpensive wax crayons, it introduced the first pack of eight Crayola colors, manufacturing them in its plant in Pennsylvania. The big sixty-four-crayon box with built-in sharpener arrived in 1958. Since 1984, the company (now called Crayola LLC) has been a subsidiary of Hallmark Cards, and it still makes its crayons in Pennsylvania. Edwin Binney's wife, Alice, is credited with the name, a portmanteau of *craie* (French for "chalk") and *oleaginous*.

Cream Cheese

Soft, spreadable cheese of the general type known as Neufchâtel has been made on farms and in homes for centuries. The conversion of that locally variable product into a branded, commercially produced commodity can be attributed to two men: William Lawrence, who'd begun mass-producing a version with a higher fat content in Chester, New York, around 1877, and Alvah L. Reynolds, who in 1880 began selling it to retail grocers downstate in the city. That same year, Reynolds was also the one who began wrapping it in foil stamped with a name in blue ink: PHILADELPHIA, capitalizing on that city's reputation for high-quality dairy products. (There are many other myths about the creation of the brand, some of which involve the dairy-producing town of Philadelphia, New York, but the world's most authoritative cream-cheese scholar, a rabbi in Santa Monica named Jeffrey Marx, has pinned this down pretty definitively.) By the end of 1880, Reynolds was selling more than Lawrence could produce, and his company soon expanded. He sold the brand in 1903 to a firm that later merged with the already successful Kraft cheese company, a chain of ownership that leads, most likely, to your morning bagel's shmear.

Credit Card

In the first half of the twentieth century, a variety of businesses, from department stores to oil companies, allowed consumers to charge purchases to their standing accounts. Over the decades, they added features to those programs that included minimum monthly payments and finance charges. In 1936, the growing airline industry created a credit system called the Universal Air Travel Plan, which was more or less a cross-industry charge account. Some of these systems depended on taking impressions from embossed metal address cards called Charga-Plates.

The real innovation came in 1949, when three men—Alfred Bloomingdale, Francis X. McNamara, and Ralph Schneider—were having lunch at Majors Cabin Grill, a restaurant at 33 West 33rd Street, next to the Empire State Building. McNamara ran a finance company called Hamilton Credit Corporation, which was on the verge of going broke because of its uncollected bills, and Schneider was his lawyer; Bloomingdale, a theater producer, was a member of the department-store family. Because McNamara's company was in such precarious shape, the men began to discuss the ways businesses could extend credit, and over the course of the lunch they realized that restaurants could share a charge system, with a third party between business and consumer handling the operation. They called over Major Satz, the restaurant's owner, and asked him what percentage he'd pay for such a system. "Seven percent," he said, off the top of his head. McNamara and Schneider launched Diners Club shortly thereafter, with some initial funding from Bloomingdale, and in the early years they did indeed charge businesses 7 percent on each transaction. A year after that first lunch, McNamara went back to Majors and charged the very first meal on the first card, No. 1000.

After a brief, shaky start during which the founders had trouble finding a bank to back them, the company

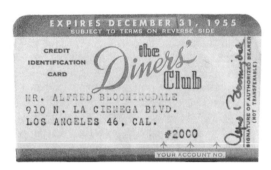

The co-founder's own card.

began to turn a profit in 1952 and within a few years went public and expanded from restaurants to hotels, retail stores, and other businesses. In 1958, it gained competition in a still-growing field from American Express, whose early cards were purple rather than today's familiar green, and BankAmericard (now Visa). Diners Club, owned by Discover, is still around today, albeit as a relatively small part of the credit-card universe.

Credit Default Swap

Before its infamous role in the 2008 global financial crisis, the credit default swap (CDS) was conceived as a way to make banking less risky. In 1994, JPMorgan bankers in New York faced a problem: Their major client, Exxon, required a multibillion-dollar line of credit to prepare for a potential fine related to the *Valdez* oil spill. Because Exxon had excellent credit, the bank would make little money extending the line of credit and would be forced to tie up a lot of capital in reserves to back up such a large loan.

Eventually, a young JPMorgan banker named Blythe Masters and her colleagues came up with a solution: a swap, wherein the bank would make the loan but

another financial institution (in this instance, the European Bank for Reconstruction and Development) would agree to bear the default risk. If Exxon failed to repay—a very unlikely circumstance—the EBRD would make JPMorgan whole for its loss. JPMorgan therefore did not need to hold extensive reserves to back the loan and could use its capital for more profitable business.

This was a novel application of an existing financial concept. Derivative contracts had long been used to simulate real-world financial events and hedge real-world financial risks. You could buy an interest-rate swap or an exchange-rate swap that would protect your business from exposure to unexpected changes in the financial environment. Now it was possible to buy a derivative that moved credit risk itself from one institution to another. And after JPMorgan created this bespoke product to help with its big loan to Exxon, it and other banks expanded and commoditized the concept, selling credit default swaps in a wide variety of contexts to many users beyond just banks.

It's possible to see how these would make the system safer rather than less so. Banks are at risk when they have excessively concentrated exposure to specific clients, regions, or industries that can get into trouble. Products that help banks spread those risks more widely and offload risks that are excessive could, in theory, make the financial system more stable and resilient. But there were still problems. One was the rise of the so-called naked CDS, a credit default swap bought by speculators who didn't actually have credit exposure to the entity whose credit was being insured. This created perverse incentives in bankruptcies; a CDS holder could actually stand to make money if the insured entity failed to pay its debts, which runs against usual principles that prohibit overinsurance. In other words, you don't let people buy property insurance on other people's houses, lest they be incentivized to burn them down.

Another problem is that while CDS shifts credit risk,

(8) The Best Time to Get a Cronut

From Dominique Ansel, baker

"We make several hundred Cronut pastries fresh each morning, and guests can purchase **two per person** in store. We recommend guests arrive in the morning (we open at 8 a.m. Monday through Saturday, and 9 a.m. on Sunday) as we typically sell out by late morning or early afternoon. Usually, if you visit **in the morning close to the opening,** you'll be able to get them.

"There's also an online preorder system so you don't have to wait in line: Each Monday at 11 a.m., we release preorders at **cronutpreorder .com for orders two weeks out.** You can preorder up to twelve Cronut pastries per person."

---

it doesn't make it go away and may even cause it to become less visible. This problem played a significant part in exacerbating the 2008 financial crisis. The major insurer American International Group had sold credit default swaps against $78 billion worth of collateralized debt obligations, effectively insuring its counterparties against the risk that there would be extensive defaults in various kinds of loans, especially residential and commercial mortgages. Then, when real-estate prices fell sharply, AIG's ability to make all the payments it would owe to cover defaulted loans came into question. Ultimately, the federal government had to bail out AIG.

CDS does play a useful role in the financial system when applied appropriately, and bank regulators around the world have taken steps to preserve helpful uses of the CDS while cracking down on its abuses. U.S. banks are no longer allowed to speculate in a CDS with their depositors' money, for example, and a CDS is increasingly required to be traded through public clearinghouses. Increased financial supervision of nonbank entities like AIG is supposed to protect against a variety of risks, including those related to CDS. But it remains uncertain whether these reforms will be effective in reducing our economic exposure to future financial crises.

Credit Reporting Agency

Manifest Destiny, meet the real-estate bubble: In 1837, after years of offering low rates on Western lands taken from Native peoples, banks in New York raised interest and cut back on lending, prompting a bad recession. Between 1839 and 1843, over 40 percent of American banks tanked, unemployment hit double digits, and the economy took seven years to recover.

A partial solution to that volatility came from Lewis Tappan, a Manhattan wholesaler and a Calvinist who hated the idea of credit and preferred, as in the Bible, to deal in cash. Tappan did have a history in credit, though, using loans in the 1830s to navigate around a boycott of him and his brother by southern dry-goods dealers angered by the Tappans' staunch abolitionism. After the crash, the brothers determined that if credit was necessary for America's expansion, they might as well be the ones to try to sanitize it of its unpredictability. In the summer of 1841, Lewis founded the Mercantile Agency using their contacts in the abolitionist movement to estimate the personal character and credit information of potential debtors. Naturally, the reports weren't all that accurate in the South, where the Tappans' anti-slavery mission excluded them from business.

But by 1844, the agency had almost 300 clients and quickly expanded into Boston, Philadelphia, and Baltimore. It also had quite the list of alumni: Abraham Lincoln, Ulysses S. Grant, Grover Cleveland, and William McKinley all served as correspondents determining the likelihood a debtor would default. Having determined that the freedom of slaves was a worthier cause than the accuracy of credit reports, Tappan retired from the Mercantile Agency in 1849 to serve as treasurer for the American Missionary Association, which he'd co-founded in 1846, to establish churches for freed slaves and help finance what eventually became the system of historically Black colleges and universities. And the Mercantile Agency eventually became Dun & Bradstreet, a New Jersey–based analysis firm with almost $2 billion in assets.

Cronut [8]

New York isn't exactly a stranger to food phenomena, but these days the line between fad and phenom is a much harder one to cross. That's why it's amazing that the cronut, a cross between a filled doughnut and a croissant invented by French-born pastry chef Dominique

*The cronut from
Dominique Ansel Bakery.*

Ansel, has managed to maintain its iconic status. It made its debut at his Soho bakery on May 10, 2013, heralded by Hugh Merwin on *New York*'s Grub Street blog in a post headlined "Introducing the Cronut, a Doughnut-Croissant Hybrid That May Very Well Change Your Life." Every day thereafter for several years, the so-called Frankenpastry—deep-fried and cream filled, with its specific method of manufacture a trade secret until the publication of Ansel's 2015 cookbook *The Secret Recipes*—attracted lines of New Yorkers and tourists alike that snaked down Spring Street and around the basketball court on the corner. Though the day's cronuts no longer sell out by 9 a.m. or appear on Craigslist at a 700 percent markup, Ansel has maintained their novelty by changing the flavors monthly. Other bakers have since tried their own repurposings of croissant dough, including a croissant-muffin hybrid called a cruffin. Cronut clones (clonuts?) can be found everywhere now, even at Dunkin'.

Crossword Puzzle

The big bang of across-and-down happened in the New York *World*, Joseph Pulitzer's paper, on December 21, 1913 (a Sunday, of course). Arthur Wynne was the newspaperman who devised the grid you see here, with "FUN" at its apex. Over the next few years, puzzle solving became a bona fide fad among young people, right up there with flagpole sitting and goldfish swallowing. In 1924, to capitalize on the craze, Richard Simon and Max Lincoln Schuster launched their namesake publishing firm with the best-selling *Cross Word Puzzle Book*, which came with a pencil attached to the cover. (Still publishing that series, S&S is now up to *Crossword Puzzle Book No. 257*.) The New York *Times* got into the game in 1942, hiring Margaret Farrar—who had edited many of the S&S books—as its first puzzle editor. Her successor Will Shortz, only the fourth person to hold the job, also runs the world's premier gathering of solvers, the annual American Crossword Puzzle Tournament.

The "Fun" supplement of the Sunday New York World *on December 21, 1913, included the first crossword puzzle. (Solution on page 349.)*

From

**DEPARTMENT-STORE
HOLIDAY WINDOW DISPLAY**

to

DRY CLEANING

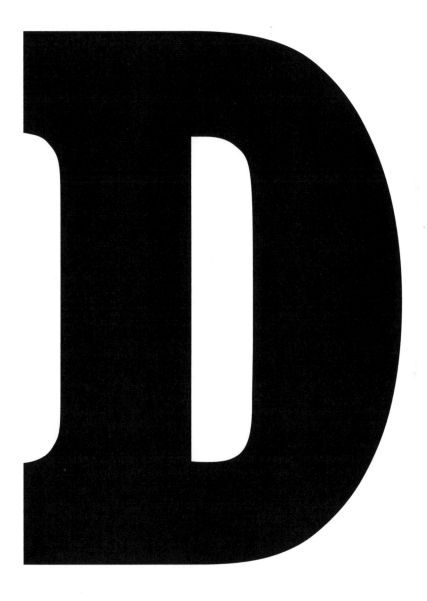

*Disco: At GG's Barnum Room on
West 45th Street, 1979.*
PHOTOGRAPH BY BILL BERNSTEIN

(1) Five Rare and Fantastic Disco Records

Chosen by Jeff Ogiba and Michael Polnasek of Black Gold Records

» **Marta Acuna,** "Dance, Dance, Dance" (12-inch single, 1977): "This ethereal cult dance classic was notoriously dismissed by its producer, Patrick Adams. Record collectors passionately disagree."

» **Donna McGhee,** *Make It Last Forever* (LP, 1978): "The soulful Brooklynite began her career as a gospel singer before creating this treasure. 'Make It Last Forever' earnestly whispers McGhee's sexual innocence as the New York City disco scene was peaking."

» **Ramsey & Co.,** "Love Call" (single, 1979): "Mainor Ramsey formed Ramsey & Co. with the purpose of playing some fun local New York gigs, but in the process, he recorded what would become an impossibly rare party great."

» **Loose Joints,** "Is It All Over My Face" (12-inch single, 1980): "Recorded by the New York experimental producer Arthur Russell, it hits the beats-per-minute sweet spot of 120, perfect for mixing

Department-Store Holiday Window Display

Macy's was not yet in Herald Square in 1874. It was still a dry-goods store in its original location at Sixth Avenue and 14th Street, although it already had as its logo the red five-pointed star (based on a tattoo that R. H. Macy himself had on his arm) it uses to this day. There, a December tradition began behind the large plate-glass windows (themselves a relatively recent technological innovation) that would continue to attract shoppers and spectators for decades to come. Some nameless marketing person put up a display of porcelain dolls re-creating scenes from Harriet Beecher Stowe's best-selling novel *Uncle Tom's Cabin*. This preceded the era of mass-media advertising, and an arresting window display really was enough to draw shoppers and enhance sales. A gimmick was born.

North of Macy's along Sixth Avenue, a chic mercantile district was beginning to take shape. Eventually known as "Ladies' Mile," it was convenient to lower Fifth Avenue's mansions and later to the elevated train. Its department stores—Siegel-Cooper, Arnold Constable, Stern Brothers, Lord & Taylor, B. Altman—were enormous. By 1883, the tableaux in those windows as well as Macy's started to move, first using steam and spring power, and then electric motors. When Lord & Taylor moved up to Fifth Avenue early in the new century, its display-window platforms were on hydraulic lifts so they could be staged in the basement and then raised into place. In the middle of the twentieth century, virtually every American city's downtown had a department store with such window displays, and a couple of generations brought their children, nostalgically, to see them.

They still do, although most of those downtowns have lost their local department stores as the paired forces of suburbanization and specialty retail (and, after those, Amazon) have hurt the business. New York, being large and still heavy on pedestrian life, has resisted those trends somewhat, but it too has thinned out, gradually losing Best & Company, B. Altman, Bonwit Teller, Stern's, Ohrbach's, Abraham & Straus, and Gimbels as the twentieth century drew to a close. A second wave, in the late 2010s, took down Barneys and Lord & Taylor. The family December outing now has four long-running destinations: Saks Fifth Avenue, Bloomingdale's, Bergdorf Goodman, and, of course, Macy's.

Deuterium

Every chemical element on the periodic table—that is, each of the 94 irreducible natural substances that make up the universe, plus about twenty-four that have been coaxed briefly into existence in laboratories—has variant forms. They're called isotopes, and they differ by the number of uncharged particles, called neutrons, in their atomic nuclei. Some isotopes are unstable and emit radiation as they decay into other materials; others last more or less indefinitely.

There were only a couple of known isotopes by the 1920s, barely two decades after the era of nuclear physics began. In 1929, Harold Urey, a chemist at Columbia University, remarked to a Berkeley chemist, who had been involved with the discovery of two oxygen isotopes, that the only more important discovery in the field would be a hydrogen isotope. He continued to think about that, and, in July 1931, published a paper in the *Physical Review* that suggested a method involving mass spectroscopy that would determine whether such a substance existed. A few months later, he had it cold, and he published his study in April 1932, naming the substance "deuterium" for its neutron-proton nucleus, double the weight of the more common hydrogen one. (It's informally called "heavy hydrogen.") Two years later, he received the Nobel Prize in chemistry.

Why does this matter? Broadly, Urey's research increased our knowledge of the structure of the atom, leading to many other discoveries (including tritium, a

as it played, which helped it stay on heavy rotation at Manhattan discos like the Loft and the Paradise Garage."
» **Jackie Stoudemire,** "Invisible Wind" (12-inch single, 1981): "Highly sought after. It still moves most who have the fortune to hear it. A whimsical disco-boogie crossover with angelic female vocals, dreamy strings, and a groovy break."
» **Liquid Liquid,** *Optimo* (12-inch EP, 1983): "As the disco fad was dimming, Liquid Liquid released this EP, which includes the famously sampled track 'Cavern.' An uncredited use sent the band's label, 99 Records, into a lengthy court battle that would bankrupt and dissolve them."

third hydrogen isotope, isolated at Cambridge University shortly thereafter). More specifically, deuterium is useful in medicine as a tracer that allows scans to follow reactions. But its future is more intriguing: One of the great hopes of humanity rests on the workability of fusion power, the alternative method of nuclear-energy generation that produces little to no radioactive waste. Unlike conventional fission reactors, which are fueled with rare and hard-to-handle enriched uranium, fusion reactors can run on hydrogen isotopes. Deuterium is relatively abundant in the oceans. It is possible to envision a green future in which it, fused with tritium, powers the planet.

Digital Ad Exchange

Today's expansive and complex online advertising ecosystem (with the big exception of Facebook) runs on ad exchanges, meaning that all of the web's ad inventory is basically stored in one bucket, and any advertiser, big or small, can bid on a spot on your browser's display. That innovation was the brainchild of a little New York company called Right Media, founded by a former employee of the early internet-advertising firm DoubleClick (and a onetime personal trainer) named Mike Walrath. Right Media's ad exchange was the business model that enabled the growth of the web, allowing any nascent website to sell an ad slot.

As the exchanges evolved, one less desirable consequence was the insatiable appetite for customers' personal data, which advertisers use to help decide how much to bid for any given set of eyeballs. "The buyer decides, in a computer process, 'I know who Mike Smith is. I got a cookie on his machine,'" said Michael Smith, then the senior vice-president of revenue, platforms, and operations at Hearst Magazines Digital Media. "I know he travels every other week. I have this Singapore Airlines ad. I think his attention is probably worth about two-tenths of a cent right now; that's what I'm going to

bid.' The exchange permits them to make that decision literally in the instant that the user is waiting for the page to load." A process that typically involves thousands of companies, including ad servers, data brokers, publishers, and advertisers, takes less than a tenth of a second.

This algorithmic system, the enormous heir to Right Media and DoubleClick, is called programmatic advertising, and it accounted for two-thirds of the global digital display advertising spend by 2019, according to the marketing agency Zenith. At the same time, the explosion in programmatic has triggered a backlash, as the unintended (or unheeded) consequences of a marketplace run by robots become clear. In 2017, YouTube faced a string of scandals as advertisers discovered their ads were running on violent and racist videos, and Procter & Gamble cut over $140 million in digital advertising due to concerns about fake impressions and "brand safety."

Major publishers are rediscovering the virtues of doing deals with a human touch, while Europe's General Data Protection Regulation, which heavily restricts user-data collection, is forcing the data-driven ad-tech industry to consolidate. Right Media did not survive. Yahoo bought it and in 2015 finally pulled the plug on the exchange. But the company's DNA lives on in the New York tech scene—and in the ad that appears next to virtually everything you read online, and in your general loss of privacy in the digital era.

Disco [1]

NOTE: *Rising from underground New York clubs like the Loft in the early 1970s, where the crowds were racially mixed and largely gay, disco music deployed heavy bass lines, repetitive synths, string sections, and spiky guitars to spread a particular brand of sophisticated hedonism across*

② **Grub Street's Favorite Pizza Slice in New York**

Joe's Pizza *(7 Carmine St.):* This workaday Greenwich Village shop is the consummate New York slice parlor, first and foremost for its uncanny, unparalleled consistency. This can be attributed to high turnover. Slices fly off the counter, and new pizzas are constantly being baked, guaranteeing freshness. That brings up another essential fact: **Joe's is always busy, but it's never a pain to get in and get out.** The ideal slice joint shouldn't be a major commitment. Cooked so it's a few shades shy of burned, the thin crust provides that slightly yeasty tang, bends easily, and has a pudgy, puffy, nicely browned end. The cheese blisters, with occasional golden freckles, and the sauce has the brightness of fresh tomatoes. **The sauce and cheese are laid out evenly and in just the right amount** so you're getting the ideal ratio with every bite. It is precisely what your younger self thought all New York slices were like.

America. But before the Latin-inflected partner dances of Saturday Night Fever (set in Bay Ridge, Brooklyn), before the midtown celebrity mecca Studio 54, and before the Village People's campiness hit the heartland, Gloria Gaynor was already on the verge of stardom. In 1974, her cover of the Jackson 5 song "Never Can Say Goodbye" from her debut album reached No. 1 on Billboard's *first-ever dance-disco chart, and her biggest hit, "I Will Survive," is an unbeatable dance-floor staple to this day. Here, she reflects on the scene during disco's early days.*

When I started doing "Never Can Say Goodbye," Barry White was really the only person doing disco music. That type of music wasn't really coming to the fore yet, but discothèques were happening. It was an economic problem: There was a recession, and people didn't want to go to regular clubs and spend the cover charge. Clubs that used to do cabaret shows were taking out their seating and putting in dance floors. Barry White and I decided we were going to supply places like that with music that was specifically for dancing.

Play Street was the first disco club I performed in. There was the Garage, and Xenon. There's another place I'm trying to remember—I loved it because from the dressing room on the second floor, you came down a set of winding stairs out of a cloud of smoke and right onto the stage.

My first time performing at Studio 54, I didn't know they had a catwalk. When I got onto the stage, it was really long and narrow. The only real space to move was on the catwalk. I absolutely loved it. I'm kind of a daredevil. I felt like the queen of disco that night. I did always love dancing. I remember when I was a kid, my mother used to say, "You can't wash the dishes, you can't scrub the floor, but you can dance." Later, I loved watching modern-dance performers, like Gregory Hines.

But more than anything else, disco was about the music itself. It was so upbeat, and it gave people much-needed relief from life itself—from the pressures and concerns of the day. It gave you an opportunity to shake it all off. I always tried to choose songs that were lyrically upbeat so that people walked away with a sense of freedom and release. That's why disco music, as I've often said, is the only type of music ever to bring together people from every nationality, creed, color, and age group.

Later, disco got a reputation for being not that serious. But I think people who heard the music didn't even realize what it was doing for them. I wish I could tell the people who tried to perpetuate that idea to relax and enjoy it. Why not just chill?

Discount Store

As affluent New Yorkers began buying homes in the suburbs after World War II, a recently returned Navy veteran named Eugene Ferkauf realized they were also furnishing those homes at a furious clip. In a walk-up on East 46th Street in 1948, he opened E. J. Korvette, selling discounted luggage, electronics, and appliances at extremely small margins that, in volume, turned out to be a great business. (There is a pervasive and entertaining and entirely incorrect legend that the store's name was a condensation of "Eight Jewish Korean-War Veterans," referring to the company's founding partners. In fact, as Ferkauf repeatedly explained, the *E* was for Eugene, the *J* was for his deputy Joe Swillenberg, and the last name was a reference to his Navy service aboard a type of ship known as a corvette.) The success of the first store quickly led Ferkauf to expand it to a small chain with five locations in Manhattan staffed with a bunch of his buddies from Brooklyn's Tilden High School.

In 1953, Ferkauf opened a much larger store in Carle Place, Long Island. It was the first of the retailers we now call big-box stores, with piles of consumer goods that beat every traditional competitor on price. In 1962, Korvette's was doing $400 million in annual business with profits well over 20 percent. By 1966, the company had more than 100 stores, and Ferkauf sold his share for $20 million. Korvette's remained a retail power-house into the 1970s, after which competition from the likes of Kmart plus some poor management decisions drove it out of business. Its DNA remains intact, how-ever, in at least one immense descendant: In 1960, the Arkansas retailer Sam Walton came to New York and took a good close look at the Korvette's operation, incor-porating what he saw into the management of his own nascent company, Wal-Mart.

Dollar Slice [2]

By a widespread metric, the price of a slice of thin-crust non-artisanal New York pizza roughly keeps pace with the single-ride subway fare (*see also* PIZZA). As of 2018, the latter was $2.75, and the former was about the same—at most places. In 2008, however, when the fare was two bucks, a slice joint called 2 Bros. Pizza opened on St. Marks Place offering a slice for $1. The response inspired the owners to make the price permanent, and very soon a competitor, 99¢ Fresh Pizza, arose.

There are now more than a dozen such places scat-tered throughout Manhattan. A lengthy price war between the 2 Bros. outpost on 38th Street and the neighboring Pizza King, in which prices briefly dipped to 75 cents, proved unsustainable. Price aside, the defining characteristics of dollar pizza are that it is okay but not great, the amenities at the restaurants (if you can call them that) are zilch, and for broke folks and drunk students, it's the best thing going.

Double Dutch [3]

Most histories of double Dutch—the dual-jump-rope style that requires extremely fast footwork and straddles the line between sport and dance—say the game indeed came from Holland, landing in New Amsterdam in the seventeenth century. Its popularity waxed and waned over the next 300 years, as jumping rope, first an activity primarily for boys, shifted to girls. By the early 1970s, double Dutch had nearly gone extinct, along with potsy (a.k.a. hopscotch), ring-a-levio (a hybrid of tag and hide-and-seek), and various other New York street games that faded away under the dual pressures of car traffic and television (*see also* SKULLY; STICKBALL).

That was when two New York cops, David Walker and Ulysses Williams, had the idea of reinvigorating double Dutch as a community-building youth-outreach gesture. They pulled in some funding through the efforts of radio personality Vy Higginsen, and on Val-entine's Day 1974, 600 mostly African-American middle-schoolers participated in the world's first double-Dutch tournament. Starting in 1978, a championship team known as the Fantastic Four out of Corlears Junior High School on the Lower East Side became (and remain) cultural ambassadors for the sport, drawing sponsor-ships and making TV and press appearances.

Today, a pair of leagues founded by Walker (the Amer-ican Double Dutch League and the National Double Dutch League) and an international group administer championships, some of which have been held on the Lincoln Center plaza and at the Apollo Theater. Although the sport's home base—and arguably its heart and soul—remains in New York, competitive teams have sprouted up all over the world, notably in France and Japan.

Doughnut

Deep-fried sweetened dough is ancient and cross-cultural, but the history of the doughnut itself has repeatedly circled through New York City. Washington Irving (*see also* KNICKERBOCKER) claimed that it arrived in America through New Amsterdam, when it was

Double Dutch in East Harlem, 1998.
PHOTOGRAPH BY
BRUCE DAVIDSON

known as the *olykoek*, or "oil cake." (The hole came later, reportedly introduced by a mother-and-son pair of cooks in New England.) As a mass-produced, widely available treat, its roots lie in Harlem with Adolph Levitt, a Russian immigrant who in 1920 came up with a machine that formed rings of dough and dropped them into hot fat. He ran it behind a window in his uptown bakery, and crowds gathered to watch it do its thing. By 1931, he'd opened another branch in Times Square. He soon expanded the business into a national chain called Mayflower Coffee Shops, selling not just doughnuts but diner food. It lasted until the 1970s, by which time its competitors, notably Dunkin' Donuts and Krispy Kreme, had blanketed the country with their little round carb bombs. In the twenty-first century, a small and delicious artisanal-doughnut movement took root in New York, led by the Lower East Side's Dough-nut Plant, which offered intense flavors such as matcha green tea and tres leches. Subsequently, the baker Dominique Ansel introduced a wildly successful addition to the genre, made of multilayered flaky dough via a proprietary secret method (*see also* CRONUT).

Dow Jones Industrial Average

Taking the measure of the stock market with one easy-to-grasp number was the brainstorm of Charles Dow and Edward Jones, who founded their namesake publishing company in 1882 and began to issue a report called the "Customers Afternoon Letter" (which later evolved into *The Wall Street Journal*). One year into its publication, Dow worked up a running tally of railroad and industrial stocks into a single figure, updated hourly, and called it the Dow Jones Railroad Index. Valuable as it was, it did not reflect the broader stock market, so he decided to do a similar gauge of solely industrial companies' stock prices. He first issued it on May 26, 1896, and it opened at 40.94. It incorporated the prices of twelve companies' shares, many of which—U.S. Rubber; National Lead; Tennessee Coal, Iron, and Railroad—reflected the priorities and products of their time.

How the index became shorthand for "the stock market's performance today" was surely driven by the primacy of Dow Jones and *The Wall Street Journal* in the financial-news business, especially during the stock boom of the 1920s. At its peak in September 1929, the

Dow stood at 381.17. By July 1932, in the deepest trough of the Depression, it was at about 41.

The average was computed hourly by hand into the 1960s, as paper tape with printed prices poured from the stock ticker. Dow Jones legend has it that Arthur "Pop" Harris, the man charged with its computation, constantly suffered from paper cuts. By then, the index had been expanded to 30 companies, and its makeup continues to adapt with the industrial landscape.

In 2012, Dow Jones sold off the business to a joint venture led by Standard & Poor's, which today administers many such indices. The Dow Jones Industrial Average, explains S&P chief commercial officer Jamie Farmer, is "a bit of an anomaly" among them today because its computation requires no elaborate computer modeling. It's a pretty simple weighted average, one that could in theory still be calculated with pencil and paper. (That simplicity is maintained in order to ensure consistency across more than a century of data.) What has changed is the economic composition of the lineup, making the term *industrial* a bit misleading. Today, for every flat-out manufacturer or resource extractor on the roster (Caterpillar, 3M, ExxonMobil), there's a company like Goldman Sachs or Disney that exists well outside traditional heavy industry. In 2018, the last of the Index's original twelve companies, General Electric, was removed and replaced with Walgreens.

Downtown

What *uptown* means depends on who you are. If you're Lin-Manuel Miranda, it means Washington Heights. If you were Duke Ellington, it meant Harlem. If you were movin' on up from Queens like George Jefferson, it meant East 85th Street, where the swells live. If you were a CBGB punk in 1977, it meant "anything above 14th Street, and the hell with all of it—I'm not going."

Downtown, though, is clear: the dense core of any city, where business is transacted by day and (in the past generation, though not much before that) culture and restaurants and bars come to the fore at night. It's "down" because Manhattan is a long, skinny island, with office towers and loft spaces at the bottom and brownstones and apartment buildings to the north. There's no "down" to downtown Detroit or Moscow or Tokyo, unless you want to argue that it's at a low elevation by the water's edge. But c'mon—it's downtown because you take the subway *down* to Canal Street or Wall Street or Fulton Street.

In the latter part of the twentieth century, *downtown* took on a secondary meaning: the parts of the city—Greenwich Village, Soho, Tribeca, the East Village, the Lower East Side—where creativity was allowed to flourish, where things were cooler. Broadway theater was played under a proscenium arch and perhaps had a spangly kickline; downtown theater was done on the cheap, in a little black box, and was weird and arty. Uptown restaurants had white tablecloths and prime cuts; downtown restaurants had unlisted numbers and menus full of offal or specialties from one particular region of China or molecular-gastronomy bizarreness. This uptown-downtown distinction has, today, begun to blur to the point of unrecognizableness, as the ostensibly artier districts downtown are today hardly younger and no less bourgeois or cheaper than uptown ones. Most of the genuine cool down there has been priced out and has resettled across the river. (*See also* "BROOKLYN.")

Drag Ball *see* VOGUING

Dry Cleaning

"Letters patent being granted under the Great Seal of the United States of America unto Thomas L. Jennings, Tailor, 64 Nassau Street, New York"—thus ran a line in the New York *Post* of March 27, 1821. This was most likely the first U.S. patent issued to an African-American (the first few years of the country's patent documentation is thin), and it was for a system of "Dry Scouring Clothes, and Woollen Fabrics in general, so that they keep their original shape, and have the polish and appearance of new." We'd call it "dry cleaning" today, and Jennings's advertisement says the technique "also removes stains from cloth." Jennings was a free man, but his wife, born in slavery, was an indentured

servant; he made enough money off his invention to buy her freedom. Their daughter Elizabeth Jennings Graham came to prominence as a very early civil-rights activist. In 1854, she was put off a streetcar by the conductor because of her race, and she sued and won, beginning the integration of the city's mass transit system and prefiguring the Montgomery bus boycott of a century later.

From
EASTER PARADE
to
"EYES ON THE STREET"

*Escape artist: Harry Houdini gets
out of a straitjacket, ca. 1910.*

① **How to Make the Perfect Hollandaise**

From Chef Jaime Young, Sunday in Brooklyn

"In my opinion, **the most important step is your setup. It should be mixed over a double boiler.** It's important to keep the water at a light simmer. If the water boils, it could scramble the yolks, which you do not want. Make sure to whisk the yolks constantly and cook them to about 160 degrees Fahrenheit. The butter should be clarified and warm. **Before emulsifying, it's important to add some liquid to help suspend the fat and create the emulsion.** I use a bit of hot sauce and lemon juice. When you begin to emulsify the butter into the egg-lemon mixture, steadily pour the butter at a slow pace, adding it in stages along with a few drops of water to help stabilize the emulsion. Once you've made the sauce, keep it in a warm place. If it gets too cold, it may separate."

Easter Parade

As early as the fourth century A.D., St. Gregory of Nyssa noted that Easter Sunday inspired people to come out in their best clothes. Since then, there have been annual religious parades, mostly in Europe, to convey the rebirth that comes with spring, and in the 1870s, those walks were codified into a spring fashion ritual in New York. On April 14, 1879, the *Times* was able to report that good weather the previous day had "tempted those who had provided themselves with Spring attire to indulge in the luxury of taking part in the annual display," adding that "Spring bonnets were worn by every lady promenader." It became very much a fashion-driven event, so much so that milliners and dressmakers would attend to take notes and make sketches in order to knock off the styles. A Harlem parade soon followed, as did, eventually, Irving Berlin's song "Easter Parade" (1933) and the musical of the same name (1948) starring Judy Garland and Fred Astaire. Today, the parade—held on Fifth Avenue in the 50s—has lost its link to contemporary fashion but remains a place for participants to show off their most outrageously ornate headwear.

Egg Cream

No egg! No cream! But perhaps you knew that. The quintessential New York soda-fountain drink has many paternity claims, but all of them trace back to the early-twentieth-century Jewish community on the Lower East Side. The firmest origin story comes from Louis Auster, who owned a couple of local candy stores—the original was at Stanton and Lewis Streets—and said he started mixing up seltzer, syrup, and milk around 1900. By the time of his death in 1955, Auster was said to be selling 3,000 egg creams a day.

The Harvard sociologist Daniel Bell, a Lower East Side native, disputed this entire narrative in *New York* in 1971. He insisted that his own uncle Hymie, proprietor of a candy store on Second Avenue, had invented the drink around 1920, and that in his early version it was indeed enriched with—wait for it—eggs and cream. Eventually a rival candy-store owner, also named Hymie, had adulterated the recipe and undercut the original Hymie's prices, driving him out of the egg-cream game. Maybe it's true.

Although you can order vanilla or (yuck) strawberry variants of the egg cream, the canonical version is chocolate-flavored and made with Fox's U-Bet syrup, which has been produced in Brooklyn since 1900. You put three ounces of milk in a tall glass, fill nearly to the top with cold seltzer, and stir with a long spoon. (It will fizz up.) Add a few squirts of U-Bet, and stir again.

The seltzer is correctly mixed in before the syrup rather than after, so the foamy head is white and bubbly rather than brown and sticky. (A lot of people get this wrong.) Refinements include extra-fizzy seltzer shot from a glass syphon bottle (*see also* SELTZER) and the seasonal kosher-for-Passover version of U-Bet made with cane sugar instead of corn syrup. True maniacs concoct their own chocolate syrup. Most important is that you drink it right away. An egg cream is delightful when fresh, flat and unpleasant fifteen minutes later.

Eggs Benedict [1]

Until 1967, it was believed that eggs Benedict—that exceedingly rich breakfast dish consisting of a poached egg, ham, hollandaise sauce, and an English muffin—was invented at either Delmonico's or the Waldorf Hotel. In the latter case, a man by the name of Lemuel Benedict was credited with first ordering the dish in hopes of curing a killer hangover. But then came 1967, when the New York *Times* received a letter from one Edward P. Montgomery, who bemoaned the current "concoction of an overpoached egg on a few shreds of

*Easter Parade on Fifth
Avenue, ca. 1940.*

PHOTOGRAPH BY RUTH SONDAK

ham" being served at most American restaurants. He claimed his mother had gotten the recipe used by the dish's true inventor, their family friend Commodore Elias Cornelius Benedict, a Wall Street banker. (A "real trick," Montgomery says, is to assemble all the components "when they are à point.") Whether Lemuel or Elias Cornelius first brought us this brunch staple may forever remain a mystery, but at the very least, this city drove one (or both) of these men to take breakfast to an entirely new level.

Electrical Grid

Thomas Edison's great invention that made modern life possible was not the incandescent lightbulb itself. Rather, it was the business and infrastructure that fed those lights: the network of power plants, overhead wires, and construction and maintenance and billing people that all supported the use of electricity. The first functional bulb came out of Edison's lab in 1879; the next year, the Edison Electric Illuminating Company was incorporated and given a franchise to light up New York. (Two other companies, Brush Electric Illuminating and United States Illuminating, made separate deals with the city to handle streetlights.) On September 4, 1882, direct current flowed from the dynamos in Edison's new plant, the world's first, at 257 Pearl Street. It served 82 customers with about 400 lights. Many other small companies quickly followed. In the late nineteenth century, most of these were bought and, after a dizzying series of mergers and deals, formed a couple of large syndicates. Eventually, the Consolidated Gas Company—which had been a major source of New Yorkers' illumination and energy when gaslight ruled—entered the electricity business by gaining control of those syndicates, and in 1936 it changed its name to Consolidated Edison.

Electroclash[2]

Between 2001 and 2003, electroclash, a short-lived but influential music movement that combined elements of techno and punk into retro, danceable beats, dominated New York club life. Centered in Williamsburg, where the artistic and bohemian scenes had moved as Manhattan became too expensive and noise averse, the

(2) **The Essential Electroclash Playlist**

Chosen by Fischerspooner's Casey Spooner and Warren Fischer

- ▸ **Space Invaders Are Smoking Grass,** by I-F
- ▸ **Frank Sinatra,** by Miss Kittin & the Hacker
- ▸ **Come to Me,** by DMX Krew
- ▸ **Emerge,** by Fischerspooner
- ▸ **Disco Rout,** by Legowelt
- ▸ **Fuck the Pain Away,** by Peaches

- ▸ **Nite Life,** by Adult.
- ▸ **La Rock 01,** by Vitalic
- ▸ **Father,** by Anthony Rother
- ▸ **Tribulations,** by LCD Soundsystem
- ▸ **Euro Trash Girl,** by Chicks on Speed
- ▸ **NY Excuse,** by Soulwax

scene had a vaudevillian, performance-art quality that put a high value on inventive, charismatic personas, humor, theatrical showmanship, and DIY style. (The 1982 cult film *Liquid Sky* was a common underlying reference.) It was perhaps the first electronic-music movement that was welcoming to women, and the scene was marked by an openly gay sensibility. Although it has European roots, electroclash was incubated in and indelibly identified with New York.

In 1997, a Dutch producer named I-F released "Space Invaders Are Smoking Grass," a track that hyper-fetishized '80s New Wave music and made those retro beats feel new. It was followed the next year by the French group Miss Kittin & the Hacker's two anthems, "1982" and "Frank Sinatra." And by 2000, two prominent acts had emerged in New York that drew on these influences. One was Peaches, whose album *The Teaches of Peaches* was full of a filthy-mouthed, unapologetic sexualized feminism (its most famous track is titled "Fuck the Pain Away"). The other was a fluid group known as Fischerspooner, created by Casey Spooner and Warren Fischer, which at times could include as many as twenty members performing at Warholian rock-opera events mixing comedy, shock, meta-critique, sex appeal, and showbiz razzle-dazzle. They played galleries instead of music venues and quickly became darlings of the contemporary-art world, supported by gallerists Gavin Brown and Jeffrey Deitch and then–MoMA PS1 curator Klaus Biesenbach.

The producer and DJ Larry Tee, already well known for co-writing RuPaul's unlikely 1993 hit "Supermodel (You Better Work)," popularized the movement's portmanteau name. After seeing Peaches and Fischerspooner, he later said, he thought of *electro*, an '80s term. But this new electro embodied many different elements, from the funk of the Detroit Grand Pubahs, to the politics of Chicks on Speed, to the sexuality of Peaches. "To me it felt like a clash of ideas and sounds."

In 2001, he put together the first electroclash music festival, bringing together all the new acts in one place, then started a record label, Mogul Electro. His own band, W.I.T. (short for "Whatever It Takes"), was fronted by a bombshell downtown "It" girl, Melissa Burns. Other prominent acts included A.R.E. Weapons, Felix Da Housecat, Avenue D, and ADULT.

Within a year, the scene had a clubhouse, LUXX, a dive bar on Grand Street in Williamsburg that could fit 200 people and was frequented by international celebrities and fashion stars. Among other groups that broke out there, Scissor Sisters, a band led by Jake Shears that went on to become one of the top-grossing electroclash acts, earned a Grammy nomination for its disco cover of Pink Floyd's "Comfortably Numb." The band's self-titled debut album was the best-selling album of 2004 in the U.K.

By then, tastes back in Brooklyn had begun to shift toward emerging neo-punk bands like the Strokes. Still, Peaches and Felix da Housecat keep performing, Jake Shears starred in *Kinky Boots* on Broadway in 2018, and Casey Spooner has become an Instagram star. Much of the style, sound, and sassy posturing of the electroclash scene lingers in the mainstream, adopted by the likes of Lady Gaga.

Elevator

Contemporary life in New York City depends on a few crucial bits of infrastructure, like cheap electrical power, the rail system, the Catskills aqueducts, and—less flashy but absolutely necessary—the elevator. Without it, you can't raise buildings over six or seven stories, and Manhattan as we know it would not exist.

Setting aside its progenitors like rope-and-pulley haylofts, the first elevator shaft in New York can be dated to 1853, and, oddly enough, it substantially predates the invention of the device itself. When the iron-and-railroads magnate Peter Cooper endowed and planned the main academic building of Cooper Union, he foresaw that a mechanized lift lay in the near future. Even though no such machinery was available, his architect left a round shaft open between the floors of his new structure. Some years after the building was completed in 1859, his son, Edward Cooper, put together a steam-engine lift and added an elevator cab.

By that time, the breakthrough had been made. In 1852, Elisha Graves Otis, an inventor in Yonkers, had figured out a safety catch that would prevent an elevator cab from falling should its cables snap. In 1854, at New York's Crystal Palace exhibition, he showed it off dramatically by standing on a demonstrator hoist and

Elisha Graves Otis demonstrates his first elevator at the Crystal Palace, 1853.

ordering the rope supporting it to be cut. After building several installations meant for freight, Otis added a passenger elevator to the E. V. Haughwout department store at the corner of Broadway and Broome Street in 1857, and the race to make ever taller buildings began to escalate.

Those safety catches are nearly fail-safe, but on one terrifying occasion, they did indeed fail. On July 28, 1945, a B-25 bomber crashed into the seventy-ninth floor of the Empire State Building, setting it afire and killing fourteen people. The impact severed the cables of one elevator, which free-fell nearly eighty floors into the subbasement. Two women onboard were badly injured but survived: The buildup of air pressure beneath the elevator cab slowed its fall just enough to save them, and the quarter-mile or so of thick steel cable beneath it bunched up, unexpectedly creating a sort of springy cushion. The operator, Betty Lou Oliver, returned to the building and rode the elevator five months later.

El Morocco *see* CAFÉ SOCIETY; NIGHTCLUB

Empire State Building *see* SKYLINE

Escalator

The town of Saugus, Massachusetts, can claim the *idea* of the escalator, owing to a moving-stairway design by a resident named Nathan Ames in 1852, but he never actually built one. New York City gets the nod because of the work of Jesse W. Reno, whose "inclined elevator" idea was patented in 1892, then built and installed at Coney Island's Old Iron Pier four years later. Passengers stepped onto T-shaped cleats, in a kind of standing version of a chairlift arrangement, and rode all of seven feet.

Subsequent refinements by Reno and inventors working with the Otis Elevator Company added stair treads and moving handrails. In fact, an Otis employee named Charles Seeberger coined the word *Escalator* (capitalized and trademarked at first). The oldest escalators still running in New York, and among the world's last with wooden treads, are rumbling along on the upper floors of Macy's 34th Street store, where they were installed between 1920 and 1930. Some of the longest in town are in the subways, including one that carries passengers 172 feet down to (or up from) the 34th Street–Hudson Yards subway station, opened in 2015.

Escape Artist

This is possibly a unique selection, in that the inventor of the job was its definitive (and perhaps only) practitioner. Harry Houdini, born Erik Weisz in Hungary, moved to Milwaukee at the age of eight, came to New York young, and established a career on the vaudeville circuit, performing in partner acts first with his brother Theo and later with his wife, Bess. In the early 1900s, he was likely the biggest star in the world, a celebrity before radio, eclipsed only by rising names of the cinema like Charlie Chaplin and Buster Keaton. The word *tricks* was barely enough to describe what he did; whereas magicians performed card and coin and cigarette magic (which he could also do quite well), Houdini went for big-and-bigger-scale acts that at least seemed, and in some cases were, life-threatening. Getting out of handcuffs while underwater, sometimes suspended by his feet; allowing himself to be sealed in local bank vaults or jail cells while on tour in Middle America; twisting himself out of tight straitjackets; even being sealed in a coffin and lowered into a pool—it all contributed to a unique act that was athletically demanding and purely American in its death-defying nature. He would on occasion stay behind a curtain for ten minutes, twenty minutes, half an hour, ratcheting up the tension in the theater as the audience began to assume that he had been injured or worse. Audience members were known to cry out for his release. Then he would burst forth, to cheers and relief.

Houdini got rich doing it, making more than almost any other entertainer of his time, and ran his business out of a brownstone at 278 West 113th Street that was packed with paperwork, touring equipment, and books about all kinds of tricks, flimflams, and magical arts. His expertise turned him into a great debunker, and he relished unmasking scam-artist psychics and spiritualists. He toured up to the end of his life: While on the road in October 1926, his appendix burst (legend has it that a fan had unexpectedly socked him in the stomach, a trick he normally prepared for by tensing his abs), and he died on Halloween. His body was shipped back to New York in the glass-topped coffin he'd used for one of his escapes. He's interred at Machpelah Cemetery in Glendale, Queens. Since then, Houdini's admirers have conducted annual séances on Halloween, hoping to hear from him. So far, they haven't.

His magnetism reportedly lay in live performance. There are films of Houdini at work, but they just don't quite convey it. Periodically, one of today's magicians—David Copperfield, say—reenacts one of the great Houdini escapes, say, from the Water Torture Cell, on television, but with the mediation of the TV camera and the unwillingness of today's audience to wait half an hour for the tension to build, a lot of its power is gone. The original escape artist remains alive as a personal brand, his name instantly recognizable, instantly identified with escape.

Ex-Lax

The man who used a spoonful of chocolate to make the laxative go down was named Kiss. A year or so after he graduated from Columbia University's pharmacy program in 1904, Max Kiss fell into a shipboard conversation with a doctor who mentioned Bayer's new drug phenolphthalein, which relieved constipation. He spent the next year working up a formulation; mindful of children who resisted swallowing their repulsive spoonfuls of castor oil, he embedded the phenolphthalein in chocolate and introduced his product in 1906. The company he founded, Ex-Lax, was slyly named, and not solely because the words imply "excellent laxative." It's a play on a Latinate phrase Kiss picked up in Hungary that describes political deadlock: *ex-lex* is a condition under which the constitution is temporarily suspended and parliament is dissolved, during which everything stalls and no legislation can, uh, move.

By the mid-1920s, Kiss had opened a big Ex-Lax factory at 423 Atlantic Avenue in Brooklyn, and he remained chairman of the company until his death in 1967. Today, the brand is owned by the giant pharmaceutical company Novartis, the product no longer contains phenolphthalein (turns out that it's carcinogenic), and the building, like so many industrial sites, has been converted to condominiums. It's surely the only luxury apartment building with a wall of laxative memorabilia displayed in the lobby.

"Eyes on the Street"

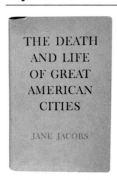

THE DEATH AND LIFE OF GREAT AMERICAN CITIES

JANE JACOBS

The first words of Jane Jacobs's *The Death and Life of Great American Cities*, published in 1961 by Random House, are "This book is an attack." She wasn't kidding. In paragraphs of sturdy carpenter's prose, Jacobs sawed up and dismantled virtually every prevailing thought in the world of urban planning. The era's dominant idea called for "slum clearance," the demolition of swaths of neighborhoods in favor of modern housing projects; Jacobs argued for keeping as much of the old as possible, intermingling it with the new. Those new towers were typically set back from the sidewalk, surrounded by lawns; Jacobs argued for the vitality of sidewalk frontage. Planners referred to "wasteful streets" and tried to eliminate them, forming superblocks; Jacobs argued for smaller blocks and more streets instead.

Most of all, she said, what made cities work was their untidy mix of functions. Planners of the day preferred to segregate retail from residences and offices, and Jacobs argued that doing so was a colossal mistake, one that was contributing to the rising crime rates in American cities. A street that was all offices would be dead by night, thus putting people at risk of being robbed. A street that housed only office workers would be silent by day, as in the suburbs, and not very interesting. In the ideal urban neighborhood—Jacobs cited the West Village, where she lived, as well as the North End in Boston and a number of others—parents with small children were out and about early, shopkeepers were active by day, office workers came home in the early evening, restaurants and bars stayed open into the night, and all of them, almost inadvertently, kept watch over the block. They were, in her pithy phrase, "eyes on the street"—the neighborhood's "natural proprietors," people who had a stake in its preservation and cared about it and who functioned as auxiliary security guards, maintaining order by their mere existence. This kind of social fabric, Jacobs argued, was almost impossible to build from scratch, which was why tearing down blocks of 80-year-old buildings and putting up slabs to replace them often created more despair and crime than before.

Jacobs's book was indeed received as the attack she said it was, particularly because she and a few other Greenwich Villagers went up against Robert Moses, New York's all-powerful planning czar, when he proposed a broad elevated highway (*see also* HIGHWAY, ELEVATED) across lower Manhattan, with a sunken access road cutting directly through Washington Square Park. Moses was aggrieved to have been challenged by, as he put it, "a bunch of *mothers*"; he grew even more so when they won, stalling his plans and preserving the area that later became known as Soho (*see also* LOFT LIVING).

A generation later, the Jacobean approach had come to be—and remains—a principal way of thinking about urban design. Yet it is often honored in a piecemeal, poorly understood way. Old low-rise neighborhoods are preserved and rehabbed (*see also* LANDMARKS LAW), but in the process they become expensive (*see also* GENTRIFICATION), which in turn means local hardware stores and bookstores and laundromats and other necessary businesses give way to boutiques that are not particularly useful except to visitors. Property developers put up towers that honor the street line, with storefronts along the sidewalk as they should be, but in doing so they give the whole block to one supersize retailer and sweep away the older, smaller frontage that might house a mixed set of businesses. When that happens, there are fewer eyes on the street—at least organically. Nowadays, building owners try to make up the difference with security desks and video cameras.

From
FAÇADE LAW
to
"FUHGEDDABOUDIT"

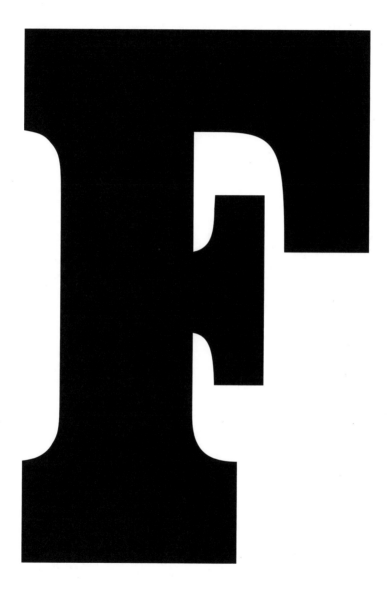

*Fandom: New York Comic Con attendee
Mei Velasco dressed as the Joker, October 2019.*
PHOTOGRAPH BY NATHAN BAJAR

① **How to Navigate New York Comic Con**

From Dimitrios Fragiskatos of Anyone Comics

»» Check the whole schedule ahead of time and make a plan. "If you're a fan of someone who draws a line, they might be at their booth most of the time, they could be signing at a lower-profile publisher or bookstore's table at another point in the day. This could mean a shorter line and more time to spend with them."

»» Carry as little as possible. "Going through security will be a pain, and wading through the crowds will be a pain. Minimize your discomfort by having less to look through and less for people to bump into. I'm not saying don't bring books to get signed or dress up, but don't bring your entire box for Frank Miller to sign—and cosplayers, don't bring weapons!"

»» Every day has its benefits. "To me, Thursday is the best day. Every exhibitor is fresh and enthusiastic, no one has to cancel the rest of their appearances because they're sick, and there are fewer attendees around. But Sunday is the best day to get good deals. If the item you want

Façade Law

Grace Gold was her name, and she was 17 years old, a first-year student at Barnard College. On the evening of May 16, 1979, as she walked past 601 West 115th Street, a chunk of masonry broke off a seventh-floor lintel and hit her in the head. She died five minutes later.

The building had been flaking apart for some time, and it was not the only one. The combination of age and poor maintenance in a city gone broke meant that many old structures had crumbling concrete and rusting cast iron. Within a year, the City Council passed (and Mayor Ed Koch signed) Local Law 10, requiring that all New York buildings over six stories high have their façades inspected every five years. Now revised and called Local Law 11, the statute has become even more important as age creeps up on the city's postwar apartment buildings, many of which have sheer brick curtain walls that can become unstable over time. Although the law is not ideal from an architectural-preservation standpoint— landlords have been known to jackhammer carved details off their buildings rather than repair them— Chicago, Philadelphia, and many other cities have followed with similar ordinances.

Fandom[1]

It all began, as so many stories beloved by geeks do, with an improbable name: Hugo Gernsback. Born Hugo Gernsbacher in Luxembourg in 1884 and emigrating to Manhattan in 1904, he, like so many pioneers of nerd culture, was a Jew who adopted a new moniker in order to fit in with the Gentiles. Gernsback was eminently a man of the Roaring Twenties, a self-made (and self-remade) man, always ready to invest in a new scheme, tuned in to the flash of consumer capitalism, and— perhaps most important—obsessed with technology and the march of progress. He sold mail-order electrical equipment, started one of the country's first commercial radio stations, and wrote about the concept of television before the invention even existed. But his greatest achievements came in his role as publisher of an array of forward-thinking magazines about tech and the future. It was the latter endeavor that gave birth to the concept of fandom.

One of Gernsback's publications was *Amazing Stories*, launched in 1926. It's generally regarded as the first magazine dedicated to science fiction—or, as he initially called it, *scientifiction*, a term that never quite caught on. Inside, readers found reprints of stories by pioneers like Jules Verne and H. G. Wells alongside the earliest works of future legends like Ursula K. Le Guin and Isaac Asimov. Youngsters ate the stuff up and, equally valuable, began to form a community around it. Gernsback would print letter-writers' addresses along with their names, so interested parties could write to one another and circulate their own stories. He was their interlocutor and idol, and when he lost control of that magazine in 1929, they flocked to his new one, *Science Wonder Stories*. Eventually, these enthusiasts coined a term for their little community: *fandom*.

Not only did they invent the terminology, they invented the praxis. On December 11, 1929, a tiny coterie of fandom members met up in a Harlem apartment to talk about the present and future of their favorite genre and the wider world of cutting-edge science. They called themselves the Scienceers, and they were the first geek fan club. Some of them started to put out a magazine called *The Time Traveller* in 1932, filled with adolescent spaceflight dreams. The first thing resembling a fan convention was held in Philadelphia in 1936, but it attracted only a handful of attendees. The first proper "con" was the World Science Fiction Convention, organized in 1939 in conjunction with the World's Fair in Flushing Meadows, albeit held in midtown (at 110 East 59th Street, to be exact). About 200 people showed up.

survives until Sunday, ask the exhibitor if they can come down on the price. It'll be worth it for them to bring one less item back with them. Friday is great if you want to attend a ton of panels. Saturday is great if you're basic."

» **Eat elsewhere.** "The convention food is overpriced. Step outside to get a cheaper meal. (Not at the McDonald's; it's crowded as all hell.) You'll see cosplayers and creators doing the same, so it won't feel like you left at all."

» **Be part of the comics ecosystem!** "You want to learn to make comics? Go to the how-to panel. If one of the artists has a style you dig, go to their table. Buy a commission; watch them draw the Ant-Man you asked for. They'll tell you about the book they drew. Go to the comic-store tables and get that book. Take a picture with cool costumes along the way. Go visit Paul Rudd and get that drawing of Ant-Man signed. Actors love the comics their movies inspired—trust me!"

All that would be enough to confirm New York's hold on the title of fandom's birthplace, but one more event makes it indisputable: In 1964, the first declared comic-book convention was held in Greenwich Village. (*Game of Thrones* author George R. R. Martin claims he was the first to sign up to attend.) These days, San Diego Comic-Con is the most prominent of the fan conventions, and the World Science Fiction Convention (now known as Worldcon) moves from city to city every year. But New York's influence is set in stone: The comics awards in San Diego are named after a Brooklyn boy, cartoonist Will Eisner, and Worldcon's awards for excellence in sci-fi are called the Hugos.

Fashion *see* SEVENTH AVENUE

Federalism

As a mode of government featuring both centralized and regional layers of authority, federalism aims to strike a rough parity between the two. Although the general idea has been with us since the time of Hellenistic Greece, the modern conception of federalism originated in the eighteenth-century equivalent of a New York City tabloid feud.

In 1787, the American republic was still operating under the Articles of Confederation, a "league of friendship" between largely independent sovereign states that gave the central government little power. From the perspective of New York's Alexander Hamilton and his aristocratic allies, this arrangement had a lot of flaws. For example, when the merchant class tried to shift the burdens of repaying the Revolutionary War debt onto subsistence farmers (forcing many to sell their land to aristocrats at bargain-basement prices) and those farmers responded by violently rebelling, there were no federal troops to force them into submission. What's more, some of the 13 states had enacted constitutions that awarded power to non-rich white men. (They did not go so far as to empower women or people of color.) Thus, Hamilton and his fellow Founding Fathers pushed for the enactment of a new, federalist constitution for the U.S. republic that would allow for a strong central national government. These "federalists" insisted it was possible to combine the best features of regional autonomy (e.g., the protection of quaint local customs such as enslaving human beings) with those of national rule (e.g., being able to violently suppress unruly peasants).

Not everyone agreed. After the Constitution was drafted and sent to the states for ratification, an anti-Federalist writing under the pseudonym Cato started bashing the proposal in the New York City press. Hamilton responded by teaming with John Jay and James Madison to write a series of pro-Constitution articles under their own Roman pseudonym, Publius, and addressed their arguments directly to the people of New York. These "Federalist Papers" detailed the virtues of keeping a strong national government in tension with state and local authorities. Ultimately, Hamilton won his highfalutin flame war, and the U.S. Constitution was ratified. Over the ensuing centuries, it would become a model for democratic constitutions the world over, thereby exporting the "made in NYC" model of federalism to nations as disparate as Australia, Yugoslavia, and Venezuela.

Federal Reserve System

The most powerful financial institution on earth isn't in midtown (JPMorgan Chase), and it's not between One World Trade Center and the Hudson River (Goldman Sachs). It's housed in a neo-Florentine limestone-and-sandstone palazzo between Nassau Street, Maiden Lane, Liberty Street, and William

② The Essential New York Reading List

Chosen by New York *literary critic Molly Young*

➻ **The House of Mirth,**
   by Edith Wharton (1905)
➻ **Time and Again,**
   by Jack Finney (1970)
➻ **Passing,**
   by Nella Larsen (1929)
➻ **Five Flights Up,**
   by Toni Schlesinger (2006)
➻ **Story of My Life,**
   by Jay McInerney (1988)

➻ **Lush Life,**
   by Richard Price (2008)
➻ **Underworld,**
   by Don DeLillo (1997)
➻ **Invisible Man,**
   by Ralph Ellison (1952)
➻ **Money,**
   by Martin Amis (1984)
➻ **Rosemary's Baby,**
   by Ira Levin (1967)

Street. (It's also the fulcrum of *Die Hard With a Vengeance.*) The Federal Reserve Bank of New York is first among equals in the twelve branches of the federal central-banking system and, in the Fed's early years, was essentially its power base, largely setting the monetary policy for the country.

The U.S. was late to monetary governance—two abortive attempts were made in 1791 and 1816 with the Philadelphia-based First and Second Bank of the United States. And between the Civil War and World War I, American finance was mainly in a state of anarchy, with thousands of banks cobbled together into a ramshackle network with no overarching entity like the German Reichsbank or the Bank of England. Booms, panics, and collapses happened nearly every decade as this free market swooped and dived.

That started to change when a group of bankers, economists, and politicians pushed for reform, and New York financiers like Paul Warburg of Kuhn, Loeb & Co. and JPMorgan partner Henry Davison took a leading role. After years of political wrangling, the Federal Reserve that emerged in 1914 was dominated by Benjamin Strong, who left his position as the president of Bankers Trust to become the New York Fed's first president. The early Fed held the reserves of its member banks, issued Federal Reserve notes (i.e., money), and even lent to banks.

By the 1920s, Fed banks realized that by buying and selling U.S. government debt, they could move interest rates up and down, foreshadowing the Fed's current "open market operations," its signature task (one carried out in New York). The forerunner of today's Federal Open Market Committee (on which the New York Fed president always has a seat) was chaired by Strong. The Fed was designed with its power divided among a board of governors in Washington and in the regional branches dispersed from Boston to San Francisco. But thanks to Strong's geographical and social proximity to the titans of American finance, his connections to financiers in Europe, and his knowledge of central banking, he quickly came to dominate the institution.

While Federal Reserve power eventually settled in Washington, the New York Fed is still where the action is—at least compared with its branches in Chicago, Cleveland, or Kansas City. Presidents of the New York Fed have gone on to become Fed chair (Paul Volcker) and Treasury secretary (Tim Geithner). And in our age of bailouts and international crises, the New York Fed's oversight of and financial connections with its local financial industry—which happen to include, well, Wall Street—gives it unique power and influence. When the Fed does business with Wall Street, it does it in New York.

The buying and selling of bonds that determine the federal funds rate happens through the New York Fed, as do the more exotic bailout, rescue, and economic-support plans. It's no coincidence that the LLCs set up to facilitate JPMorgan Chase's emergency purchase of Bear Stearns and the bailout of AIG were named after Maiden Lane. And although precious metals no longer have the central place they once did in the global financial system, the New York Fed looks like a fortress for a reason: Its vault, built on bedrock some eighty feet below street level, holds 12 million pounds of gold bars.

Felt-Tip Pen *see* MAGIC MARKER

Feud, Literary [2]

Edgar Allan Poe was a drunk, an ephebophile, a hoaxer, and an itinerant literary vagrant, and he invented the art of literary shit talk as we know it in America. Born in Boston and raised and educated in Virginia, he devised the detective story while living in Philadelphia in 1841 and, soon after, moved to New York City, where his polemical, personal tract "The Literati of New York

City" was serialized over six issues of *Godey's Lady's Book* in the summer and fall of 1846. Poe named names, described faces, called out frauds, and spared no one whose tastes he deemed too "Flemish" or style too "bizarre." With a fondness for the deprecating double negative, Poe isn't entirely ungenerous in his appraisals. His mission was to expose the gulf "between the popular 'opinion' of the merits of contemporary authors and that held and expressed of them in private literary society." He delivered the raw truth about his peers: "The most 'popular,' the most 'successful' writers among us (for a brief period, at least) are, ninety-nine times out of a hundred, persons of mere address, perseverance, effrontery—in a word, busy-bodies, toadies, quacks." One of those quacks was Henry Wadsworth Longfellow, but he was spared the full treatment because he lived in Cambridge, Massachusetts, where, due to his position at Harvard, he had "a whole legion of active quacks at his control." The controversy over Poe's breaking ranks lasted months.

It also started a tradition of calling out literary quackery. In 1935, Mary McCarthy and Margaret Marshall took aim at the reviewers of their day in a five-part series for *The Nation* called "Our Critics, Right or Wrong." It effectively put McCarthy, then 23, on the map, and she would remain one of the country's most cutting critics for more than five decades. In 1959, Elizabeth Hardwick wrote an essay for *Harper's* called "The Decline of Book Reviewing," which became the blueprint for *The New York Review of Books*. That same year, Norman Mailer took aim at his fellow novelists in his collection *Advertisements for Myself.* The essay "Evaluations: Quick and Expensive Comments on the Talent in the Room" rated J. D. Salinger as "no more than the greatest mind ever to stay in prep school" and James Baldwin as "too charming a writer to be major."

For a brief decade or two, writers were a staple of television chat shows, not as pundits but as personalities,

and often those personalities clashed on air. On the *Dick Cavett Show*, Mailer called Gore Vidal "a liar and a hypocrite" for comparing him to Charles Manson. "It hurts my sense of intellectual pollution," Mailer said. "As an expert, you should know about that," Vidal replied. (Although they were epic feuders, neither participant was exclusive: Vidal carried on a long-simmering battle with Truman Capote, and Mailer fought it out with Tom Wolfe, Michiko Kakutani, and virtually everyone else in New York.) In 1979, Cavett asked McCarthy which writers she thought were overrated, and she turned the subject to Lillian Hellman. "I said once in an interview that every word she writes is a lie, including *and* and *the*," McCarthy said. Hellman sued her for more than $2 million, a libel case that ended only with Hellman's death in 1984. (The feud was later portrayed in a play by Brian Richard Mori, in which Cavett starred as himself.) Social media, of course, is the ultimate in feud-enabling technology. If a day goes by without a literary dustup, it's only because some outside entity has writers united in their disgust.

Fifth Avenue

see COOPERATIVE APARTMENT BUILDING; PENTHOUSE; ROBBER BARON; SOCIALITE; TRUMPISM

Flagel

Back in the '90s, the Atkins diet craze hit gluten with the force of a high-glycemic food coma, and a certain dense breakfast staple (*see also* BAGEL) became Exhibit A. So New York's enterprising bagel purveyors improvised: Unlike other enemies of a low-carb diet, like doughnuts and pasta, bagels could be made healthier without affecting their most important part—the outer crust—by either scooping out the innards or flattening a smaller amount of dough out to the regular diameter.

Purists ridiculed scooping as "utterly sacrilegious," but flattening proved a more artful solution. Former *Village Voice* food critic Robert Sietsema has argued that Tasty Bagel, a legendary outpost in Bensonhurst, Brooklyn, boiled the inaugural flagel in the mid-'90s. But Tasty's owner, Joe Geraldi, downplays its role, saying customers simply kept special-requesting "just a flat bagel." Meanwhile, Bagel Boss—a chain founded in 1975 by Mel Rosner, who styled himself a "bagel innovator, not an imitator" and purportedly invented the chocolate-chip variation—claims it has been serving a flagel since 1999. In 2010, the company officially trademarked the name.

In reality, bagels had been deflating for decades, their bakers inspired by old-world flatbreads, among them the Middle Eastern *laffa*, Turkish *simit*, Lebanese *ka'ak*, and especially the elongated Jerusalem bagel. Rosner got his start making bialys, the flat oniony rolls that many non–New Yorkers might mistake for flagels, although their crust is quite different.

Flat breadstuffs ultimately popped up all over town— at Russ & Daughters, Pick A Bagel, David's Bagels, Zaro's, H&H Midtown—lending them staying power after all the fad dieters got back to carbs. Thinner than a hero roll, and therefore more merciful on an eater's jaw, flagels grew popular during the rise of the all-day bagel sandwich in the early aughts. As with the bagel it modernized, the flagel has undergone changes, such as when the bagel-sandwich craze itself got caught in the industry-wide "supersizing" wave and lots of flagels followed suit. Today, many are the same weight as traditional bagels, only flatter.

Flashmob

The origins of the flashmob—a brief gathering of hundreds of people at a random site, arranged purely as a befuddling prank—can be dated with precision. On May 27, 2003, the writer Bill Wasik ("bored and therefore disposed towards acts of social-scientific inquiry," he wrote some years later) created and then forwarded an email to about sixty people, telling them to convene upon a Claire's accessories store near Astor Place the following Tuesday at 7:24 p.m. and disperse at 7:31. The point was not to do anything in particular; the point was to show up for the sake of showing up, creating a harmless sight gag or physical punch line.

That first one didn't go as planned, because the cops heard about it in advance and dispersed the flashmobbers. But another, two weeks later, indeed came together (two hundred people in the Macy's rug department for no evident reason), and a lightly anarchic, if somewhat pointy-headed, fad was born. That July, an organizer in Boston called for hundreds of people to enter a department store, each one claiming to need a greeting card to send to "my friend Bill in New York." More events in other cities followed. The ones Wasik himself arranged ran ten minutes or less, all the better to leave barely a trace as the (always benign) mob dissipated.

In the outsize amount of media coverage surrounding these events, Wasik cited as a forebear Stanley Milgram, the social psychologist known for his experiments in obedience that had asked people to administer electric shocks to others, as well as Allen Funt's reality-TV progenitor *Candid Camera*. Certain styles of performance art, notably the 1960s "happenings," were similarly part of the trend's DNA. Yet the flashmob was uniquely attuned to its time and place, particularly to the aughts' hipster ethos of ironic detachment, wherein fine distinctions among small things mattered, yet large issues could be dispatched with a "yeah, whatever." The flashmob participant took the event seriously enough to show up, while taking very little else, including the flashmob itself, very seriously at all. And like everything hipster-adjacent, it drew the attention of the corporate world. By 2005, the flashmob had been co-opted by the Ford Motor Company, which began arranging "flash

(3) The Essential Greenwich Village Folkie Playlist

Chosen by Hap Pardo, director of musical operations at Cafe Wha?

» **Tell Old Bill,** by Dave Van Ronk: "The mayor of Macdougal Street!"

» **House of the Rising Sun** (traditional): "Chas Chandler of the Animals popularized this song, but everyone was playing it back in the day in this neighborhood."

» **See That My Grave Is Kept Clean:** "Originally by Blind Lemon Jefferson, recorded by Bob Dylan, Dave Van Ronk, and many others in the '60s."

» **If I Had a Hammer:** "By Pete Seeger; made popular by Peter, Paul and Mary."

» **John Henry** (traditional): "This was recorded by a ton of people, including Woody Guthrie and Dylan."

» **Little Bit of Rain,** by Fred Neil and Karen Dalton: "Dylan used to back them up at Wha."

» **Motherless Child,** by Richie Havens: "He owned Cafe Wha? for a few years in the late '60s and early '70s."

---

concerts" to market its automobiles. Barely a year after Wasik's first experiment, *flash mob* popped up in the *Concise Oxford English Dictionary*.

FM

The electrical engineer Edwin Armstrong is hardly a household name, but this native New Yorker changed the soundscape of America (*see also* RADIO BROADCASTING) not once but three times over. In 1912, he developed what's known as the regenerative circuit, which (broadly speaking) allowed a radio to receive weak signals without a lot of extra electronics. He followed that up in 1918 with the superheterodyne circuit, which eliminated a lot of the squeals and chirps that plagued early radio tuners, thus accelerating radio's shift from a hobbyist attic medium to a mainstream living-room fixture. And in 1933, from his lab at Columbia University, came his biggest breakthrough of all: frequency modulation, an entirely new way of encoding information into a broadcast signal that was far more resistant to interference. Whereas AM signals were perpetually full of static, FM was not.

Armstrong spent the next decade and a half trying to hang on to his invention. Although he'd grown wealthy licensing his earlier designs to the giant Radio Corporation of America, he and the company could not come to an agreement over FM, and RCA eventually offered its own knockoff circuits based on his idea. Armstrong sued and spent years in court and many thousands of dollars. In 1954, he cracked under the strain and leapt from his thirteenth-floor window on East 52nd Street. Within the year, the respective legal teams settled and Armstrong's widow received approximately $1 million.

Although the early FM receivers were imperfect—the tuners tended to drift off the signal as their electronics warmed up, requiring repeated adjustment—solid-state technology resolved that problem in the 1950s (*see also* TRANSISTOR). The new broadcast band gradually came to be the main destination for classical music, jazz, and eventually popular music. In 1978, the band Steely Dan even recorded an ode to it, titled "FM," with the refrain "No static at all!" Today, the AM radio dial is nearly all news and talk; FM is where the music is.

Folkie [3]

For many listeners, "folk music" began in the late 1950s at sleepaway camp, a relatively low-cost, vaguely socialist, sanity-saving respite from the urban parent-child continuum. After sunset, a "counselor," usually a young man with a cantorial voice or a lank-haired woman strumming a Sears Silvertone guitar, led campers in renditions of "The Midnight Special," "Swing Low, Sweet Chariot," and, of course, "This Land Is Your Land."

It never crossed most of these kids' minds that many of their "folk songs" had originally been sung by enslaved African-Americans and sharecroppers and Celtic-Appalachian dirt farmers. (Some did associate them, vaguely, with leftism and commie rabble-rousers like Woody Guthrie, who had THIS MACHINE KILLS FASCISTS written on his guitar.) A mere three years later, these same adolescents would be sitting in bohemian Greenwich Village coffee houses like Le Figaro and Caffè Reggio, boldly ordering double espressos. Attired in woolly red-and-black Pendleton jackets and corduroy caps, they cast their budding intellectual-political lot in with the revolution. No mindless rock and roll there. They were folkies.

From roughly 1957 through the early 1970s, the intersection of Bleecker and Macdougal was the undisputed nexus of what came to be called the American folk-music revival. San Francisco, Boston, and Chicago had their protest singers, but the Village was the hothouse, the mecca. Some, like Bob Dylan, Joan Baez (who graced the cover of *Time* magazine in 1962), and Peter, Paul and Mary (whose eponymous debut album topped

99

*Bob Dylan and
Joan Baez, 1964.*
PHOTOGRAPH BY
BARRY FEINSTEIN

Heather Holliday, Coney Island sword-swallower.

the *Billboard* charts for six straight weeks that same year) became voices of the civil-rights movement, appearing before the multitudes at the 1963 March on Washington opening for Martin Luther King Jr.'s "I Have a Dream" speech.

For the rest, it was a scene. The 14-year-old folkie could emerge from the West 4th Street station, a six-foot scarf wrapped around his or her neck, with every chance of seeing Dave Van Ronk, Phil Ochs, Eric Andersen, Janis Ian, Patrick Sky, Mark Spoelstra, Happy and Artie Traum, Carolyn Hester, John Sebastian, Richie Havens, Richard and Mimi Fariña, Odetta, Buffy Sainte-Marie, Guy Carawan, Gil Turner, Peter La Farge, Tom Paxton, or Jean Ritchie, not to mention Doc Watson and an endless supply of hat passers who lived in local walk-ups. With the bomb ready to drop, someone was always protesting something at the Gaslight, Gerde's Folk City, the Bitter End, Cafe Wha?, the Night Owl, the Cafe Bizarre, or any of the clubs whose leases, everyone said, belonged to Mafia landlords. The focal point of the scene was the Folklore Center, operated by Izzy Young at 110

Macdougal Street, just steps from the Kettle of Fish (at No. 114), a Kerouac-era bar adopted by harder-drinking folkies. There one could buy guitar picks, issues of *Broadside* and *Sing Out!*, or a copy of Lead Belly's *Last Sessions* or Harry Smith's epic *Anthology of American Folk Music*, a six-LP collection of Depression-era 78s. Every "real" Villager knew that here, in these scratchy interfaces with the vanished past, the true hidden American songbook resided, not in that commercial schlock turned out in midtown (*see also* BRILL BUILDING).

Van Ronk called Young's place a "clubhouse": "If you had no fixed address, you would have your mail sent care of the Folklore Center ... it became a catalyst for all sorts of things." Indeed, one cold day in 1961, in its tiny back room, Van Ronk came to share a microphone with the 19-year-old Bob Dylan, who had recently arrived in the Village with a suitcase full of apocrypha about being an orphan and running away from the circus. "Want to do that 'Fixin' to Die'?" Van Ronk asked, referring to a wrenching blues number written by Bukka White while he'd been imprisoned in Mississippi in the 1930s. Then

④ **How to Swallow a Sword**

From sword-swallower, strongman, and Coney Island USA Sideshow School professor Adam Realman

"How do you swallow a sword? Very carefully! **It requires mind and body control.** If you flip that switch in your head that says, *Yes! I will accomplish what I set out to do*, then guess what: You actually will be able to swallow a sword. That's the mental. The physical is the series of gag points that your body has—the epiglottis, the esophagus, the sphincter, the stomach. When the sword passes down each one, you're going to feel like retching. You need to learn to control those.

"You start with a training implement, something softer than a sword, more flexible, so that, should you be able to get it down and you retch or move, it will bend along with your body and not puncture your esophagus. I've taught people who within minutes have managed to get the training implement down. Conversely, I've taught people who just can't ever, because they don't believe in themselves."

the two young white singers from relatively well-off backgrounds bashed into a tune of ultimate powerlessness, harmonizing on lines like "I'm looking funny in my eyes, an' I believe I'm fixin' to die / I know I was born to die, but I hate to leave my children cryin.'" In 1963, Columbia released *The Freewheelin' Bob Dylan*, featuring "Blowin' in the Wind," "Masters of War," and "A Hard Rain's A-Gonna Fall." The album's cover showed a windswept Dylan and his girlfriend, Suze Rotolo, running through the dirty snow on Jones Street, summing up the scene in a single frame.

In 1965, Dylan, then one of the world's biggest pop stars, recorded the single "Positively 4th Street," the final kiss-off to the place that had made him. He'd already gone electric; now he was abandoning protest, calling some of his most famous works "finger-pointing songs." Its well-known opening zinger, "You've got a lotta nerve to say you are my friend," left a lot of people wondering if he meant them. More likely it was the scene itself, with all those purist rules Dylan could no longer abide. A few years later, he'd be living in Malibu.

The Village folkie scene didn't die just then (the war in Vietnam continued to rage, and there were many versions of Leonard Cohen's "Suzanne" left to be sung). It was just that the neo-hobos who'd come to town with guitars on their back, people like Jimi Hendrix, who led the house band at Cafe Wha? in 1966 under the name Jimmy James and the Blue Flames, were now making the kind of music you could dance to.

Fountain Pen

Hard to imagine a time when the only self-contained writing implement was a pencil or a stick of chalk or charcoal. Yet barely 150 years have elapsed since scribes were liberated from the mess of the open inkwell and its dip pen, made at first from a quill and subsequently with a steel nib. A few unproduced or variously flawed products aside—including a potentially usable 1847 model built and patented by Walter Hunt, better known for another pointy invention (*see also* SAFETY PIN)—the great cursive leap can be attributed to a Brooklyn resident named Lewis Waterman. He'd been selling some of those flawed early pens, and in 1884 he patented the key improvement: a variable-depth fine groove in the nib that fed ink slowly and evenly, through capillary action, from an internal reservoir to the paper. Even though fountain pens have long since moved from everyday writing tool to baroque enthusiast niche product, they all still work that way.

Freak Show [4]

The first presentations of abnormal people and animals date to sixteenth-century Europe, where unusual bodies were seen as comical, rather than frightening or grotesque, and freak shows were lighthearted affairs that accompanied church feasts and holidays. But New York turned freak shows into something else entirely: more extreme, profit driven, fantastical, and cruel. And for that, we can thank P. T. Barnum.

The home of freak shows as we know them was Scudder's American Museum on the corner of Broadway and Ann Streets in lower Manhattan. Barnum bought Scudder's, renamed it after himself, and began exhibiting people there in 1842. By that time, such displays had been gaining popularity in "scientific" museums around the country. They were often framed as educational, but Barnum saw something bigger: commercial potential.

He put a wide range of people on display, going well beyond the nonnormative bodies that freak shows had once featured. And crucially, he wasn't afraid to fabricate outlandish—and often racist and ableist—stories to pull in gawkers. Barnum displayed individuals with ambiguous gender traits, entire Native American and Chinese "families," and the wildly tattooed. In his telling, unusual characteristics became outsize spectacles: "the largest Mountain of Human Flesh ever seen in the form of a woman," the "mammoth infant," and the "living skeleton." One of Barnum's earliest draws was Joice Heth, a formerly enslaved woman who Barnum claimed was 161 years old and the onetime nurse of George Washington. Heth fascinated the public and helped establish Barnum's reputation, while he made up a series of tall tales to keep popular interest fixed on her.

Barnum actually managed to make freak shows highbrow. Through a constantly rotating series of human "exhibits" and by paying scientific "experts" to back up his claims, he turned his museum into the ritziest place in New York, one where visiting dignitaries wanted to be seen (it was across the street from Astor House and a few blocks from Delmonico's, which didn't hurt, either). But he also wasn't above marketing his shows to the threepenny press aimed at working-class readers. His publicity strategy is credited with the spread of freak shows across the country over the next hundred years, but by the mid–twentieth century, the public's understanding of disability had started to shift and the events fell out of favor. Even now, though, Barnum's legacy hasn't entirely disappeared. The Coney Island Circus Sideshow advertises "Freaks, wonders, and human curiosities!" daily throughout the summer season.

Free Verse

Like many revolutionary writers, Walt Whitman was at first self-published, printing 795 copies of the first edition of *Leaves of Grass* at his own expense and putting them on sale on July 4, 1855, when he was 36. The book's explicit sexual content made it controversial. A fellow poet said Whitman should have burned the volume. *The Saturday Press* called for its author to commit suicide. Ralph Waldo Emerson admired the book but wrote to Whitman advising him to tone it down. Whitman was fired from a clerkship in the Department of the Interior because the secretary thought he wrote smut. But the book's content was less radical than its form. Taking his sense of rhythm from the King James Bible but adhering to no regular meter, Whitman was writing free verse.

Free verse is defined by an irregularity in the recurrence of a poem's stresses and rhymes. The irregularity is persistent and can be seen on the page as well as heard by the ear when the poem is spoken aloud. Detractors sometimes dismiss it simply as "rhythmical prose." There were precursors to Whitman's experiments, notably the liberal use of blank (i.e., unrhymed) verse by John Milton in *Paradise Lost* and the long, religious poem "Jubilate Agno," which Christopher Smart wrote in a madhouse between 1759 and 1763 (and of which only thirty-two pages survive, first published in 1939). Though Whitman was largely derided, even shunned in his lifetime, his influence immediately registered in America and Europe. Baudelaire, Rilke, Hopkins, and Eliot became practitioners and advocates of this seemingly nonformal form.

Like many innovations that do away with traditional constraints, free verse is often said to be democratizing, and it did become the dominant mode of poetry in the twentieth century. From William Carlos Williams's short line through Allen Ginsberg's homages to Whitman to the "American Hybrid" style in vogue at the turn of the new century, it has become not so much a way for poets to escape the rules but to invent, and instantly reinvent, their own.

Friends see SITCOM

Frozen Custard

When it's made the classic American way, ice cream calls for milk and cream, sugar, and some churning to add air (*see also* SUPERPREMIUM ICE CREAM). The French add egg yolks; the Italians, in their gelato, use more milk than cream and stir it less, for a dense smoothness. Early in the twentieth century, however, four Pennsylvania brothers, the Kohr family, introduced an extremely delicious variant. The oldest, Archie, usually gets the credit for tinkering with the ice-cream maker they'd purchased and creating their frozen custard— basically an ice-cream mixture with whole eggs and not so much churned-in air, served slightly less cold than the standard scooped product—though other Kohrs claim they were involved to various degrees. In 1919, they hauled their machine to Coney Island and set up shop.

Coney Island, just then, was itself facing change as it turned from a fancy seaside resort for aristocrats to one frequented by the masses. (The subway reached Coney Island that same year, jump-starting this social leveling.) The nickel cone was the perfect accompaniment to a middle-class day at the beach, and the Kohrs' frozen-custard business soon expanded up and down the East Coast with 48 stores by 1960. Competitors sprung up too: In Coney Island, the preponderance of these were owned and operated by Greek immigrants. Most of them served a standard complement of flavors (vanilla, chocolate, pistachio) plus a signature unique alternative (maple walnut, say, or banana).

With Coney Island's physical decay after the 1960s— not to mention the increasing presence of "soft serve," that ersatz, eggless, nearly tasteless stuff offered at Dairy Queen and McDonald's—frozen custard became harder to find in New York. Its life continued mostly at the Jersey Shore and a few other niche markets, including (curiously) Wisconsin, where it built a big following at roadside drive-in shops. But that long slide was reversed in 2001, when the upscale restaurateur Danny Meyer opened his first Shake Shack hamburger kiosk in Madison Square Park. Meyer's pastry chef Nicole Kaplan developed a frozen-custard recipe for the stand's cones and milkshakes, one that used higher-quality ingredients than the old Coney Island sellers would ever have imagined. Her custard was a huge hit, and Shake Shack now serves it in more than 200 stores in 15 countries, with more to come.

Frozen Hot Chocolate

Stephen Bruce, Calvin Holt, and Patch Caradine didn't set out to found a frozen-dessert empire. They were three struggling actors and dancers who opened a café together in 1954, figuring they'd sling some coffees to pay the bills while they waited for their stage careers to take off. All their initial offerings were hot drinks, so someone—nobody quite remembers who—suggested they add a funny oxymoron to the menu: frozen hot chocolate. They came up with a recipe for a rich, slushy drink topped with whipped cream and served in a goblet, and they billed it as a secret formula.

It was not an instant hit. Early visitors to their Upper East Side café, Serendipity 3, were intrigued, if not immediately sold. But within a few years, Marilyn Monroe—then married to Arthur Miller and living a few blocks away—was coming in to sip the drink while learning lines. Andy Warhol was paying for his sugar fix with drawings instead of cash. And Jackie Kennedy found she liked frozen hot chocolate so much that she asked for the secret recipe to serve at a White House dinner. (The owners flatly refused.) These days, its fan base is somewhat less elite: Six couples have chosen to be married in bathtubs filled with the concoction. Serendipity 3 estimates it has served somewhere around 25 million such drinks, including several to Cher, who has come by and gotten them to go.

"Fuhgeddaboudit"

In 1985, the Washington *Post* writer (and future *Donnie Brasco* screenwriter) Paul Attanasio interviewed Martin Scorsese, who, in the course of their conversation, answered two questions with rhetorical utterances of exasperated resignation: "Whaddaya gonna do?" and "Forgetaboutit." The latter appears to be the first published use of a commonplace expression in the New York Italian-American vernacular that had long ago spread to the broader city population. Two years later, Tom Wolfe (*see also* NEW JOURNALISM) used it in his novel *The Bonfire of the Vanities* with the innovative twist of the phonetic spelling "Fuhgedaboudit."

By the early 1990s, it was showing up in the *Times*, and in 2004, the wisecracking, boosterish Brooklyn borough president Marty Markowitz used it on the LEAVING BROOKLYN sign that drivers can see as they roll onto the Verrazzano-Narrows Bridge. In 2016 it made it into the *Oxford English Dictionary* with three *D*'s and one *T*, plus a usage note clarifying its origins "in representations of regional speech (associated especially with New York and New Jersey)." Notably, it is a word that can be deployed as its own opposite: You can say "fuhgeddaboudit" to mean "It's no trouble at all, sir," and, in other contexts, "That's out of the question, buddy."

From
GAME SHOW
to
GUM

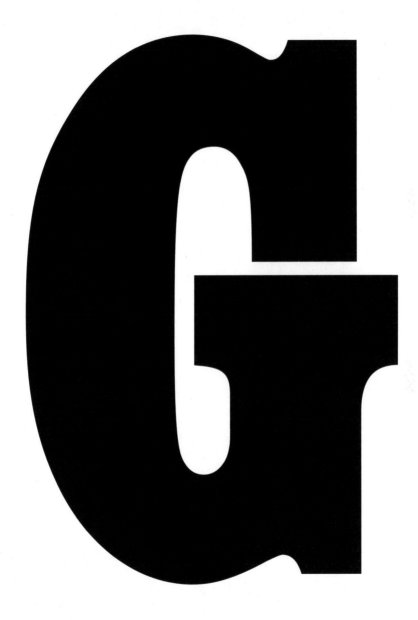

Grand Central Terminal,
2013.
PHOTOGRAPH BY PARI DUKOVIC

Game Show

After a few years of experimental broadcasts, the era of commercial television began on July 1, 1941, when NBC-owned WNBT began beaming news, sports, and entertainment programming to the few hundred New Yorkers fortunate enough to own a set. The first-day lineup included the Brooklyn Dodgers losing to the Phillies at Ebbets Field, real-life soldiers putting on a mini-play about Army life, and the very first TV game shows: *Uncle Jim's Question Bee* and *Truth or Consequences*. Both were one-time specials, video versions of existing radio hits. But the format was clearly a natural for the new medium, which was hungry for cheap, easy-to-produce live programming. A day after those pioneering telecasts, rival WCBW debuted *CBS Television Quiz*, the first regularly scheduled game show of the commercial TV era, and WNBT soon added a charades-like program called *Play the Game*. (For sticklers, the government-funded, noncommercial BBC actually got to game shows first—sort of—back in 1938. For four months that year, it broadcast *Spelling Bee*, which was exactly that: Host Freddie Grisewood, modifying a radio show of the same name, asked people to spell words.)

America's entry into World War II put a halt to the genre's growth—and slowed TV's rise in general—but game shows returned in a big way soon after V-E Day, with (slightly) more sophisticated formats. In 1946, the doomed DuMont Network introduced *Cash and Carry*, where contestants on a fake-grocery-store set picked up cans and answered questions printed on them. Over the next few years, the category began to rapidly evolve and exploded in popularity. Out in L.A., Groucho Marx took his radio hit *You Bet Your Life* to NBC, and it quickly became the first game show to finish a TV season in Nielsen's Top 10. (The game was barely the point; Groucho's banter was what made it work.) Around the same time, panel shows started to break out thanks to two big CBS hits: *What's My Line?* and *I've Got a Secret*. Both were native to television, shared a production team (the pioneering Mark Goodson and Bill Todman), and took advantage of New York's status as the world's cultural capital to deploy celebrities and socialites in a format that leaned on chat rather than trivia.

Not that quiz-style game shows were dying. A 1954 Supreme Court ruling that big-money TV jackpots didn't constitute gambling (and thus couldn't be banned by the FCC) prompted the networks to green-light prime-time spectacles such as *Twenty-One* and *The $64,000 Question*. The amiable, low-stakes Q&A of earlier shows gave way to dramatic music and isolation booths. Contestants risked thousands of dollars with each answer, returning for multiple episodes as they worked toward a life-changing payout. Within weeks of its debut in the summer of 1955, *The $64,000 Question* was the No. 1 show on TV, displacing *I Love Lucy* from the top spot for the season. Winners became instant celebrities, with some (like Dr. Joyce Brothers) using their fame to launch long-running careers.

It soon came to light that producers on a few programs, notably *Twenty-One*, had been rigging their competitions by giving contestants questions in advance and rehearsing ways to up the drama. Several big shows were canceled in late 1958 in the fallout of what became known as the Quiz Show Scandals, and for the next decade, networks largely relegated game shows to daytime TV. But after those fallow years, games recaptured their buzz in the 1970s. Old hits such as *The Price Is Right*, *Password*, and *The Match Game* were resurrected and reinvented, and new hits like *Wheel of Fortune* and *Family Feud* were created. A few legal changes helped: New FCC regulations made it lucrative for independent producers to flood the market with low-cost programming. Those cost pressures, along with the move away from live programming, helped push production of most game shows to California. But in 1999, the games returned to New York (and prime time) with the U.K. import *Who Wants to Be a Millionaire*, bringing the format full circle.

Gay-Rights Movement[1]

The gay-rights movement is often thought to have begun at the Stonewall Inn in June 1969, but New York City has been a magnet for gay and lesbian people for two centuries. It was among New York's sailors and laborers in the decades before the Civil War where "Walt Whitman, a kosmos, of Manhattan the son" (*Song of Myself*, 1855) would search for democratic love among throngs of anonymous men. As New York's nineteenth-century economy boomed, so did its downtown streets—particularly the Bowery, where pleasure palaces wooed sexual adventurers

Twenty-One, *NBC's notoriously rigged game show, 1956.*

with rooms for rent by the hour, no questions asked. Downtown bars and dance halls catered to the preferences of male "fairies," "pansies," "wolves," and "jockers," while female "lady lovers"—union organizers, schoolteachers, and reformers—paired up in "Boston marriages," pioneering a new way of living that often intersected with feminism and other forms of radical politics.

The "long-haired men and short-haired women" who laid the groundwork for the modern LGBTQ movement clustered in Greenwich Village debating everything from free love to anarchism to modern poetry. Before World War I, the Village anarchists Emma Goldman and Alexander Berkman defended homosexual rights as part of their belief in free love. Lesbian writer Djuna Barnes moved to the Village's thriving scene in 1915, and by 1920, the bisexual Carl Van Vechten threw racially

integrated parties featuring writers and artists, many of them gay, of the uptown Harlem Renaissance (*see also* HARLEM). Gladys Bentley, a lesbian who wore men's suits in her cabaret performances and ran a club uptown, and the gay poet Langston Hughes would have been frequent guests there, as well as at uptown parties hosted by cosmetics heiress and patron of the arts A'Lelia Walker, herself a lover of women and men.

New York's radical worlds also gave birth to modern sexual politics. In 1920, Village reformers—including free-love advocates Roger Baldwin and Crystal Eastman, along with activists who made their lives with women, like Jane Addams and Rose Schneiderman—founded the American Civil Liberties Union. Starting in 1933, the bisexual Eleanor Roosevelt kept an apartment in Greenwich Village, where she was surrounded by reformers like

Marsha P. Johnson (with umbrella) and
Kady at a gay-rights rally at City Hall, 1973.
PHOTOGRAPH BY DIANA DAVIES

① **17 Queer Things to Do When Visiting New York**

Chosen by Fran Tirado, writer-editor and former brand and editorial director for LGBTQ+ content at Netflix

➦ Party at **NO BAR,** the gay bar at the Standard East Village ➦ See drag at **the Rosemont** ➦ Browse the **Lesbian Herstory Archives** in Park Slope ➦ Sunbathe at the **People's Beach at Jacob Riis Park** ➦ Eat at **MeMe's Diner** in Prospect Heights ➦ Grab a drink at **Cubbyhole** ➦ Wait in line at **Via Carota** ➦ See more drag at **Branded Saloon** ➦ Try to get into **the Box** ➦ Get a tattoo at **Fleur Noire Tattoo Parlour** in Williamsburg ➦ Get a haircut at **Baddies** in Greenpoint ➦ Catch a monthly party like **Papi Juice** or **Bubble_T** ➦ Donate to a **Housing Works thrift shop** (proceeds go to HIV-affected people and other vulnerable populations) ➦ Get a zodiac-themed cocktail at **Mood Ring** ➦ Pick up tarot cards at **Catland** ➦ See even more drag at **Pieces** ➦ Buy sex toys and lube at **Babeland.**

---

politician Molly Dewson and her partner, Polly Porter. Dewson, Porter, and others were veterans of the women's-suffrage movement and, like many same-sex couples, understood themselves as married, wearing rings to symbolize a union that would not be recognized by law until the end of the century.

After World War II, militant chapters of two early gay-rights groups, the Mattachine Society and the Daughters of Bilitis, begun in 1950s California, combined to form East Coast Homophile Organizations (ECHO) in 1962. While in Greenwich Village, writer James Baldwin fused his passions for African-American and gay civil rights, and feminist Audre Lorde, then a student at Hunter College and Columbia, came out in a thriving butch-femme culture of lesbian bars. In 1965, radical homosexuals organized public protests at the United Nations. In 1966, Mattachine spearheaded a series of "sip-ins" at New York bars, most notably at Julius' on West 10th Street. (It's still there.) And in 1967, Thea Spyer proposed marriage to Edie Windsor, a long engagement that ended in a Toronto marriage in 2007 as the pair were increasingly pulled into the movement for sexual civil rights.

But it was transgender people—many if not most of them people of color—who, in the multiday rebellion at the Village's Stonewall Inn at the end of June 1969, would most effectively radicalize demands for LGBTQ rights. Stonewall became a rallying cry, a queer Declaration of Independence, and made Christopher Street visible as an East Coast gay mecca rivaling San Francisco's Castro district. A year later, the commemorative march was, de facto, the first Pride Parade, giving rise to similar parades worldwide that served both as public affirmations of visibility and as places for people to out themselves. After Stonewall, the closeted New York physician Howard Brown was galvanized first to come out and then to co-organize the National Gay and Lesbian Task Force on October 16, 1973. (On Stonewall's 50th anniversary, the group would unveil the National LGBTQ Wall of Honor at the inn.) Lambda Legal defense was founded in New York in 1973, as was Parents and Friends of Lesbians and Gays, founded by Queens mother Jeanne Manford after her activist son, Morty, was brutally beaten.

In 1980, because of their efforts, New York became one of the first states to decriminalize homosexuality. By then, bohemia had moved across town to the East Village, where radical artists and writers like Allen Ginsberg, Quentin Crisp, Andy Warhol, David Wojnarowicz, Ana María Simo (who would co-found the Lesbian Avengers in the 1990s), Peggy Shaw, Lois Weaver, and Sarah Schulman were but a few figures who lived or worked. By 1984, Tompkins Square Park, formerly a site for nineteenth-century labor rallies, and the Pyramid Club on Avenue A, became the launching ground for Wigstock, an annual celebration of gender transgression by and for drag queens.

Downtown New York became a center of resistance to the Reagan administration when some of the earliest cases of AIDS were detected by a Greenwich Village doctor in 1981. As the plague spread, the East and West Villages and Chelsea gave birth first to the Gay Men's Health Crisis and then to a highly effective direct-action collective (*see also* ACT UP). The LGBTQ community built institutions to advocate for and deliver basic services to the suffering. AIDS also pushed LGBTQ activists to challenge discrimination more broadly, targeting for reform institutions like marriage, parenting, medicine, and prison.

Discrimination in benefits after the attacks on the World Trade Center (*see also* 9/11 ERA) also exposed that, without national marriage equality, the patchwork of domestic-partnership and civil-union laws passed in the 1990s was inadequate. In 2003, New Yorker Evan Wolfson founded Freedom to Marry, which joined existing groups to win marriage equality in 2011. With the backing of these groups, Edie Windsor, recently widowed after more than forty years with Thea Spyer, filed a lawsuit in Manhattan's federal court to be recognized as a spouse and regain $350,000 in taxes levied on Spyer's estate. When she won in June 2013, in a 5-4 decision that affirmed the right to same-sex marriage in every state, it would close one chapter in the history of gay rights, a history that two centuries of LGBTQ New Yorkers can justifiably claim as their own.

General Tso's Chicken

There really was a general named Tso Tsung-t'ang (in today's preferred Pinyin transliteration, Zuo Zongtang). But the nineteenth-century Hunanese military hero most assuredly never tasted the dish that bears his name: battered, deep-fried chicken chunks coated in a heavily sweetened, lightly chili-peppered glaze, which Americans consume by the ton. Hunanese cooking is hot, salty, meaty, and not especially sugary, and no native of the region would call this dish representative.

He or she might, however, recognize its predecessor. In 1955, for a U.S. admiral's visit to Taiwan, a Hunanese chef named Peng Chang-kuei made up a chicken entrée. On a whim, he named it for the general. As Peng later told the cookbook author Fuchsia Dunlop, it was "Hunanese in taste and made without sugar." He continued to serve it in his restaurant in Taipei, and in the early 1970s, as regional Chinese cooking began to gain a foothold in New York (*see also* IMMIGRATION), chefs who'd eaten there started adapting it to American tastes. The city's first Hunan restaurants—Uncle Tai's Hunan Yuan, Hunam, and Shun Lee Palace—each offered versions of Peng's original, but in particular at Hunam, the chef Tsung Ting Wang eventually (according to the New York *Times*) "crisped up the batter and sweetened the sauce, producing a taste combination that millions of Americans came to love." He called it General Ching's chicken, either honoring or ripping off Peng's General Tso.

In 1973, Peng himself moved to New York looking to get in on the Hunan trend and was apparently surprised to find his dish adopted and transformed. Nonetheless, he jumped into the game, opening Uncle Peng on East 44th Street, which did not do well, then Yunnan Yuan on East 52nd Street, which flourished in part because Henry Kissinger, the secretary of State, was known to be a regular. There, the signature dish—in its sweet-and-crispy incarnation—became wedded to the general's name for good, and a billion takeout orders

followed. Peng eventually took the dish back to Taiwan, where he opened a chain of restaurants whose menus included the American-style innovation and kept serving it for many years thereafter.

Gentrification

In a 1964 essay on the affluent sheen then transforming London, the British sociologist Ruth Glass described the way "the middle class, upper and lower" were methodically invading working-class neighborhoods, fixing up "shabby, modest mews and cottages" and turning them into "elegant, expensive residences." She saw this as a problem but not a disaster, a trend that was actually evening out the city's stark social divisions. Yet she was recounting an irreversible, traumatic process that would shape cities for decades to come, and she casually tossed into her diagnosis a term she'd invented, set off by scare quotes: "Once this process of 'gentrification' starts in a district, it goes on rapidly until all or most of the original working-class occupiers are displaced, and the whole social character of the district is changed."

It took more than a decade before the New York *Times* applied that English-sounding word to this city (has any American ever unironically referred to "the gentry"?), but the trend it defined was by then in full swing. In 1969, *New York* had detailed the challenges of buying and fixing up brownstones in cheap but iffy neighborhoods (*see also* "BROOKLYN"; BROWNSTONE ROWHOUSE; "EYES ON THE STREET"), reporting that the Park Slope Betterment Committee "keeps an eye on brownstones in the neighborhood as they become available and relays the word" and also "sponsors a cocktail party for bankers." The subtext is clear: Banks refused to write mortgages in largely African-American neighborhoods, but exceptions could be made for affluent, white "pioneers." Policy also began to support the idea of fixing up old houses rather than replacing them with high-rises. In 1965, the city created the Landmarks Preservation Commission (*see also* LANDMARKS LAW), which quickly designated Brooklyn Heights as the city's first historic district, and in 1978, Congress enacted the federal Historic Tax Credit, allowing landlords and homeowners some relief toward the cost of renovating an old property. Suddenly, spiffing up brownstones and Art Deco apartment buildings had financial as well as aesthetic appeal.

First came a trickle of hardy eccentrics who were willing to stake small fortunes on rickety structures and risky renovations. Gradually, they multiplied, and in the 1970s, most observers saw the current as a welcome antidote to the years of abandonment and demolition that had caused New York's population to drop by nearly a million in the previous decade. But already some saw it as a portent for the next kind of crisis. "To date, gentrification has too often meant the blunt dispersal of the least privileged," the historian Fergus Bordewich wrote in 1979. Over the next four decades, New York incubated, amplified, and continually redefined the phenomenon, which became recognized as an urban ill. In a city perennially obsessed with real estate, the fight over who lives where has become a proxy for racial and class conflict, for the tension between memory and development, and for the inequities splintering the entire country.

From the beginning, it was a two-faced trend. Neighborhoods that had become derelict and dangerous during the crisis years were improving; businesses opened, crime dropped, drug dealers drifted away, parks got cleaned up, and taxes started flowing. But simultaneously, many low-income residents had to decamp—again. Slumlords generally provide little or no upkeep in exchange for accepting federal-housing-aid vouchers and financially shaky tenants. Now they had an alternative: Force out the poor, renovate, and raise rents exponentially. As soon as some landlords in any given neighborhood went that route, it was in the interest of them all to follow suit. The mechanism is so consistent that the coverage of gentrification over the years is a repetitive litany. The place-names change, but the arguments, complaints, and "longtime resident" quotes remain the same.

Although the mechanisms of gentrification have been studied intensively, debate still rages on its root cause and how to address it. One faction holds that it's simply a part of historical cycles of urban change; neighborhoods rise and fall in prestige and cost, even when their basic attributes—schools, public transit, and housing stock—remain the same. A second group sees it as the product of discrete, deliberate policies that can be reversed by political action, just as redlining (that is, the onetime government practice of writing off certain neighborhoods as too risky for mortgage loans, most often those

inhabited by Black and brown people), disinvestment in urban cores, federally funded highways, and the mortgage-interest deduction created a gulf between suburbs and urban slums. The third school of thought sees gentrification as both a weapon and a symptom of an all-out war that the global power elite wages on the poor.

Missing from all this is a set of proven, practical tools to control gentrification. Every New York mayor since the 1970s has used subsidies and rent regulation as bulwarks against eviction, yet similar policies have had nearly the opposite effect at different times. The Koch administration turned over large swaths of blighted city property in the South Bronx to private developers, which helped stabilize the area and allowed residents to remain; twenty years later, Mayor Bloomberg used a robust affordable-housing program and targeted rezonings to guide private investment toward areas he saw as ripe for development (the Greenpoint-Williamsburg waterfront, for instance). That strategy resulted in tall, deluxe towers sprinkled with affordable apartments and a rapid climb in real-estate prices—not just gentrification but hypergentrification, producing "everycity" areas that are essentially devoid of history and character.

The same duality is true of just about any neighborhood improvement. A better school, a cleaned-up park, a pleasant plaza, working streetlights, fresher produce at the market—residents can spend years accumulating these public luxuries only to find that outsiders have noticed and want in too. That's the cruel irony of New York's success: The city needs so much work, but every time a piece of it gets done, someone sees each crumb of improvement as a signal that it'll soon be time to leave.

George Washington Bridge

see SUSPENSION BRIDGE

Getaway Car

According to legend, gangster Harry Horowitz, a.k.a. Gyp the Blood, was known to make $2 bar bets claiming he could snap a man's back over his knee. On July 16, 1912, at the direction of a crooked cop, Horowitz shot gambler Herman "Beansie" Rosenthal outside the Hotel Metropole on West 43rd Street, killing him. After the murder, Horowitz and his accomplices hopped into a gray Packard and sped away. It's said to be the first time a getaway car was used.

When detectives tracked Horowitz down at a hideout on Ridgewood Avenue in Brooklyn, the gangster asked to change into his finest suit—he wanted to look sharp in the newspaper photographs. Two years later, Horowitz and his accomplices were electrocuted at Sing Sing.

Gin Rummy

The scene: the Knickerbocker Whist Club, a "masculine affair" (according to *The New Yorker*) headquartered at Madison Avenue and 42nd Street. The characters: Elwood T. Baker, accountant, bridge teacher, and lifetime member of the club, and C. Graham Baker, Elwood's son, a cartoonist and the future writer of such screenplays as *Speed and Spunk* and *Walls and Wallops*.

Allegedly, the two Bakers holed up at the Knickerbocker in 1909 to collaborate on inventing gin rummy. It's descended from the larger family of rummy games, all based on picking up some cards and putting down others to try to form sets, or "melds," of three or more cards that either share a rank (e.g., kings) or a suit and sequence (e.g., the king, queen, and jack of hearts). Mahjongg and various Chinese card games dating back to the 18th or 19th centuries are based on a similar foundation of picking up cards and putting down others to form melds. And in the late ninetieth century, game scribe R. F. Foster mentioned a game called conquian, rummy's parent, as "a great favourite in Mexico, and in all the American states bordering upon it, especially Texas." In devising their version, the Bakers combined some rules from existing kinds of rummy with those of conquian and smoothed out the edges. The younger Baker is credited with the name; the story goes that he saw "rum" in the name and added another liquor.

The game wasn't an immediate hit, and its hometown can't rightly be credited with its success. What really made gin rummy popular was Hollywood. The game is quick to play and can be put down and easily picked up again later, and by the 1940s, it had caught on among actors waiting around between takes. Gin became so popular it was name-dropped in movies and shown onscreen, whether or not the context called for it. *The Sea Hawk*, set in Elizabethan England, contains a scene of the queen herself playing gin rummy with the Earl of Essex.

Gossip Column [2]

There was no other newspaper quite like the New York *Evening Graphic*. It was founded in 1924 by Bernarr Macfadden, a health nut and publisher of bodybuilding and true-crime magazines. At the time, the business of tabloids (*see also* TABLOID NEWSPAPER) was new, and New York City had two of the first ones, the *Daily News* and the *Daily Mirror*. Macfadden saw room for a third, differentiated by its sensationalism and vulgarity. The *Graphic* was, of course, a big hit, soon selling 350,000 copies a day, though people were ashamed to admit they read it. And much of their attention went to its star columnist, Walter Winchell.

Born Weinschel—poor and Jewish in East Harlem in 1897—Winchell came up in vaudeville as a song-and-dance performer. In the teens, he began collecting little showbiz news items and posting them backstage at the theater where he was performing. That led to a column in a small trade paper called *The Vaudeville News*, which in turn got him hired by the start-up *Evening Graphic*. "Your Broadway and Mine," as his column was first known, made its first appearance there on September 20, 1924, and it was chatty and filled with anecdotes and jokes. Gradually, broader news items infiltrated the pages, and in 1927, Winchell turned over the

▶ **"You need a doorman who is pleasant,** because everybody is sending you a book, a CD, a script they think is going to be fabulous, a picture of themselves."
▶ **"And you need to be younger than I am** if you're starting out, so you don't keep writing about Elizabeth Taylor."

Monday edition of the column to news that was, at the time, considered distasteful and privacy invading: elopements, pregnancies, betrayals. The public ate it up, and when Winchell moved to the big time—William Randolph Hearst's *Daily Mirror* and the thousand-plus papers to which Hearst could syndicate the column—it was said that he took 200,000 of the *Evening Graphic's* readers with him. In his post there, he was widely considered one of the most powerful people in America.

There were rivals. Louella Parsons's column, which predated Winchell's and covered the movie business, soon began to move gossip as well, and she eventually gained a competitor herself in the more glamorous Hedda Hopper. "Cholly Knickerbocker," the pseudonymous society columnist of the Hearst papers, began to do the same. Leonard Lyons and Earl Wilson produced columns somewhat like Winchell's but with less ferocity and vindictiveness. Winchell, though, remained the emperor of this world, first aligning himself with President Franklin Roosevelt, then eventually sliding over to the anti-communist right, building up some careers while destroying others with a swipe. Only when he himself overstepped, aligning with the red-baiting senator Joseph McCarthy, did the public turn on Winchell, and his power finally began to wane through the 1950s. The *Mirror*, his home paper, shut down in 1963, dealing Winchell his professional death blow. When he died in 1972, only one mourner—his formerly estranged daughter, Walda—attended his funeral.

The gossip column as a form outlived him, of course, and others rushed in to fill the demand, notably the TV gossipseuse Rona Barrett. After Rupert Murdoch bought and wildly revved up the New York *Post* in 1976, he commissioned a high-energy new column in a tabloid that was itself already pretty high-energy. Named for its original location in the paper, "Page Six"—which eventually resettled on page eight or page ten—was soon loved and feared and obsessively read,

especially during its heyday under Richard Johnson. Nor was it alone at the *Post*: Cindy Adams's celebrity coverage dealt in its own exclusives from her Park Avenue milieu. Across town, Liz Smith's column in the *Daily News* continued a slightly more high-toned tradition in which celebrities felt a little safer. In 1991, the impending divorce of Donald and Ivana Trump dominated them all for weeks (*see also* TRUMPISM); in 1992, the Woody Allen–Mia Farrow–Soon-Yi Previn scandal did the same. Three years later, the O. J. Simpson murder trial effaced any remaining line between celebrity scandal and hard news. Quite a bit of the coverage of that story was delivered from court by the Los Angeles newscaster Harvey Levin, who later founded TMZ, which is inarguably a descendant of the *Evening Graphic*. So are the gossip-and-news sites of the type that originated with Gawker Media (*see also* NEWS BLOG) and its imitators, and, perhaps, the quick-twitch outrage culture of Twitter.

Gotham

In 2000, *GQ* commissioned the typographers Jonathan Hoefler and Tobias Frere-Jones to draw a new sans-serif typeface. Inspired by mid-century signage around New York City—especially the chunky letters reading PORT AUTHORITY on the Eighth Avenue bus terminal—Frere-Jones began scouting liquor stores and other bold sign-bearers. The font he subsequently drew was highly geometric, with the *O* nearly a perfect circle, but certain letters, such as the capital *G*, didn't quite conform, adding flair and playfulness to the look. Looking for a name that used the set's distinctive

(3) Where to
See Graffiti Art
in New York

*Chosen by Museum
of Street Art
(MoSA) curator
Marie Cecile Flageul*

➻ **Keith Haring**, *Crack
Is Wack (128th St. at Second
Ave.)*: "Haring's 1986 mural
was inspired by the crack
epidemic. It was executed
without permission but
was immediately put under
the protection of the City
Department of Parks."

➻ **Graffiti Hall of Fame** *(106th
St. at Park Ave.)*: "The artwork

in this schoolyard is visible
on weekends and when the
school is not in session. Every
year, it's refreshed with a
different artist. A great place to
experience the art of lettering."

➻ **Freeman Alley**
*(off Rivington St. near
Chrystie St.)*: "A haven for
magnificent wheat-paste
and stencils work."

➻ **Germania Bank Building**
(190 Bowery): "Covered
in graffiti, this building was once
the hangout of young SAMO
before he became Jean-Michel
Basquiat. At the base is the
first landmarked illegal graffiti
block letter by Nekst. Atop the
water tower is a Shepard Fairey
portrait of Rosario Dawson,
iconic Cubana for the LES."

---

letters, he considered Goats and Gomorrah but chose
Gotham. It was a typeface that simultaneously conveyed
sophistication without spikiness, modernity without
coldness. This made it extremely versatile and commercially successful, and the firm added multiple variants
in italics and lighter and heavier weights. (The Hoefler
& Frere-Jones company split up shortly thereafter, and
Gotham is now sold by the former's firm, Hoefler & Co.)

Gotham gained visibility when it appeared on the
cornerstone of One World Trade Center, but most people came to know it in 2008 when the campaign of
Barack Obama adopted it for its logo and printed matter. Shepard Fairey used it on his HOPE poster of Obama,
too. Since then, Gotham has been licensed everywhere,
from Australian government documents to the logo of
New York University.

Graffiti As Art ³

Humankind has been writing on walls since the caves,
but today's global urban phenomenon of self-expression
in youth culture took hold in New York in the 1960s.
Gangs employed it to mark their territories, and teenagers, especially following the 1950s popularization of
the felt-tip pen (*see also* MAGIC MARKER), competed to
cover every available surface with their nicknames.

In 1971, a teen from Washington Heights who used
the sobriquet TAKI 183—abbreviating his Greek sur-
name, unrevealed to this day, and the street he lived on—
was profiled in the New York *Times*. In his neighborhood
and in the Bronx, ever more ambitious kids were picking
up spray-paint cans, tagging blighted buildings, and
treating the subway as a circulatory system of moving
murals. A heavily indebted city (*see also* MAYHEM),
unable to police the rail yards or scrub the cars, did little
to stop them. No less a figure than Norman Mailer hailed
these outsider artists in a 1974 essay, "The Faith of Graffiti," comparing them to Giotto and Michelangelo.

Looking for a support system, the graffiti artist Hugo
Martinez set up the collective United Graffiti Artists in
1972 as "an alternative to the art world." But the Establishment was already absorbing those outsiders: The
writer MICO was showcased at Soho's Razor Gallery in
1973, selling a painting for $400. Graffiti writers and
their artist friends, too, used the language of art history.
The artist and film director Charlie Ahearn compared
the elaborate lettering known as "wild style" to Cubism.
Another graffiti writer, Lee, called wild style "sculpture
in motion." The artist John "Crash" Matos, ticking off the
institutions that hold or have shown his works—MoMA
and the Brooklyn Museum among them—described
museums as "the last stop on the subway line."

The music and fashion worlds, enamored of street
culture and running somewhat in parallel, also hooked
up with graffiti artists. In 1980, Matos organized a show,
"Graffiti Art Success for America (GAS)," at Stefan Eins's
South Bronx nonprofit Fashion Moda that included
major players like Fab 5 Freddy, Futura, and Lady Pink.
That same year, Fashion Moda partnered with the artist
collective Colab to mount the legendary "Times Square
Show" of 100 artists in an abandoned massage parlor,
pairing uptown graffiti writers with the downtown likes
of Jenny Holzer and Kiki Smith.

More attention came in 1983 with the release of *Wild
Style*, a feature film about the hip-hop scene, and *Style
Wars*, a Sundance Grand Jury Prize–winning PBS documentary. New York art buyers like Sidney Janis and
the artist Martin Wong saw merit in the work of these
young rebels and assembled collections that would go
on to form major museum exhibitions. The greatest
crossover from the street to the white cube was the
Brooklyn-born Jean-Michel Basquiat, known by the tag
SAMO ("same old"), who rocketed to fame in his early
twenties after appearing in the Times Square show.
Keith Haring's 1986 *Crack Is Wack* mural is preserved
by the City Parks Department on a handball court at

128th Street and Second Avenue, and his final work, an altarpiece using his signature graffiti characters, is at the Cathedral Church of St. John the Divine.

The 2010s saw two landmarks in graffiti history, for better or for worse. In 2017, a 1982 canvas by Basquiat sold for $110.5 million at Sotheby's New York, unseating Andy Warhol as America's highest-priced artist, and a few miles away in Queens in 2013, a developer white-washed the legendary outdoor graffiti museum known as 5Pointz, eager to raze the building and put up luxury apartments. If New York is the birthplace of graffiti as we know it, the lot near MoMA PS1 that housed 5Pointz might be its grave.

Grand Central Terminal [4]

First of all: a taxonomic note. Grand Central Station is the midtown post office. Grand Central station, with a small *s*, is the subway stop underneath. And Grand Central Terminal—that last word used specifically because it's at the end of the line—is the Beaux-Arts monument to the great age of rail travel at 42nd Street and Park Avenue, designed by Warren & Wetmore with assistance from Reed & Stem, with golden constellations on the turquoise concourse ceiling and warm, creamy Indiana limestone nearly everywhere else.

It's a landmark, of course, but its beauty belies its sheer engineering achievement. Walk between Madison and Lexington Avenues anywhere from 45th to 100th Street, and apart from a slight rise in the street level, you'd never know you were crossing a broad tunnel that funnels rail service in and out of the city. Grand Central is merely the tip of an immense public work, one that stretches several miles all but invisibly. New York would simply not work without it; it would also be unthinkable to construct it today, and indeed Grand Central could not even have been built much later than it was because subsequent development would have blocked its path.

The current terminal is the third on that spot. The first, an awkward pile of Victoriana called Grand Central Depot, built by Cornelius Vanderbilt for his New York Central & Hudson River railroads, opened in 1871. It was soon overwhelmed by passengers and was replaced in 1900 by a much larger structure (one that was actually called Grand Central Station, because its trains continued downtown). But even that wasn't enough, and, after a horrible crash in the tunnel in 1902, there was a push to rebuild everything and to replace steam locomotives with electric-powered trains.

On its opening day in February 1913, the terminal stood alone, surrounded by low-rise buildings. That changed quickly as its presence spurred real-estate development along 42nd Street and up Park Avenue. (A basement tenant, the Grand Central Oyster Bar & Restaurant, opened that first year and is still shucking away.) Within 20 years, the 56-story Chanin Building, the 77-story Chrysler Building, and the 55-story Lincoln Building rose on the neighboring blocks. Midtown, in great measure, arose around Grand Central Terminal.

By the 1950s, as the real-estate value of the site grew and auto and air travel clobbered the long-haul railroad business, Grand Central began to seem anachronistic. (Its crosstown cousin, Pennsylvania Station, was demolished starting in 1963; *see also* LANDMARKS LAW.) Several proposals for skyscrapers to replace the terminal were shot down, although the Pan Am Building—now MetLife—was built right up behind it, its escalators feeding into the concourse. Another building, tentatively called 175 Park Avenue, probably would have replaced the terminal itself had it not been for the intervention of Jacqueline Kennedy Onassis, who lent her immense public profile to the Municipal Art Society's push to save it. The fight ended up in the courts, and in 1978's *Penn Central Transportation Co.* v. *New York City*, the United States Supreme Court, by a vote of 6-3, upheld Grand Central's landmark designation.

*A subway car
graffitied by
NOC 167 reaches
96th Street, 1981.*
PHOTOGRAPH BY
MARTHA COOPER

④ **Where to Play Tennis in Grand Central Terminal (No, Really)**

The **Vanderbilt Tennis Club** is a fully functional tennis center on Grand Central's fourth floor, above the concourse. It has one full-size hard court, two small practice courts, locker rooms, a pro shop, a workout room, and a ball machine. Rates vary from $200 to $280 an hour, and the place is open till 2 a.m., every day of the year.

By then, the building was in rough shape, having suffered years of shoddy maintenance and awkward modifications. A decade-long restoration began in the 1980s, and the terminal—with reconfigured and improved shops and food vendors—was rededicated on October 1, 1998. By that point, it was purely a commuter-rail and subway station, the final long-haul Amtrak trains having departed in 1991. An enormous subterranean level, bringing the Long Island Rail Road to the terminal for the first time, is being dug and is slated to open around 2022. Curiously, neither the city nor the state owned Grand Central until the MTA finally bought the building in 2020. Before then, it was paying rent under the 400-year lease once owned by one of Vanderbilt's companies, its expiration scheduled for 2274.

Grid, Street

New York was, early in the nineteenth century, sprawling crazily into wherever it could find the space. Alarmed at the chaos but confident that the rambunctious city would continue to surge outward, officials appointed a surveyor, John Randel, to mark off Manhattan Island into regular rectangles formed by 11 north-south avenues and 155 cross streets.

Ancient Romans, Spanish colonists, and the London architect Christopher Wren had all considered the checkerboard the ideal city form, but New York's iteration, from an 1811 map known as the Commissioners' Plan, was farseeing in its balance of orderly growth and inherent randomness. It imposed no hierarchy of boulevards, highways, or alleys, provided no ceremonial plazas, and allowed for no monuments, or even parks. (The "large arms of the sea which embrace Manhattan Island render its situation, in regard to health and pleasure . . . peculiarly felicitous," the commissioners declared. Who needs a park when you're nestled between rivers?) Instead, Randel carved up miles of rough topography into an unyielding matrix. As the city marched northward, the grid forced farms, streams, mills, breweries, groves, churches, and villages into straight lines and right angles. Many were horrified to watch this Cartesian nightmare advance on irregular nature and romantic coastlines. "These magnificent places are doomed," wrote Edgar Allan Poe in 1844. "The spirit of Improvement has withered them with its acrid breath."

It took decades. Workers obliterated escarpments, sometimes leaving isolated shacks or farmhouses teetering on what was left of a hill. Tenants were dispossessed, and property owners cashed in on the windfalls that new streets brought. Only one meandering country track remained, shifted and widened so that it sliced diagonally across the grid: the Bloomingdale Road, later rebaptized Broadway (*see also* TIMES SQUARE).

The grid leveled more than topography. It encouraged a rational jumble in which rich and poor, home and store, and church and stable shared the same stretch of sidewalk. By dividing the city up into more or less equivalent chunks of square footage, it seeded the land for future development, making it easy to price and predict what could be built on any given lot. Wealthy enclaves and slums materialized anyway, of course, but they had a tendency to shift, sometimes even trading places. As the city expanded beyond the commissioners' original vision, so did the grid, marking off the flatlands of Queens into vacant rectangles ready to receive future multitudes. It also became the template for virtually every American downtown and for urban expansions as far away as Barcelona and Sapporo, Japan.

In the twentieth century, the New York–style grid practically defined cities, its regularity contrasting with the suburbs' squiggly drives and road hierarchies. It has remained remarkably resilient, partly because its apparent rigidity allows for enormous flexibility: You can build a skyscraper on the same block that once contained only tenements. It also optimizes the city for walkers, who can choose from several (or many) equally direct routes between any two points. The dense mesh keeps a lot of land permanently off the real-estate market—more than a quarter of New York's land area is composed of streets—which means that one of the fundamental urban experiences is using, and fighting over, space that belongs to the public, and always will.

Gum

The first commercial chewing gums were made of spruce-tree sap or paraffin wax, and they were awful. In 1869, the Mexican general Antonio López de Santa Anna—the same one whose forces won the Battle of the Alamo—was living in exile on Staten Island, where he connected with Thomas Adams, a local inventor. They intended to create a rubber substitute that Mexico could export, and experimented with chicle, a viscous tree sap the Mayans had been using as a chew for thousands of years.

The rubber project didn't work out, but after Santa Anna sold him a big pile of chicle and went back to Mexico, Adams and his son had the idea of forming it into balls and offering it at a local drugstore, where it was a minor hit. Chicle later became the fundamental ingredient in Adams's candy-coated product, which he called Chiclets. Not long after, he joined with a partner, William Wrigley, whose place in chewing-gum lore (not to mention with the Chicago Cubs) was soon cemented.

From

HALAL CART

to

HOT DOG

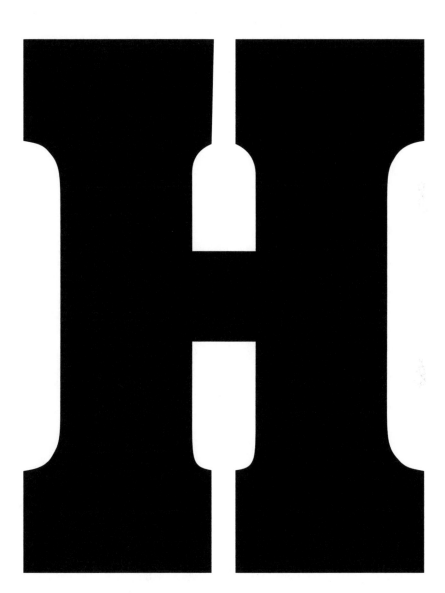

*Hipster totems ca. 2010: trucker hat, ironically enjoyed
Pabst Blue Ribbon, fetishized analog LP, "natural" smokes.*

PHOTOGRAPH BY PLAMEN PETKOV

Halal Cart

On corners all across New York, the faint but distinct smell of griddled, curried meat wafts through the air. The carts and vendors are varied, but the dish they prepare is the same: halal chicken or lamb satisfying Muslim religious requirements, turmeric-hued rice, maybe some shreds of iceberg lettuce and a few slices of tomato, all covered in a mix of rich white sauce and spicy red sauce. The combination—variously and casually referred to as "halal food," "chicken and rice," or just plain "street meat"—is now a staple of the city, as central to New York's food scene as hot dogs or pretzels ever were, even though it didn't exist in its current form until 1990.

"Street food has always been that entry-level job for immigrants, whether it was Italians and pizza or Greeks and gyros," says Zach Brooks, founder of the recommendation website Midtown Lunch. "When Egyptian and South Asian immigrants started arriving in the '80s and '90s, they took over the mantle of these carts. Around the same time, the taxi business started being taken over by a lot of Muslims. The place where people picked up and dropped off their cabs was centralized in Midtown West, where a lot of these carts were."

One of those carts was Trini Paki Boys, at 42nd Street and Sixth Avenue, which opened in 1990. "My husband and I both grew up eating chicken and rice, and both of us love spicy food. He is from Pakistan, and I am from Trinidad," explains Fatima Khan, who ran the cart with her husband, Abdul Sami Khan. "We knew the cuisines would go together, his rice with my curry chicken." The cart gained a cult following among New Yorkers and accolades from foodie publications. The Khans' cart featured a range of specialties, like Trini curry chicken and oxtail stew, but as other vendors began experimenting with their own versions, street meat settled into its tried-and-true form, even if the specifics are often closely guarded. "We keep our white and red sauces a secret," says Muhammed Khan, Fatima and Abdul's son, who took over management of the cart. "There are so many copycats."

Another early innovator, the Halal Guys (Egyptian-born Muhammed Abouelenein, Ahmed Elsaka, and

The Halal Guys cart at 53rd Street and Sixth Avenue.

PHOTOGRAPH BY E. WESTMACOTT

Abdelbaset Elsayed), started with a single cart on the corner of 53rd Street and Sixth Avenue and eventually franchised out to include cafeteria-style dine-in restaurants in eighty-six locations across the country and around the world with more in development.

Halligan Bar

Virtually every fire department in the U.S. buys its men and women the same handheld tool: a forged-steel bar, a couple of feet long, with a forked chisel at one end and a right-angled adze and spike at the other. It's called a Halligan bar, and it's used for anything a firefighter may encounter on the job. It can pop open a door, break a window and clear the frame of glass shards, bash through a Sheetrock wall, and provide the leverage to open a stiff water valve. The FDNY chief Hugh Halligan designed and patented it in 1948, improving on a cruder predecessor known as a Kelly tool (invented a generation earlier by another New York fire captain, John F. Kelly). Among the Halligan's advantages is the way it locks on to a firefighter's ax for easy carrying. The paired tools are known among firefighters by a term that reeks of brawny charm: "the Irons."

Hall of Fame

Before the Baseball Hall of Fame in Cooperstown, or the Basketball Hall of Fame in Massachusetts, or the RV/MH Hall of Fame and Museum in Indiana, there was the Hall of Fame for Great Americans. Built on a New York University campus in the Bronx (now Bronx Community College) in 1901, the Hall of Fame for Great Americans is an outdoor gallery displaying bronze busts of 96 prominent citizens.

The Hall was intended to highlight the achievements of scientists and scholars alongside military heroes. It's old—one might say antiquated—and its roster is almost entirely white and male. Among those honored are Susan B. Anthony; Harriet Beecher Stowe; Elias Howe, who patented the sewing machine; Louis Agassiz, the Swiss-American credited with discovering the Ice Age; and generals William Tecumseh Sherman and Ulysses S. Grant. No one has been inducted into the Hall since the 1970s, but some have been removed. In 2017, the city took down the busts of Robert E. Lee and Stonewall Jackson.

Hare Krishna

In 1965, as many young Americans were looking for a deeper meaning beyond middle-class conformity, A. C. Bhaktivedanta Swami Srila Prabhupada—a 69-year-old ex-pharmacist veteran of Gandhi's civil-disobedience movement in India and a follower of a Hindu guru who tasked him with bringing his teachings to the Anglophone world—stowed away on a cargo ship, arriving in New York with a few Indian rupees and a box of Sanskrit texts.

After a short stint living on the Bowery, the swami found a storefront on Second Avenue in the East Village and started what would become the first Krishna Consciousness temple outside of India, leading workshops on the Bhagavad-Gita, the ancient text that underpins much Hindu belief. Prabhupada preached that, through meditation and chanting and a renunciation of some temporary pleasures of the material world, including alcohol and drugs, one could serve the deity Krishna and obtain a state of spiritual ecstasy in the present.

Prabhupada's big splash in New York occurred in Tompkins Square Park a year later, when the Beat poet Allen Ginsberg joined him and a crowd of followers for a now-iconic public *kirtan* (a group chant of the Hare Krishna mantra) that got written up in the New York *Times*. A plaque commemorates the occasion under the elm tree where they met. This moment marked the start of the International Society for Krishna Consciousness (ISKCON). Throughout the '70s, it grew in cities across the U.S., where the sight of chanting, saffron-robed Hare Krishnas, the men shaved bald save a topknot, became a common symbol of the various countercultural crusades sweeping the nation during and after the Vietnam War and Watergate. It gained in fame when the former Beatle George Harrison became an acolyte and recorded his hit 1970 homage, "My Sweet Lord." ISKCON also alarmed suburban parents who worried that their children might be brainwashed. Many likened it to a cult, and for a time, the "deprogramming" of former members became a hot cottage industry.

In the 1970s, the group operated out of a large head-quarters in midtown Manhattan that included a commune, hotel, and gift shop. In 1977, after Prabhupada died, ISKCON faced financial difficulties, later selling the Manhattan property and splitting into three branches in New Jersey, upstate, and in downtown Brooklyn. It also had to contend with sexual-abuse scandals in boarding schools it runs in the U.S. and India. In very recent years, internal tensions have arisen over whether, and how, to sell the Brooklyn space and build a new temple in Queens, where many current members live. Meanwhile, Hare Krishnas still serve a free weekly vegetarian lunch in Tompkins Square Park under a banner reading "FOOD FOR LIFE," and small pods of the group have sprung up in other parts of the city, assuring that orange robes and droning chants remain part of the urban landscape.

Harlem [1]

Like New Breukelen and Staaten Eylandt, the village of Nieuw Haarlem began as an independent entity established by the Dutch and only belatedly incorporated into New York City. (The Haarlem for which it's named is a good-size city in the Netherlands.) Its redefinition as a center of (and perhaps shorthand for) African-American cultural and intellectual life came much later. In its first developed state, when its rows of brownstones were built, it was a German-American area; around the turn of the twentieth century, the Germans moved on, and it became a mostly Eastern European Jewish enclave with a few middle-class African-Americans. It was crowded but not as much as the Lower East Side, and it was somewhat more affluent with patches of racial segregation.

The dramatic shift began in the years before World War I, when the population turned over again. Jewish residents were starting to move down to the Upper West Side, and tens of thousands of Black Americans from the South, fleeing Jim Crow laws and looking for work, flowed into New York. Many Caribbean Blacks joined them as well. There was, as you'd expect, vigorous and openly racist pushback against people viewed as "interlopers." Around 1900, Philip Payton, a young Black property manager, began running, and eventually buying, buildings as white owners bolted. He saw Harlem as a place of opportunity for African-Americans: It had better housing stock than the tenements downtown and

provided a chance to start fresh. "The very prejudice which has heretofore worked against us," he wrote, "can be turned and used to our profit." By the 1920s, Harlem was a mostly Black neighborhood—albeit still one with a certain amount of white property and business ownership, a state of affairs that was not without tension.

As in so many striving enclaves, a dynamic local culture sprang up. The creative flowering known as the Harlem Renaissance may have had a number of starting points. Was it sparked by the return of African-American soldiers from World War I expecting their rights and finding them limited? The rising popularity of jazz, which broadened the white acknowledgment of Black culture? The Great Migration itself? Marcus Garvey's establishment of the Black-nationalist Universal Negro Improvement Association and African Communities League in 1914? The writings of W.E.B. Du Bois published around that time? The extraordinary dinner held in March 1924 at the Civic Club on West 12th Street, when the community's top writers and publishers (Du Bois, Langston Hughes, Alain Locke, Jessie Fauset, and Countee Cullen, among many others) came together with their counterparts in the white Establishment (Eugene O'Neill, H. L. Mencken) to celebrate Black authors and poets? All were part of the movement's beginnings, along with much more.

The upshot is that, in this era, a lot of Black New Yorkers, living principally though not exclusively in Harlem, began writing, painting, performing, and generally making art that did not accept or proceed from familiar stereotypes of subservience like minstrelsy. Instead, their work was proudly Black, a characterization summed up in a phrase popularized by the Washington, D.C., philosopher-writer Alain Locke: "the New Negro." His anthology by that name, published in 1925 and including some of his own work, posited that pride in identity and the rejection of an automatic assumption of submissiveness should be African-Americans' default worldview.

Although Locke became known as the philosopher, perhaps the godfather, of the Harlem Renaissance, he was hardly its only sage. Langston Hughes produced some of its greatest poetry and criticism and wrote a column for the Chicago *Defender*, probably the country's most significant African-American newspaper. Zora Neale Hurston wrote novels, nonfiction, and satirical short stories, and, from her background as an

① **The Essential Harlem Reading List**

Chosen by Thelma Golden, director of the Studio Museum in Harlem

» **Cane,** by Jean Toomer
» **The Weary Blues,** by Langston Hughes
» **Passing,** by Nella Larsen
» **The New Negro,** edited by Alain Locke
» **Home to Harlem,** by Claude McKay
» **Blue Blood, Plumes,** and **Blue-Eyed Black Boy,** by Georgia Douglas Johnson

» **God's Trombones,** by James Weldon Johnson
» **Plum Bun,** by Jessie Redmon Fauset
» **The Blacker the Berry,** by Wallace Thurman
» **Black No More,** by George S. Schuyler
» **Harlem Renaissance: Art of Black America,** by Mary Schmidt Campbell

anthropologist, collected Caribbean folktales that informed her work. James Weldon Johnson, variously a Broadway songwriter and U.S. consul whose activism led to his role as executive secretary of the NAACP, found time to experiment with fictional autobiography and verse forms inflected with the stylized language of Black preachers. (Also worth noting: There was, for the era, an unusually wide acknowledgment of gay and lesbian relationships, although it fell well short of full acceptance.) Most of all, the vibrant Harlem jazz scene began to catch the ear of the rest of the country and then the world, equaling those in New Orleans and Chicago in reach and influence. The American music we know today is hard to imagine without Duke Ellington's so-called jungle music, played by Black performers for all-white audiences, at the Cotton Club in the 1920s. Among white sophisticates, wrote Hughes, "the Negro was in vogue."

The financial crash of 1929 made it more difficult for artists and musicians to earn a living, though plenty of great books by Harlem Renaissance writers came out in the '30s, including Hurston's 1937 masterpiece, *Their Eyes Were Watching God.* The Apollo Theater opened in a formerly whites-only burlesque house in 1934 and has booked virtually every great African-American artist since then. A riot that shook Harlem in 1935 seemed to mark the end of something. Most of all, much of the neighborhood's distinctive culture (and some of its food; *see also* CHICKEN AND WAFFLES) just got adopted by white America. Big-band popular music gradually subsumed its jazz influences, for example, as Duke Ellington and Count Basie begot Harry James and Glenn Miller. Plenty of Harlem Renaissance artists continued to work, but the next generation's creations felt different and more radical—and some of their proponents came to criticize their forebears, suggesting that they had been too quick to adopt the manner and interests of white society.

The Great Depression was especially tough on Harlem, not least because the neighborhood was redlined by the federal government—that is, declared too risky for mortgage loans, crushing its property values for decades thereafter. After the Second World War, a new kind of Black pride began to move to the forefront in the arts and in the culture at large, one that explicitly and politically demanded parity through the civil-rights movement. Malcolm X's leadership role was largely centered in Harlem, although he lived in East Elmhurst, Queens, and on the night Martin Luther King Jr. was assassinated in 1968, Mayor John Lindsay memorably went straight to Harlem, where he spent the evening walking the streets and talking to residents. It was a gesture of solidarity, albeit a pretty paternalistic one, that did not go unappreciated; it is often said that Lindsay's walk made the difference between Baltimore's and Washington, D.C.'s, destructive riots and New York's relative stability.

In this era, New York City as a whole was getting poorer, losing jobs and well-off white residents to the suburbs. Black New Yorkers, always more vulnerable to economic stressors, once again got hit hard. Even as Harlem's cultural influence in music (*see also* HIP-HOP), athletics (*see also* HOOPS), fashion (*see also* STREETWEAR AS LUXURY FASHION), and literature continued to grow, its physical manifestation was (aside from a few fastidiously kept enclaves of Black affluence like Sylvan Terrace) dangerous and decaying. Many blocks had bricked-up old houses and vacant lots. Widespread dealing and use of heroin and then cocaine left the neighborhood devastated, its social fabric held together by informal support networks of neighbors, social-services workers, small-business owners, and grandparents.

The sharp drop in crime citywide in the 1990s and its attendant rise in property values soon began to hit Harlem hard in a different way. Brownstones that had been left to rot were in no time being bought up and rehabbed. In the early days of this transition, architectural showplaces and burned-out shells sometimes occupied the same block. With affluence, perhaps inevitably, came another demographic change (*see also* GENTRIFICA-TION). The 1990 census counted 672 white people in central Harlem; a 2008 tally recorded nearly 13,800, and around that time, Blacks ceased to be the majority of its residents. One can imagine a future, not unlike that of the nearly vanished Jewish Lower East Side, in which the neighborhood's African-American cultural institutions—the Schomburg Center for Research in Black Culture, the Studio Museum in Harlem, Dance Theatre of Harlem, and, of course, the Apollo—memorialize its contributions after its creative population has moved elsewhere.

Harlem Shake

Before it was called the Harlem Shake, New York's most popular shimmy was called the "albee," so named for Harlem resident Al B, known since 1981 for running onto the court at the Entertainer's Basketball Classic tournament at Harlem's Rucker Park and flailing around. The dance, which its creator later described as "an alcoholic shake" inspired by Egyptian mummies, has enjoyed waves of popularity since, with Sean "Puff Daddy" Combs featuring it in his '90s music videos and Baauer's 2012 viral hit "Harlem Shake" setting off a wave of think pieces about the way Al B—who'd died in 2006, at 43—got left out of the narrative.

Hedge Fund

Near the end of the Depression, a 38-year-old sociology graduate student trudged off to Akron, Ohio, to research his dissertation on industrial relations. Few would have predicted greatness for this not-so-young man. But over the next decade, Alfred Winslow Jones turned his dissertation into a book, which led to a story in *Fortune*, which yielded him a job at the magazine, which became Jones's initiation into the business world and led to the

founding of the first hedge-fund company, A.W. Jones & Co., in 1949. Yes, the low-rent precincts of sociology, the Rust Belt, and journalism all played a part in creating the financial rocket ship of our times.

The term Jones used was *hedged fund*. It promised the Shangri-la of investment strategies: profit without risk. Using a metric he called "velocity" (a precursor to what is now called "beta," the measure of how closely a stock's movement tracks the broader market), he split his holdings into two groups—good stocks, which tended to rise faster than the market in good times and fall slower than the market in bad times, and bad stocks, which did the opposite. He took long positions in the former and short positions in the latter, theoretically ensuring that he'd make money whether the market went up or down.

Elegant as it was, it was a difficult strategy to sustain. Who, after all, likes driving with one foot on the brake? When the market is humming and every jackass is cleaning up, it takes superior discipline to stay hedged and make less. But except for the occasional lapse, Jones had that discipline, eking out a dependable margin that, amplified with borrowed money, produced superior returns. His system demanded humility. It meant admitting that one couldn't outsmart the market.

Jones was a private man with an intellectual bent. John Brooks, the author of *The Go-Go Years*, the definitive account of Wall Street in the '60s, depicts him as a folk hero who resisted the era's hot-money schemes yet still emerged with a fortune. This being Wall Street, even a revered figure like Jones had, shall we say, his short sellers. Barton Biggs, who once worked for him in the '60s, contests the purity of the Jones creation myth in his book *Hedgehogging*. The great founder of hedge funds, Biggs claims, was a stock picker with highbrow pretensions who happened to have enough pull on the Street to gain access to privileged information. The hedging system was a cover for run-of-the-mill sleazy practices, and any crusading regulators who tried to cap

OCTOBER 21, 1968

New York

40 CENTS

Wall Street's New Way To Make Money

The Hedge Fund

such practices were still decades in the future.

It's hard to say what really goes on inside any hedge fund, much less one that existed forty years ago, but Jones's career trajectory hardly makes him look like a rank profiteer. He often took time away from the firm to serve in summer Peace Corps missions and even tried to create a "reverse Peace Corps," in which aid recipients would send their own volunteers back to the U.S.—as a hedge, in a sense, against creating a culture of inferiority among developing countries. According to Brooks, Jones put "his most profound efforts into work not in the cause of profit but in that of humanity." (When Biggs retired after thirty years at Morgan Stanley, what did he do? He started a hedge fund.)

Many of the twenty-first century's new billionaires have been hedge-fund managers, owing to the extremely lucrative fee schedule known as "two and twenty": They are paid 2 percent of the net value of the fund each year, plus 20 percent of the profits. As buyers and sellers of any kind of financial instrument that will allow the management of risk, they have indirectly contributed to the creation of financial products that chop up debt in new ways (*see also* CREDIT DEFAULT SWAP), including things like the subprime-mortgage funds whose implosion led to the 2008 financial collapse.

Jones died in 1988, but his firm lives on as a so-called fund of funds, directing hundreds of millions of its clients' dollars to firms that employ Jonesian principles. "I'd say a lot of the industry is still based on the long-short model," said Robert L. Burch IV in 2008. He's Jones's grandson, and he runs the firm with his father, Jones's son-in-law, operating his own tiny hedge fund on the side. "You just hear a lot less about them." That may be because such assiduous risk avoidance has gone out of style. If Jones was obsessed with beta, today's investors are all about "alpha," the singular pursuit of the above-market return, which is based on the conviction that you can, in fact, outsmart the market.

High Line, The *see* POSTINDUSTRIAL PARK

High Schools, Public Elite

The most successful and influential public high schools in the U.S., hands down, are not the ancient Boston Latin School or the sleek suburban campuses of Westchester, Chicagoland, or Greater Los Angeles. They are the three elite public institutions of New York City: Stuyvesant High School, the Bronx High School of Science, and Brooklyn Technical High School. In a century-plus of educating New Yorkers of all socioeconomic classes (and a much shorter history of coeducation; Brooklyn Tech did not admit girls until 1972), they have produced a long list of authors, CEOs, members of Congress, and movie stars and a wildly disproportionate number of scientists, scholars, doctors, and mathematicians. You could compile an encyclopedia nearly the size of this book about their collective accomplishments, but here's one representative metric: Those three exemplary public schools (graduating only a few thousand kids per year) have produced fourteen Nobel Prize winners.

How they did it is not rocket science (although they have produced a number of actual rocket scientists): There's a rigorous admissions test, known as the SHSAT, and the curriculum is both difficult and flexible. Roughly 30,000 kids take the test each year, and around 18 percent are offered admission. That arrangement has caused controversy over the years because it favors certain personality types and practices (grinds over brilliant creatives, plus anyone willing to endure a ruthless test-prep schedule). A couple of generations ago, Stuyvesant's student body was nearly all white. As of 2018, it was 74 percent Asian-American, with a disproportionally small number of Black and Latino students. Most observers say this is partly due to testing bias and partly cultural (because so many Asian-American immigrant families have bet their future on intense test prep and tutoring). There is talk of chucking the exam, which is unlikely to happen.

Highway, Elevated

On the far western edge of Manhattan, people and goods once moved along the waterfront by rail. It was an awkward arrangement, especially downtown, where the train was preceded by a man blowing a horn to avoid collisions. (He was called a "West Side cowboy.") As the age of the automobile dawned, the two forms of transit began to compete, but there was no way to run a highway down the railbed. A generation of planners struggled to resolve the West Side mess.

The solution was to double-deck it, and the man who got it done was New York's master builder, Robert Moses. In his usual manner, he expanded the project beyond laying a road and called it the "West Side Improvement." In order to build it, he corralled (partly in secret) a huge budget, roughly ten times the amount he revealed to the public. As Robert Caro put it in his Moses biography, *The Power Broker,* the project constituted "the transformation of six and a half miles of muddy wasteland into a park that would make beautiful the city's western waterfront" all the way up to the Henry Hudson Bridge and well beyond the city limits via the Saw Mill River Parkway. Moses had the backing of Manhattan's borough president, Julius Miller, and when the new elevated road was named in January 1931, it was called the Miller Highway.

It was not an unalloyed good. It cut off pedestrians on the West Side, particularly in Riverside Park, from access to the Hudson River. It ceded the best views to drivers, throwing shadow and exhaust down onto surface streets and the people who lived nearby. Nonetheless, every city soon built roads like it, from the Central Artery in Boston to the Embarcadero Freeway in San Francisco to seemingly half of Los Angeles. Moses ran elevated highways all over New York and knitted them together into a system that simultaneously fed, empowered, and strangled it. He wanted to ram two more straight across Manhattan, through lower Greenwich Village and near 34th Street, but they were fought off by activists (*see also* "EYES ON THE STREET").

Looming as it was, the Miller Highway turned out to be undersize for the age of the automobile, in part because it had narrow entrance and exit ramps that were oddly placed between the north- and southbound lanes. By the 1950s, it was obsolete; by the 1970s, it was in severe disrepair. In December 1973, a portion collapsed under the weight of an overloaded dump truck. The road was subsequently closed and demolished, and a complex plan to bury its replacement in a tunnel, called Westway, was stopped by environmental and cost concerns. Today, a surface street with a grassy median carries drivers up and down the West Side below 57th Street. Its descendants completely dominate places like Los Angeles and Houston, but in cities that are attempting to take back some turf from the automobile, mid-century elevated highways are being demolished and replaced. Gone are both San Francisco's Embarcadero Freeway, where the route is now shared at street level by cars and trolleys, and the Central Artery in Boston, where the once grim right-of-way chopped through the middle of the city has become a one-and-a-half-mile-long park.

Hip-Hop [2]

Cities are a lot like bodies. Streets and highways are veins and arteries. Cars and pedestrians pass through like blood cells. Proper circulation keeps cities alive; cut off access, and rot sets in. Robert Moses—the famed "master builder" of New York City and, by extension, the whole of the urban United States—tended to cities as a doctor treats a patient. Through an urban-planning campaign that stretched from the 1920s to the 1970s, Moses sculpted the New York City we've come to know, for better and for worse (*see also* CAST-IRON BUILDING; "EYES ON THE STREET"; HIGHWAY, ELEVATED; LANDMARKS LAW). Moses is the reason there's a functioning zoo in Central Park, a baseball stadium in Queens, public beaches and state parks from Wantagh to Thousand Islands, and bridges and highways connecting the five boroughs. But his ruthless, classist, frankly racist practices also made Moses the architect of tremendous division. His projects frequently decimated neighborhoods and shoveled families into public housing that displaced Latino and African-American residents with surgical precision. "Urban renewal is Negro removal," the writer James Baldwin quipped in the 1960s.

Hip-hop is the child of the disorder that Moses visited on communities of color. His Cross Bronx Expressway bulldozed hundreds of homes and cut a dividing line through the borough that families with cars and means used as a trail out of the crowded city and into quieter lives as commuters in New Jersey and Long Island. White flight precipitated decay in Bronx neighborhoods like Morris Heights. Buildings emptied, property values plummeted, and crime spiked. By the 1970s, gangs like the Black Spades, the Ghetto Brothers, and the Savage Skulls gave teens raised in the dilapidated areas a sense of identity and a means of protection. Bronx youths created their own infrastructure and then their own culture.

Hip-hop was birthed in the summer of 1973, when Jamaican-born Bronx kid Clive Campbell, a.k.a. DJ Kool Herc, cleverly crossed Kingston dancehall and sound-system culture with thriving American funk music. Herc, who was DJing his sister's late-summer birthday party one night in the rec room of their building at 1520 Sedgwick Avenue in Morris Heights, decided to show off a trick he'd been practicing in private. Instead of playing songs all the way through, he cued up two copies of the same record, zeroing in on the dance break and using two turntables to run the part back on a continuous loop, like a merry-go-round. He was looking for the perfect beat, whittling leaner, tighter dance-floor routines out of existing hit records. Herc's isolation of the white-hot instrumental sections of James Brown and Incredible Bongo Band records is the backbone of the sound of rap music. Catchy, repeating instrumental passages were fertile ground for dancers and rappers alike. The practice made maestros out of children who couldn't afford instruments and weren't given a musical education. The music made party planners out of anyone who could jack enough juice to power turntables, microphones, and speakers.

Early hip-hop culture was a genius multimedia found-art exercise. Street artists (*see also* GRAFFITI AS ART) tagged their names on wrecked buildings and spread their work on passing train cars. Rappers and DJs cut up their parents' records to give voice to a new generation of inner-city blues. Rockers and breakers (*see also* BREAK-DANCING) gave Nureyev and Baryshnikov stiff competition on cardboard floors. Time and practice created professionals. Toasters became MCs. DJs became producers. Dancers became crews. As records like the Sugarhill Gang's "Rapper's Delight," Kurtis Blow's "The Breaks," and Grandmaster Flash and the Furious Five's "The Message" took off in the late 1970s and early 1980s, hip-hop slipped into the national consciousness. Documentaries like *Style Wars* showcased the limitless creativity and effortless style of New York City street artists and performers, while the box-office success of scripted motion pictures like *Beat Street*, *Krush Groove*, and *Breakin'* carried the culture out to the moviegoing public worldwide (albeit somewhat churlishly in the case of *Breakin'* and the shaky sequels and knockoffs it inspired).

Krush Groove lent greater visibility to party promoter Russell Simmons, producer Rick Rubin, and soon-to-be superstars LL Cool J and Beastie Boys, the first emissaries of the hip-hop superpower Def Jam Recordings, founded in 1984. Def Jam upped the ante on the gains made by producer and executive Sylvia Robinson's Sugar Hill Records—which had released singles by the seminal Sugarhill Gang, Treacherous Three, and Grandmaster Flash and the Furious Five—by focusing its attention on full-length studio albums. The first great rap full-lengths had been delivered by Kurtis Blow, who, after making the first commercially successful rap record, 1979's "Christmas Rappin'," proved a rapper could carry an entire project with his self-titled 1980 debut, and by the Furious Five, whose songwriting and turntablist chops in the singles "The Message" and "The Adventures of Grandmaster Flash on the Wheels of Steel" had carried over onto 1982's *The Message*. But barring opuses like Run-DMC's self-titled debut and Whodini's *Escape*, both released in 1984, early rap was a field of great singles and patchy albums. A new class of rhymers and producers changed that. LL Cool J's *Radio* introduced the world to the Queens kid's youthful arrogance. The Beastie Boys' *Licensed to Ill* made rap stars out of three Jewish punk rockers. Salt-N-Pepa's *Hot, Cool & Vicious* and their platinum-selling single "Push It" were important strides for women in the culture.

Fruitful live engagements like Run-DMC's Raising Hell Tour and the Beasties' opening slot on Madonna's Virgin Tour in the mid-'80s added pop fans and middle-class suburban teens to the blend of Bronx and Manhattan kids and downtown onlookers who composed the early hip-hop audience. Each tour attracted new eyes and ears, and each creative stroke opened new paths of expression. A happy accident in a Times Square studio caused producer Marley Marl, of the Queens-based Juice Crew, to swipe the drum track off an older record, and the art of sampling was born. Rap music quickly evolved from the coarse synth and drum-machine textures of the early-'80s records into a lusher, more organic sound. Greatness in hip-hop production became a question of who had the keenest taste and the best record collection as well as who'd mastered torque and finesse.

Sampling transformed the onetime Los Angeles dance-music maestro Dr. Dre, of the electro pioneers World Class Wreckin' Cru, into the architect of the plush gangsta funk of N.W.A, Dre's own *The Chronic*, and his protégé Snoop Dogg's *Doggystyle*. By the early 1990s, hip-hop had grown from an accidental inner-city latchkey-kid culture into nationwide art and commerce with distinctive regional flavors. An expanding library of end-to-end great studio albums suggested the young folks creating them hadn't fallen for a new fad; they'd arrived at the future of American music.

Notoriety brought success and strife in equal measure. The more households the Black-activist Public Enemy and the gun-toting N.W.A beamed into, the more puzzled parents felt threatened by the music. As future Second Lady of the United States Tipper Gore's Parents Music Resource Center turned up the pressure on rock and pop music it deemed explicit, obscenity trials endangered the future of 2 Live Crew, whose 1989 album *As Nasty as They Wanna Be* pushed a conversation about offensive rap lyrics centered on its crass lead single, "Me So Horny." The group also came under fire for its version of Roy

Orbison's "Oh, Pretty Woman," released on the clean version of *Nasty* not long after Orbison's death without permission from Acuff-Rose, the country-music publishing titan that owned the rights.

Wars over decency and sampling would plague hip-hop from the 1980s into the early 1990s, when rap producers' freewheeling, Wild West attitude toward intellectual property broke down as new legal practices were introduced. Records containing explicit lyrics had to display parental-advisory notices on the cover. Samples had to be cleared by the parties who owned the copyrights. The latter policy quickly placed an expensive premium on psychedelic, sample-filled collage art like Public Enemy's *Fear of a Black Planet* and the Beastie Boys' *Paul's Boutique*. Going forward, rap producers either shelled out big money for recognizable samples, as Dr. Dre and flashy New York hitmakers like Bad Boy Records head Sean "Puff Daddy" Combs dutifully did; dug deeper for more obscure and affordable sounds, as the architects of East Coast jazz and conscious rap would over the next decade; or simply resorted to programming everything themselves. On the East and West Coasts, the young megastars 2Pac and the Notorious B.I.G. and their respective camps became embroiled in a war of words that would ultimately claim both rappers' lives in tragic shootings in the mid-1990s. As that battle raged, other regions surged to the fore.

Hip-hop's passage from the 1990s into the new millennium saw the culture gain a powerful footing in new territories. The tongue-tying fast raps of Midwest rhymers like Bone Thugs-N-Harmony and Twista set the stage for the lyrical dynamism of Eminem. Atlanta's OutKast wove funk, blues, rock, and soul into indelible hit records. Nelly blew up out of St. Louis infusing gangsta-rap stories with nursery-rhyme melodies. Lil' Kim, Foxy Brown, Eve, and Trina snatched power back from male rappers whose lyrics treated women like objects. Missy Elliott, Timbaland, Pharrell Williams, and Chad Hugo invigorated rap and R&B with outré sounds and unflappable style. New York and California not only were home to haughty tough-guy rap sensations like 50 Cent, DMX, and Xzibit but also were breeding grounds for indie artists who'd been squeezed out of airplay as rap radio became big business and media conglomerates snatched up stations, demanding they play only the music that retained ears and sold advertising. Rap indie labels like

Run DMC, Hollis Queens, 1984

"This is less what hipsters would have (Neutral Milk Hotel) and more what they should have. And by 'hipsters,' I mean: people who seek to cultivate a lifestyle around meaningful, often idiosyncratic, sometimes (but not necessarily) obscure art. This is music for insecure people who also have their (bleeding) hearts in the right place and just want to live a big life but are also scared of other humans. Cool albums that show you speak the same language with fellow weirdos you probably want to fuck (or at least want to want to fuck you)."

IN NO PARTICULAR ORDER:
- **Pet Sounds,** by the Beach Boys
- **White Light/White Heat,** by the Velvet Underground
- **Blue Lines,** by Massive Attack
- **Fear of a Black Planet,** by Public Enemy
- **Surfer Rosa,** by Pixies

Definitive Jux, Anticon, and Stones Throw Records have kept smart, weird, insular rap afloat through dramatic changes in the look and feel of the culture that have come to pass since the 1990s.

The hip-hop scene of the past decade may not sound much like the stuff piped out of stereo systems in the twentieth century, but it bears some strong familial resemblance. The trap generation recalls the ingenuity of the 1970s class as it records and produces in bedrooms and closets on pilfered, cracked beat-making software. The amateurish, exploratory spirit of the early-1980s rap sensations is on display as today's young rappers sort out their skills and strengths through public trial and error. The DIY distribution tactics of the 1990s southern-rap pioneers are mirrored in self-released street albums and mixtapes. The culture changes, but the fundamentals—beats, rhymes, life—hold steady. One constant, as hip-hop culture rolls out of its fifth decade, is the disadvantaged youth hurtling past insurmountable odds. Hold them back, and they'll simply find a way over, under, or around you.

Hipster [3]

Before it was the defining subcultural persona of the 2010s, the hipster was a Black subcultural figure of the late 1940s, best anatomized by Anatole Broyard in a 1948 essay for *Partisan Review* called "A Portrait of the Hipster." A decade later, the hipster had evolved into a white subcultural figure (*see also* BEATS, THE). This hipster—the reference here is to Norman Mailer's 1957 essay "The White Negro," published in *Dissent*—was explicitly defined by the desire of a white avant-garde to disaffiliate itself from whiteness, with its stain of Eisenhower, the bomb, and the corporation, and achieve the "cool" knowledge and exoticized energy, lust, and violence of Black Americans. (*Hippie* itself was originally an insulting diminutive of *hipster*, a jab at the sloppy kids who hung

around North Beach or Greenwich Village after 1960 and didn't care about jazz or poetry, only drugs and fun.)

In both the Black and white incarnations, the hipster in essence had been about superior knowledge—what Broyard called "a priorism." He insisted hipsterism had developed from a sense that minorities in America were subject to decisions made about their lives by conspiracies of power they could never possibly know. The hip reaction was to insist, purely symbolically, on forms of knowledge they possessed before anyone else, indeed before the creation of positive knowledge—a priori. Broyard focused on the password language of hip slang.

The return of the term after 1999 reframed the knowledge question. *Hipster*, in its revival, referred to an air of knowing about exclusive things before anyone else. The new young strangers acted, as people said then, "hipper than thou." At first, their look may have overlapped enough with a short-lived moment of neo-Beat and '50s nostalgia (goatees, fedoras, *Swingers*-style duds) to help call up the term. But these hipsters were white and singularly unmoved by race and racial integration.

Indeed, the early-aughts hipster inverted Broyard's model to particularly unpleasant effect: trucker hats; undershirts called "wifebeaters," worn alone; the aesthetic of basement-rec-room pornography, flash-lit Polaroids, and fake-wood paneling; Pabst Blue Ribbon; "porno" or "pedophile" mustaches; aviator glasses; Americana T-shirts from church socials and pig roasts; tube socks; the late albums of Johnny Cash; tattoos.

These were the most visible emblems of a small and surprising subculture that thrived in Williamsburg and the Lower East Side, where the source of a priori knowledge seemed to be nostalgia for suburban whiteness. As the White Negro had once fetishized Blackness, the White Hipster fetishized the violence, instinctiveness, and rebelliousness of lower-middle-class "white trash."

By 2003, though, an overwhelming feeling of an end to hipsterism permeated the subculture. The wifebeaterwearer's machismo no longer felt subversive, and while the more sinister strain of White Hipster style started to diminish, the artistic concern with innocence turned from human absolution to the fragile world of furry creatures, trees, and TRS-80s. Suddenly, a "green" hipster had succeeded the white. The points of reference shifted from midwestern suburbs to animals, wilderness, plus the occasional Native American. Best perhaps to call this the Hipster Primitive, for linked to the Edenic nature-as-playground motif was a fascination with early-1980s computer electronics and other rudimentary or superannuated technologies.

Music led the artistry of this phase, and the period's flagship publication, the record-review website and tastemaker Pitchfork, picked up as *Vice* declined. In Pitchfork-approved bands, listeners heard animal sounds and Beach Boys–style harmonies; lyrics and videos pointed to rural redoubts, on wild beaches and in forests; life transpired in some more loving, spacious, and manageable future. Women took up cowboy boots, like country squiresses off to visit the stables. Men gave up the porno mustache for the hermit or lumberjack beard. Flannel returned, as did hunting jackets in red-and-black check. Scarves proliferated unnecessarily, conjuring a cold woodland night (if wool) or a desert encampment (if a kaffiyeh). As CDs declined, LP records gained sales for the first time in two decades. The most advanced hipster youth even deprived their bikes of gears.

Through both phases of contemporary hipsterism, and no matter where their adherents identify themselves on the knowingness spectrum, there exists a common element essential to their identity: their relationship to consumption. Adopting the rhetoric but not the politics of the counterculture, hipsters convinced themselves that buying the right mass products individualizes them as transgressive. The neighborhood organization of hipsters—their tight-knit colonies of similar-looking, slouching people—represents not hostility to authority (as among punks or hippies) but a superior community of status, where the game of knowing-in-advance can be played with maximum refinement.

Home Security System

In the mid-1960s, as urban crime rates rose and rose again (*see also* MAYHEM), New Yorkers grew nervous and fearful in their homes. Marie Van Brittan Brown, an African-American nurse in Jamaica, Queens, assisted by her electronics-expert husband, Albert, patented a new type of security device: a video camera that could be attached inside a door and was height-adjustable along a set of peepholes, allowing it to catch the faces of tall and short visitors alike. The camera feed went to a video monitor, wirelessly, and a remotely released lock could open the door from within. We've been buzzing people into our buildings ever since. Today's internet-enabled Ring doorbell is a hyperconnected version of the Browns' influential invention—as is, arguably, the surveillance state.

Hoops

"Basketball belongs to the cities," Pete Axthelm wrote fifty years ago in *The City Game.* He was being modest: At the time, basketball belonged to New York. Since its invention in Springfield, Massachusetts, in 1891, there haven't been many innovations in basketball history that can't somehow be traced to the five boroughs.

The aspect of the sport most treasured by New Yorkers has been and always will be the playground game. With more than 1,800 outdoor courts scattered across the city, concrete half-courts became incubators for generations of talent and a streetball tradition richer than anything the Knicks have achieved in the past half-century. Many of New York's earliest stars, like Nat Holman, known as the "world's greatest basketball player" in the 1920s, came

④ **The Best
Hot Dog in NYC**

Chosen by New
York's *"Underground
Gourmet"* columnists,
*Rob Patronite
and Robin Raisfeld*

In *When Harry Met Sally...,*
what Sally is having during the
"I'll have what she's having"
gag (*see also* ROMANTIC COMEDY)
is a turkey sandwich, but
most people remember it as
pastrami. Yet if anything were
to inspire someone to unleash
ecstatic moans while dining
at Katz's, it would be the
hot dog. **Everything you**

**want in a frankfurter, you'll
find at Katz's:** a good amount
of char, some flavor-enhancing
mojo imparted by a greasy old
griddle, the essential natural-
casing snap, a tongue-tingling
jolt of salt, and a garlic-forward
blend of spices that finds its
gustatory counterpoint in
the soft, bland roll that cradles
it. Some deli aficionados we

know go to Katz's solely for
the dogs. Other super-*fressers*
consider a proper full-course
dinner chez Katz to consist
of the following: amuse-bouche
(hot dog), appetizer (potato
knish), intermezzo (swig
of Dr. Brown's Cel-Ray), main
course (pastrami sandwich),
salad course (coleslaw),
and dessert (hot dog).

from Jewish and Irish enclaves and learned to pass, drib-
ble, and shoot in neighborhood parks from the Lower East
Side to Brownsville, Brooklyn.

The playgrounds of Harlem (*see also* HARLEM)
produced fewer athletes who'd eventually be recognized as pioneers—owing to the segregation and quotas
that stained the college and pro sport—but the quality
of play was without equal anywhere in the world.
"There was no question that they were better than NBA
players," said Satch Sanders, an eight-time NBA champion with the Boston Celtics, of the competition he
witnessed in Harlem summer leagues and pickup
games as a teenager in the 1950s.

Over the years, those tournaments became a proving
ground. Future Hall of Famers like Wilt Chamberlain,
Dave Cowens, Allen Iverson, and Kobe Bryant made
pilgrimages to the New York asphalt. Locals who gave
the NBA stars all they could handle—Earl Manigault,
Joe "the Destroyer" Hammond, Pee Wee Kirkland, Ed
"Booger" Smith, and countless others—became legends,
guys who never made the league but, according to local
lore, were better than most pros. Harlem native Kareem
Abdul-Jabbar once called Manigault the "best basketball player in the history of New York City," and Manigault's nickname, "the Goat" (tidily enough, an acronym
for "greatest of all time"), became a go-to term for
superlativeness, as well as an inescapable emoji. The
Knicks could stay hopeless forever, but as long as crowds
are pressing up against chain-link fences to watch summer hoops at Harlem's Rucker Park, the Cage at West
4th Street, Inwood's Dyckman Park, and Brooklyn's
Soul in the Hole, New York will still be the mecca.

Hot Dog [4]

How contested are the origins of the term *hot dog*?
Enough that, in 2004, three of America's top word historians wrote a 300-page monograph debunking the

biggest myths. It wasn't coined at a New York Giants
baseball game or a Madison Square Garden bicycle race,
where the famous *Evening Journal* cartoonist and
slang-slinger extraordinaire Tad Dorgan supposedly
tried sketching "dachshund sandwiches" in 1906 only
to realize he couldn't spell *dachshund*. Rather, it was at
1890s Yale, where immature students loved joking
about sausages filled with dog meat.

Fortunately, the man who served the first hot dog has
a more palatable story. Many believe he was a German
immigrant, Charles Feltman, who sold it from a pushcart in Coney Island sometime between 1867 and 1871,
possibly with the help of a local baker, Ignatz
Frischmann, who fashioned its special oblong bun.
Today, Nathan's Famous is the name most New Yorkers
know, and the young Nathan Handwerker got his start
in 1915 slicing buns at the restaurant Feltman founded.
Years later, company brochures declared that Feltman
was "widely known to have invented the hot dog,"
although his menus never employed that term. They
used either "dachshund sandwich" (after the shape) or
"red hot" (after the color and temperature).

Challengers to Feltman's legacy are many, the crowd
favorites being the Giants concessionaire Harry Stevens
(debunked) and the St. Louis sausage purveyor Anton
Ludwig Feuchtwanger. The latter supposedly served his
franks with gloves so patrons' hands would stay clean,
but one day he switched to a cheaper, far tastier wedge
of bread, possibly at his wife's insistence. (Getting to
utter "Feuchtwanger" when talking about wiener-making
no doubt aids his popularity.)

Feltman's restaurant sold millions of hot dogs a year
until its closure in the 1950s. The property became part
of Coney Island's Astroland park, and in 2010 the building that housed the original Feltman's kitchen was torn
down. But hungry New Yorkers can still buy hot dogs
from one of the city's 4,200 street vendors inspired by
his pushcart.

From
IBOGAINE
to
"IVY LEAGUE"

*The incubator: originally for chickens,
then for preemies.*
PHOTOGRAPH BY JAMIE CHUNG

Ibogaine

The psychoactivity of the iboga tree, a perennial rainforest shrub native to western Central Africa, was discovered by the Pygmy tribe of Central Africa, who ate its bark to induce visions and heal an assortment of ailments. They passed the knowledge on to the Bwiti tribe of Gabon, who passed the knowledge to French explorers, who brought it back to Europe. Some four decades later, French scientists extracted the main alkaloid from the iboga plant and called it ibogaine; some three decades after *that*, they began marketing it as a stimulant called Lambarene. But the drug also had anti-addictive properties, which were discovered in New York by a Bronx-born NYU film graduate named Howard Lotsof. Lotsof was a heroin addict who experimented regularly with hallucinogens. In 1962, when he was nineteen, he got his hands on ibogaine in the form of a white powder—which he promptly swallowed. The ensuing trip lasted thirty-two hours, during which he didn't use heroin once. When it ended, he realized he hadn't experienced a single withdrawal symptom. He then persuaded six heroin-addicted friends to try the drug, and afterward, five of them immediately stopped using heroin. Lotsof dedicated the rest of his life to pioneering the anti-addictive applications of ibogaine—lobbying public officials, pharmaceutical companies, and researchers and even persuading the FDA to approve a clinical trial in the mid-'90s (which was never completed due to, among other impediments, concerns over cardiotoxicity). Though the drug remains illegal in the United States, its efficacy in treating the patients who were given the chance to try it is indisputable: In the terminated trial, twenty-seven of the thirty-three subjects demonstrated significantly lower withdrawal scores and decreased opiate cravings.

Illuminated Advertising Sign

It lit up Madison Square in 1892 from the north side of a hotel at 23rd Street and Fifth Avenue. Eighty feet high, that first sign spelled out MANHATTAN BEACH—SWEPT BY OCEAN BREEZES in 1,457 lightbulbs. By 1900, it had been replaced with the first such sign to advertise products: fifty-seven varieties of preserved foods and condiments, the display topped with a 43-foot-long flashing illuminated pickle that read HEINZ. The sign lasted only a few years because the edifice on which it hung was demolished. In 1902, the Flatiron Building rose in its place (*see also* SKYLINE).

I Love Lucy *see* SITCOM

I ♥ NY.

Hoping to counteract New York City's bad public image, the New York State tourism board in 1976 asked Milton Glaser—the graphic designer who, a decade earlier, had co-founded *New York* (*see also* NEW YORK MAGAZINE; NEW JOURNALISM)—to come up with a logo to accompany its new ad campaign. Glaser presented a typographic design that was approved by the agency Wells Rich Greene and the state's William Doyle. A week afterward, Glaser later recalled, he was "doodling in a cab" and, with a red crayon on the back of an envelope, scratched out three letters and one glyph. When he got to a phone, he called Doyle and said, "I have something better."

What he'd drawn was a simple rebus that, at first, might not have seemed as perfect as it turned out to be.

It's hard to convey aloud without saying "I Heart Enn Wye." But I♥NY has the makings of an ideal logotype: It is concise, graspable, and cheery. From a graphic-design standpoint, it works at any size, whether on a billboard or the side of a pencil, and it is flexible because the letters can be stacked into a square or laid out in a row. Glaser gave the trademark to New York at no charge, calling it a public service for his state and his hometown.

It's knocked off everywhere now. The state of Virginia later stuck a heart into its preexisting "Virginia Is for Lovers" slogan (it became LO♥ERS). The heart-for-love logo is nearly universal, having been knitted into sweaters, molded into Christmas ornaments, and plastered on anything it can be plastered on. (There are some dumb versions that superimpose the word LOVE onto the heart.) Glaser's original back-of-the-envelope taxicab sketch is now in the collection of the Museum of Modern Art. And, of course, cell-phone users communicate in such hieroglyphics all day every day in the form of emoji.

Immigration [1]

The first immigrants to what became the United States arrived from the west rather than the east, over the now-vanished land bridge at the Bering Strait that allowed the future native population of North America to walk over from Asia. The first people known to live in Manhattan were here about 9,000 years ago, but they moved on as the food supply became scarce. A second people, the Lenape (now often referred to as the Delaware people and principally relocated to a reservation in Oklahoma), resettled the area around 1000 B.C.E. and lived well, farming and sustaining themselves on the harbor's abundant seafood.

The European explorers who would begin the process of driving them out first touched this land in the sixteenth and early seventeenth centuries: Giovanni da Verrazzano, Henry Hudson, Peter Minuit. Each was

followed by ships, by land claims, by settlement and resettlement and trade. The first old-world descendant to live on Manhattan Island was Juan Rodriguez, a member of a Dutch trading ship's crew who arrived in 1613. Born in the Dominican Republic to an African mother and a Portuguese father, he was thus the first Black New Yorker, the first Latino New Yorker, and the first European New Yorker. Like millions of people who came after him, he came to visit, liked it, and insisted on staying in Manhattan when the rest of his party headed home.

For the next two centuries, there was no formal procedure to admit arriving foreigners. People just disembarked and found a place to live. (Or were brought here involuntarily: Slavery was fully legal in New York until 1799 and was gradually abolished over the next thirty years.) It took a few decades after the founding of the United States to formalize "immigration" as an actual thing. Record keeping began in 1820, at which time most immigrants were from England and Scotland. The first massive wave crested during the Irish potato famine, which began in 1845. Roughly half a million Irish entered the U.S. within five years, and because New York was the country's biggest port of entry, the lion's share of them came through here; approximately half of those stayed in town. A hundred thousand German immigrants came over during the same period. By 1860, the foreign-born population of today's five boroughs had topped 540,000—nearly half of the total population of 1.16 million—and was growing fast. With that volume came the need for systemization, and on August 3, 1855, the country's first immigration center opened at the bottom tip of Manhattan. Occupying the shell of a disused fort called Castle Clinton (which had formerly been on a little island until the channel was filled in), it was called the Emigrant Landing Depot at Castle Garden and was run jointly by New York State and the city.

The numbers of immigrants were big in the 1840s

and 1850s but were dwarfed by what was to come a generation later. Around 1880, the economy of Southern Europe, particularly Italy, went sour, aided by another agricultural blight and the changes wrought by the Industrial Revolution. At the same time, Eastern and Southern European Jews began to come under attack as a newly invigorated climate of anti-Semitism took hold. In both cases, people began to leave for America— not a few hundred thousand in total but a few hundred thousand per year. The port city where most of them landed could not possibly house that many people, but the city needed vast numbers of hands to fill its factory jobs and wash dishes and cut hair and lay bricks, and New York absorbed a lot of the flood. In 1860, the already immigrant-swelled population of Manhattan had been 805,658. In 1900, it was 1.44 million.

Castle Garden was soon overwhelmed. (Bad management and corruption at the center didn't help.) At the same time, Americans' fear of the newcomers led to concerns about the importation of disease and bad behavior. The solution was, effectively, a quarantine. A new, larger station was constructed a few hundred yards offshore on Oyster Island, so called for its abundant shellfish. Renamed Ellis Island and over time septupled in size by the addition of landfill, it became the country's official arrival spot on January 1, 1892. The latest arrivals' stories played out under the eye of an extremely tall immigrant Frenchwoman, sturdily built of copper and iron and carrying a torch and a tablet. The Statue of Liberty was still gleaming like a penny and nearly brand new; she had not yet acquired her green patina.

After a fire leveled the first Ellis Island structure in 1897, it was rebuilt, larger and more ornate, with an adjacent hospital added soon after. At its peak, around 1907, more than 1 million people a year came through Ellis Island—"12 new Americans a minute," as a New York *World* headline put it. Newcomers were checked for illnesses (mainly tuberculosis, cholera, and trachoma, a highly contagious form of pink eye) and questioned. *Are you a polygamist, an indigent, an anarchist?* Most people made it through processing in a few hours, but some were kept in the island's hospital for weeks, and a relative few were sent back overseas. (One thing Ellis Island's clerks did not do was actively rename families. That's a myth. The truncation and Anglicization of surnames was largely done by immigrants themselves, that scene in *The*

Godfather Part II notwithstanding.) The first person through was an Irish teenager named Annie Moore.

The influx slowed during World War I. By then, the casual prejudice against immigrants—which had been part of their experience for a long time, starting with signs reading HELP WANTED, NO IRISH NEED APPLY in shop windows and continuing with various bans on Jews and Italians and other groups—had coupled with the increasingly robust eugenics movement, and President Calvin Coolidge was willing to go along. The Johnson-Reed Act, also known as the Immigration Act of 1924, nearly slammed the door shut. It set country-by-country quotas for future arrivals based on the rates of immigration in 1890 rather than more recent years, thus keeping out virtually all the Jews, Italians, Hungarians, and Greeks whose numbers had exploded thereafter. In the subsequent four decades, barely anyone was admitted except citizens' relatives and a few wartime refugees. Ellis Island soon became a quiet shell of itself and was closed for good in 1954, by which time it had processed 12 million people. Forty percent of today's Americans have an ancestor who came through there.

The tide came back in again in 1965, with federal passage of the Immigration and Nationality Act. (In a nice historical turn, Emanuel Celler, who, as a young Jewish congressman from Brooklyn had fought the passage of the 1924 act, was still in office 41 years later. He sponsored the bill, then stood at the signing alongside President Lyndon Johnson as the new law superseded the old.) The new rules didn't throw the gates wide open, as they had been a century earlier, but they did rebalance the demographics of who was coming in. The numbers of arrivals from China, India, South Korea, Africa, and Latin America soon began to climb. They weren't coming by ship anymore, of course; instead they came through Kennedy airport or San Francisco International, and although they were more easily settled anywhere in the country (because they could catch a connecting flight to, say, Dearborn or St. Paul), a lot of them stayed put in the big coastal cities. To take one representative population as an example, in 1960 there were 19,789 Chinese-born Americans in New York City. In 2020, there were nearly 400,000. There are more immigrants in New York now—roughly 3.1 million—than ever before.

*Arriving,
ca. 1905.*
PHOTOGRAPH BY
EDWIN LEVICK

The invisible dog: a one-joke novelty turned curiously enduring product.
PHOTOGRAPH BY
PETE MCARTHUR

146

② **The Definitive
Details of the
Ivy League Suit**

*Described by
J. Press chief
merchandising officer
Robert Squillaro*

"The suit that has been traditionally worn by Ivy League attendees and grads is the classic three-roll-two undarted 'sack' suit. It features **lightweight internal components, a natural shoulder, and a center hook vent. The trousers are flat front.** Solid colors, subtle stripes, or plaids are the patterns of choice."

Incubator

"Incubators are not a new invention," said the New York *Times* on March 15, 1894. "They have been used for years with great success in hatching chickens." Entirely new, however, was the idea of warming up a newborn premature baby, and that was what a scientist named W. G. Robinson had done in the back room of a shop on East 26th Street. Robinson was a leading surgical-instrument maker, known for his research in the very early understanding of germ theory, and had built incubators for bacterial cultures. In 1893, he learned of a baby boy, Joseph Grevert, born three months premature, and put him into what was called the "brooder," a glass case three and a half feet long, heated to 100 degrees Fahrenheit. Its warmth was believed to have saved the child from certain death.

Less than a year later, Robinson did it again, this time for the premature daughter of a millionaire from Murray Hill named Edward Clarence Haight, whose wife had died in childbirth. This time, he got a significant amount of press owing to the prominence of the Haight family—and because Robinson later sued him for back rent on the incubator.

Invisible Dog

There are novelty crazes that stick around past their expiration date (the Hula Hoop comes to mind) and then there are ... others. Around 1972 or so, it was the invisible dog's turn. Basically, it was a leash stiffened with a thin steel rod so you could walk around while appearing to have a pet where there was no pet. It didn't last, but it did prompt guffaws and chortles for a few years on city streets and seaside boardwalks alike.

Two inventor-entrepreneurs laid claim to the invisible dog, though neither was exactly its creator. One was S. David Walker (such an appropriate name!), a

New York novelty manufacturer who resettled in Kansas City; he'd started out as a pitchman selling trick card decks to amateur magicians and later got into the decorative-foil-balloon game early and lucratively. The other was George Zorbas, a World War II veteran who manufactured the leashes in a Brooklyn factory at 51 Bergen Street. (The building now houses an arts center called the Invisible Dog.) But the invisible dog made his first nonappearance well before that. In 1963, Allen Funt came up with the idea and constructed one for *Candid Camera*, his prankster TV show that pioneered an entire genre. In the segment, an actor walks the streets of New York with his petless leash as startled bystanders gape and a hidden movie camera catches their reactions.

Iron, Electric

A clothes iron—a "flatiron," colloquially—used to be a triangular slab of metal that you heated on a fire, repeatedly, as you worked. The New Yorker Henry Seely, an associate of Thomas Edison, was the man who figured out that tucking an electrical resistance element inside would heat up the tool flamelessly. He and his business partners, R. N. Dyer and Samuel Insull, received the patent on June 6, 1882. The world has been ever so slightly less wrinkly ever since.

"Ivy League" ²

The term for the athletic association of eight elite universities in the Northeast (Harvard, Yale, Princeton, Brown, Cornell, Dartmouth, the University of Pennsylvania, and Columbia) is newer than you think. Most histories credit a sportswriter from the New York *Herald Tribune* named Caswell Adams, citing his use of the term in print, slightly disparagingly, for the first time in 1937. But a few references precede his. Stanley Woodward, a colleague of Adams's on the *Trib*'s sports desk, had used the term *ivy colleges* a couple of years earlier, and a 1935 AP story about Brown University's induction into the group referred to it as "the so-called 'Ivy League'" that was "in the process of formation." Given that both the AP and the *Trib* were just a few blocks apart in midtown, the term didn't have to travel far to gain wider use. The eight schools signed their football-league agreement in 1945 and finally started playing under that name in 1956.

By then, the name *Ivy League* was established to denote not just the universities' athletic teams but the exclusive schools themselves, becoming colloquial shorthand for the ruling elite. As such, the term even extended to a style of men's clothing. The "Ivy League suit," a.k.a. the sack suit—an unflashy, single-breasted American cut, usually with three buttons (the top one unused and only half visible behind a rolled lapel), straight out of the window display at Brooks Brothers or J. Press—came to dominate businesswear in the 1950s and 1960s in large part through its association with the eastern American Establishment, as epitomized by the Kennedys. Its popularity has waxed and waned in the decades since, but it never disappears. A story told at Brooks Brothers involves a customer who returned a new suit several years back after the pants had worn out prematurely. It turned out he'd accidentally switched them with those from an almost indistinguishable suit he had purchased in 1957.

From
JAYWALKING
to
JUNK BONDS

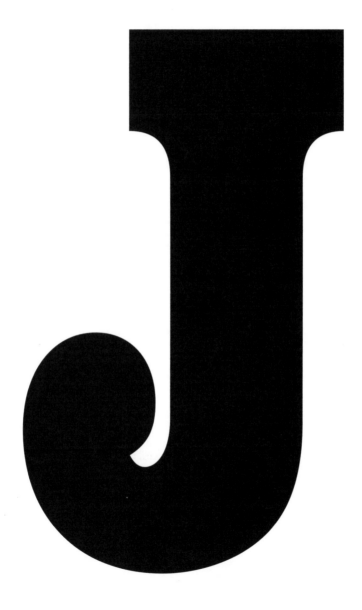

Jell-O: pioneered by Peter Cooper.
PHOTOGRAPH BY JOE LINGEMAN

① **How to Love
Your Jeans**

*From Jeff Rudes, CEO
and creative director
of L'AGENCE*

▸ **Get a good fit.**

"A jean is the most emotional piece of clothing in a woman's closet: When she looks in the mirror, she loves the way her butt looks; people tell her how great she looks; her significant other tells her how hot she is. What does all of this have to do with finding the right jeans? When shopping, be willing to spend some time on the treasure hunt. Take the time to try on different fits and be open to suggestions from the salespeople. You may love a fit that you weren't expecting."

▸ **Make them last.**

"The good thing is jeans don't need much care: Wash them as recommended. Depending on whether you want them

Jaywalking

At the turn of the century, a "jay" was a rube, someone who didn't know how cities work, a person who'd bump into you on the sidewalk while gawking at the sights. Or, of course, someone who'd step into the street without looking. With the advent of the automobile, "jaywalking" turned from annoying to life-threatening, linguistically shifting the blame for any injury from driver to pedestrian. By 1915, New York's police commissioner, Arthur Woods, was using the term while proposing a law requiring pedestrians to cross only at street corners. The *Times* both editorialized against it and published a vehement letter suggesting that "It is time for pedestrians to assert themselves and to prevent the issuing of ukases by certain czars who are appointed to represent and protect and not to tyrannize." Woods didn't get his ban; New York's jaywalking law wasn't enacted until 1958.

But before and since, New Yorkers have claimed the God-given right to cross the street wherever they goddamn please. In fact, filmmakers have on occasion used such a moment to establish the nature of a New York movie character. In the opening credits of *Shaft* (the 1971 original) Richard Roundtree exits the subway and strides across Times Square, glaring and cursing as drivers screech to a halt. And of course the quintessential moment of onscreen jaywalking came in 1969 with *Midnight Cowboy*, as Dustin Hoffman's Ratso Rizzo, mid-crosswalk, is nearly hit by a cab and slaps the hood, shouting, "I'm walkin' here!"

Jazz *see* BEBOP; HARLEM

Jeans, Designer[1]

Blue jeans—rugged denim pants reinforced with copper rivets—were born as a workingman's uniform and, for a century, varied little from the 1873 originals invented by Jacob Davis and Levi Strauss. Over time, others, like rockers, artists, and students, came to appreciate jeans. But no one mistook them for fashion until the age of disco.

In 1976, New York icon Gloria Vanderbilt—heiress to one of America's great fortunes and a former model, artist, and designer—was approached by Warren Hirsch, manager for the Indian garment manufacturer Mohan Murjani, whose company was based in New York and for whom Vanderbilt had already designed some blouses. As Vanderbilt recounted it, "Warren came to me one day and said, 'The Murjanis have oodles of blue denim tucked away somewhere. How about designing Gloria Vanderbilt jeans?'" The decision to collaborate felt uncannily right to her. "'Yikes, Warren,' I said. 'You must be a mind reader. There's been nothing on my mind lately but *jeans*.' And that's how it all began. I knew exactly what to do and how to do it."

*"I'm walkin' here!" Dustin Hoffman at
Sixth Avenue and 58th Street, 1969.*

looking aged or dark and clean, they will usually outlast you."

» **Don't worry about a too-tight pair.**

"In the '70s, when it was all about rigid, non-stretch denim, you'd lie down on the floor, pull in your stomach, and use a hook to pull up the zipper. Now, with stretch denim, it's much easier to get your jeans on."

Together, Murjani and Vanderbilt transformed the humble blue jean into an epoch-defining fashion status symbol. Vanderbilt's imagination took fire thinking about jeans, which she saw as a kind of magical, infinitely versatile garment: "Jeans are, without doubt, not only most comfortable to wear, but ... have an almost fairy-tale quality. And once they are perceived in that way, ideas you may never have thought possible pop into your mind."

Vanderbilt jeans walked a fine line between sexy and accessible. Made of stretch denim, they fit more snugly than classic jeans and hugged the derrière. ("They fit like the skin on a grape!" promised one TV ad.) But they were also comfortable and wearable for the average woman. Their elasticity afforded more "give" and breadth of movement, and their wide size range accommodated full figures as well.

But the real key to the jeans' success was Vanderbilt herself. While other companies also succeeded in the '70s and '80s jeans market (notably Calvin Klein, Jordache, and Sasson), Vanderbilt's was the only brand with a public image guaranteed to confer high-society glamour. The jeans were inextricably tied to her identity. Her embroidered signature embellished the back pocket, and on the front coin pocket sat her trademark logo, a swan, in gold thread. A blitzkrieg promotional campaign drove home her tight connection to her product; Vanderbilt starred in many print and media ads (the tagline: "It's a million-dollar look!").

She made countless personal appearances across the country, dispensing fashion and decorating advice to crowds of waiting fans. In the first year alone, sales of her jeans (priced around $36 a pair) reached $30 million. When asked to consider the role her own star power played in all this, Vanderbilt invoked the slightly mystical interpretation she seemed to favor: "A designer creates and represents an image people are drawn to for whatever mysterious reason. They are interested in the designer's taste if it brings beauty into their lives. A magic is suddenly available which has not been discovered before."

Her design empire would expand to include other fashion items as well as perfume and home goods. But nothing caught on like Gloria Vanderbilt jeans in the late 1970s, when, as comedian Gilda Radner put it, Vanderbilt took "her good family name and put it on the asses of America."

Jell-O

The nineteenth-century railroad magnate Peter Cooper—variously the founder or namesake of Cooper Union, Cooper Square, Peter Cooper Village, the Cooper Hewitt, and a variety of other enterprises—can take responsibility for another, humbler, much jigglier invention. Among his entrepreneurial businesses was a glue factory, which provided the rendered horns and hooves for "Cooper's refined American isinglass," more generally known as gelatin. A patent for powdered gelatin that Cooper took out in 1845 calls for adding sugar and a flavoring; his suggestions included lemon, lime, clove, allspice, cinnamon, and peach pit (which approximates almond). He also proposed adding eggs, making him an undersung flan pioneer.

It's worth noting that, although Cooper's product was successful, it didn't carry the Jell-O name. Nor was Jell-O even the first fruit-flavored gelatin-dessert mix. The earliest such product, invented by an immigrant New York confectioner named Leo Hirschfeld in 1895, was called Bromangelon. It dominated the market for a couple of years before Pearle Bixby Wait of LeRoy, New York, started selling a competitor called Jell-O. Her new product gradually sank its competitor with better ads, not to mention a much catchier name. Hirschfeld apparently learned from his experience; his subsequent, much more euphoniously trademarked invention (*see also* TOOTSIE ROLL) is still around.

Gloria Vanderbilt at Murjani, maker of her namesake jeans.

PHOTOGRAPH BY
CHAN YUEN-MAN

Junk Bonds

Mike Milken had an appropriate goal for a young, middle-class Californian born on the Fourth of July: As a teenager, he decided he would be a millionaire by age 30. To do so, he attended UC Berkeley in the late '60s, turning away from campus activism and toward the study of credit—specifically, the work of W. Braddock Hickman. A former president of the Federal Reserve Bank of Cleveland, Hickman had determined that, when adjusted for risk, a collection of low-grade bonds could outearn a blue-chip portfolio. Though the risk of default on a junk bond—one determined by S&P or Moody's to be below "investment grade"—is high, its yield soars above that of an investment-quality or a government bond when it does pay out.

In 1969, the summer after his graduation, Milken moved to New York to research low-grade bonds and soon became head of the new "junk department" at Drexel Burnham Lambert. Here, he pioneered the use of junk bonds as a highly profitable, even vital organ of an investment bank; indeed, Milken's low-grade revolution was a key factor in DBL's rapid growth to one of the five largest American banks of the 1980s. By 30, Milken easily hit his seven-figure goal, earning an estimated $5 million a year.

However, Milken was a little *too* relaxed in his approach to financial regulation. By 1979, he was under close scrutiny by the SEC; in 1986, he was implicated in illegal actions, including insider trading, stock manipulation, stock parking, and fraud. His behavior drew the SEC's attention toward Drexel Burnham Lambert and a criminal probe from U.S. Attorney Rudy Giuliani. In 1989, a federal grand jury indicted Milken on ninety-eight counts of racketeering and fraud, resulting in six guilty pleas, a ten-year Club Fed sentencing, a lifetime ban from securities, $200 million in fines, and a $400 million settlement with investors.

Milken wound up all right—he served less than two years, transitioned to a life of philanthropy, was pardoned by President Donald Trump (*see also* TRUMPISM), and as of 2020 was the 494th-richest person in the world, with a valuation of $3.7 billion. Drexel Burnham Lambert did not do nearly as well. Giuliani threatened the bank with a RICO indictment in 1986, and after subsequent losses, DBL filed for bankruptcy four years later.

*Michael Milken at
Drexel Burnham
Lambert, mid-1980s.*
**PHOTOGRAPH BY
JIM MCHUGH**

From
KELLY TOOL
to
KNICKERBOCKER

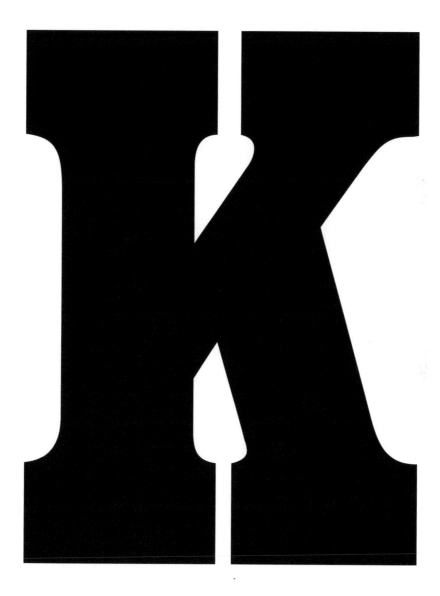

Klieg lights, deployed in memory of 9/11.
PHOTOGRAPH BY MICHEL FRIANG

① **How to Make a Key-Lime Pie**

From Steve Tarpin of Steve's Authentic Key Lime Pies

➤ **Start With the Crust.**
"Only graham-cracker crumbs and butter, period. From scratch, crumb one package of crackers in a blender or food processor, and pour in one stick of melted unsalted butter. Mix and mush into a 10-inch pie pan, then bake. We prebake our crust (375° for 6 to 7 minutes; what you're looking for is nice browning) and use the 'fill and chill' method for our custard."

➤ **Picking the Limes.**
"We use only Key limes, which can be difficult to find. Ripe ones are yellow in color and close to the size of a golf ball. The supermarket variety is extremely immature, but Mexican groceries might prove a good opportunity. Same goes for standard Persian limes—the tight, hard ones are far from ripe. Either is better than bottled juice, which is recommended for stripping paint or removing rust, not for food."

➤ **Assembling the Pie.**
"Most important is *slowly* incorporating the lime juice (a half-cup) into your

---

Kelly Tool *see* HALLIGAN BAR

Key-Lime Pie[1]

Surely, a dessert named for the Florida Keys, incorporating Florida citrus, declared the official state pie of Florida, and offered on every menu south of Tallahassee cannot be a New York invention. As it turns out, recent research suggests it is.

The defining ingredient of Key-lime pie is a can of sweetened condensed milk, which thickens into a smooth custard when mixed with acidic citrus juice. That discovery has generally been attributed to a Florida cook ("Aunt Sally") from the 1860s. But the first published recipes for Key-lime pie are much newer, dating to around 1940. In 2017, the baker and food writer Stella Parks republished the earliest known reference: a nearly identical 1931 recipe made with lemons rather than limes that came out of the Borden Company's food-science lab at 352 Madison Avenue. As Parks wrote in her book, *BraveTart: Iconic American Desserts,* the formula depends upon an industrial-style product and process that doesn't work with regular milk (which would curdle) but is "exactly the sort of recipe a food scientist would develop."

It will not surprise you to learn that a contingent of Florida food historians would like to prove her wrong. The Key-lime truthers suggest that Borden picked up and modified Aunt Sally's formula, but their documentation is thin. (Parks thinks it went the opposite way, when some Floridian saw the Borden recipe and substituted limes for lemons.) It is more than plausible that this bit of Americana came not from a southern auntie but a Manhattan corporate entity (*see also* MADISON AVENUE), looking to goose the sales of its product.

Klieg Light

You can ascribe this one to the Kliegls, Anton and John (who used the extremely old-fashioned abbreviation "Jno" for his name), Bavarian immigrants who founded the Kliegl Brothers Universal Electric Stage Lighting Company in 1896. Working from buildings on West 50th Street in the Theater District, the company in 1911 introduced a carbon-arc light as the first practical way to illuminate an indoor motion-picture set. It was initially called a Klieglight, and the shared *L* eventually migrated off the end of the family name. By the time John died in 1959, the firm had lit up the Metropolitan Opera House, Madison Square Garden, the naturalist William Beebe's deep-sea diving vessel (*see also* BATHYSPHERE), and movie studios from Mexico to India. The Kliegl company eventually moved to Long Island City, then farther out on Long Island to Syosset, and it went dark for good in the mid-1990s. "Kliegl"—minus one letter, lowercased, and often with its vowels incorrectly flipped—outlived the firm, and has entered Merriam-Webster's dictionary as the term for any such light.

Knickerbocker

"Old Knickerbocker Dutch" is what historically inclined New Yorkers say when referring to aristocratic families that have been here since the seventeenth century. Although "Knickerbocker" was indeed the name of a family up in the Hudson Valley, Washington Irving essentially made it up in his satire *A History of New-York from the Beginning of the World to the End of the Dutch Dynasty,* published in 1809 and ascribed to the author "Diedrich Knickerbocker." A best seller, the book gave shape to the legends of New Amsterdam, and the term stuck as a general descriptor of local lineage, like "Main Line families" in Philadelphia or "Brahmins" in Boston. Irving's circle of writer friends, which included James

sweetened condensed
milk (one can) and egg
(four yolks) mixture, allowing
the chemical action of the
lime's acid to thicken
the custard. Overmixing will
destroy that process. We
do not bake our filling. Insert
raw-egg warning here!
You can easily pasteurize
egg yolks."

Fenimore *"The Last of the Mohicans"* Cooper, became known as the Knickerbocker Group, and the magazine they frequently contributed to was called *The Knickerbocker, or New-York Monthly Magazine.*

By the early twentieth century, the word was a widespread nickname for anything New York–y. Knickerbocker Beer—brewed by Yankees owner Jacob Ruppert in a giant brick complex on Third Avenue—was a local barroom staple. You could stay at the Knickerbocker Hotel in Times Square. "Cholly Knickerbocker," his first name spelled as a New Yorker might pronounce "Charlie," represented several successive pseudonymous writers of a society column in various newspapers that eventually settled in the New York *Journal-American* (*see also* GOSSIP COLUMN). After that paper closed in 1966, the column's current writer, Aileen Mehle (*see also* SOCIALITE), took it to several other outlets, writing as "Suzy Knickerbocker" until her retirement in 2005.

In George Cruikshank's illustrations for Irving's book, as well as the later ones by other artists, the Dutch wear baggy short trousers. These became known as knickerbockers, later shortened to *knickers*, the word still used in American English for knee breeches and in Britain for women's underpants. In the 1840s, the baseball players who wore these abbreviated puffy pants gave this name to one of the sport's first teams, the New York Knickerbockers (*see also* BASEBALL). A century later, New York's first pro basketball squad (*see also* HOOPS) adopted the same name, although when the Knicks won the NBA championship in 1970, Walt Frazier and Bill Bradley most definitely did not wear the pantaloons to match.

DIEDRICH KNICKERBOCKER.

The mythical proto–New Yorker.

From

LABOR LAW

to

LONG-PLAYING RECORD

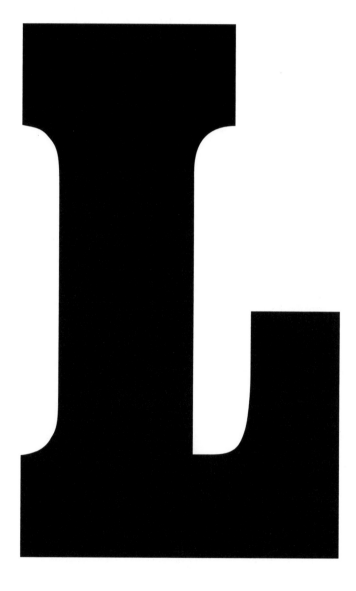

The Lindy Hop, demonstrated by
Leon James and Willa Mae Ricker, 1943.
PHOTOGRAPH BY GJON MILI

Labor Law

To understand why 146 people died in Manhattan's Triangle Shirtwaist Company fire in 1911, you should start with greed. A killing greed that locked the factory's workroom doors for fear the women inside would steal a few rags. A negligent greed that allotted one fire escape for all those workers and kept it in such shoddy shape that it collapsed under their weight. Greed did not start the fire, did not push burning women out of the windows down to the pavement nine floors below, but it was an accelerant in more than one sense. The fire not only galvanized activists in New York, it helped transform American labor law.

In the years leading up to the fire, the labor movement had been organizing garment workers into unions. Mostly women, the daughters of immigrants or immigrants themselves, workers in New York City's garment factories lacked robust workplace protections as well as the social connections necessary to capture the attention of the political class. But the bodies were difficult for anyone to ignore. The Triangle Shirtwaist tragedy made labor practices visible that were often opaque, at least to the city's educated elite. At the same time, it advanced the idea that workplace dangers could have legislative solutions. Both working-class women and well-off reformers like Frances Perkins lobbied New York politicians to prevent factory fires by amending the laws. Three months after the Triangle blaze, New York created the Factory Investigating Commission, which had the statutory authority to uncover fire hazards, occupational disease risks, and sanitation.

Workplace-inspection regimes soon spread to other industrial states, including Illinois and Massachusetts. Later, the election of reformers like Al Smith and Franklin Delano Roosevelt to the governorship of New York ensured that a system of workplace-safety standards would continue to take shape as part of a broader push to protect employees from their bosses. Perkins, who witnessed the fire from Washington Square Park and who would later become FDR's secretary of Labor, remarked that the day of the blaze was "the day the New Deal was born." Decades later, the Occupational Safety and Health Administration, or OSHA, would continue their work.

Not all the regulations we now regard as basic labor protections originated with the Triangle Shirtwaist fire or with New York organizers, but the disaster was an inflection point. "You got a consensus that says people shouldn't have to risk dying to make a living," says the Dartmouth College historian Annelise Orleck. Greed may be part of the human condition, but labor law can prevent it from taking lives.

Landmarks Law

When workers began smashing up Pennsylvania Station in 1963, they were also laying the foundation for the modern preservation movement. The demolition of that grand and gracious structure, designed by McKim, Mead & White and just over 50 years old at the time, struck even futurist New Yorkers as a barbaric act and was followed two years later by the equally unthinkable destruction of a set of Fifth Avenue mansions known as the Brokaw houses. Public opinion was particularly swayed by a photograph, first appearing in the New York *Times* in 1966, of the station's broken-up statuary and columns where they were dumped in the Meadowlands. The costs of historical amnesia suddenly seemed too high for a civilized city to bear, and within months a never-again bill was making its way through the City Council. The statute Mayor Robert Wagner signed in 1965 empowered a new Landmarks Preservation Commission to protect individual buildings and entire neighborhoods, for the first time enshrining New York's architectural history into law.

It was too late for Penn Station, but the commission moved quickly to protect Wyckoff House, a 1652 Dutch farmstead in Canarsie, Brooklyn, now a museum. It also designated Brooklyn Heights the city's first historic district—a sharp rebuke to Robert Moses, who, a decade earlier, had hoped to flatten its brownstones to make room for the Brooklyn-Queens Expressway. The LPC has so far ordained 149 historic districts across the five boroughs and ten times that many individual landmarks (but only 120 interiors). More than a quarter of Manhattan's buildings are protected in one way or another.

That broad jurisdiction comes with severe limitations, however. The LPC can protect a building's architectural character but has no jurisdiction over what happens inside it. Office buildings get converted to condos, clothing stores give way to restaurants, mixed-

Penn Station stonework dumped in the Meadowlands, 1966.

PHOTOGRAPH BY
EDDIE HAUSNER

① **5 Perfect Lap-Dance Songs**

Chosen by StripXpertease owner and instructor Kimberly Smith

"The perfect lap dance song is *slow*! Your adrenaline will make you dance faster, so slow is key. And never, *ever* lip-sync! When you lip-sync, you're paying attention to the song. Your attention should be on your subject! Plus, unless it's one to three words at an appropriate time, like 'I want you,' it just looks like you're distracted."

➻ **Brain,** by Banks
➻ **Sleep Sound,** by Jamie xx
➻ **Cola,** by Lana Del Rey
➻ **Bitter Poem,** by Cold War Kids
➻ **Lies,** by the Black Keys

income neighborhoods gentrify into affluent preserves, and the commission must confine itself to fussing over railings and windows. For that reason, in much of New York, the more a neighborhood changes, the more it looks the same.

While the landmarks law, the first of its kind in the country, became a model for many cities, it remained controversial. On the 50th anniversary of its enactment, the Real Estate Board of New York, the voice of developers and landlords, blamed LPC overreach for driving up prices and aggravating a citywide housing shortage. The law also fortified the preservationist movement, which evolved from a loose club of nostalgists and antiquarians into a well-resourced network of architects, planners, lawyers, and scholars, plus a changing cast of celebrities. This group could do more than complain: It knew how to pitch the commissioners with a solidly researched argument and, when necessary, shame them into action. Yet many questioned its independence. The writer Tom Wolfe attacked LPC as a collection of lackeys who did the bidding of City Hall and its clan of moneyed real-estate tycoons. The agency, he fulminated in a 2006 *Times* op-ed, was "packed with expirees who would gladly disintegrate, if necessary, to avoid casting so much as a shadow on any of the mayor's plans."

As it navigated between hostile poles, the LPC also had to adapt its preservationist mission to a constantly changing context. Once the obvious landmarks from the nineteenth century and earlier were safely under its wing, the commission started approaching the more unresolved present. Only buildings at least 30 years old are eligible for landmarking, but by the turn of the millennium, the commission predated many of the buildings it was charged with protecting. And when it came to modern architecture, it could be almost arbitrarily selective: Skidmore, Owings & Merrill's Lever House earned landmark status, but the firm's elegant Union Carbide Building at 270 Park Avenue did not. Wolfe's

venom was inspired by the commission's refusal to hold hearings on 2 Columbus Circle, an eccentric and initially much-mocked modernist building that Edward Durell Stone had designed for A&P heir Huntington Hartford's art collection in 1964.

With its slow-moving bureaucracy, underfunded staff, and sometimes haphazard processes, the LPC often has trouble keeping up with a fast-changing city. In 2005, the Municipal Art Society compiled its "30 Under 30" list of candidates for landmarking. Among them was Tod Williams and Billie Tsien's American Folk Art Museum, which was built in 2001 and demolished a decade later, long before the law could intervene. But the commission can be nimble when it chooses: In 2018, a developer floated a plan to strip much of the masonry façade from Philip Johnson's postmodernist AT&T Building at 550 Madison Avenue, a structure that is more important than beloved. LPC stepped in and designated the tower a landmark, sending the architects back to square one for a more modest alteration. Though the Landmarks Law was enacted to protect the past, it winds up guiding the future.

Lap Dance [1]

The tale of the Melody Theatre has everything: a disgraced politician, porn stars turned strippers (and vice versa), and the invention of the lap dance. Its history begins in 1973, when Al Kronish, an enterprising accountant, convinced Fred Cincotti, an assistant DA for the State of New York, and Steven Katz, the 28-year-old heir to a construction empire, to invest in a brand-new strip club in Times Square. It would be called the Melody Burlesk, and, compared with the other dives in the neighborhood, this place would be classy. But Kronish's aspirations were short-lived: A year earlier, *Deep Throat*, starring Linda Lovelace, had earned mainstream notoriety (*see also* X-RATED FILM, GOLDEN AGE

OF) and strip-club audiences became thirsty for increasingly bawdy live acts. In response, Kronish began inviting members of the rising class of porn stars to put on shows at the Melody. In 1978, the club introduced Mardi Gras, a raucous weekend event where, for the first time, strippers interacted directly with the audience, grinding on their laps for just $1 per sitting. Word spread, men began lining up down the block to get one of these newfangled "lap dances," and things pretty much devolved from there into illegal sex acts with audience participation. In 1982, Cincotti and Katz, making $20,000 a week ($51,000 today), were indicted on a charge of "promoting prostitution" and were painted in the press as nothing more than well-to-do pimps. The Melody Theatre shuttered in 1998, but the lap dance lives on.

Late-Night Talk Show

Most of the late-night-talk-show format was cemented in 1962, when Johnny Carson's *Tonight Show* (he'd taken over from the popular host Jack Paar) was first broadcast from NBC's 30 Rockefeller Plaza studios. Its (initial) 11:15 p.m. time slot, the host monologue, the celebrity interview segments and guest performances, the focus on comedy—*The Tonight Show* became the gold standard for what late night could be. But the series itself grew out of a few earlier TV experiments.

Broadway Open House, an NBC variety show hosted by comedians Morey Amsterdam (briefly) and Jerry Lester, started airing from 30 Rock in May 1950. Although it was broadcast for only about a year, its 11 p.m. slot had demonstrated that there might be an audience for late-night programming, and its format included many pieces of what would later become *The Tonight Show*, especially the inclusion of topical daily comedy. (It also created a sensation out of Lester's sidekick, a bosomy blonde airhead character who went by the single name Dagmar.) In 1954, NBC began broadcasting *Tonight Starring Steve Allen* from the Hudson Theatre in New York. Allen's *Tonight* established most of the late-night-talk-show formula that Carson would later refine, including the monologue, celebrity interviews, and comedy segments in which the cameras occasionally left the studio. In his first monologue, Allen had announced that *Tonight* would run "forever," and the clip of his saying that was often replayed on the show's anniversaries to celebrate its legacy. In Allen's bit, though, the line was meant as a joke about the show's run time, from 11:30 p.m. to 1 a.m. Allen told the live audience that the theater had been especially selected because "it sleeps about eight hundred people."

In 1972, Carson's *Tonight Show* left New York and resettled in "beautiful downtown Burbank." Los Angeles was where the bookable stars were, where the business was centered, where you didn't have to deal with the technical hassles of broadcasting out of an office tower from the 1930s. Aside from *The Dick Cavett Show*—which at various times aired in the morning, early evening, and prime time, but spent its most memorable six years opposite Carson—and *Saturday Night Live*, which went on the air three years later (*see also* SKETCH COMEDY), the late-night game had left town.

The boomerang began to come around in 1982 with the premiere of NBC's *Late Night With David Letterman*, which started at 12:30 a.m. on weeknights. Letterman the antic ironist was in some ways the antithesis of Carson the cool showbiz pro, and the show—masterminded by the genius writer-producer Merrill Markoe—regularly sent Dave out into the city to talk with New York shop clerks, taxi drivers, deli owners, and general weirdos, echoing the old Allen bits, which Letterman openly spoke

Backstage at Donna Karan, 1985.
The black bodysuit, a slightly
modified leotard, was one of her
versatile Seven Easy Pieces.

of admiring. When he took his act to CBS, the Ed Sullivan Theater, and the 11:35 p.m. slot a decade later, the New York–iness of the show remained intact. And everyone followed. Comedy Central's *The Daily Show*, first with Craig Kilborn and then Jon Stewart and Trevor Noah, was broadcast from New York; so were, later, *Last Week Tonight With John Oliver* on HBO and *Full Frontal With Samantha Bee* on TBS. And Jimmy Fallon, taking over *The Tonight Show* in 2014, moved it back from California into Studio 6B at 30 Rockefeller Plaza, the very same room where Paar and Carson had worked—at least until he started broadcasting from home during the 2020 pandemic (*see also* QUARANTINE).

Leotard As Streetwear

The ascent of the leotard—invented around 1859 by French aerialist Jules Léotard—from lowly rehearsal garment to sleek streetwear essential dates back to the mid–twentieth century and the creative synergy of two freethinking female artists living in New York City: modern-dance pioneer Martha Graham and fashion designer Claire McCardell. By the 1940s, Graham was firmly established as a revolutionary choreographer known for rejecting ballet's physical constraints and fairy-story plots in favor of a more organic, deeply bodily style built on woman-centered myths, gravity, and breath. Eschewing tutus and pointe shoes, Graham dancers went barefoot and wore sculptural, unadorned costumes consisting often of jersey tube dresses over leotards, or leotards with attached skirts. For Graham, the body took precedence over any garment. "Costume… must reveal the beautiful line of the waist, the hips, the shoulders," she wrote. A style icon herself, Graham inspired young women around the country to emulate her pared-down, body-centered look.

McCardell shared Graham's minimal aesthetic and began incorporating dance looks into her designs in the 1940s, including jersey separates, flat ballet slippers (which she commissioned from Capezio), and, of course, leotards. Her look seemed to encapsulate an essential quality of postwar new-world womanhood; by January 1950, *Vogue* was touting the American woman's "frugal, spare silhouetted American Primitive Look that Martha Graham helps her to visualize and Claire McCardell and Capezio help her to achieve," a look that included a "skimpy jersey jumper over a skimpy leotard." The dancer look was born—deeply American in its athletic free-spiritedness, deeply New York in its restrained beauty.

From there, these versatile, torso-molded onesies became staples of athleisure, workwear, and even evening dress, kept in runway rotation for generations. Disco lovers wore them under Lycra wrap skirts in the 1970s, Donna Karan layered them under power suits in the 1980s, and they returned full-force in 2016, when clingy bodysuits were made by brands ranging from Maison Margiela to H&M, perhaps inspired by the U.S. women's gymnastics team's victory at the Olympics.

Lincoln Center for the Performing Arts

The postwar years were a peak era for European high culture in New York. At last, the city was mighty enough to keep up with Paris, London, and Amsterdam, supporting orchestral music and opera on a grand scale. The local audience had been beefed up by the previous generations' immigrants, especially Germans, Austrians, and Hungarians who appreciated the music and art they knew from Berlin, Vienna, and Budapest. Now, with the increasing affluence of the city's bourgeoisie, its cultural institutions could come into full flower. For that, they needed new facilities. Carnegie Hall, home of the New York Philharmonic, was acoustically impeccable but aging, and its owner planned to knock it down and put up a skyscraper. The Metropolitan Opera House was hopelessly outdated, with backstage space so inadequate that sets were stored on the sidewalk under tarps between performances. For twenty years, the Met had wanted to move—at one point, its new home was going to be the heart of Rockefeller Center—but it never worked out. At the same time, Fordham University was looking to add a campus in Manhattan. City-planning czar Robert Moses took all this in and envisioned a giant arts center,

the first swath of "a reborn West Side, marching north from Columbus Circle and eventually spreading over the entire dismal and decayed West Side." (Which is to say he wanted to demolish and redevelop everything and bottle up the poor in a few housing projects.)

A plan formed, backed by philanthropist John D. Rockefeller III (the brother of New York's governor), to have three institutions at the core of the arts center surrounding a central plaza. Philharmonic Hall was to be designed by Max Abramovitz, the Met's new opera house by Wallace Harrison, and the New York State Theater, for New York City Ballet, by Philip Johnson. Their disparate aesthetics soon put them at loggerheads, and it took all of Johnson's diplomacy to get everyone to agree to a consistent roofline and matching travertine marble cladding. The opera house was decorated with huge murals by Marc Chagall. Auxiliary buildings housed performance spaces for Lincoln Center Theater, a new home for the Juilliard School, a chamber-music space called Alice Tully Hall, and the New York Public Library for the Performing Arts. Fordham got its campus next door, and a small park and bandshell were put in adjacent to the Met.

When opened, largely between 1962 and 1966, Lincoln Center was not particularly well reviewed. The new buildings, especially the opera house, were certainly more practical than their predecessors: They had enough bathrooms, patrons' traffic flow was generally better, and finally the Met had enough backstage space. Yet because the complex was modern and swoopy and hard edged, traditionalists (quite a few of whom were opera-, symphony-, and balletgoers) dismissed it as an ugly comedown, glitzy rather than timeless. That impression was reinforced after a few concerts in Philharmonic Hall, where the acoustics were revealed to be dramatically inferior to Carnegie Hall's, dry at best and painful at worst. A few years later, the stereo magnate Avery Fisher donated $10.5 million to have the interior

② **How to Lindy Hop**
*From Margaret
Batiuchok,
co-founder of
the New York Swing
Dance Society*

"You alternate between eight- and six-count steps. The leader chooses which step comes next. You can do a whole dance using only six-count steps (many did in the '50s) or only eight-count steps, though that would be rare. To get the full richness of the dance, you use both. You can learn the basic rhythm pattern in an hour, but **to really dance the Lindy, it takes lessons and lots of practice.** You'll dance with everyone in the room, so you want to avoid accidents— whether getting stepped on or crashing into someone."

reconstructed and his name put on the building, after which it sounded better if not actually good. In 2015, David Geffen donated $100 million for another rehab.

Tastes change, and for all of New Yorkers' mixed feelings about Lincoln Center at the start, it has grown on them. Some of that is acceptance of its high-kitsch postwar style, which has become familiar rather than revolutionary, even a little bit retro-cool. Renovations in the 2010s helped, particularly as they made the center's gathering areas more useful and comfortable. And it's impossible not to appreciate the plaza on a concert night. Watch the procession moving through it in the half-hour before a performance is to begin, and you see something extraordinary: Well-dressed people straighten up and slow down, as if they themselves are stepping onstage; the fountain at the center splashes; they meet up, form groups, chat. It's the closest thing New York has to the Piazza San Marco. Then, if they're inside the opera house, another bit of razzle-dazzle: A moment before the curtain, a switch is thrown and the crystal-and-gilt starburst chandeliers glide up to the ceiling and dim. Everyone gets the message, cell phones are shut off, and the city falls away as the music starts.

Lindy Hop [2]

Whereas the fox-trot was all about getting close and dancing "cheek-to-cheek," the Lindy Hop was a major departure. According to legend, the Harlem-born dance resulted from a mistake made by performers George "Shorty" Snowden and Mattie Purnell at a dance marathon in 1928. The two got separated, then danced their way back to each other, sending observers into a frenzy. These breakaways turned into the Lindy Hop, named for Charles Lindbergh's "hop" across the Atlantic a year earlier, a canvas for improvisation that took Harlem and eventually the rest of the country by storm. "What's great about the Lindy is you can bring your own feeling to it and be expressive," said Margaret Batiuchok, a founder of the New York Swing Dance Society who wrote her master's thesis on Lindy Hop history. "Like jazz, there's improvisational sections, and it's just a wonderful, joyful dance that people see and they want to do."

"Little Magazine"

In Mary McCarthy's telling, the modern American "little magazine"—home to the culture's most ambitious, obscure, and lengthy discourse—was born in 1934 in an apartment in Greenwich Village, as was the New York intellectual. The apartment belonged to Philip Rahv, who, along with William Phillips, would relaunch *Partisan Review*. There had been plenty of socialist publications (*Masses* and its successor, *The New Masses*, for example) and a few magazines devoted to modernism (e.g., the *Little Review*, which published the first excerpts of Joyce's *Ulysses* in the U.S.), but it was *Partisan Review* that fused leftist politics with modernist aesthetics. The fusion was embodied by New York intellectuals themselves, who took turns arguing (in letters) with Trotsky when they weren't reading new translations of Kafka. The first relaunched issue of *Partisan Review* included Delmore Schwartz's story "In Dreams Begin Responsibilities," in which a man dreams he's in a movie theater watching his parents' Brooklyn courtship on the screen and yells at them to stop because their union will only lead to misery.

The *Partisan Review* crowd was mostly but not entirely Jewish: Rahv, Phillips, Schwartz, and Lionel Trilling were the leading lights; McCarthy, Dwight Macdonald, and Anatole Broyard were notable exceptions. Their ranks were bolstered by the elder literary figure Edmund Wilson and later by émigrés fleeing Nazi Germany like Hannah Arendt. In the arts, they overturned the patrician, conservative, and largely southern New Critics, while their Trotskyist politics turned to

*Chuck Close working
on* Keith *in his Greene
Street loft, 1970.*
PHOTOGRAPH BY
WAYNE HOLLINGWORTH

staunch anti-Stalinism and, after Stalin's death, liberal anti-communism. Several journals were spawned in *PR*'s wake, among them Macdonald's *politics*, which opposed U.S. entry into World War II, and Irving Howe's social-democratic *Dissent*. Many in the *PR* circle made their living with day jobs at glossies, like James Agee at *Fortune*, or reached a larger audience in *The New Yorker*, which sent Arendt to Israel to cover Adolf Eichmann's trial, and many later found a home at the *New York Review of Books*, a more diffuse, academic-leaning miscellany founded in 1963.

In the 1960s, the third and arguably last generation of New York intellectuals included Susan Sontag, Philip Roth, and Norman Podhoretz. Before taking the magazine he edited, *Commentary*, from left to right, Podhoretz wrote a book, *Making It*, about the desire for success among his peers, whom he referred to as "the Family," scandalizing them and getting himself ostracized (it's one of the reasons he became a conservative). But success and fame were indeed their destiny, as Sontag's and Roth's careers demonstrated; before they turned 40, both became too big to fit into the little magazines. That may be one reason young writers keep starting such journals (the past 20 years have seen the birth of *n+1*, *The New Inquiry*, and *Jacobin*) even when print is said to be dead: They're a good little way to get famous.

Loft Living

NOTE: *Chuck Close was one of the first artists to live in a converted industrial loft in downtown Manhattan. Now famous for his large-format photorealist paintings of his friends and fellow artists (twelve of which are installed uptown at the new 86th Street station on the Q line), Close moved to 27 Greene Street, just above Canal, in 1967, when he came to the city as a young man. Here, he details his experiences at the intersection of two fundamental New York forces: art and real estate.*

What had your building been before you moved in? An underwear-manufacturing business. They had one set of machinery on the floor, and belts on three

or four pulleys that could be engaged to power the sewing machines. I was on the fifth floor. No elevator. Rats and rags.

Did you have to build it out? We had no heat or hot water. We slept under electric blankets, and we'd go to my friend Don Nice's loft on Spring Street to take a shower. I'd just gotten married, and I didn't see her body till spring. [*Laughs*] Philip Glass did the plumbing—he was a better composer than he was a plumber. When I came, I paid $150 a month rent for 2,500 square feet, and artist friends of mine laughed because they were paying $50.

I stole gas. I went down in the basement and I'd run the meters backwards and reverse the flow, and then when the guy came to read the meter, I'd take the connection hose off and run it the other way. I was very good at putting dust on the top of the valve so it wouldn't show that I had opened it.

People weren't allowed, at first, to live there. So the biggest sham, which was great, was your bed, which slid into a platform. You'd call that your "model stand." And everybody had a hole cut in the staircase wall to see who was coming in.

The neighborhood looks so empty in old photographs. One by one, the factories moved out, and some of the most beautiful cast-iron buildings were torn down because they couldn't pay the property tax (*see also* CAST-IRON BUILDING).

How long did you stay there? In 1970, a loft became available in a co-op building on Prince between Mercer and Greene—that's where Jerry's restaurant was, but first it was a cuchifritos place. So we bought the building, six of us, for $100,000. We each came up with $5,000 to make a $30,000 down payment. I borrowed from my wife's father and started paying him back. Tony Shafrazi put up the Sheetrock on my ceiling one summer when I had a teaching gig on the West Coast. He defaced my ceiling before he defaced *Guernica*.

The rest of [the co-op] wanted to sell the [ground-floor] restaurant for, like, five or six thousand, so we'd have to pay less, and I said, *Don't be a fool! We're going to be able to rent that space for a lot more now that the neighborhood's changing.* So luck prevailed: Within two years, it was paying $100,000 a year in rent. So I was so brilliant! [*Laughs*] Everyone in the building got a check every month instead of paying rent.

Was it dangerous at night? Cabdrivers didn't want to let my wife off, but it was quite safe. We'd walk the streets at night, and every three or four or five blocks we'd see a light on—"Oh, hey, someone else lives there." And then the city made that area artist residency. Two people, two floors of a building. When a building burned—they had wooden interiors—the fire department did not want to go in [if nobody lived there]. They'd just let them burn. It was called Hell's Hundred Acres. So when there was an artist-in-residence, you'd put a sign outside: "AIR 3." That meant artist in residence, living on three.

Were there grocery stores and restaurants? What was everyday life like? There was a Grand Union up on West Broadway at Spring. And everybody had a cart—you'd take the Grand Street bus, and on the far east side, there was a co-op for vegetables and stuff. But there were only two places [to eat]. There was Fanelli's, and there was the Broome Street Bar. We were really between the two Little Italys.

Elizabeth Murray had the first children in what became Soho, and Leslie and I had Georgia in 1973, relatively early. And then there were artist child-care groups. There wasn't any money to be made in the art world, nor was there any fame to be merchandised, so everybody helped everybody. It was an amazing moment.

They tried to open a juice bar across the street from Fanelli's—that was code for a place where you could go and smoke pot and take drugs. And Fanelli, who was at this point 78 years old or thereabouts, had pictures of boxers and the chief of police on the walls; all the police would go there to drink. Fanelli said, "We're not gonna have any goddamn juice bar, whatever the hell that is," and he went over and let them know that the Mafia would be making a visit if they chose to open. And then later Fanelli's became—we called it Loser's Lounge. No serious artist ate or drank there anymore. They'd go up the street to Broome Street Bar or up to Max's Kansas City.

There were garbage trucks everywhere because the garbage companies would park on the street. They were Mafia, so once in a while all the trucks from one company would get set on fire by another company. (*See also* MAYHEM; MOB, THE.)

When did you leave? I moved out of the building in 1984 because my daughter was in school on 88th Street every day. I sold the loft—for which I'd paid $5,000 and lived rent free—for $400,000, and I was able to buy an apartment on Central Park West.

But my studio was always downtown. I commuted. I had a loft on West 3rd Street, owned by NYU, which was advertising "Study where the artists live"—while they were evicting us! I sued them. We got 60 grand each to leave. And I bought a loft on Lafayette, which was the biggest crack street. I bought it for $50K. I still have that loft.

Long-Playing Record

"It is quite unnecessary to point out to the gramophone addict the shortcomings of the instrument," wrote a *Times* music reviewer in 1931. The "greatest nuisance with which we have been labouring," he explained, was that the then-ubiquitous 78-rpm records could play only about five minutes of music per side. To hear an entire symphony, a listener had to constantly pause the music to flip or replace discs. To solve a problem that obviously bedeviled audiophiles, record-company engineers had been trying to develop a longer-playing record. In 1931, to great excitement, RCA Victor released one capable of playing 30 minutes of music—but it was riddled with technical problems. The discs were made of an insubstantial material, and the record players' pickups (the part that holds the needle) were known to tear them after a few uses. Customers grew so upset these failures were pulled from the market.

In 1939 CBS, headquartered in New York City, bought Columbia Records and assembled a crack team of engineers to attempt another long-playing record. They worked on it for a couple of years until World War II broke out and research came to a halt. Engineers picked the project up again after the war, experimenting with groove size and pitch control to fit as much music as possible on each side of the disc. Finally, in 1948, they produced an LP that played for 22.5 minutes per side, long enough that the vast majority of pieces in the classical repertory could be fit onto an album. The label's first LP release was Mendelssohn's moody, lyrical Violin Concerto in E-Minor—a 100-year-old composition delivered by cutting-edge technology. Within a few years, 78s had all but disappeared from the market.

5×7 Enlargement (Our 1...

NIGHT OWL

DAILY NEWS

WANTED

Son of Sam

Stories on page 3

ECONOMICAL
DEPENDABLE
FILM
DEVELOPING

Photo Service

From

MACY'S THANKSGIVING DAY PARADE

to

MUSICAL THEATER

Mayhem: The summer of 1977 brought a
blackout, fires, looting, and the Son of Sam serial killings.
PHOTOGRAPH BY CHARLES FRATTINI

Macy's Thanksgiving Day Parade

The thing about a parade is, if you're not in the front row at the curb, you can't see the marchers. Unless, of course, they are oversize and elevated high above the street. That was the breakthrough idea, in 1928, of Tony Sarg, a designer and illustrator widely known for his puppeteering. Macy's had inaugurated its Thanksgiving Day parade four years earlier, intending it to kick off the holiday shopping season. At the start, its signature displays were caged zoo animals, which brought with them all sorts of problems (they scared small children, for one). Sarg's idea was to replace them with enormous balloons filled with helium, the extremely lightweight gas that had fairly recently started to be produced in quantity. They were controlled, like upside-down marionettes, by operators holding ropes. At first, they represented generic characters, elephants and birds and such; five characters from the *Katzenjammer Kids* newspaper comic strip and then Felix the Cat, a couple of years later, were the earliest branded balloons. (Mickey Mouse joined in 1934.) After the parade, they were released and allowed to float away and could be returned to Macy's for a reward once they returned to earth. Starting in 1931, Newark's main department store, Bamberger's—which Macy's owned—launched a Thanksgiving Day parade with balloons of its own. That lasted until 1957.

Nearly a century later, Bamberger's is gone, but Macy's endures and the balloons have become an even bigger part of the show. There are roughly twenty of them each year, their presence paid for out of the promotion budgets of animation companies and brand strategists, their backstories narrated on NBC by the punny Al Roker and crew. They have not always been benign: In 1997, when high winds pulled several balloons off course, the Cat in the Hat snagged and knocked over a lamppost, injuring four spectators, one almost fatally. In 2019, when the day was once again windy, the balloons were nearly grounded, but the parade marched on—as does the bizarre habit, in surprisingly widespread use among New Yorkers (listen for it), of calling the event "the Macy's Day parade."

Madison Avenue

Toward the end of the nineteenth century and into the twentieth, advertising moved from being a local, straightforward endeavor to a business that was professionalized, wily, and increasingly informed by the emerging science of human psychology. Early megacorporations (General Motors, Coca-Cola, Standard Oil) needed to sell products and establish their brands, so they engaged outside help—the newish innovation known as the advertising agency. Those early firms were initially scattered around the country, but eventually most of the business coalesced in Chicago and New York. The pioneering J. Walter Thompson agency, the first to have its own creative department and later the first to conduct market-research surveys, got its start in 1878, operating from the old New York *Times* building on Park Row. A few years later, the George Batten Company, progenitor of BBDO, opened on the same block.

With the rise of mass communications—first magazines, then radio and television—and their concentration in New York, the ad business flourished in the city and soon began to migrate uptown, and particularly to Madison Avenue. In 1917, J. Walter Thompson moved to 244 Madison, becoming one of the first agencies with an address on the avenue; Young & Rubicam followed a few years later. By 1930, one-quarter of the American Association of Advertising Agencies' members were based on Madison Avenue, and the eponym began to come into wide use.

The Great Depression and the Second World War were inherently tough on the ad business, based as it is on spending, especially disposable-income spending. After the war, however, that changed in a hurry as American consumerism took off. Advertising fed the beast, and the field itself was invigorated during this period, now known as the creative revolution. Whereas earlier advertising had tended to sell a product itself rather than the lifestyle that goes with it (and it was rarely funny), as the world got more dense with branding messages, ad-makers needed new tools to cut through the noise. The breakthrough talent was Bill Bernbach, a principal in the firm Doyle Dane Bernbach. (It existed in contradistinction to its rival, David Ogilvy's agency, which was founded on the principle that hard data should do the bulk of an ad's work.) In 1949, DDB's ads for its first client, Orbach's department store, created a minor sensation by using an image of a man leaving the store carrying a cardboard cutout of his newly dressed-up wife under the tagline "Liberal

Lemon.

This Volkswagen missed the boat.

The chrome strip on the glove compartment is blemished and must be replaced. Chances are you wouldn't have noticed it; Inspector Kurt Kroner did.

There are 3,389 men at our Wolfsburg factory with only one job: to inspect Volkswagens at each stage of production. (3000 Volkswagens are produced daily; there are more inspectors than cars.)

Every shock absorber is tested (spot checking won't do), every windshield is scanned. VWs have been rejected for surface scratches barely visible to the eye.

Final inspection is really something! VW inspectors run each car off the line onto the Funktionsprüfstand (car test stand), tote up 189 check points, gun ahead to the automatic brake stand, and say "no" to one VW out of fifty.

This preoccupation with detail means the VW lasts longer and requires less maintenance, by and large, than other cars. (It also means a used VW depreciates less than any other car.)

We pluck the lemons; you get the plums.

One of DDB's breakthrough ads for Volkswagen, 1960.

Trade-in." (Creative, perhaps; sexist, unquestionably.)

The real turning point, though, came with ads for DDB's most famous client: Volkswagen. The Beetle was an ugly-duckling car from a nation that, only a few years earlier, had been the mortal enemy of civilization. (Adolf Hitler himself had specified the design of a durable little "people's car" that could be built and run inexpensively.) Starting in the late 1950s, DDB's Bob Gage, Helmut Krone, and Julian Koenig created almost from scratch an entirely new image for the Volkswagen: that it was a car for thinking consumers, that its unchanging profile was a not a bug (so to speak) but a feature because it didn't go out of date, that its value lay in its durability and practicality. The ads themselves were clever and spare, with lots of white space and simple black-and-white photographs; the most famous one showed a Beetle over the single boldface word *Lemon*. Never in a million years would General Motors have allowed that word, describing an unreliable junker, near a Chevrolet ad. (A bit of copy underneath explained that VW in the photo had come off the assembly line with a blemish on the glove compartment and thus could not be sold, emphasizing the company's quality-control operation.) DDB rolled the dice and created an icon. Increasingly, the image of the sellout ad man, bound to his drab client's wishes, his gray flannel suit, and his two cocktails on the 5:05 back to Larchmont, was giving way to a more flamboyant figure.

This kind of lively thinking turned DDB into the "hot shop" of its time, and its approach began to proliferate. Over the next couple of decades, one of the agency's alumni, the flamboyant and high-profile art director George Lois, created taglines like "When You Got It—Flaunt It" (for Braniff International airlines) and "I Want My MTV." Pepsi-Cola tried to differentiate itself as a youthful alternative to Coca-Cola ("For those who think young"), and Coke eventually countered with the legendary "I'd Like to Teach the World to Sing"

television spot. Mary Wells Lawrence, of Wells Rich Greene, created "I can't believe I ate the whole thing" and "Plop plop fizz fizz" for Alka-Seltzer. TBWA's Absolut Vodka campaign took a nearly tasteless product sold in a nondescript bottle and turned it into a totem of upscale life, while Apple Computer's *1984*-inspired ads with Chiat\Day successfully pitted a small start-up against giant IBM. But although DDB was based at 350 Madison, the term *Madison Avenue* was beginning to reflect the past rather than the future. More and more agencies were almost perversely taking offices elsewhere as if to duck the cliché. In the 1970s, they started looking eastward to Lexington (where J. Walter Thompson had long since resettled) and Third Avenues.

Advertising's creative revolution never exactly ended. Like many successful rebellions, it simply ceased to be revolutionary as it took over the mainstream. The outlaw quality of the 1960s ad business couldn't be sustained forever; agencies can do this kind of outré work only when the client accepts it on faith, fearlessly, and today, most clients are more controlling and not so inclined to just say yes. Doyle Dane Bernbach (now DDB Worldwide) has been rolled up into a conglomerate with the self-parodying name Omnicom, one of the last few big agencies with an actual Madison Avenue address. (After 87 years, Young & Rubicam moved across town to Columbus Circle in 2013.) And anyway, the entire ad business has had to contend with a wild new change with the rise of the internet: Actual data that show whether ads are seen, who's seeing them, and whether they pay any attention at all. The biggest ad agency in the world is, pretty much, Google.

The story of the industry's golden age is now mostly encapsulated in the shorthand "Mad men," referring to Matthew Weiner's TV series set at a fictional agency quite a bit like Bill Bernbach's. Many of the old real-life Mad men disdain it: They say Don Draper's pitches aren't nearly as good as the real thing and there wasn't

as much drinking and sex in the agencies of their time. Image supersedes reality once again.

Mafia, The *see* MAYHEM; MOB, THE

Magic Marker

Sidney Rosenthal, a tinkerer-inventor working in Richmond Hill, Queens, is responsible for those squiggles on your office whiteboard. In 1952, he figured out how to feed a wide felt wick from a glass vial of ink. (Earlier patents for felt-tip pens exist, one dating to 1910, but they were not effectively commercialized.) Rosenthal called his handiwork a Magic Marker, and his company, Speedry Chemical Products, soon had a hit on its hands, among warehouse workers, artists, kids, and anyone who wanted to write on anything besides paper. By 1958, a competitor, Carter, had introduced its similar Marks-a-Lot line, provoking some legal tussles between the two; in 1966, Rosenthal sold Speedry, and the company itself was renamed Magic Marker Corporation. Today the trademark is owned by Binney & Smith, the Crayola people (*see also* CRAYON).

Makeover[1]

In 1910, Elizabeth Arden, a Canadian expat born Florence Nightingale Graham, opened her first salon on Fifth Avenue, its door painted red "so everyone would know where to find us." From her menu of treatments that promised self-improvement, her well-to-do guests could choose to be pummeled and rolled, creamed and steamed, rouged and coiffed. By the end of its second decade in business, the Red Door housed a Department of Exercise, through which women could engage in a low-impact regimen of stretching and rhythmic movements, and after Arden moved up the street to a new location, the salon included a full gymnasium. Patrons may have walked in looking drab, but they walked out reborn a few hours later. However transitory, the change instilled hope and newfound confidence—and the idea of the makeover was born. The concept and catchy name gained significant attention when *Mademoiselle* magazine published a feature on this metamorphosis in 1936.

A nurse named Barbara Phillips read the story, in which the New York makeup artist Eddie Senz took readers through the techniques he performed on actresses, encouraging readers to follow along. Phillips had her own ideas, and wrote to *Mademoiselle* (saying "I am as homely as a hedgehog") with the suggestion of performing these changes on a noncelebrity, namely herself. In the November 1936 issue, she was featured as the magazine's first-ever makeover. They removed her glasses, capped her teeth, covered her hair with a wig, and put her in a ball gown. This second feature was an even bigger smash than the first, so much so that it was covered in *Time,* and the gown she wore was duplicated and marketed nationally as "the Cinderella Dress."

Senz got a recurring column out of that feature, showing his "befores" and "afters" with their various shortcomings ameliorated, and the *Mademoiselle* Makeover became a contest, for which women would send photographs of themselves looking as unattractive as possible in order to be chosen. By the '60s, the magazine's team of editors and experts would travel the country, making over teachers, nurses, and students, eventually including the series as part of its annual "College" issue. *Glamour* soon followed with its monthly "Please Make Me Over" page, as did *Allure* in 1991, when editor Linda Wells wisely hired makeup artist Kevyn Aucoin, known for his transformative prowess. In the late '90s, *Jane* magazine included a regular "Makeunder" page, turning the concept on its head with the belief that too much was, in fact, just that, neutralizing the makeup, and subduing the big hair.

The makeover continues, of course, to be offered in full-service salons, in magazines, on reality TV, and on YouTube and other websites, in which women creatively make over themselves. The promise of a "new you," and all the implications associated with a haircut and a professional makeup application, is a dream that doesn't appear to be dying anytime soon.

Manhattan

Take two parts rye or bourbon (purists would use the former), one of sweet vermouth, and a dash of bitters; add ice, stir till the drink is chilled and slightly diluted, strain into a glass, drop in a cherry, and then down the hatch. The booze historian Philip Greene argues persuasively that the Manhattan was the first modern cocktail—that is, one not derived from a punch, neither too sweet nor too straight up, and possessing both balance and flavor complexity. Endless arguments have been fought over the precise site and date of its creation, but the case best borne out by historical sources says it was invented by a bartender at the Manhattan Club, at 96 Fifth Avenue, near 15th Street, in the 1870s. The first known references appear in newspapers from 1882. (A widely repeated and probably spurious story holds that the drink was invented for a banquet given by a socialite named Jennie Jerome—a.k.a. Lady Randolph Churchill, Winston Churchill's mother.) The Manhattan is now a staple of craft-cocktail menus, made with a high-quality rye and garnished with a premium Luxardo preserved cherry.

Manhattan Project *see* ATOMIC BOMB

Mass Defense *see* OCCUPY MOVEMENT

Maternity Clothes

Until the twentieth century, women who were pregnant dressed however they could, making or ordering loose-fitting shifts and wraps and staying out of public view when possible. In 1904, a Lithuanian immigrant, Lena Himmelstein Bryant, began selling belly-accommodating clothing out of her shop at 1489 Fifth Avenue, near 120th Street. A misspelling on her application for a business loan turned Lena into Lane (simultaneously making her name more Gentile-sounding), and Lane Bryant was thereafter the name of her business. Her unique product line spread via word of mouth, aided by ads bearing the legend "The Kind of Garment You Never See in a Department Store." By 1910, Lane Bryant was operating just off Fifth Avenue in the Garment District (*see also* SEVENTH AVENUE), at 19 West 38th Street.

Bryant's firm eventually moved beyond maternity wear into another formerly invisible market: clothes for women described today as plus-size and back then as "stout." That turned out to be another lucrative move, which gradually superseded the maternity-clothing lines. By 1917, Lane Bryant was a million-dollar business; by 1923, $5 million. Today, it's a chain of 700 stores and the biggest plus-size retailer in the world.

Mayhem

New York City started—or so goes the legend—as a con game. In 1626, a Dutchman from Utrecht named Peter Minuit stood on a rock and bought Manhattan Island for goods worth 60 guilders, or $24. The cash went to the chief of the Canarsie tribe, whose principal residence was on Long Island; Manhattan then was mostly Weckquaesgeek territory. The Dutch thought they'd snookered the Indians out of their land, and the Canarsies accepted payment for use of an island to which they didn't really have a claim. In short, New York City is the product of a business exchange in which each side thought it had hoodwinked the other. This explains a lot.

America is, at its root, a violent and debaucherous country. The westward push of Europeans and the displacement of indigenous people were often brutal, predicated on rape and murder. By the 1630s, the pirate and privateer Abraham Blauvelt had established New Amsterdam as his base of operations. A quarter of the city's buildings were taverns, breweries, or other sources of alcohol, and, this being a seaport with transient sailor populations, prostitution was everywhere. The author Russell Shorto describes a casual encounter between a trio of armed farmers and a local sentry that escalated (after one of the former insulted the latter with the command "Lick my ass") and ended in a stabbing and a court date. "Clearly," he wrote, "the New Netherland settlers were quite unlike their fellow pioneers to the north, the pious English Pilgrims and the Puritans ... governed by godly morality." New Amsterdam's records are filled with accounts of sexual transgression and public intoxication.

This didn't change after the English came in and the city started to grow uptown, although the bad behavior did begin to coalesce, somewhat, into certain districts. The most notorious, developing in the early nineteenth century, was known as the Five Points. It began alongside a nice little lake called the Collect Pond, sitting next to an intersection of five city streets that gave the area its name. The pond had attracted industry and become foul with sewage, and in 1811 it was filled in and eliminated. Soon the fill began to sink and the pond's stink reemerged, whereupon the surrounding neighborhood lost its respectable residents, becoming the worst slum in New York. Its denizens, jammed in tightly, were principally Irish immigrants, with some African-American former slaves among them as well. Street gangs and machine politicians—you can see Martin Scorsese's depiction of them in *Gangs of New York*—took over for decades. In one visit, you could place bets, buy sex, get conned in a faro game, and be rolled for your money after it was all over.

The city eventually condemned Five Points, erasing it from the map—it now lies more or less under the courthouses at Foley Square—but that was hardly the end of the behaviors that categorized it. As the Irish immigrant population that constituted a lot of poor New York began to assimilate and leave its enclave neighborhoods, other street gangs, often also based in ethnic allegiances, stepped up in their place. (On the Lower East Side, broadly speaking, the Bowery divided them: Italians to the west, Jews to the east. Comparable divisions took hold uptown and in Brooklyn.) The loose gangs of the nineteenth century gave way to somewhat more structured ones in the twentieth—first the Italian Black Hand and eventually the Five Families of the Mafia (*see also* MOB, THE) and the killing-for-hire operation known as Murder, Incorporated, cemented in pop culture by the rum-running operations of Prohibition.

The rise of organized crime didn't necessarily make the neighborhoods where it operated more dangerous than they already were. There were killings, and there was a certain level of run-of-the-mill street crime present because the population was mostly poor. But if you were an ordinary resident of the Lower East Side and you played by the local rules, staying on your turf and avoiding conflict—or if you were a shopkeeper and paid protection money, either to the racketeers or a crooked cop—you were perhaps as safe as anyone. The gangsters, in fact, functioned as a shadow police force. Even in the Depression, then again during wartime, crime rates in New York were as low as they'd been since measuring began.

That stasis began to crack in the 1950s, when headlines about "juvenile delinquency" began to appear. The triple forces of job loss to other states, emigration to the suburbs, and general shifts in family structure, accelerated by the rise of hard drug use, began to have a noticeable impact. Unlike the gangsterism of the 1930s, which could in a perverse way be romanticized—gun molls, honor killings, *Guys and Dolls* craps games and toughguy patois—this wave included old people's being clubbed for their grocery money, and there was nothing remotely charming about that. "We confront an urban wilderness more formidable and resistant and in some ways more frightening than the wilderness faced by the pilgrims or the pioneers," Robert Kennedy said in 1966. As the city's population thinned out, the murder rate rose, and rose again. In 1950, there were 294 murders in the five boroughs. In 1960, there were 482. In 1970, the total reached 1,117. In 1980, it hit 1,814.

By then, many people felt the city was in free fall. Middle-class swaths of the Bronx, Brooklyn, and the Lower East Side were depleted, leaving buildings unrentable, abandoned by their owners to avoid property taxes, and left to burn or rot. The families remaining in those areas were the poorest poor, often Black and Hispanic, people who had to get by with whatever everyone else had left behind. Drugs saturated the neighborhoods, putting a generation of young people at high risk. Their relationships with police (mostly white and decreasingly local) were sometimes helpful but more often toxic. "The South Bronx" became widespread shorthand for an urban place where you could, in the popular imagination, get shot just for stepping out of your door, a new Wild West that marked the end of civilization. Movies were made about it, one of which (set in a police precinct) was called *Fort Apache, the Bronx*. The perception of total urban collapse was both driven by racism and a little overblown but also dispiritingly accurate. The citywide blackout in 1977 led

② **Walk the Giant Chelsea Galleries**

From New York *art critic Jerry Saltz*

"**Larry Gagosian** has one massive space anchoring 24th Street and another on 21st Street. **Pace Gallery** built an entire building on 25th Street and is always open for business. (The Who played opening night!) **Hauser & Wirth** has dozens of locations, including a gigantic warehouselike building on 22nd Street. And nearby on 19th and 20th Streets is the ever-expanding gallery empire of **David Zwirner.** Visits to any of these will reward viewers with jaw-dropping amounts of wide-open space and works of famous artists, often including Picasso, Monet, Jeff Koons, Chuck Close, Jean-Michel Basquiat, and Julian Schnabel.

---

to patches of looting and the perception of much more. During the 1977 World Series, Howard Cosell saw a plume of smoke near Yankee Stadium and announced, "There it is, ladies and gentlemen, the Bronx is burning" to a national audience. The image stuck.

Life for middle-class urbanites was better but still not great. Mugging—a street robbery, by threat of force or with a knife or gun—became the quintessential shared New York experience. Even in well-off, pleasant neighborhoods, people avoided walking at night, and Central Park was considered a risky place after dusk. Women walking on midtown sidewalks in broad daylight knew to wear their purses slung across the body rather than on one shoulder, lest they be grabbed. Men avoided keeping a wallet in a back pants pocket. If you dozed on the subway, you might awaken to a razor-sliced hole in your coat and your money gone. Chain snatchings, in which someone would grab your necklace, snap it, and run, were rampant. When the MetroCard was introduced to replace the transit token in 1993, many people's first reaction was "It's dangerous to take out a wallet in the subway." An abandoned, ruined automobile was a commonplace sight on a Manhattan street, and a graveyard of stripped stolen-car carcasses formed on the bank of the East River near the Brooklyn Bridge. In 1990, the murder count peaked at 2,245 people.

And then something changed. Already, aggressive federal prosecution under new racketeering regulations had begun to break the grip of the mob on various businesses, and its influence was waning. But some combination of a newfound job base in the dramatic growth of financial services, increasing wealth, more effective crime-fighting techniques, and other cultural shifts (*see also* "BROKEN WINDOWS" POLICING) caused the numbers to turn. Between 1990 and 2010, the murder tally fell from 2,245 to 534, a 76 percent drop. Comparable changes took place in every other violent-crime category: robbery, burglary, rape, assault. Most other American cities saw their numbers decrease over the same period, but nowhere else was it nearly as dramatic. And incredibly, that was not the end. By 2018, it had nearly been halved again, to 289. The place whose very identity was "only the toughest survive" had become the safest big city in America.

Which did not mean disorder was gone, of course. The new ironed-smooth New York began to curl up and crinkle at the edges as you went out into the boroughs. The South Bronx was better than before, yes, but it was still a hard place to live. The city's de facto segregation between Black and white did not get much better. And that divide, one of class as well as race, became broader rather than narrower; public schools and parks in affluent neighborhoods got financial buttressing from their well-off users, who could supplement their budgets and volunteer help, whereas those in poorer neighborhoods were left behind, unrenovated and decaying. Perhaps this was a stage on the road to fixing New York's ills, but more likely it reflected the intractability of the growing rich-and-poor gap. One might also say that it proves New York to be not entirely domesticable, no matter how many brownstones that had fallen into ruin are re-renovated into luxury single-family homes. Quite a few young people—those who weren't here in the 1970s—speak fondly of the bad years, wishing they could spend time there, when apartments were cheaper and the city (as they perceive it) felt more "authentic" and "dangerous." A striking number of old-timers agree with them.

Megadealer [2]

With its massive concentration of wealth, New York City has provided fertile ground for the rise of the supersize art dealer—known to art-worlders by just one name (Larry, David, Marian) and for turning their mom-and-pop shops into globe-spanning operations. And though many top dealers have raced to open multiple locations

"Also don't skip **Matthew Marks's three galleries;** maybe you'll see work by geniuses like Jasper Johns or Robert Gober. At **Sikkema-Jenkins & Co.,** be on the lookout for the electrifying work of MacArthur-winning artist Kara Walker. For photography, never miss **303 Gallery,** where the art form was rediscovered in the 1990s, and **Metro Pictures Gallery,** where the world-famous master of disguise Cindy Sherman has shown since the early 1980s. Finish the day with a walk along the High Line directly above and be treated to the greatest curated outdoor program in the United States, if not the world."

worldwide, even those who didn't start in New York soon moved to Gotham or set up an outpost here.

This development began after World War II, when New Yorkers such as Leo Castelli and Betty Parsons moved from their predecessors' modus operandi of dealing mainly in individual artworks to exclusively representing a stable of artists so the dealer's investment could bear fruit for both. This was not without precedent: French dealer Paul Durand-Ruel, who worked with the Impressionists, put artists on stipends and aimed to represent them exclusively. (He also opened a gallery in New York after the Civil War, exploiting postwar industrial wealth and the new concept of art as an investment asset.)

The king of the megadealers may be the self-made Larry Gagosian, who opened his first gallery in West Hollywood in 1978 and landed in a former truck dock in Chelsea, then an ungentrified warehouse neighborhood, in 1985. Gagosian also blazed a trail by taking a more mercenary approach. He was among the first to make a killing in the hypercharged 1980s market by showing rising artists like David Salle and Jean-Michel Basquiat and facilitating multimillion-dollar deals on brand-name modern and contemporary artists between the world's wealthiest collectors.

Castelli was Gagosian's mentor and introduced him to deep-pocketed clients including Condé Nast owner S. I. Newhouse. He early on cultivated major collectors like the entertainment magnate David Geffen, the cosmetics heirs Ronald and Leonard Lauder, and the newsprint millionaire Peter Brant, enabling him to pull off exhibitions of works from major private collections and museums both. In the '90s, he lured the notoriously perfectionist (and pricey) artist Jeff Koons to work with him by finding backing for his sculptural series "Celebration," kicking off a long-standing relationship. Today Gagosian has eighteen galleries, five in Manhattan. In 2016, *The Wall Street Journal* estimated his annual revenue at $1 billion.

Gagosian's rarefied competitors include the Pace gallery, which migrated to 57th Street from Boston in 1963 and now has ten locations and about $900 million in annual revenue, and David Zwirner, who opened his seventh location in 2020 (four are in Manhattan, where he got his start in Soho in 1993) and whose annual revenue in 2017 was estimated at a half-billion dollars. Some of the most renowned dealers operate from fewer venues but have the allegiance of artists who dominate both the market and critical discourse. Painter Gerhard Richter, among the best-selling artists alive, has remained for years with Marian Goodman, who set up shop in her native New York in 1977 and also represents major figures like Maurizio Cattelan and the filmmaker-artist Steve McQueen. As her peers set up outposts all over the globe, Goodman was content to operate solely from midtown until 1995, when she expanded to Paris (and to London in 2014). But not everything about the rise of these New York giants is beneficial. Small and midsize galleries—including some in New York pummeled by the rising costs of real estate and those anywhere who lose their best sellers to the megadealers—have gone to work for the titans or thrown in the towel entirely, robbing the market of a key element in the art world's ecosystem. Their departure from the business often leaves non-superstar, modestly successful artists, particularly those who are no longer young, with nowhere to show.

Microphone, Condenser

 On the earliest sound recordings, before the technology was electrified, a singing voice would emerge like a howl from inside a locked closet—muffled, desperate, and indistinct. The process favored the loudest blasts, so orchestras sounded like they consisted exclusively of trombones. The problem was that in an acoustic recording system, as sound waves hit a diaphragm

*Larry Gagosian, the
mega-est megadealer
of them all.*
PHOTOGRAPH BY
CHRISTOPHER STURMAN

186

attached to a conical horn, causing a stylus to cut grooves into a wax cylinder, the vibrations degraded at every step. What started out as a strong yet subtle signal wound up a scratchy mess.

That changed in 1916 thanks to Edward C. Wente, an engineer who worked for Western Electric at 463 West Street. (That building, a West Village hothouse of inventiveness, became Bell Laboratories in 1925 and was converted to an artists' subsidized-housing complex in 1970 [see also WESTBETH ARTISTS COMMUNITY].) Wente came up with the condenser microphone, in which sound waves activate a lightweight metal membrane that flutters next to a metal plate. As the space between the two surfaces varies, the amount of stored electrical charge they carry—called capacitance—rises and falls. When that tiny electrical variation is amplified, even a quiet murmur can be preserved and transmitted without losing its lifelike quality. Speech sounds like speech, music like actual music.

The condenser mic was refined and developed for commercial use in the mid-1920s, and it revolutionized daily life on several fronts. The telephone, Wente's original focus, became a household and office object now that the people on either end of the line could conduct conversations instead of shouting matches. The microphone's acoustic precision also turned music into a mass medium with live performances broadcast on the radio and recorded ones distributed on disc. Wente complemented his microphone with two more inventions: the ribbon-light valve, which married sound to film, and a moving-coil speaker that made it possible to fill a large room with loud but accurate sound. Link these components—mic, valve, and speaker—together into one apparatus, and what you get is talkies. Without Wente on West Street, Emma Stone might still be miming oohs and aahs, à la Louise Brooks.

Minimalist Music

Minimalist music was born in California but grew up in New York. Its bright drones and polychrome pulsations saturated the culture of downtown Manhattan so completely that it's impossible to imagine Soho in the '70s without them.

Two composers can lay claim to having launched the movement: La Monte Young, whose 1958 string trio stretched out sustained notes so long that time seemed to go on vacation, and Terry Riley, who in 1964 combined endless repetition, slow buildup, improvisation, and unchanging harmony into the landmark piece *In C*. But minimalism acquired a distinctively New York accent in 1965, when Manhattan-born Steve Reich composed *It's Gonna Rain* for magnetic tape, based on the twin concepts of looping and phasing. Reich recorded a street preacher's sermon, made identical loops of one brief passage, and played them on different tape machines, which in those days unavoidably ran at slightly different speeds. As the loops slipped out of alignment, the musical snippet of speech acquired a weird, unpredictable quaver.

As these early experiments added up, it became clear that composers had developed new principles for assembling music's basic ingredients; instead of story, contrast, passion, variety, climax, and conclusion, minimalists offered a cool, continuous unfurling. This demanded fresh ways of hearing. The experience, Reich wrote, was like "placing your feet in the sand by the ocean's edge and watching, feeling, and listening to the waves gradually bury them."

Reich's main rival for the role of movement leader was his friend Philip Glass, a fellow cabdriver and downtown denizen. Realizing that the musical Establishment had no place for them in the 1960s, both men formed and trained ensembles that specialized in their styles. But the two veered in different directions. Reich sought structural purity and expressive clarity in works like *Clapping Music* and *Drumming*. Glass wrote *Music in Twelve Parts*, wrapping surfaces full of color, lushness, and sonic variety around a basic frame. When he composed the score for the nonnarrative opera *Einstein on the Beach* in 1975, he harnessed the language of artless simplicity to grand, complex spectacle.

Set off against the academic complexity of "uptown" music, minimalism first created its own counterculture, with concerts in Soho lofts and art galleries, then developed an international reach, infiltrated the Carnegie Hall and Lincoln Center Establishment, and spread to pop music, film, and car commercials. A lot of the music of the past 50 years depends on those long, long tones over a constant *plunk-plunk-plunk-plunk*. And the movement's own story, much like one of Glass's early works, goes on and on, mutating from an avant-garde into a stockpile of clichés and influencing post-minimalist generations. One strand led to the Velvet Underground, David Bowie, and Japanese techno, another to the busy, historically ambitious operas of John Adams, a third to the film scores of Hans Zimmer. Minimalism became maximized.

Mr. Potato Head

George Lerner, a Brooklyn toy inventor, was the man who put a face on a spud. His original Mr. Potato Head, drawn up in prototype in 1949, was not much like today's. It called for an actual potato, and its plastic eyes, lips, ears, and tobacco pipe bore sharp spikes so they could be jabbed into place. The eyebrows and hair were made of felt and were intended to be pinned on. The face, at least by today's toy standards, could be a little bit demonic looking.

There were reportedly misgivings in the immediate postwar years about the waste of food this product potentially entailed, but in 1951, a modestly sized Rhode Island toy company, Hassenfeld Brothers, bought the design and the next year began advertising the Mr. Potato Head Funny-Face Kit on TV in the world's first toy commercial. (The slogan on the box: "Any Fruit or Vegetable Makes a Funny Face Man.") In 1953 he was joined by a spouse, Mrs. Potato Head. A son, Spud, and a daughter, Yam, followed. The instructions on the British version of Mr. Potato Head suggested that, if pressed, one could also use a beetroot.

In 1964 Mr. Potato Head went all-plastic, shedding his dependence on an authentic tuber. (This was possibly a relief to the thousands of parents who had discovered rotting vegetables in their children's bedrooms.) In this new form, he and the missus were successful enough that Hassenfeld introduced a whole line of their produce-aisle friends. Cooky the Cucumber, Pete the Pepper, Oscar the Orange, and Katie the Carrot each had slightly different, slightly disturbing facial features. So did various potato-complementing associates: Frenchy Fry, Mr. Ketchup Head and Mr. Mustard Head, Willy Burger, Frankie Frank. There was even a custom-branded Dunkie Donut-Head.

Over the years, Mr. Potato Head has seen his proportions change and his various accessories get larger to conform to government safety regulations, lost his pipe and become a spokespotato for smoking cessation at the behest of the U.S. surgeon general, and had a major role in the *Toy Story* movies. Lerner—who drew a royalty on every Mr. Potato Head sold—started his own toy company with a partner, Julius Ellman, and their firm, Lernell, is still in business, operated by Ellman's sons under the name Giapetta's Workshop. Hassenfeld Brothers also did okay. Its name was condensed to Hasbro (*see also* SCRABBLE), and it's one of the largest toy-makers in the world.

Mob, The [3]

One tends to think of *the mob* or *the mafia* as a catchall term for crime organizations, but the actual Mafia—founded in 1282 in Sicily—is merely one large group among many. The Camorra held power in Naples, the *vorovskoi mir* ("thieves' world") in Soviet Russia. Crooks in virtually every country have banded together for the sake of greater lawbreaking efficiency, often first as street gangs and then in more complex structures, especially in the past century or so. Given New York's position as a nexus of immigrant cultures, it's no surprise that a lot of those groups made their American landfall here. The Mafia itself got its first toehold in America in 1881, when a group of seven gangsters fled Sicily after one of them, Giuseppe Esposito, had murdered more than a dozen prominent local men. (Esposito, who settled in New York and then New Orleans, was eventually caught and sent back to Italy for trial.)

Around 1900, in New York's Lower East Side and a few other ethnic enclaves—where loosely affiliated street gangs had already conducted their business for generations (*see also* MAYHEM)—a particular network of Italian immigrant criminals known as the Black Hand began to shake down local residents and merchants. It was more or less a protection racket (one whose methods you

③ **Three Famous Rub-Out Joints Where You Can Still Eat**

» **Da Gennaro (former home of Umbertos Clam House)** (129 Mulberry St.)
At the original location of Umbertos—which has since moved twice, and is now across the street—the Profaci family hitman known as "Crazy Joe" Gallo was shot to death at his own birthday party in April 1972. The restaurant had just opened, and one local told the *Times*, "Just goes to show, you shouldn't try new places."

» **Sparks Steak House** (210 E. 46th St.)
On December 16, 1985, Constantino Paul Castellano, boss of the Gambino crime family, came for lunch and was gunned down in a coup.

» **Rao's** (455 E. 114th St.)
Albert Circelli and Louis Barone of the Lucchese family were dining here on December 29, 2003, when Circelli started heckling a young Broadway star's impromptu performance. Barone demanded that Circelli stop, and when he refused, Barone shot him dead.

can see fictionalized in *The Godfather Part II*, where the white-suited character named Fanucci demands that Vito Corleone "wet my beak"). To combat the Black Hand, the New York City Police Department set up a task force led by Lieutenant Joseph Petrosino—who, on an evidence-gathering trip to Sicily in 1909, was murdered for his efforts. You can still see his name on Petrosino Square, at Kenmare and Lafayette Streets.

The shakeout between the Camorra and the Mafia in New York began in 1915, after the murder of Giosue Gallucci and his son led to an exchange of hits that left 23 members of both groups dead. By its end, the former (which was ever so slightly less brutal and thus at a competitive disadvantage) was basically defunct and was absorbed by the Mafia, which was then perfectly placed to take advantage of Prohibition, enacted in 1919. It was an ideal set of circumstances in which to form a shadow economy by providing a black-market product that people really wanted at a premium price without taxation. The old neighborhood gangs began to divide the turf and create territories, hastened by an intramural Mafia battle for control known as the Castellammarese War. A concurrent shakeout in Chicago led to the primacy of Al Capone's gang.

By the 1930s, most American cities had a crime organization in charge of rum running, gambling, and various other mobbed-up businesses. New York, being much larger, spread that work among the Bonanno, Lucchese, Gambino, Profaci (a.k.a. Colombo), and Genovese organizations, the so-called Five Families, also known as the Commission. Charles "Lucky" Luciano, who established the Commission and ran the Genovese gang, oversaw its links with the enforcement organization known as Murder, Incorporated, the widely publicized contract-killing arm of the mob. This was not a Sicilian Mafia organization per se; it was mostly a Jewish group, headed by Louis "Lepke" Buchalter. (It was also affiliated with the hired killer Dutch Schultz until he threatened to go rogue in 1935 and the Commission had him shot dead.) Within various other New York communities, different organized-crime groups held power of their own: the tongs of Chinatown, for example.

Mayoral reform efforts—notably by Fiorello La Guardia—and state and federal prosecution were, at first, only modestly effective against all of this, for a variety of reasons. Even after Prohibition came to an end in 1933, there were plenty of businesses, including prostitution and gambling, in which the mob was providing services people wanted one way or another. Loan sharks, for better or worse, were there for those who couldn't borrow from a bank. Your average New York precinct house was also pretty corrupt—street cops were often on the take, and local businesses were sometimes faced with a choice of paying off the police or the gangsters for protection. Sometimes the mobsters seemed like a more attractive bet. Mob influence also infiltrated the Democratic political machine and a variety of otherwise legal New York industries: trucking, the produce and fish markets, concrete production, commercial garbage collection, the nightclub business. Many gay bars were mob controlled, in part because the gangsters could keep the cops away for a price, in part because the gangsters could extort the owners and clientele under threat of public exposure. It's been said that each New Yorker once paid a small daily fee to the mob, hidden in the slightly elevated price of every retail purchase or restaurant meal.

But the government pushed back and won in some instances: Murder, Inc., was broken up after one of Buchalter's deputies, Abe "Kid Twist" Reles, turned state's witness. (Reles, after he'd incriminated several underbosses and was preparing to talk about bigger fish, died from an ostensibly accidental fall out a window.) In the late 1950s, the links between the Democratic Tammany Hall machine finally gave out, and Albert Anastasia—who held power over the dockworkers union—was killed on the orders of the Gambino family, consolidating its power over the aging heads of the Five Families. Robert Kennedy, as attorney general in his brother's administration, stepped up prosecution efforts as well. In one curious turn, Joe Gallo, a boss in the Profaci family, advocated for opening up the ranks to African-Americans in order to broaden the talent pool and the family's reach (leading to Nicholas Gage's book *The Mafia Is Not an Equal Opportunity Employer*). Gallo's colleagues did not agree, and he was shot to death during a lunch at Umbertos Clam House in Little Italy in 1972.

The real change, though, came with the passage of the Racketeer Influenced and Corrupt Organizations laws in 1970. Known as RICO, they gave government lawyers broader power to prosecute groups as well as individuals and take their assets. Over the next decade, as the turf wars continued among the Five Families, the U.S. Attorneys' offices began to take larger and larger bites out of the mob. In the Southern District of New York, the most prominent prosecutor, Rudolph Giuliani, built his future career on a record of indicting and (mostly) convicting the heads of these families. John Gotti, the Gambino chief who was the last superpower in the New York Mafia, received a life sentence in 1992. Vincent "the Chin" Gigante, the Genovese-family boss known for ordering a hit on Gotti—and for ambling around Greenwich Village in his bathrobe—was convicted in 1997 and died in prison. Generational change helped weaken it further: The children and grandchildren of powerful mobsters often went to college, abandoning what was effectively the family firm in favor of straight businesses, leaving nobody to run them. They moved to the suburbs, too, where they couldn't keep an eye on one another quite as easily.

The Italian mob still exists in New York, albeit in vastly shrunken form, confined mostly to drug trafficking, loan sharking, and a few other fields. It now coexists with the New York arm of its Russian equivalent, which operates in similar realms and is also known for complex money-laundering operations. Today the actual presence of organized crime in the city is overshadowed by its perceived presence, owing to its popular fictionalized versions. *The Godfather*, Mario Puzo's 1969 novel, and Francis Ford Coppola's trilogy of films adapted from it introduced its culture and lingo (*consigliere, capo*) to outsiders, leaning on a vision of the Mafia's brutal glamour and deep sense of family ties. So did Martin Scorsese's film *GoodFellas*, so did David Chase's award-winning TV show *The Sopranos*, and so did about a thousand other books and films and songs. After *The Godfather*'s release, more than a few mobsters were said to have remodeled their behavior and even their accents on those of the fictional Corleones.

Modern Art[4]

The Armory Show opened in New York on February 17, 1913. By the time it closed, less than a month later, nearly 90,000 people, by far the largest audience that had ever attended an exhibition of contemporary art in this country, had come to the 69th Regiment Armory on Lexington Avenue at 25th Street to see it; the last day drew over 10,000 visitors in the wake of enormous waves of publicity. Former president Theodore Roosevelt attended. When the show traveled to Chicago, the attendance was estimated at 188,000. American art can be divided into Before and After the Armory Show: Before it, art was being made in the U.S. but not with the same drive, ambition, confidence, and world-changing vision. After it, the advancements of European artists mixed with the already impressive work of a handful of Americans pushed art in this country into a completely new existence.

Originally dubbed the "International Exhibition of Modern Art," the show included around 1,200 works by

④ **Works From the Armory Show You Can See at the Metropolitan Museum of Art**

1.　　　　　　　　　2.　　　　　　　　　3.

more than 300 artists and was organized entirely by a group of young American painters and sculptors. Two-thirds of the pieces were by Americans, but the Americans weren't the ones who produced this genesis moment. This was the first in-the-flesh, in-depth look at the art of Picasso, Braque, Picabia, Cézanne, Kandinsky, Kirchner, Courbet, Daumier, Degas, Derain, Gauguin, van Gogh, Léger, Manet, Monet, Munch, Pissarro, Redon, Renoir, Seurat, Toulouse-Lautrec, Archipenko, Bonnard, Brancusi, Duchamp, Matisse, and many others. How significant was the show? Salon impresario Mabel Dodge wrote to Gertrude Stein that it was "the most important public event … since the signing of the Declaration of Independence." She predicted it would cause "a riot and a revolution and things will never be the same afterwards." One New York critic wrote that "American artists did not so much visit the exhibition as live at it." Albert Barnes, Henry Frick, and the Met bought work from it, and the founding of MoMA and the Whitney stems directly from those 26 earthshaking days.

Artists may have been thunderstruck, but nonartists exploded an atom bomb of anger. The New York *Times* headlined a story "Cubism and Futurism Are Making Insanity Pay." (There were no Futurists on hand, however; they were invited, but their leader, Filippo Marinetti, wouldn't allow his artists to mingle with Cubists.) The participants were lambasted as "paranoiacs," "degenerates," and "dangerous." The show was like "visiting a lunatic asylum"; it was filled with the "chatter of anarchistic monkeys." The art was "epileptic." Matisse came in for especially harsh criticism. (More, even, than Duchamp's sensation-causing *Nude Descending a Staircase, No. 2*.) Conservative American painter William Merritt Chase clucked that Matisse was a charlatan, and when the show reached Chicago, provincial art students tried him in absentia for "artistic murder, pictorial arson … criminal misuse of line." They burned copies of

his paintings and tried to burn him in effigy but were thwarted by local authorities. Critics opined that Matisse's "poisonous" works were "the most hideous monstrosities ever perpetrated." And what of the president? He barked that the art was "repellent from every standpoint" and concluded that there was "no reason why people should not call themselves Cubists, or Octagonists, or Parallelopipedonists, or Knights of the Isosceles Triangle … one term is as fatuous as another."

Most art historians today say American artists in 1913 were yokels and the Armory Show marked the arrival of European sophistication on our shores. Although the U.S. was behind the curve, Americans did know change was afoot. Between 1907 and 1913, more than 60 exhibitions of "modern art" were held in New York. Alfred Stieglitz had opened a tiny gallery at 291 Fifth Avenue in 1905 that had almost as big an effect as the Armory Show, championing Americans like Georgia O'Keeffe, John Marin, Paul Strand, and Marsden Hartley. Stieglitz also showed Europeans like Picasso, Matisse, Brancusi, and even Duchamp's world-changing urinal turned on its side, *Fountain*. By 1913, Americans were—apart from the academicians—keen on the European vanguard. Numerous Americans had studied, worked, or exhibited in Europe, including many women. (Almost 20 percent of the Americans in the Armory Show were female—a better ratio than we often see today.) One thing the Armory Show revealed was that a number of "modern" American artists—realists like William Glackens, Robert Henri, and George Bellows, with their vernacular street scenes and pictures of prostitutes and boxers—were in a different universe than their European counterparts. Indeed, all but a few of the American artists trying to be "modern" were desperately trying to do it without Cubism, Fauvism, or Futurism.

But the Armory Show was a blast of fresh air for those American artists who had already gleaned what counted as "modern art" since the 1870s. Marin's mad,

4.   5.

1. **Young Sailor II,** by Henri Matisse
2. **Porcupines,** by Robert W. Chanler
3. **Moonlight Marine,** by Albert Pinkham Ryder
4. **Factory Village** (now titled **The Factory Village**), by J. Alden Weir
5. **Carrying Coal** (now titled **Stevedore**), by Mahonri Young

quasi-Cubistic watercolor of New York's St. Paul's Chapel was in the show; ditto Oscar Bluemner's flat planes depicting the Hackensack River. Edward Hopper's paintings, which aren't exactly "modern," already show signs of the implacable isolation that would later make his paintings quake. Maurice Prendergast's street scenes had completely digested Impressionism. More than this, many of the other American artists included in the Armory Show—among them Hartley, Mary Cassatt, Agnes Pelton, Stuart Davis, Elie Nadelman, Charles Sheeler, and Joseph Stella—felt as if they were now part of something much bigger than a little local New York struggle. They were citizens of a new international avant-garde.

Modern Dance

What makes a dance "modern"? The same thing that makes a painting modern—a de-emphasis on narrative and representation and a turning toward the material of the work itself. In the case of dance, the material is movement, shape, gesture, emotion, and the body itself. Modern dance is also defined as a historical movement, primarily developed from the 1920s through the 1960s. It's an Expressionist, muscular style that rejects the refinement of Western classical dance, being energized by the twisting torso (rather than the drifting arms) and focusing its movements on the floor rather than the air, where, in ballet, a dancer is meant to float.

First came the prophet: Isadora Duncan. In 1896, Duncan traveled to New York from San Francisco to perform with Augustin Daly's theatrical company. She had already begun developing her new, instinctive method of dancing—a primal, expressive movement she claimed was "the art which has been lost for two thousand years." She rejected almost everything about ballet: its emphasis on formal steps, its corsets and its shoes. But she became frustrated with Daly's melodramas and

started presenting her dance concerts in high-society New York living rooms, trying to find aristocratic patrons. And while Duncan later fled to Europe, where her iconoclastic work was more fully embraced, she returned to America in 1914 for a seminal season at the New York Century Theatre—where she spent nearly her entire savings on $2,000 worth of heavy-scented lilies for decorations. In both her bohemian life and her ecstatic art, Duncan wore free-flowing unstructured garments; her hair was down, her feet were bare. She insisted that in dance, movement should be organic, that every gesture should dictate the next. And so her own movements dictated the future: 120 years later, all modern dance is infused with her spirit.

While Duncan tied her work to classical Greece— many of her gestures were imitations of images from vase paintings—the other protomodern master choreographers, Ruth St. Denis and Ted Shawn, looked further east (St. Denis based many of her dances on "Oriental" and Indian movement) and to Americana. Together they formed Denishawn Dance in Los Angeles and, through their wildly successful Denishawn School of Dancing and Related Arts, trained the woman who would come to define modern dance: Martha Graham. In 1923, disappointed with commercial tendencies among the Denishawn company, Graham struck out on her own and, in 1926, founded the Martha Graham Center of Contemporary Dance on New York's Upper East Side. Soon she and her dancers began performing her often harsh modernist works (stark sets, simple costumes) throughout New York, transforming dance in the same way lightning transforms dry grass.

Like Duncan, Graham took inspiration from classical Greece—her *Errand Into the Maze*, for example, was loosely based on ideas about the Minotaur. And like the Denishawn team, she took inspiration from Americana, working with composer Aaron Copland and designer Isamu Noguchi for another of her masterpieces,

Appalachian Spring. Dancing well into her 70s, she eventually crossed over into the mainstream and was named *Time* magazine's Dancer of the Century in 1998, becoming known in circles that would normally never care about experimental dance. More important, over the course of 181 choreographic works, Graham refined her technique of contraction and release, developing a vivid, percussive, energetic method that would "increase the emotional activity of the dancer's body." Even in her most lyrical pieces, effort was at the marrow of Graham's project; every dance was meant to be a "graph of the heart."

The lineage of American modern dance largely descended from Graham and her fellow ex-Denishawner, Doris Humphrey. In 1928, Humphrey moved to New York, where she developed her own modern-dance technique rooted in fall and recovery, or the "arc between two deaths," as she described it. With the exception of the great Alvin Ailey (who was trained by Lester Horton and founded his own company in New York in 1958), the major figures of the third modern-dance wave were often connected to one of the two women: José Limón started as Humphrey's student and eventually employed her as artistic director in his own company; Paul Taylor danced for Graham for several seasons in the mid-'50s while choreographing for his own troupe. Taylor's minimalist work veered eventually into postmodernism, playing with silence and obstruction—his 1975 *Esplanade* explores the poetry of everyday movements like walking. Another Graham dancer, Merce Cunningham, would stride even further from her dramatizing elements, moving fully into the avant-garde and embracing elements of chance and, later, computer-assisted choreography. When you watch the dispassionate, silvery movement of the Cunningham company, nothing could seem more divorced from the Expressionistic work of the high moderns. Still, you can see glimmers here and there. It's in the twist of a torso, the flash of a bare foot.

Mortgage-Backed Securities

In the 1970s, Lewis Ranieri, a mailroom employee who'd graduated to the trading floor at Salomon Brothers, began "securitizing" mortgages that weren't eligible for grouping under the loan companies Fannie Mae or Freddie Mac—i.e., consolidating them and selling them to investors as securities in a new secondary market. In the '80s, Ranieri normalized these securities by going to Congress to allow pension funds and banks to invest. The congressional okay opened them up to huge swaths of the market: By 1986, the private-label mortgage-backed security was worth $150 billion. "Mortgages are math," said Ranieri, and to do the homework, he hired Ph.D.'s to determine the most efficient methods of selling them. These became collateralized mortgage obligations, or CMOs—high-yield, low-risk collections of mortgages layered into "tranches" of risk designed to protect the more stable bonds in the group. In 1987, Wall Street's Drexel Burnham Lambert, the lion of the junk-bond market, invented the similar collateralized debt obligation, or CDO.

It took almost 30 years, but these three concepts would merge in the housing boom of the mid-2000s. This bubble was built on mortgage-backed securities and CDOs with unstable mortgages, offering high returns and artificially low risk thanks to the rating agencies. When housing prices peaked in 2006, homeowners could not refinance, adjustable-rate mortgages caused higher monthly payments, and delinquencies ballooned. Then the mortgage-backed securities went down, banks were stuck with billions in collapsed CDOs, and the recession hit. "I will never, ever, ever, ever live out that scar that I carry for what happened with something I created," Ranieri told *The Wall Street Journal* in 2018. "It did so much damage to so many people."

Movies [5]

Pictures began to move, commercially speaking, at Thomas Edison's laboratory in West Orange, New Jersey, in the 1880s and early 1890s. One of the first public demonstrations was held on May 9, 1893, at the Brooklyn Institute of Arts and Sciences—today's Brooklyn Museum—where audience members lined up, peered into the little window of a machine, and watched a few moments of a blacksmith at work. (The Brooklyn *Eagle* reported the next day that the experience could "excite wonderment.") The next year, the first "kinetoscope parlor," with coin-op versions of those machines, opened at 1155 Broadway, essentially creating the original moviegoing experience.

In 1894 and 1895, a few of Edison's ex-employees and competitors made short films in Brooklyn and Manhattan, and on April 23, 1896, Edison demonstrated his Vitascope system (which he hadn't invented himself but had recently acquired) at Koster & Bial's Music Hall, located on the block of 34th Street where Macy's is today. He screened dancers, crashing surf, and a short boxing comedy and soon established a studio on West 28th Street. Edison was, very soon, joined by a lot of people who really wanted to direct. By 1905, movie production had become a proper industry, and most of it happened in New York. American Mutoscope, later known as Biograph, was headquartered first near Union Square and then in the Bronx; it launched the career of the great director D. W. Griffith. Adolph Zukor's Famous Players Film Company operated out of a converted armory on West 26th Street (which, incredibly, is still a television studio; Rachael Ray's cooking show is shot there). Carl Laemmle started the Independent Moving Pictures Company, headquartered in New York and shooting across the river in Fort Lee, New Jersey.

In the earliest days, the films they made were reenactments of famous historical events, but after a few years, they began to shift to fictional stories—miniature plays, a few minutes long. Many of those were shot in studios and are universal in setting rather than specific to city life. Most have also been lost, and those that survive are often of historical interest but not so lively as cinema. One little exception is a 1901 Edison production called *What Happened on Twenty-Third Street, New York City*, shot near the brand-new Flatiron Building and showing wind from a subway vent kicking up a young woman's skirts, uncannily like Marilyn Monroe's a half-century later in *The Seven Year Itch*. Another short film documents a trip uptown on the subway, shot from the front car. It's from 1905, when the IRT was a year old, and you can watch it on YouTube.

The '10s and '20s allowed the movies to grow up somewhat. The "two-reeler," running twenty minutes or so, became a dominant form of comedy, and hundreds of these films were produced in New York. Famous Players merged with another studio, Lasky, and eventually took the name of its distributor, Paramount. Independent Moving Pictures also merged with several firms, becoming Universal Pictures. But the end of New York's status as the movie capital was coming into view. Early film was best shot in bright sunlight—the emulsion was not as light-sensitive as it became later—and New York had a long, gray winter. Also, Edison's royalty collectors were extremely strict, and in the days before cross-country communication, it would be easier to dodge them at a distance. By 1920 or so, the industry was shifting its business to Southern California, which had endless sunny days and a wide variety of locations (desert, beach, mountains) in which to shoot. The arrival of talkies in 1927 more or less killed the New York location shoot because crowds and traffic noises made hash out of the audio tracks. For the next twenty years, New York as a presence in the movies was almost completely re-created elsewhere. The noir gangsters, the screwball-comedy heiresses, and the Park Avenue antics of Nick and Nora Charles in *The Thin Man*—all existed principally on the back lots of Los Angeles.

Until 1947, that is, when Jules Dassin and his producer Mark Hellinger made the daring decision to return to New York and shoot their film *The Naked City* in its streets. Some short sequences for other movies had been shot here, notably for *The Lost Weekend* a couple of years earlier, but Dassin would shoot most of his outdoors in New York and in real city apartments, culminating in a chase sequence on the walkways of the Williamsburg Bridge. (To avoid drawing large disruptive crowds, they often concealed their cameras and microphones with makeshift structures and inside trucks.) The location shoot added a vast amount of verisimilitude and atmosphere to the film.

Yet, a few great moments aside (like 1957's *Sweet Smell of Success*, partly shot in and around Times Square), New York as a real backdrop did not quite come roaring back until after 1966. That was when Mayor John Lindsay, having learned that the city's tortuous permit process was causing filmmakers to stay away, created a single agency, now called the Mayor's Office of Film, Theater & Broadcasting, to cut the red tape. An immediate increase in the number of local productions followed.

As it happens, this could not have come at a better time for cinema, because the social dynamics of New York in the 1970s and 1980s turned out to be solid gold for filmmakers. Over the next fifteen years, the big movies shot here—and they were unmistakably, indelibly made *here*, not in California—established both the tragedy of broken-down New York and its cracked-mirror beauty, and along the way they set a new standard for filmmaking grit. Consider this extremely incomplete, entirely compelling list: *Mean Streets, Rosemary's Baby, The French Connection, Midnight Cowboy, Panic in Needle Park, Taxi Driver, Serpico, Shaft, Dog Day Afternoon, Annie Hall, The Taking of Pelham One Two Three, The Warriors*, and, at the tail end of this era, *Do the Right Thing*. Martin Scorsese, in particular, became the bard of this befouled city; Woody Allen, his emotional polar opposite, portrayed New York as a charming, magnetic place rather than a dark one.

As the city recovered and grew wealthier in the 1990s (and after Miramax set up shop here, bringing a powerhouse independent company to the birthplace of the industry), the somewhat warmer cinematic view of New York began to supersede the grittier one; *When Harry Met Sally...*, *Crossing Delancey*, *Metropolitan*, and even, perhaps, *Home Alone 2: Lost in New York* were harbingers. At a distance from the mainstream, portrayals of the city in films like Spike Jonze's claustrophobic *Being John Malkovich*, released in 1999, could get weird and often surreal. But in the twenty-first-century multiplex, the upper-middle-class, aspirational New York more familiar from sitcoms and novels reigned over all, as in the angsty couplings of Noah Baumbach's films and the fashion-magazine intrigue of *The Devil Wears Prada*. Though not in *every* movie: Jennifer Lopez's stripper character in *Hustlers* is shaking down those callow investment bankers for as much as she can get.

Muckraking

When Theodore Roosevelt coined the term *muckraker* in a 1906 speech, he didn't mean it as a compliment. "The man with the muck rake"—an image he borrowed from the English writer John Bunyan—was, to his thinking, a journalist operating down in the mud, one obsessed with the worst aspects of society. Of course, the muckrakers themselves saw it differently. The term soon became shorthand for a lefty activist-journalist of the Progressive Era who was crusading against inequity or corruption. Ida Tarbell (on the business practices of Standard Oil), Jacob Riis (on slum conditions), Lincoln Steffens (on civic corruption), and Upton Sinclair (on unsafe food practices, among other subjects) epitomized the genre, and all spent their peak career years living and working in New York City. Two magazines, also headquartered here, were arguably the central publishers of the early muckrakers' work: *McClure's*, where Steffens and Tarbell often wrote, and *Collier's*, whose 1905 publication of one of Sinclair's exposés, "Is Chicago Meat Clean?" led to the passage of the landmark Federal Meat Inspection Act the following year.

Although neither magazine survives—*McClure's* went bankrupt, became a women's magazine, and folded in 1929, and *Collier's* closed, after a long twilight, in 1957— the muckraking tradition outlasted them. At *The Village Voice* (see also ALT-WEEKLY), for example, Wayne Barrett was a perpetual irritant to the administration of Mayor

Rudolph Giuliani and dove deeply into the practices of the Trump Organization (*see also* TRUMPISM). WikiLeaks and the Intercept are arguably digital-age descendants of the muckrakers. And the investigative unit at the New York *Times* now does it all day, every day.

Muffins, English

Surely they're ... English? Nope. Those are crumpets. But in 1874, an Englishman in New York named Samuel Bath Thomas started baking a crumpet variant from a yeast batter. The resultant baked good was a little more breadlike and fluffy than its British sibling. His Chelsea bakery, briefly on Ninth Avenue and then at 337 West 20th Street, very quickly reached its capacity and eventually grew into a national brand. (Today Thomas' is owned by the Bimbo Bakeries conglomerate.) In 2006, renovations to the 20th Street structure revealed a brick oven still extant underneath the backyard. The building, now a co-op (*see also* COOPERATIVE APARTMENT BUILDING), has been renamed the Muffin House.

Mugging *see* MAYHEM

Musical Theater[6]

If you want to be finicky, you could trace musical theater back to the ancient world, when, in the fifth century BCE, it emerged from chanting and verse. We had chorus lines before we had shows to put them in. But when we think of musical theater now, we think of Broadway's much-tinkered-with recipe of a cohesive play, or "book," interspersed with songs (which often advance the story) and expressed with razzle-dazzle. There are musicals like *Evita*, *Falsettos*, and *Cats* that are "sung-through" like operas, and musicals like *Jersey Boys* and *Mamma Mia!* whose songs barely graze the plot. The balance of dancing, dialogue, and song changes in every combination, and even now people can disagree on whether a show is a "play with music" or a "musical." But you can always tell where the line is, and those lines were all drawn in New York.

The modern American book musical evolved in the nineteenth century out of revues, Gilbert-and-Sullivan-style operettas, and plays sprinkled with hit songs. *The Black Crook*, a huge hit in New York in 1866, usually gets credit for being the form's first "true" example, and its origin story is classic: Two impresarios booked a Parisian ballet company into the huge Academy of Music, but the Academy burned down; meanwhile, a melodrama had booked another large local venue, so the ballet impresarios and the melodrama's playwright joined forces and called it a show. The spectacle-filled result packed the 3,200-seat Niblo's Garden (at Broadway and Prince Street) for 474 performances and was revived and toured for decades to a totally unprecedented degree, proving that in New York, even a huge property fire is opportunity knocking. That same year, *Black Domino/Between You, Me and the Post* was the first show to call itself a "musical comedy," and in 1860, *The Seven Sisters* had innovated with scene changes, a book, songs, and special effects. But *The Black Crook* had all the basics: a unifying book, some purpose-written songs, and the actors themselves (rather than a cameo troupe) performing the musical numbers. Its original tunes, like "You Naughty, Naughty Men," hint at the reason for its runaway business. The ballet dancers did not wear a lot.

By the early twentieth century, the block of West 28th Street between Fifth and Sixth Avenues (*see also* TIN PAN ALLEY) was churning out hits by the likes of Irving Berlin, which then found their way into theatricals, and offering work to future icons like Victor Herbert and George Gershwin. The super-producer Florenz Ziegfeld soon dominated the scene with his star-making *Follies*, while now-vanished forms like minstrel shows, acted by both Black and white performers, and vaudeville variety acts swept the nation. The ne plus ultra of song-and-dance men, George M. Cohan, soon brought vaudeville to the "legitimate" stage, creating beloved musical comedies that sat at the core of America's sense of itself: He was a "Yankee Doodle Dandy." He sang "You're a Grand Old Flag." He crooned "Give My Regards to Broadway," turning the street into a metonym for patriotic pride. George and Ira Gershwin, Richard Rodgers and Lorenz Hart, Cole Porter—all were writing dazzling lyrics full of surprise and vivid comedy. Shows and their songs

Chita Rivera and Liane Plane in the original Broadway production of West Side Story, 1957.

6 **Where to See a Broadway Star Dining Postshow**

From New York *theater critic Helen Shaw*

➤ **Joe Allen Restaurant** *(326 W. 46th St.)*: "It's been there since 1965, plenty of time to gather posters for its wall of flops. Visit to meditate on your show's imminent death."

➤ **Sardi's** *(234 W. 44th St.)*: "Since theater is always vanishing, stage folks love a place with tradition; Sardi's has been here since 1927."

➤ **The Lambs Club** *(132 W. 44th St.)*: "Eavesdrop on producers toasting their success or drowning their sorrows."

➤ **Café Un Deux Trois** *(123 W. 44th St.)*: "Big and boisterous; the right place to eat giant slabs of country pâté and hoover up skinny French fries, while actors from the Belasco next door come to complain about how all the theaters east of Broadway do worse business."

➤ **West Bank Cafe** *(407 W. 42nd St.)*: "I can't go in there without falling over Jonathan Groff."

became more tightly integrated, and the Broadway signature became sparkle and craft.

Then came the hammer blow: 1927's *Show Boat.* During the interwar years, lyricist-librettist-producer Oscar Hammerstein II had wondered if there was a way to reclaim some of the majesty of grand opera while still remaining "sufficiently human to be entertaining." The composer Jerome Kern wanted to stage Edna Ferber's sweeping novel about people working on a riverboat, and his and Hammerstein's vivid adaptation brought a seriousness of intent to the musical—here was opera, vernacular entertainment, and popular musical comedy, all joined into one. According to historian Larry Stempel, "There simply was no cultural frame of reference at the time adequate to describe the piece." Our theatrical history divides into before *Show Boat* and after: The musical had finally made its claim as art.

But the Depression followed, sending writers and performers west to Hollywood and pausing the advancement of the form. Not until a decade and a half later did another Hammerstein show raise the American book musical to international preeminence. Rodgers and Hammerstein's 1943 *Oklahoma!* was thematically akin to *Show Boat* in the way it used folk idiom, rather gravely framed the American story, and focused on landscape as an encompassing metaphor for the democratic project. But *Oklahoma!* was also a definitive formal step forward. Its speech segued gracefully into song to signal heightened emotion, move the story along, and explicate characters, rather than being an interruption or ornament. Music and drama were finally blended, as was the mix of high and low art the musical had long promised. *Oklahoma!* was both a wildfire commercial success and a critical one. As the globe moved into a long period of American influence, theater carried at least one part of the message out—and the musical's hundred-year invention was complete.

The corresponding golden age leaned heavily on the Rodgers and Hammerstein canon—*South Pacific, Carousel, The King and I, The Sound of Music*—and many of their shows were turned into films. The mid-century love for movie musicals gilds them even now: Cinema is why we have such live-wire contact to the greats like *Guys and Dolls* (1950), *My Fair Lady* (1956), *West Side Story*, and *The Music Man* (both 1957). Bearing such cultural weight, musicals became a site to negotiate changing ideas of American values. They got sweet for kids (*Annie*) and groovy with rock and roll (*Hair*) while elevating Stephen Sondheim, who is still the fiercest, least sentimental intellect ever to grapple with the musical. In 1970, he and director Harold Prince joined forces for *Company* and stormed through the rest of the decade with one groundbreaking show after another—all excitingly modern, psychologically precise, and anti-nostalgic, the acid that eats through layers of paint to show the form beneath. And anti-sentiment must obviously call into being its antithesis, the Foreign Big Emotion Musical, which would include *Les Misérables* and everything by Andrew Lloyd Webber.

When you look at the American musical today, you're looking into a refracting mirror showing images of ages past: jukebox musicals (bombastic entertainment marathons much like nineteenth-century shows that exploited popular hit songs), Disney movies made into stage versions, golden-age revivals, new investigations in the realist mode (*Next to Normal, Dear Evan Hansen*), and Hammersteinian attempts to get a handle on the country itself (the immense hit *Hamilton*). And although musical theater is principally a Broadway product these days, it still starts downtown: The Public Theater, which developed and launched *Hair, A Chorus Line, Hamilton*, and *Bloody Bloody Andrew Jackson*, and New York Theatre Workshop, which originated *Rent* and *Hadestown*, sit very close to where the old Niblo's Garden once stood.

From
NANNY STATE
to
NUYORICAN

New Wave's "It" girl, Deborah Harry, 1978.
PHOTOGRAPH BY MARTYN GODDARD

Nanny State

The British term *nanny state*, first used in the 1960s and popularized in the Thatcher era, describes an intrusive (usually liberal) government deciding what's best for its citizens and restricting the choices it disagrees with. It's a shrewd coinage, because *nanny* carries with it both a draconian, forcing-medicine-down-your-throat quality and a pursed-lips kind of fussiness, along with an overtone of distancing wealth and privilege.

If any leader has epitomized the nanny state for Americans, it is Michael Bloomberg, mayor of New York from 2002 to 2013. Bloomberg ran as a Republican but governed as a centrist, pro-business, technocratic Democrat. Trained as an electrical engineer, he held a somewhat unusual belief (for a politician) in the transformative power of data and placed a high emphasis on results. He therefore sized up two public-health crises—smoking-related illness and obesity rates—and assessed how much leverage he had to affect them. Starting in 2003, he and the City Council banned smoking in bars and restaurants (apart from a few cigar- and hookah-centric places) and most other indoor spaces where people congregate. An enormous amount of criticism erupted, citing personal liberty, the ancient social ritual of smoking and drinking with friends, the potential effect on business, the notion that it would put off international visitors, and more. He (and the council) stood firm, and virtually no one stopped going to bars or restaurants. A dozen years later, the smoking rate in New York had fallen by more than a third, to 13.9 percent. In public-health terms, that is a profound outcome. Most significant, many cities and states have followed suit, including those with robust tobacco cultures: Rome, Paris, even North Carolina.

Then came the overreach. In 2012, the Bloomberg administration attempted to repeat its success by announcing a ban on the sale of sugary beverages—soda, mostly—in cups larger than 16 ounces. There were loopholes (like exemptions for 7-Eleven's Big Gulp and similar grocery-store offerings regulated by the state rather than the city), but a lot of places, including movie theaters, would have been affected, and this time the forces arrayed against the ban were more effective. (They had a better case. It's hard to argue that even a little bit of tobacco smoking is harmless, whereas the occasional big soda truly is.) Critics pointed out that

Bloomberg's own habits—extra heavily salting his fries, say—appeared hypocritical. The "nanny state" charges became overwhelming, industry-backed groups challenged the ban in court, and a judge declared it to be outside the Board of Health's regulatory power.

By that time, Bloomberg was no longer mayor, having been replaced by Bill de Blasio (who also supported the soda ban). It might have been largely forgotten, a hiccup in a mayoralty that was otherwise pretty successful, but when Bloomberg made a brief, unsuccessful lunge at the presidency in early 2020, "the soda ban" was, for a few weeks, back on everybody's lips. It was an easily grasped and potent symbol of annoyingly overprotective government in a country where the per capita consumption of soda is 39 gallons per year.

National Rifle Association

 Troubled by Union soldiers' lack of marksmanship training, New Yorkers George W. Wingate and William C. Church founded the National Rifle Association in 1871 to teach young men to shoot. Wingate was a Brooklyn lawyer, and Church was a journalist who'd been the publisher of the New York *Sun* and, for a time, a Washington, D.C., correspondent for the New York *Times*. Both men had served in the Union ranks during the Civil War and believed their organization should "promote and encourage rifle shooting on a scientific basis." With funding from the state, the pair purchased a farm in Queens—land that is now the Creedmoor Psychiatric Center—and built a rifle range.

In 1907, the NRA moved its headquarters to the nation's capital. Four years later, after a grisly murder-suicide near Gramercy Park, Tammany Hall boss "Big Tim" Sullivan proposed a bill in the New York State Senate outlawing unlicensed concealed handguns. "I believe it will save more souls than all the preachers in the city," said Sullivan. The Sullivan Act passed with an overwhelming majority. Though the NRA was in favor of gun control at the time, the organization tried for years to repeal and replace the Sullivan law with a less restrictive one, claiming it had "the effect of arming the bad man and disarming the good one to the injury of the community." A century later, the

NRA continues to have an adversarial relationship with its birthplace. In 2018, New York attorney general Letitia James, who was the city's public advocate at the time, described the NRA as "a terrorist organization," and in December 2019, the NRA argued before the United States Supreme Court that New York City's gun laws were too restrictive.

Neoconservatism

Everybody agrees on where it all began: In Alcove 1, adjacent to the City College cafeteria in the late 1930s, where anti-Stalin left-wing students gathered to take their lunch and debate politics. (The Stalinists occupied Alcove 2.) Just where it all went wrong, or whether it did at all, has been a point of intense dispute ever since.

The denizens of Alcove 1 were largely though not exclusively Jewish by religion and Trotskyist by philosophy. (That is, they supported the Bolshevik revolution in the Soviet Union but believed it had soured somewhere on the way to Stalin's gulag.) From that point of departure, nearly all of them moved rightward to varying degrees, and many went on to occupy prestigious jobs in academia and intellectual journalism. But ultimately, the most famous product of Alcove 1 was an oppositional, reactive political ideology, or sub-ideology, often applied situationally, that formed the basis for what decades later would be called the neoconservative movement. In contrast to traditional, small-government conservatives, its adherents would approve of some massive federal interventions such as the New Deal, and, far from being isolationist, would espouse, often to the point of fanaticism, the use of military force abroad. Undergirding such decisions were a strong belief in American-style democracy and conventional morality.

Perhaps the most politically influential early neocon was Irving Kristol, who graduated from CCNY in 1940. Over the next twenty years, he abandoned Trotskyism for New Deal liberalism, and in 1965, he and fellow alcove veteran Daniel Bell founded *The Public Interest*, a highbrow journal of domestic policy devoted to what were at first friendly critiques of Lyndon Johnson's Great Society programs. The founding ethos of *The Public Interest* was hardheaded realism and a respect for rigid, empirical inquiry. But Kristol soon wandered from these moorings; he grew annoyed, then perhaps obsessed, with

the New Left and its attacks on traditional morality and the moral legitimacy of American foreign policy. Bell (still a liberal) quit the journal, and Kristol began to attract a large collection of disillusioned former liberals and leftists.

In 1973, the socialist Michael Harrington called them "neoconservatives," a coinage that may not have perfectly described their political orientation but did perfectly predict it. By then, the movement had attracted such names as Norman Podhoretz, Jeane Kirkpatrick, and Nathan Glazer, and the neoconservatives at first directed their energies toward defending the old, New Deal faction of the Democratic Party against the insurgent New Left. After Hubert Humphrey—the old liberal who had been alienated from antiwar liberals by his association with President Johnson and the Vietnam War—lost the 1968 election to Richard Nixon, they founded the Coalition for a Democratic Majority in 1972 and tried, unsuccessfully, to nominate the anti-communist senator Henry "Scoop" Jackson in 1976.

The neocons found that their revulsion for the left on culture and foreign policy overwhelmed their residual domestic-policy liberalism, and by the 1980s, almost all of them had joined the Republican Party. And since the GOP was enjoying a political ascent, the neocons seemed to embody a major source of its appeal (a sense that Democrats had veered too far left on culture and foreign policy) and to have supplied the party with the brainpower necessary to govern. The successful end of the Cold War made neocons appear prophetic, even though in reality they had hyped up Soviet power and dismissed the possibility that the USSR might disintegrate on its own. By the second Bush administration, the movement had so thoroughly permeated Republican doctrine that it was difficult to separate it from old-fashioned conservatism. This culminated in the political and cultural pinnacle of neoconservatism: the Iraq War.

Strictly speaking, the war was not a purely neoconservative brainchild. Several of its architects—Dick Cheney, Donald Rumsfeld, George W. Bush—had only loose connections to the movement, and many moderates and liberals also endorsed the war. Still, the neocons argued for regime change in Iraq more fervently than they had ever argued for anything, jingoistically cheering on the greatness and goodness of American military might and dismissing its hand-wringing skeptics. The war demonstrated that the neocons had, at minimum, massively overlearned the lessons they had drawn from the Cold War. The Republican Party's bright young minds were now its sinister masterminds.

It took until 2016 for the price to finally come due. Donald Trump ushered into the party a new faction of "nationalists" who openly disdained the neoconservative program of crusading military intervention. Trump's nationalists also carried more than a whiff of anti-Semitism and racism. And neocons were disproportionately represented among the conservative intellectuals who refused to support Trump (John Podhoretz, Bret Stephens, David Frum) or even left the party altogether (Max Boot, William Kristol). By the Trump era, the political standing of neoconservatism was as uncertain as it had been since the phrase was invented. Last in, first out.

New Journalism[1]

Tom Wolfe always said Gay Talese was the first to figure it out. Talese may agree, but he dislikes the term. You can argue that Joseph Mitchell beat them both to it, and John Hersey, too, and Lillian Ross, and maybe Nellie Bly. No matter: The arrival of the so-called New Journalism happened when the tired conventions of feature writing were abruptly and unexpectedly blown up. Around 1962, a select few writers at the New York *Herald Tribune*, *Esquire*, and occasionally *The New Yorker* and *Playboy* and a couple of other outlets began adopting devices formerly confined to short stories and novels—vivid scene painting, emotional richness, pop-culture awareness, the unapologetic presence of the writer, lots of dialogue—and applying them to nonfiction articles. The groundbreaking piece, according to Wolfe, was Talese's profile of Joe Louis, which ran in *Esquire* in June 1962; Wolfe was knocked flat by how much more vivid it was than Talese's work at his home paper, the *Times*. (You couldn't really *write* at the *Times* then, when its joylessness was not only accepted but encouraged; *see also* NEW YORK TIMES, THE.) Wolfe's own breakthrough came a year later in *Esquire* with a feature about the car-customizing culture of Southern California. As he told it, he'd been stuck on deadline; told his editor, Byron Dobell, that he'd deliver his notes for someone else to write up; and drafted overnight a wild, stream-of-consciousness 49-page memo. The next day, Dobell told Wolfe that he was striking "Dear Byron" from the top and running the rest of it in the magazine.

Wolfe was the showiest of the writers in this clique but was hardly alone, especially as a certain one-upmanship started to kick in. Joan Didion, on the West Coast, began delivering reports from the edges of the counterculture and Hollywood that incorporated references to her own ragged mental state into her paradoxically vigorous prose. Talese's massively reported 1966 profile "Frank Sinatra Has a Cold," whose subject had refused the writer any access, became an avatar of the form. Truman Capote turned a thrill-killing murder in Kansas into the 1965 "nonfiction novel" *In Cold Blood*. In 1968, after the *Trib* had folded and its Sunday magazine carried on as *New York*, its editor, Clay Felker, continued to treat it as a showcase for the New Journalism (*see also* NEW YORK MAGAZINE). Nora Ephron absolutely dismembered the fussbudget culture of what she called the Food Establishment in a story for *New York*, "Critics in the World of the Rising Soufflé (or Is It the Rising Meringue?)." Jimmy Breslin wrote for Felker, hilariously and pungently, about blue-collar New York politics, and in 1969, he and Norman Mailer mounted a half-joking mayoral campaign of their own. Wolfe's 1970 story about the Black Panthers' fund-raiser at Leonard Bernstein's apartment, "Radical Chic: That Party at Lenny's," took a blade to the era's radicalism.

The flamboyance of the New Journalism pissed people off, and some (though not all) of its practitioners got a little *too* close to writing fiction. Often it wasn't a case

VOLUME V, NO. 7   FEBRUARY 14, 1972   40 CENTS

New York

Weather
Fresh mass of new information, driving out occluded front of old notions about what "journalism" does and doesn't do. Better reader insights likely today and tomorrow despite high winds and occasional storms of protest.

THE BIRTH OF 'THE NEW JOURNALISM': EYEWITNESS REPORT BY TOM WOLFE

PARTICIPANT REVEALS MAIN FACTORS LEADING TO DEMISE OF THE NOVEL, RISE OF NEW STYLE COVERING EVENTS

[1] THE FEATURE GAME
By TOM WOLFE

I doubt if many of the aces I will be extolling in this story went into journalism with the faintest notion of creating a "new" journalism, a "higher" journalism, or even a mildly improved variety. I know they never dreamed that anything they were going to write for newspapers or magazines would wreak such evil havoc in the literary world . . . causing panic, dethroning the novel as the number one literary genre, starting the first new direction in American literature in half a century . . . Nevertheless, that is what has happened. Bellow, Barth, Updike—even the best of the lot, Philip Roth—the novelists are all out there ransacking the literary histories and sweating it out, wondering where they now stand. Damn it all, Saul, the *Huns* have arrived . . .

God knows I didn't have anything new in mind, much less anything literary, when I took my first newspaper job. I had a fierce and unnatural craving for something else entirely. Chicago, 1928, that was the general idea . . . Drunken reporters out on the ledge of the *News* peeing into the Chicago River at dawn . . . Nights down at the saloon listening to "Back of the Stockyards" being sung by a baritone who was only a lonely blind bulldyke with lumps of milk glass for eyes . . . Nights down at the detective bureau—it was always nighttime in my daydreams of the newspaper life. Reporters didn't work during the day. I wanted the whole movie, nothing left out . . .

I was aware of what had reduced me to this Student Prince Mauldin state of mind. All the same, I couldn't help it. I had just spent five years in graduate school, a statement that may mean nothing to people who never served such a stretch; it is the explanation, nonetheless. I'm not sure I can give you the remotest idea of what graduate school is like. Nobody ever has. Millions of Americans now go to graduate schools, but just say the phrase—"graduate school"—and what picture leaps into the brain? No picture, not even a blur. Half the people I knew in graduate school were going to write a novel about it. I thought about it myself. No one ever wrote such a book, as far as I know. Everyone used to sniff the air. How morbid! How poisonous! Nothing else like it in the world! But the subject always defeated them. It defied literary exploitation. Such a novel would be a study of frustration, but a form of frustration so exquisite, so ineffable, nobody could describe it. Try to imagine the worst part of the worst Antonioni movie you ever saw, or reading *Mr. Sammler's Planet* at one sitting, or just reading it, or being locked inside a Seaboard Railroad roomette, sixteen miles from Gainesville, Florida, heading north on the Miami-to-New York run, with no water and the radiator turning red in an amok psychotic overboil, and George McGovern sitting beside you telling you his philosophy of government. That will give you the general atmosphere.

In any case, by the time I received my doctorate in American

Tom Wolfe in 1968: Participant and observer in a time of change.

studies in 1957 I was in the twisted grip of a disease of our times in which the sufferer experiences an overwhelming urge to join the "real world." So I started working for newspapers. In 1962, after a cup of coffee here and there, I arrived at the *New York Herald Tribune* . . . This must be the place! . . . I looked out across the city room of the *Herald Tribune,* 100 moldering yards south of Times Square, with a feeling of amazed bohemian bliss . . . Either this is the real world, Tom, or there is no real world . . . The place looked like the receiving bin at the Good Will . . . a promiscuous heap of junk . . . Wreckage and exhaustion everywhere . . . If somebody such as the city editor had a swivel chair, the universal joint would be broken, so that every time he got up, the seat would keel over as if stricken by a lateral stroke. All the intestines of the building were left showing in diverticulitic loops and lines—electrical conduits, water pipes, steam pipes, effluvium ducts, sprinkler systems, all of it dangling and grunting from the ceiling, the walls, the columns. The whole mess, from top to bottom, was painted over in an industrial sludge, Lead Gray, Sub-way Green, or that unbelievable dead red, that grim distemper of pigment and filth, that they paint the floor with in the tool and die works. On the ceiling were scalding banks of fluorescent lights, turning the atmosphere radium blue and burning bald spots in the crowns of the copy readers, who never moved. It was one big pie factory . . . A Landlord's Dream . . . There were no interior walls. The corporate hierarchy was not marked off into office spaces. The managing editor worked in a space that was as miserable and scabid as the lowest reporter's. Most newspapers were like that. This setup was instituted decades ago for practical reasons. But it was kept alive by a curious fact. On newspapers very few editorial employees at the bottom—namely, the reporters—had any ambition whatsoever to move up, to become city editors, managing editors, editors-in-chief, or any of the rest of it. Editors felt no threat from below. They needed no walls. Reporters didn't want much . . . merely to be *stars!* and of such minute wattage at that!

That was one thing they never wrote about in books on journalism or those comradely blind-

(continued on page 30)

of wholesale fabrication but instead a "composite"—a character drawn from several people's lives and words. Others were known to condense, enhance, or similarly mess with quoted dialogue. Nik Cohn, writing in *New York* in 1976, completely manufactured the central character of a piece about a disco in Brooklyn, a story so compelling it became the basis for *Saturday Night Fever*. You could argue that these were just lapses as a new form got on its feet or that they were worth the trade-off, that being more truthful could come from being less factual. You could also argue that, in less capable hands, these "techniques" served as an excuse to be lazy and shoddy. By the 1980s, the term "New Journalism" carried with it a stain of disrepute. Inevitably, though, the old journalism subsumed the new, imbibing its vigor while rejecting its less conscientious aspects. Most of today's magazine writers (print and digital alike) are far more careful about their quotes. But they absolutely aspire to write vivid scenes and longer, richer stories than most newspapers can run, and the best of those stories endure because they have the sweep and power of great fiction.

News Blog

NOTE: *Elizabeth Spiers, the author of this entry, was the founding editor of Gawker.com, writing daily on the site from 2002 to 2004.*

In July 2002, an English serial entrepreneur named Nick Denton started a gadget blog called Gizmodo and then, in December of that year, launched a New York–centric gossip blog called Gawker. (I was Gawker's first editor.) Blogging was in its infancy but not entirely new. There have been endless, often tedious, debates about when blogging began and who began it, and there's not much consensus. Early pioneers include Justin Hall and Dave Winer, whose respective blogs, Links.net and DaveNet, debuted in 1994, and Jorn Barger, whose blog was called Robot Wisdom and who invented the term *weblog*.

But Gawker Media's blogs made two inroads: They were fundamentally news-driven, designed to break news as well as comment on it, and they were commercialized, their revenue generated by advertising. It's unsurprising that for-profit, ad-supported news blogs would originate in New York City, home to the advertising business (*see also* MADISON AVENUE) and the headquarters of many major media companies, and that, once proven successful, the model would be heavily adopted by both indie media companies and traditional news organizations.

The initial response to news blogs wasn't wholly positive. For many bloggers, the form's commercialization was unwelcome, and they viewed it as a potentially corrupting force. As for the traditional media types, news blogging's journalistic aspirations presented a threat; they implied that one didn't need the imprimatur of a large, established media company to credibly break news. In the early days, Gawker wasn't generating enough revenue to be impressive as a business, and the stories it broke were fairly small-scale—personnel changes at Condé Nast and the New York *Times*, minor celebrity news. But as Gawker's reach and influence expanded (mostly well after I left), some of the original criticisms faded and the Gawker model became something to emulate. Bloggers began to monetize their own sites as standalone media entities, specializing in topics or beats to help brand themselves, and media companies began to add blog or bloglike elements to their offerings.

Gawker became a source for a certain type of breaking news and a rapid response to aggregated stories. Its influences in this area are traceable to aggregation blogs that were popular at the time, mostly run by individuals—Jim Romenesko's media blog, published by Poynter, and Glenn Reynolds's right-leaning political site Instapundit, for example, which collected relevant news links as they were published, often at high volume. Jake Dobkin and Jen Chung's Gothamist, also born in New York City, focused on local interests, first as aggregators and later adding original reporting. Sites run by political commentators and journalists, like Josh Marshall's Talking Points Memo, would generate scoops occasionally, and their proprietors eventually transformed them into full-blown independent companies employing full-time journalists.

Gawker itself also adapted. At its peak, it had tens of millions of unique visitors and a couple hundred employees, and by 2014 it was generating $45 million in annual revenue. But in 2016, it filed for bankruptcy after having been sued out of existence by Hulk Hogan over its publication of a video clip of the wrestler having sex with the wife of his best friend, Bubba the Love Sponge. (This is not a sentence the first editor of Gawker would have envisioned writing in 2002.) Hogan, whose real name is Terry Bollea, was being financed by Silicon Valley billionaire Peter Thiel, who, angry with Gawker's coverage of himself, had paid for Bollea's legal fees with the intent of putting Gawker Media out of business. He was successful. Yet the news-blog model—conversational, topical, news-driven blogging that's commercially sustainable—lives on, in many of the sites mentioned here and in the DNA of many independent and traditional media companies. Not to mention, of course, in a lot of threads on Twitter.

Newsweekly

NOTE: *Edward Kosner, the author of this entry, was the chief editor of* Newsweek *from 1975 through 1979 and of* New York *from 1980 through 1993.*

In 1923, two youthful, ambitious former colleagues from the *Yale Daily News*, Henry Luce and Briton Hadden, birthed the slick newsmagazine *Time*, simultaneously creating the inverted mock-Homeric, rat-a-tat language known as "Timestyle" that was the hallmark of its early years. ("Backward ran sentences until reeled the mind … where it will all end, knows God!" as Wolcott Gibbs parodied in *The New Yorker*.) Despite this and other adolescent eccentricities—not to mention Hadden's death at 31, just six years into the magazine's life—*Time* became one of the most innovative and successful journalistic creations of the twentieth century. Luce went on to found *Fortune* in 1929, relaunch *Life* in 1936, and create *Sports Illustrated* in 1954, the bulwarks of its parent company, Time Inc. Along with the New York *Times*, the major radio and later TV networks, book publishers like Alfred A. Knopf and Simon & Schuster, and Madison Avenue's advertising wizards, Luce's empire helped make New York City the unrivaled media capital of the world.

Early on, Hadden cobbled together issues mostly by rewriting clippings from the *Times* with an insouciant touch. The magazine was to be called *Facts*, but the founders switched the name to *Time* before its launch to suggest that busy executives could catch up on the news of the week in barely an hour. The cover of the first issue went to the grizzled Speaker of the House, Joseph G. Cannon, framed by Grecian scrollwork. The distinctive red border wasn't introduced until four years later.

Over the years, the magazine grew into a major enterprise with a big, well-paid staff of adroit writers (virtually all men), diligent fact-checkers (virtually all young women), haughty editors, and bureaus staffed by correspondents all over the world. *Time* was essentially a giant rewrite desk. Files of research for stories from the bureaus would flood into New York each week, where they would be smelted into crisp narratives by the writers, then buffed to a high sheen by top editors. The result of all that labor was a polished 60,000 or so words that managed to be both informative and, at its best, a pleasure to read.

Luce ruled his realm with a strong ideological hand. *Time* stories carried no bylines and all seemed to be written by the same deft pen. There were no editorials, but Luce's politics infused everything. The magazine was Eastern Establishment Republican, favoring presidential candidates like Wendell Willkie in 1940 and Dwight Eisenhower a decade later. It disliked the New Deal and was strongly anti-Communist; Chiang Kai-shek and his Chinese nationalists were an obsessive cause. *Time* astutely covered everything from art to Zen Buddhism, and the mix was a hit with readers. Its "Man of the Year" was an instant icon. Circulation of the domestic and international editions zoomed into the millions before long.

For its first decade, *Time* had the field nearly to itself. Founded by a *Time* defector in 1933, *News-Week*, as it was called for its first five years, was pallid competition. So was *U.S. News & World Report*, based in Washington and even more conservative than *Time*. Then in 1961, Philip Graham, who ran the Washington Post Co., bought *Newsweek* and installed Osborn Elliott, a young *Time* veteran, as the editor. When Graham took his own life two years later, his wife, Katharine, stepped up as publisher. With the Graham family's bigger ideas and budgets, Elliott transformed the magazine into a formidable challenger to *Time*, based just a few blocks west in midtown.

Newsweek used the basic newsmagazine system invented at *Time* but added columnists with provocative opinions and provocative scooplets in the breezy front-of-the-book "Periscope" section. Trying to exploit *Time's* reputation for conservative bias, *Newsweek* bragged in

a successful slogan that it "Separates Fact From Opinion," though in reality its coverage had a distinctly liberal tinge. The magazine covered the civil-rights movement and anti-Vietnam protests more sympathetically than *Time* and broke newsmagazine tradition by editorializing in special issues for Black rights and against the war. When President Kennedy was killed in 1963, *Newsweek* published a memorable special edition with a soulful portrait of JFK on the cover; *Time*, which had something of a fetish about not putting dead subjects on its cover, chose the new president, Lyndon Johnson, instead.

I worked at *Newsweek* for sixteen years, starting just a few months before that Kennedy issue in 1963, and edited the magazine from 1975 to 1979, participating in the two magazines' rivalry. *Time* editors treated *Newsweek* as if it didn't exist. At *Newsweek*, we referred to *Time* as "Brand X" and mocked its pretensions. When Luce staged an intellectual extravaganza he proclaimed "The National Purpose," we called it "Flipper: The National Porpoise."

Newsweek was quicker to switch its cover to catch breaking news, hop on trends, and spotlight new stars in entertainment and the arts. It stood out in its coverage of the Watergate scandal in the early 1970s, one of the high points of its sparring with *Time*. At the peak, from the 1960s into the '80s, *Time*'s circulation topped 4 million, a million more than *Newsweek*'s. Both magazines were highly profitable, and both spent lavishly, sometimes chartering planes to develop color photos of major events en route and dispatch them to printing plants around the globe. Top editors toured overseas bureaus in high style and interviewed world leaders as fellow grandees. It was a wonderful ride and produced some memorable journalism.

In the digital age, weekly servings of the news—no matter how polished and stylish—had diminishing appeal. With losses growing, *Newsweek* tried to reinvent itself yet again. The Graham family sold it in 2010 for

$1 plus liabilities of about $40 million. It merged with Tina Brown's Daily Beast website, ceased print publication, and then was revived by yet another owner with a print run of barely 50,000 copies a week.

Time Inc. was, for a while, better positioned to handle the digital media world. Having already merged with Warner Communications in 1989, it joined with America Online in 2000 in one of the most misguided deals of the dot-com era. The magazine was spun off with the rest of Time Inc.'s titles in 2014, bought and absorbed by the Meredith Corporation in 2018, and then quickly flipped to a tech billionaire for $190 million. Long gone are the gaudy, glory-draped days of willful news mogul Luce's inspired invention.

New Wave[2]

New Wave began as a critical catchall term describing the exhilarating guitar music fomenting in New York City in the late '70s. But by the end of the next decade, what had been something of a pejorative term for bands on the less abrasive, more commercial end of the punk spectrum had embedded itself into the fabric of mainstream music, soundtracking epochal youth-culture films of the '80s like *The Breakfast Club*, *Pretty in Pink*, and *Sixteen Candles*. The first wave hit at CBGB, where the eclectic band roster included Blondie and Talking Heads, whose quirks and pop smarts yielded platinum albums and chart-topping singles as they drifted from straitlaced rock and roll to parts unknown. Blondie's "One Way or Another" typified New Wave's median sound: It's undeniably hooky and easy to dance to, with a dollop of lovable weirdness and a dusting of synths.

Bands around the world picked up on Debbie Harry and Chris Stein's playbook, adding their own edits. London singer-songwriter Gary Numan leaned into electronics, powering songs like "Cars" and "Down in the Park" with melodies on synths made by the American keyboard manufacturer Moog Music. The Police scored early hits with "Roxanne" and "Message in a Bottle" and experimented with Caribbean sounds on records like 1979's *Reggatta de Blanc* (literally "white reggae"), adding slick adult contemporary pop to the palette on 1983's *Synchronicity*. Elvis Costello and the Attractions threaded in pub rock and power-pop sounds. New Wave's borders were open, and that gave bands room to grow and evolve. By their fourth album, Talking Heads had traded the jerky punk-funk of "Psycho Killer" for polyrhythmic Afrobeat. Costello made a soul album (1980's *Get Happy!!*) and a folk album (1986's stately *King of America*) and collaborated in later years with orchestras, string quartets, and musical luminaries including Burt Bacharach and the Roots.

New Wave raided the charts at the dawn of MTV in 1981 thanks to indelible hooks and impeccable style; the first video the fledgling channel played was British New Wave duo the Buggles' "Video Killed the Radio Star." But as the tides of culture shifted in the '90s, interest in the genre dipped, and though it had created space on the charts for rockers to be offbeat and unique, '90s kids prized relatability in their music, not showmanship. New stars like Kurt Cobain and Alanis Morissette hated kitsch and artifice. It was an allergic reaction to '80s camp, and the remnants of that decade were dethroned like royalty in a revolution.

New York Magazine

New York was not the first city magazine. *Philadelphia*, founded in 1908, and *Los Angeles*, in 1961, preceded it. So did *The New Yorker* and *Cue* and various newspapers' Sunday magazine sections. What it did invent, however, was a particular combination of politics and culture coverage packaged with enthusiastic affection for material goods, written in the knowing, forward voice and skeptical yet forward-looking attitude of New Yorkers. And

not just any New Yorkers: *New York* was aimed at those who were making it but were not hereditary gentry, those who were still in the game, the successful upper-middle-class strivers. It revolutionized the magazine world, creating a form that came to dominate during the next half-century. It even went so far as to mold New York City itself—or a small slice of it, at least—in its own image.

It began in 1963 with the dying New York *Herald Tribune*'s Sunday magazine, newly revamped and renamed *New York*. Trying to save itself, the paper's management had decided that if it couldn't outdo the *Times* on every front, it could at least outwrite it. The editors James Bellows and Sheldon Zalaznick, joined very soon by an *Esquire* editor named Clay Felker, began assigning stories to Tom Wolfe, Jimmy Breslin, and other talented people around the newsroom. *New York* soon became the buzziest magazine in the city, especially after Wolfe published a long, hilarious piece in 1965 making light of *The New Yorker*'s self-regard. After the *Trib* folded, Felker and the graphic designer Milton Glaser (*see also* I♥NY) relaunched the magazine as a stand-alone weekly, premiering on April Fools' Day 1968. Its first issues included stories by Gloria Steinem (then still more reporter than activist), Breslin, Wolfe, Gail Sheehy, and Nora Ephron, all doing significant reporting about urban life, trends, politics, and culture (*see also* NEW JOURNALISM). It had a robust arts section too, one where Judith Crist reviewed movies thoughtfully and John Simon reviewed theater viciously. But *New York* also ran a shopping section, "Best Bets," reflecting trends and tastes among urban sophisticates. In another influential column, "The Underground Gourmet," Glaser and his friend Jerome Snyder reviewed good, cheap ethnic restaurants—a thing that, somehow, nobody else was doing.

That mix was fresh and timely. There was a little bit of consumer culture in the *Times* (on the "women's page"), and the pioneering newspaper *PM* had run good shopping and service coverage in the 1940s. *New York* was a bit like *PM,* in that it too had a smart and knowing tone and a well-defined sense of its politically and culturally engaged consumer-reader, but its glossy-magazine format allowed for much longer and more writerly stories. *The New Yorker* had mostly (apart from its fashion column, "On and Off the Avenue") been a little disdainful of shopping, even though it was packed with ads, and its readers were increasingly suburban with little interest in the physical city, let alone its restaurants. Felker and Glaser and their writers, by contrast, wrote for the unabashed urbanite, the person who fought to remain in New York, even though it was maddening and exhausting and seemed to be disintegrating (*see also* MAYHEM), and who sought out its pockets of unique greatness: a really good bar, a secret discount house on Orchard Street that sold Pucci at half-price, a brand-new, potentially world-changing Off Broadway play, the best (rather than a merely good) shoe-repair shop or upholsterer or noodle parlor. The New York *Times*' enthusiastic coverage of all these things, introduced via rotating daily sections in the 1970s, did not come out of thin air. "We swallowed *New York,*" the *Times*' executive editor A. M. Rosenthal later admitted. "I'll steal an idea from anybody if it's not nailed down."

In this era, the giant general-interest magazines (*Life, Look, Collier's, The Saturday Evening Post*) were dying, their ads sucked away by television on one side and niche publications on the other. *New York,* it turned out, was positioned just right to fill a local yet also national piece of that void. It quickly became evident that there was a robust readership for that mix, and advertisers liked the audience too. It didn't make money right away, but by the 1980s, *New York* was pulling in something like a 20 percent profit per year.

More telling, though, is what happened to the city around it. In 1968, *New York*'s image of comfortable, bourgeois urban life was, for most people, a fantasy. The subway was falling to pieces, the crime rate was spiking, and the market (*see also* WALL STREET) was headed into a decade-long malaise. In the 1970s, New York City lost a million residents. Increasingly, however—starting in the '80s, as corporate jobs began to refill the tax coffers decimated by the loss of manufacturing, and accelerating as crime rates fell and the population began to grow again—that kind of modern-flâneur life became achievable. People, including quite a few of the global superrich,

began to move here not in spite of New York's texture but because of it. Vastly more tourists came too. Young arrivals in particular assumed and even demanded a version of the glossy life they'd seen on *Sex and the City* (*see also* SITCOM), one built around cultural literacy and political awareness but also the embrace of adults-at-play enthusiasm. *New York* had sketched that world out with such brio that its readers willed it into being. They live in *New York*'s New York now.

New York *Times,* The

The New York *Times* was, for its first few decades, a merely solid newspaper. Founded in 1851 (with a hyphen in its nameplate, as the *New-York Daily Times*), it covered the Civil War, added a Sunday edition to do so, and competed well with James Gordon Bennett's New York *Herald* and Horace Greeley's New York *Daily Tribune.* In the 1870s, a series of *Times* stories helped break the back of William Magear "Boss" Tweed's profoundly corrupt Democratic political machine. But by 1896, the paper was dying, its press run below 19,000 copies, half of them going unsold. (By way of comparison, Joseph Pulitzer's New York *World* was printing 600,000 a day.)

The *Times*' growth beyond local influence began that year, after Adolph Ochs, a 38-year-old newspaper publisher from Chattanooga, Tennessee, bought it for $75,000. By 1900 he had a majority stake, and a few years later, he moved the paper's headquarters uptown from Park Row to a new tower at 42nd and Broadway, the foot of Longacre Square, which the city renamed Times Square in its honor. How Ochs reinvigorated the paper has become a journalism legend: He made public claims to elevated levels of impartiality, authority, and correctness, reporting "without fear or favor," and—in a box at the top of the front page—"All the News That's Fit to Print." In his first month, he introduced a Sunday magazine and a stand-alone Sunday books section, and required that his reporters move from pens to typewriters. He aimed above all to make the *Times* the paper of record, and to that end he demanded—and, for the next 70 years, the paper did indeed have—tiny listings of the world's weather, every fire in New York, and shipping arrivals in the harbor, along with the news reports from around the globe. It would be, he said, a newspaper that "will not soil the breakfast linen."

To accomplish this, he hired Carr Van Anda, a managing editor who brought a new level of class and intelligence to coverage of science, art, and global affairs. (The editorial pages' stance, then as now, was somewhat liberal but not radical, essentially center-left.) He was cautious when it was called for, the coverage of the *Titanic*'s sinking in 1912 being a case in point: As other papers published poorly sourced stories that reported the ship's passengers all safe, Van Anda held back, waiting for confirmation, and got it right. By the 1930s, the *Times*' Sunday circulation was 780,000, and it was the paper of record that Ochs and Van Anda had envisioned, one with unparalleled influence in the White House and the American power structure as a whole.

Ochs's son-in-law, Arthur Hays Sulzberger, succeeded him in 1935, and despite some missteps under his leadership (notably the flawed work of Walter Duranty, the paper's Moscow bureau chief, who swallowed Joseph Stalin's propaganda and thus contributed to the cover-up of mass murder), the paper's wartime and postwar coverage contributed to its international reputation. Sulzberger's son, Arthur Ochs "Punch" Sulzberger, was considered a lightweight and was passed over for the top job after his father's death. Yet Punch turned out to be the perfect publisher when his brother-in-law died suddenly and he was thrust into the job: open to new ideas, cautious but decisive as the publishing world changed, and willing to defend his paper, expensively, against legal attack. In 1964, the Supreme Court ruled in the case of *New York Times Co.* v. *Sullivan*, a case in which an ad placed by civil-rights activists was claimed to have been defamatory to an Alabama police chief of Montgomery, Alabama. The court ruled in the paper's favor, determining a new, elevated standard for libel, requiring malicious intent. Seven years later, when Sulzberger's executive editor Abe Rosenthal wanted to publish the trove of documents that came to be called the Pentagon Papers, that too required risk, boldness, and an argument before the Supreme Court. And in the 1970s, as city magazines (*see also* NEW YORK MAGAZINE) proved that lifestyle news—coverage of food, home design, technology, shopping—could be actual news, Rosenthal introduced a rotating daily section to handle those topics in a rigorous, *Times*-y way, a quietly influential move that was eventually reflected in every daily newspaper in America.

By the 1980s, the *Times* reigned supreme in American journalism. It had become a national paper, printed all over the country, a million or more copies a day. If Walter Cronkite was (according to a misleading but famous poll) the most trusted man in America, well, the morning *Times* was where he was getting a lot of *his* news. A *Times* obituary was the definitive send-off. A *Times* theater review could close a show or save it. Even the food editor Craig Claiborne had unparalleled reach and influence. Its solemnity of intent was underscored by its relatively foursquare reading experience, and for many years it was (along with *The Wall Street Journal*) one of the last big American dailies printed only in black-and-white. Color photos finally arrived in 1997, but the news editors remained a little suspicious of humor, lively writing, or anything that smacked of unseriousness. Only on the op-ed page, where Russell Baker was one of the funniest writers in America, and occasionally in the Sunday magazine, did it loosen its tie a little. And when it botched a story—as in Jayson Blair's bogus reporting and plagiarism scandal in 2003 or Judith Miller's credulous writing on Iraq—the paper expressed its internal self-flagellation in print, transparently, sometimes on the front page.

In this era—and as "Punch" Sulzberger handed the paper off to his son, Arthur Jr.—the *Times* was as rich as it would ever be. That was soon to change. Although the company introduced a website fairly early, in January 1996, and was generally precocious about the digital future, it was, like every other newspaper, unable to get out in front of the abrupt contraction of print. In the next decade, its massive classified-ad linage and the millions of dollars that brought in every month evaporated, and display advertising began to disappear as well. After decades of growth, daily circulation peaked in 2001 at 1.19 million copies, then began to decline, first slowly, then faster. Arthur Jr. tried to avoid severe cuts and layoffs to the newsroom, slashing the corporate dividend to family stockholders, propping the company up with loans from the Mexican billionaire Carlos Slim, and selling off many of the ancillary properties it had bought over the years. The bleeding, however, was drastic. Between 2006 and 2013, the company's revenue fell by about 60 percent. In 2009, *The Atlantic* ran a solemn story sketching what would happen to the news media at large if the *Times* went out of business.

What would save it was a threefold set of shifts in its worldview. It needed to embrace wholesale that the paper edition was likely to be retired within a generation or so. It was going to have to get rid of some of its internal stratification and tribalism, its fussiness about language, and its endless in-house fetishization of what went on page one. But most of all, everyone was going to have to accept that the online *Times* was, in fact, now the *Times* itself, an international digital news outlet that readers, instead of advertisers, would have to get used to paying for. The latter initiative was led in part by Arthur Jr.'s son, Arthur Gregg Sulzberger, who had become an editor on the paper's digital team and then, in 2018, stepped up as the fifth-generation publisher of the whole thing. Imperceptibly at first, the ship started to turn. By 2019, the *Times* reported (in its own pages) that digital ad revenue had surpassed print revenue, and in the last quarter of that year, for the first time, its subscribers contributed more to the bottom line than its advertisers did. A pair of statistics from 2020 demonstrate the *Times*'s growth and relative health amid widespread decline in the rest of the industry: Its 1,700 journalists constituted roughly 7 percent of the country's entire daily-newspaper workforce, and the paper had more digital subscribers than the Washington *Post, The Wall Street Journal,* and 250 Gannett papers combined.

Nightclub

Between what is obviously a bar, what is obviously a concert space, and what is obviously a dance hall lies the hybrid known as the nightclub. The first venue that fit all three definitions is often said to be Webster Hall, a brick and terra-cotta pile at 119 East 11th Street, designed by Charles Rentz and built in 1886 by a cigarmaker named Charles Goldstein. In its early years, it was simply a hall for hire, rented for big parties and dances and often for lefty political events like labor rallies. In the 1910s, however, it became known for masquerade balls that drew the Village bohemian crowd— events that were, unusually for the time, quite queer friendly. Some of the best parties were hosted by the socialist magazine *The Masses.*

After the passage of Prohibition in 1919, Webster Hall and other legitimate bars and clubs converted into speakeasies. Simultaneously, a younger generation of well-off New Yorkers began to go out in the evenings, socializing at these places rather than at dinner parties (*see also* CAFÉ SOCIETY). The Depression and World War II dampened but did not kill the business; clubs like El Morocco and the Copacabana flourished over the next couple of decades with a celebrity clientele and a big presence in the press. Walter Winchell ran his mighty gossip column from Table 50 at the Stork Club on East 53rd Street, once calling it "the New Yorkiest place in New York." West 52nd Street became a locus of jazz clubs, loosely known as Swing Street, where the top figures of the late-1940s and 1950s scene—Charlie Parker, Dizzy Gillespie, Miles Davis—developed new musical idioms (*see also* BEBOP).

The first threat to the classic New York nightclub came from television and the nighttime domestication it engendered. Real-estate pressures hurt it, too—the clubs of Swing Street mostly gave way to skyscrapers in the 1960s, and the site of the Stork Club became a park between two towers. Overall, the small-club-with-tables experience began ceding to that of a large dance floor with a bar and much louder music: the discothèque. And the big New York discos reflected the beaten-down, dissolute nature of the city in their era; Xenon and Studio 54, the most famous of the two, were set up in raddled old Broadway theaters, one of which had recently operated as a pornographic movie house. The Saint, on Second Avenue in the East Village in another converted movie theater, catered mostly to a gay clientele that danced under a lighted dome. The old Academy of Music, on 14th Street, became the Palladium a few years later, and Danceteria, in a Chelsea loft building, was where Madonna dominated the dance floor before she was famous and dominated the soundtrack afterward. As the 1990s crested, Life (on Bleecker Street) and various places in the rapidly gentrifying Meatpacking District became, for a year or two apiece, the club of the moment.

Once again, though, the pressures of real estate, amplified by the city's new wealth, began to crush the nightclubs almost out of existence. Mayor Rudolph Giuliani's administration was at least tacitly and sometimes openly hostile to the business, perhaps because nightclubs were perceived as places that tolerated widespread drug use. Formerly quiet areas like the Meatpacking District that had been hospitable to thumping late-night music and squealing couples were becoming residential neighborhoods for the well-to-do, and the occupants of those multimillion-dollar apartments tended to be people with prominent day jobs who didn't appreciate the noise. By 2000, the nightclub business had mostly been driven to industrial stretches of Brooklyn, the far edges of Manhattan's West Side, and a few other spots like Fordham Road, where Jimmy's Bronx Cafe became an after-hours hangout for the New York Yankees. That pattern persists to this day: A new pocket of nightlife opens in a fringe area of the city, it becomes cool for a few months or years, the neighbors start complaining, and it moves or closes down, only to be superseded by the next hot boîte.

9/11 Era

The twentieth century ended, for many Americans, with a sense that we'd finally settled all that. The Soviet Union was gone, Communist China was less a threat than a trading partner, the economy was humming, and the Clinton administration had left us, after two decades of deficit spending, with a balanced budget. There was talk of "the end of history," of the dawning of the Age of Aquarius, of a world where American ideals, rather than the significantly more brutal reality they masked, might rule much of it. A modest recession kicked off by the collapse of the tech bubble in the spring of 2000 was about as bad as things were likely to get.

That all changed on the morning of September 11, 2001, when nineteen hijackers associated with the Al Qaeda Islamist network took over two airliners headed west from Logan Airport, another from Newark, and one more from Dulles. The Boston flights were redirected toward New York, and—at 8:46 and 9:03 a.m.—they struck the Twin Towers of the World Trade Center. Both buildings caught fire, trapping many people on high floors, and by 10:28 a.m., both had collapsed, killing 2,763 people on the spot and eventually poisoning many rescue workers who breathed in the toxic dust at the scene. The third airplane struck the Pentagon, and the fourth, most likely headed to the White House, crashed in Pennsylvania after passengers attempted to reclaim control of the cockpit. Including the suicidal hijackers, 2,996 people died. A few border skirmishes aside, it was the first foreign attack on the United States mainland since 1814.

The proximate source of the attackers was Saudi Arabia, although Osama bin Laden, Al Qaeda's leader, had gone into hiding in Afghanistan and was protected there by the Taliban government. His stated reason for the assault related to the American desecration of Islamic holy sites in the Middle East, but the roots of this aggression lay in various long-term grievances against the West, most obviously related to the creation of Israel in 1948. Even more broadly, Al Qaeda, like most fundamentalist movements, existed in opposition to modernity as it is lived in most Western-style democracies: largely secular government, immodest pop culture, sexual emancipation and women's liberation (relatively speaking), and cosmopolitanism.

The United States retaliated with military strikes, first on Afghanistan, then on Iraq. Estimates of the wars' full death count vary dramatically, particularly for Iraq; approximately 800,000 killed is a plausible figure. Bin Laden himself was eventually found and shot dead by American commandos in Pakistan in May 2011. As of 2020, both wartime occupations had begun to wind down, but neither had completely ended, and they had cost the U.S. approximately $2.5 trillion. In New York, after a tortuous, stop-start rebuilding process, a cluster of new skyscrapers surrounding a memorial park began to rise on the World Trade Center site, with a museum underneath.

The ultimate effects of the 9/11 attacks remain difficult to gauge because the reaction to them is still rattling the world. Evident at least is that the United States, and by extension the West, has been on emergency footing for the two decades since. New Yorkers, for a while, found themselves not regarded with disdain by the rest of the country (as is customary) but with concern and even affection. The city's fire department, having lost 343 of its people, received a particularly intense flood of affection and charity.

The small, everyday changes the attacks wrought include intense searches and scanning at airports and anti–truck bomb bollards and beefed-up security at the entrances to most office and government buildings. The NYPD gained a large anti-terrorist unit, and urban police departments all over America became highly militarized, arming and armoring themselves against an imagined next attack. At a global scale, the U.S.—in particular its big cities, and especially New York—was revealed to be

John and Nassau Streets, after the collapse of the Twin Towers.

PHOTOGRAPH BY
ARISTIDE
ECONOMOPOULOS

vulnerable in ways it had not obviously been before, and the country responded not with introspection and a step back but instead with aggression, countering brutal strength with vastly greater brutal strength.

That aggression was directed at Iraq and Afghanistan but also within. Since 2001, Americans have accepted increased surveillance by the federal government, and Congress has increasingly ceded power to the executive branch, first to George W. Bush, then to Barack Obama, then to Donald Trump. The attacks did not immediately bring down the United States, as their perpetrators had hoped. But their long-term ramifications for American democracy do not look promising. The U.S. electorate went a little mad on September 11, and it has not recovered yet, if indeed it will.

Nuyorican

In the decades surrounding World War II, after international immigration had been cut to a trickle (*see also* IMMIGRATION), a million people from the American territory of Puerto Rico—roughly a quarter of the island's population in that period—moved to New York. Most were looking for work, driven north by poor economic prospects at home. They often filled the blue-collar, lower-wage jobs the city offered in factories and restaurants, dealing with significant discrimination as they did so, particularly if their English was poor. (Robert Moses referred to these American citizens as "that scum floating up from Puerto Rico.") The writer Jesús Colón, in his book *A Puerto Rican in New York and Other Sketches*, tells the story of a man who was kicked to death in a bar in Williamsburg in the 1950s for speaking in Spanish.

By this time, swaths of the Lower East Side, the South Bronx, and north Brooklyn were largely Puerto Rican, and as the community became established in New York, so did its distinct culture. The most prominent enclave, East Harlem, became known as El Barrio, with its sprawling La Marqueta food hall on East 115th Street at Park Avenue. The neighborhood's musicians, drawing heavily on Cuban influences, almost single-handedly created a genre all their own (*see also* SALSA MUSIC). And a unique local dialect of Spanish with a particular streetwise slang developed—*pompa* for "fire hydrant," the Spanglish hybrid *voy pa'l rufo* for "I'm going to the roof."

Although the word this community often applied to itself was *Boricua*, one derogatory term for Puerto Rican New Yorkers was gradually reclaimed and turned into a badge of honor: *Nuyorican*, a portmanteau that in 1975 gave its name to the Nuyorican Poets Cafe, a performance space in the East Village that celebrated New York Puerto Rican writing and music. The Young Lords, a radical-politics organization that rose out of the Chicago streets, established three large chapters in New York, working on human-rights issues and for the Puerto Rican nationalism movement. Boricua College, founded in 1974 in Washington Heights, was the first college in the continental U.S. to offer bilingual classes in Spanish and English. With greater numbers came political power as well. In 1973, the congressman and former Bronx borough president Herman Badillo came within shouting distance of the mayoralty, and since the 1960s New York politics has had a steady and significant Puerto Rican presence, generally but not exclusively at the leftward end of the spectrum.

And, inevitably, the distinctive qualities of *puertorriqueñidad* have become absorbed into the larger fabric of the city and the nation. Sonia Sotomayor, born to Puerto Rican parents and reared in the tenements and housing projects of the Bronx, went to Princeton and eventually the Supreme Court. Jennifer Lopez, also born and raised in the Bronx, became one of the biggest stars in the world while retaining a little of her distinctive Bronx accent. (She titled her first album *On the 6*, a reference to her subway line, and her film-and-TV company is called Nuyorican Productions.) Lin-Manuel Miranda gained recognition with his Tony Award–winning musical about uptown New York, *In the Heights*, then went on to write the global hit *Hamilton*. The word once used almost exclusively for small grocery stores in Puerto Rican neighborhoods has gone national (*see also* BODEGA). A good-size museum, El Museo del Barrio, celebrates the community's art. In 2018, Alexandria Ocasio-Cortez was elected to the House of Representatives by voters in the Bronx and Queens, becoming the youngest woman ever to serve in Congress and one of the most talked-about political figures in the country. And in her campaign logo, she had foregrounded her roots, rendering her name as it might appear on a Spanish-language radical poster: *¡OCASIO! CORTEZ*.

◄▣

An arrest at Occupy Wall Street,
November 17, 2011.
PHOTOGRAPH BY CHRISTOPHER ANDERSON

① **The Essential Occupy Wall Street Hand Signals**

Identified by artist-activist Marisa Holmes

Agree
To show that you feel good about what a person is saying or doing, raise both your hands and twinkle your fingers.

Disagree
To show that you don't feel good about it, down-twinkle your fingers.

Clarifying Question
If you don't understand what a person is saying and need more clarification, make a C-shape with your hand.

Obscenity Trial, American Literary

On June 16, 1904, a twenty-two-year-old Dublin woman sat not too close to but not too far from a middle-aged Jewish man on the beach. Twilight was gathering. They could hear parishioners nearby at Mass. There were fireworks going off. It was like this:

> *And she saw a long Roman candle going up over the trees up, up, and, in the tense hush, they were all breathless with excitement as it went higher and higher and she had to lean back more and more to look up after it, high, high, almost out of sight, and her face was suffused with a divine, an entrancing blush from straining back and he could see her other things too, nainsook knickers, the fabric that caresses the skin, better than those other pettiwidth, the green, four and eleven, on account of being white and she let him and she saw that he saw and then it went so high it went out of sight a moment and she was trembling in every limb from being bent so far back that he had a full view high up above her knee where no-one ever not even on the swing or wading and she wasn't ashamed and he wasn't either to look in that immodest way like that because he couldn't resist the sight of the wondrous revealment half offered like those skirtdancers behaving so immodest before gentlemen looking and he kept on looking, looking.*

She blushes. And it was like this:

> *O, he did. Into her. She did. Done.*
> *Ah!*
> *Mr Bloom with careful hand recomposed his wet shirt.*

That's an orgasm, in case you missed it.

One reader who didn't was a New York attorney whose daughter subscribed to *The Little Review* (*see also* "LITTLE MAGAZINE"). The first excerpts from James Joyce's *Ulysses* had appeared in the magazine in 1918, by which time its editors, Margaret Anderson and Jane Heap, already had experience with accusations of obscenity. An issue with some racy fiction by Wyndham Lewis had been seized by the U.S. Post Office in 1917, and it again seized and burned copies of the first few issues that serialized Joyce. When the "Nausicaa" episode quoted above appeared, that lawyer gave his daughter's copy of the magazine to the New York Society for the Suppression of Vice, leading to the editors' arrest. At trial in 1921, their lawyer made a number of tangential, sometimes contradictory arguments: that the book relied on a knowledge of Dublin to be understood, that it was generally incomprehensible because of its author's poor eyesight, and that the passage was meant to have an inhibiting rather than corrupting effect on impressionable young readers. Three literary critics were called as witnesses for the defense. One delivered a Freudian interpretation that was lost on the three-judge panel. Another called the book "beautiful" and attested that it would not be "corrupting the minds of young girls." But a third, Scofield Thayer, editor of *The Dial*, said he probably wouldn't have published it. The editors of *The Little Review* lost, and the book's serial publication ceased in America.

But the full novel was published anyway, in Paris in 1922, by the bookstore owner Sylvia Beach. Random House held the U.S. rights and, knowing it had a masterpiece on its hands, imported copies in 1933 expressly to set off another case. It never came to trial. Impressed by Joyce's stream-of-consciousness narration, Judge John M. Woolsey in the Southern District of New York threw the case out, writing that "whilst in many places the effect of *Ulysses* on the reader undoubtedly is somewhat emetic, nowhere does it tend to be an aphrodisiac." It was the triumph of vomit over arousal. Scholars hailed Woolsey's decision as an important work of literary criticism, and the challenge effectively paved the way for new

Point of Process

When the facilitator or group has diverged from the agenda or disruptions are stalling the process, make a triangular shape with both hands.

Point of Information

To offer context or other relevant information to the group, raise your index finger.

Wrap It Up

Sometimes a participant will get long-winded. When this occurs, remind them, gently, that their time is up by circling one hand over the other.

Block

If you have a moral or ethical concern about a proposal that would cause you to leave the group, raise and cross your arms, making an X-shape.

---

modes of writing that would once have been litigated as blasphemous or obscene. From there it was only a few steps to *Lolita*, to the 1960 trial that lifted the ban on *Lady Chatterley's Lover*, to the sexually explicit novels of Norman Mailer, John Updike, and Philip Roth, and to the transgressive New Narrative movement of the 1980s and '90s. Not to mention internet porn. You're welcome, world.

Observation Deck *see* SKYLINE

Occupy Movement [1]

Occupy Wall Street—the protests born of the federal government's failure to hold to account the banks that caused the 2009 financial bust—took over lower Manhattan's Zuccotti Park in 2011. But its roots lay a generation earlier, in the Columbia University protests of 1968 and in the New York innovation known as mass defense. That April, students protesting the construction of an allegedly segregated gym and the university's Vietnam War weapons research occupied several buildings, held a dean hostage, and shut down the campus. Hundreds were arrested. Mary Kaufman, a defense attorney who had prosecuted war crimes at Nuremberg, came up with the strategy of representing the students as a collective unit, giving her leverage against the prosecutors.

Throughout the '70s and '80s, the mass-defense strategy was used in dozens of other civil-disobedience cases—for welfare mothers arrested during sit-ins, Black Panthers prosecuted for selling newspapers, Puerto Ricans occupying a church in Harlem. The model spread around the world, but New York remained, and remains, at the center of its use. Martin Stolar, who was trained by Kaufman, remembered going to the prosecutors' office after the 2004 Republican National Convention in Manhattan, where the NYPD had arrested more than 1,800 protesters, and saying, "What the fuck are you people doing? How could you let this thing go on?" He estimated that 95 percent of the charges were dismissed.

In 2011, a preplanned march on Wall Street drew about 1,000 protesters, of whom 100 or so spent the night in Zuccotti Park, a small public space near One Liberty Plaza. Their demands were somewhat inchoate, but their grievances were not: Their outrage was directed against a sharp rise in wealth inequality and its debilitating social effects. Among their distinctive innovations was the heavy use of the human microphone (in which a speaker's words were amplified by shouted repetition from the crowd, obviating the need for a public-address-system permit) and the slogan "We Are the 99 Percent." It even had an affiliated newspaper called *The Occupied Wall Street Journal*.

Occupy Wall Street held the park until November, when the NYPD forcibly removed the group, arresting many protesters. But its spirit was quickly propagated into other settings around the world—Occupy Berlin, Occupy Nigeria, Occupy Baluwatar—and took aim at related but distinct causes. It was broad enough to incorporate a Mexican hunger strike over income issues and a South African free-education movement. Moreover, its focus on income inequality signaled a tactical shift among the global left. Occupy prefigured the rise of Bernie Sanders and Alexandria Ocasio-Cortez, and that influence—pulling the Democratic Party leftward in the United States and having similar effects overseas—is only beginning to be felt.

Oral History

An oral history of an event is a first-person account told by someone who was there. Courtroom testimony is arguably oral history; so is a grandmother telling her granddaughter what life was like when she was young. You could even say that Herodotus, taking down a (semi-accurate) chronicle of Egypt from the locals before returning to Greece, did the same.

Yet this type of interview was, until the mid–twentieth century, left mostly to journalists rather than historians. One early project in the form included the WPA-funded Federal Writers' Project, which between 1936 and 1938 took down (among many other things) the testimonies of hundreds of formerly enslaved Americans. Others, notably Myles Horton of the Highlander Folk School in Tennessee, recorded the words of social activists from the early civil-rights and labor movements. Alan Lomax did similar work documenting the originators of the Delta blues, although he recorded more music than talk. They all depended on the increasing availability of portable sound recorders, first with shellac discs and spools of steel wire and later with magnetic tape. In 1948, Allan Nevins, a newspaperman turned author, founded a program at Columbia University called the Columbia Center for Oral History. He systematized the interviewing of cultural figures and preserved the conversations, creating a central archive that gave later historians models for their work.

Only a few years earlier, the term *oral history* was first applied to this type of project by an unexpected source: Joseph Ferdinand Gould, a ragged bohemian and classic New York nut who wandered downtown streets cadging food and drink in exchange for reciting poems or arguing about philosophy. He claimed he was 9 million words into writing a book titled *The Oral History of Our Time*, to be composed mainly of interviews with common folk. When the great Joseph Mitchell profiled him for *The New Yorker* in 1942, Gould briefly became a minor, if no more polished, celebrity. After Gould's death, Mitchell wrote about him again in 1964, revealing that Gould had rattled on about his book for decades but hadn't written any of it down apart from a few monologues of his own. (It later turned out that he had taken down a little but not much.) Oddly, a great history that was never recorded has given its name to millions of smaller ones that were.

PHOTOGRAPH BY BOBBY DOHERTY

Oreo

In the spring of 1912, the National Biscuit Company—
a.k.a Nabisco, often called NBC back then, before
the broadcaster came along—introduced four new
cookies. The Mother Goose Biscuit was embossed with
a character's image, like an animal cracker. The
Veronese Biscuit was a hard cookie. The Lorna Doone
was (and still is) shortbread. And the Oreo, a
mini-sandwich of chocolate cookies with creamless
crème in the middle, was a near duplicate of Sunshine
Biscuits' recently introduced Hydrox cookie. The first
two are long gone (as is the National Biscuit Company
itself; the Nabisco brand is now owned by Mondelēz);
Hydrox crumbled away in 1999 and has since been
revived at a small scale. But of course it's the Oreo that
has endured in unimaginable volume, brand-extended
to include Double Stuf, Mega Stuf, Thins, dozens of
seasonal flavors, ice-cream mix-ins, churros, hot-
chocolate mix, and God knows what else. About one-
fifth of American cookie dollars are spent on them.
The world eats 40 billion per year. Some people
batter-dip and deep-fry them.

In the early days, Oreos were made in a huge brick
Nabisco plant between Ninth and Tenth Avenues in
Chelsea. (It's now the home of Chelsea Market and the
New York 1 newsroom, and is owned by Google.) The
cookie itself has barely changed in more than a century.
The embossing was slightly redesigned a couple of
times, but the only dramatic change happened in 1997,
when the recipe was rejiggered to replace lard with vegetable shortening, making Oreos simultaneously kosher
and vegan.

Organized Crime *see* MAYHEM; MOB, THE

From

PARKING, ALTERNATE SIDE OF THE STREET

to

PUNK

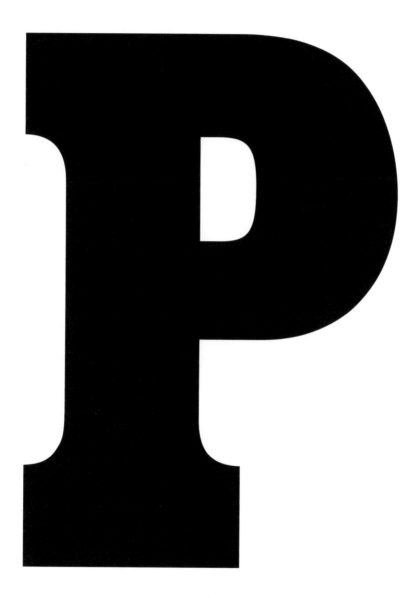

*The pastrami sandwich: You want
thin-sliced or thick?*

PHOTOGRAPH BY BOBBY DOHERTY

Parking, Alternate Side of the Street

The New York City Department of Traffic was established in June 1950 as the postwar auto boom threatened to swamp New York City in cars. Within a few weeks of its creation, the DOT was beseeched by the city's sanitation commissioner, Andrew W. Mulrain, to try out a new plan on the Lower East Side: a scheme to ban parking on each side of the street on alternating days, allowing the DOS to clean at the curbs. Fifteen hundred signs went up that July, and the law took effect on August 1. The local auto clubs predictably howled. By the end of the year, the arrangement had been expanded to the Upper West Side, and over the next few months into Brooklyn, Queens, and the Bronx. (It would have rolled out even faster, but the budget for new signs was quickly exhausted and had to be re-upped.) Within two years, the city was declaring the plan a success because of the substantial parking-fine revenue and (according to Mulrain) the cleaner streets.

Pasta Primavera

Most everyone agrees that this dish—spaghetti with a mélange of fresh spring vegetables, especially asparagus and peas, in a light, slightly creamy sauce—took off at Le Cirque in 1976. From there, the credits reel gets murky. A cook in Katonah, New York, named Ed Giobbi says he created it and served it to Sirio Maccioni and Jean Vergnes, Le Cirque's frontman and chef, before they adopted it. Maccioni has always said his wife came up with the idea. In any case, most accounts agree that Vergnes, a highly orthodox French chef, considered pasta an inferior food and delegated its preparation to others. In any case, primavera was a hit. Its lightness and minimal tomato content were a little unusual in a town still accustomed to Italian-American red-sauce restaurants (see also SPA-GHETTI AND MEATBALLS), and its preponderance of vegetables made it seem sensible to the slim and stylish set of the 1970s. (Carbs were not yet the enemy.) Gael Greene, in New York, called it "as crisp and beautiful as a Matisse" and "the best pasta in town."

By the mid-1980s, it could be found in every trattoria in America and was on its way to becoming a bit of a punch line. Like most trendy dishes gone masscult, it gradually lost the thing that made it unique; the spring vegetables that gave pasta primavera its name are essentially seasonless in most preparations, making it just another oversauced pasta option. (Capellini primavera even made it to the Olive Garden.) Le Cirque itself closed its New York dining room in 2017, having taken the dish off the menu years earlier. Its licensed offshoots in Las Vegas, Bangalore, and Dubai continue to operate, but none serves pasta primavera. That's a shame because Gael Greene was right: It is—when made with care during the actual primavera—delightful. It's so far from being chic that it's fresh all over again.

Pastrami Sandwich

In Turkey, basturma has for hundreds of years referred to a technique of pressing and drying meat with a spice paste called çemen. Those methods eventually crossed into Romania, where they were applied by kosher cooks to preserve whatever meat they were curing—sometimes goose, sometimes duck, sometimes beef. When Romanian Jewish immigrants settled on the Lower East Side of Manhattan, they adopted the local cheap cut: beef brisket. Generally speaking, the meat is "corned" (that is, cured in brine) for a couple of weeks, then dry rubbed with spices, then wood smoked, and then eaten, enthusiastically.

In 1887, a Lithuanian Jewish immigrant named Sussman Volk opened a butcher shop on Delancey Street. Soon after, a Romanian customer for whom he'd done a favor gave him a pastrami recipe, and Volk began curing his own. According to his great-granddaughter, the writer Patricia Volk, another customer finally asked for his sliced meat between two pieces of bread, and a billion deli sandwiches were born.

That's one paternity claim. Another comes from Katz's Delicatessen, which opened in 1888 under the name Iceland Brothers. (Willy Katz joined the business in 1903, his cousin soon followed, and the Katzes eventually put their name on the sign.) Yet some recent genealogical work by the writer Robert Moss has thrown both origin stories into doubt: The earliest public records of both Volk's deli and Iceland Brothers appear well after the turn of the century, suggesting that both have been pushed back to claim pastrami primacy. The two Iceland (formerly Eisland) brothers, for example, didn't even immigrate to the U.S. until 1902, and in 1888 they were 11 and 6 years old.

Volk's delicatessen closed decades ago, and today the Jewish deli is an increasingly rare bird in New York City owing to high rents, changing demographics, and a sense that using rendered chicken fat as liberally as others deploy ketchup may not be the best thing for a person. The Carnegie Deli closed in 2016. The 2nd Avenue Deli remains in business, its two locations now illogically situated on First Avenue and near Third Avenue. The Lower East Side is down to Katz's, which was recently at risk of being sold for the land underneath the building but instead has been preserved with a real-estate deal for the air rights above. In a taste test of the city's pastrami sandwiches conducted by *New York*'s editors in 1973, Katz's came in dead last behind seventeen competitors. By 2017, when a new generation of editors did a roundup, it was declared the champ.

Penthouse

In the early 1920s, as Fifth Avenue was being redeveloped, nearly all its spectacular mansions (*see also* ROBBER BARON) were torn down to make way for apartment buildings. Marjorie Merriweather Post, the cereal heiress, didn't want to sell the 54-room house she lived in on Fifth Avenue near 92nd Street. A developer eventually persuaded her, accepting her condition that the house, with a private entrance, be more or less re-created atop his new building. When 1107 Fifth Avenue was finished a few years later, Post indeed had 54 rooms on the top three floors (including the top story of the building itself) set back from the façade with a wraparound terrace: the first penthouse apartment. (The term was borrowed from the ancient French word *apentiz*, which described an outbuilding attached to the side of a structure.) The views, as you might expect, were staggering.

Because it provided exclusivity within community, and privacy in the center of it all, the penthouse came to epitomize a sybaritic lifestyle. The five twin-tower apartment buildings of Central Park West built in the 1920s and 1930s—the Majestic, the San Remo, the El Dorado, the Century, and the Beresford—each got

multiple penthouses. The great co-ops of the East Side, like 740 Park Avenue, had them as well. Lesser buildings sometimes plopped one atop the roof—little huts, essentially, that added rental or sales income plus a bit of cachet. Even after Bob Guccione named a pornographic magazine *Penthouse*, the term didn't entirely go into the gutter. The only real hit it has taken is from real-estate brokers and developers, who have been known to call any upper-floor apartment a penthouse. But they know what they're doing: Post's mega-apartment was broken up into six generous units in the 1950s, and in 2014, one floor alone—about one-third of her original layout—was sold for nearly $31 million.

Period Underpants

"I just love the taboo space," New York–based Miki Agrawal, the founder of Thinx, once explained of her mission to (profitably) destigmatize menstruation by making and selling "period underwear," panties made with a special fabric that wicks away menstrual blood. Thinx underwear is sold in a range of styles, including lace, and absorbencies, including a thong for light days and a brief that can absorb two tampons' worth for heavy days, and feels not dissimilar to wearing a pad. Its patent filing, explaining the technology, refers to layers of fabric (a "moisture-impermeable polymer layer," a "moisture-absorbent layer," a "moisture-wicking layer"), but the promise of the garment is that, if it's used as a backup, waiting too long to change a tampon will never result in a spoiled pair of underwear. Or it can enable a more radical "free-bleeding" approach, for those who, like Agrawal, are suspicious of Big Tampon.

Thinx gained notice in late 2015 when the MTA tried to pull its ads—beautifully designed in shades of millennial pink with suggestive imagery of fruit—from subway trains for being inappropriate. Thanks to Agrawal's savvy PR leveraging, Thinx became an exemplar of "period feminism," in which confronting the world frankly with the biological realities of being a woman became a political cause—sometimes slightly ironic, sometimes completely earnest. Agrawal briefly became a hero of the feminist start-up scene until, in early 2017, she was accused by female employees of sexual harassment, among other long-standing concerns about benefits and her treatment of workers, and

① **The Five Essential Pilates Ab Exercises**

From instructor Marina Kaydanova. Start each exercise from a supine position; do ten repetitions apiece.

➻ **Single leg stretch.** Pull your legs into tabletop position. Exhale as you crunch, extend the left leg to a 45-degree angle while pulling in the right knee. Then switch legs, breathing.
➻ **Double leg stretch.** Curl up your upper body, hugging your knees. Keeping the body curled, extend legs to a 45-degree angle. And breathe.

➻ **Single straight-leg stretch.** Bring your legs to a 90-degree angle. Exhale as you curl your upper body off the mat and begin to scissor your legs. Pull in the leg closer to your torso, then switch the leg out.
➻ **Double straight-leg lower and lift.** Lift your legs to 90 degrees. Curl your upper body, with your hands behind your

head. Lower your legs, holding the ab movement. Use your core to draw your legs back up.
➻ **Bicycle.** From tabletop position, curl your upper body off the mat with your hands behind your head. Twist your right elbow toward your left knee while extending your right leg, then repeat with the opposite arm and leg.

---

was removed from her role as CEO. Agrawal then pivoted to the bidet space with a new company, Tushy. But by then, period underpants had proven to be a marketable concept. Thinx continued to grow under new leadership, though so would its bevy of competitors with cutesy names, including Modibodi, Lunapads, and Knix.

Pickleback

The pickleback may have begun with Russian barflies or with long-haul truck drivers in Texas, but there's little doubt that Brooklyn put it on the world stage. In 2006, when Bushwick and East Williamsburg were still mostly industrial neighborhoods and certainly not home to two Michelin-starred restaurants, a chance meeting at the Bushwick Country Club forever changed the city's drinking culture. A southern patron—no one recorded her name—asked bartender Reggie Cunningham to give her a shot of whiskey with a pickle-juice chaser. Cunningham balked, but once he tried it he was converted, and the pickleback became a staple.

Pilates[1]

The idea behind the exercise program first known as "body contrology," for its emphasis on small, precise muscle movements, was formed when Joseph Pilates, a German-born self-defense instructor for Scotland Yard, was interned as an enemy citizen in England during World War I. Faced with extremely limited resources, Pilates created a method of working out that required very little equipment. After the war, he spent several years perfecting his new technique and developing his signature resistance-increasing apparatus, called the "reformer"; he then left Europe in 1926 for the United States, where he and his wife, Clara, established the world's first Pilates studio at 939 Eighth Avenue.

Their arrival, it turns out, was perfectly timed: The regimen caught the attention of the soon-to-be-legendary choreographer George Balanchine, co-founder of New York City Ballet, who saw that its focus on posture, mental control, and a strong central core would be perfect for dancers; they also found Pilates conditioning effective for recovering from and preventing injuries. Several of those who trained with Pilates would go on to open their own studios devoted to his technique in New York and across the country, adding their personal variations to the traditional range of movements. Its popularity among Hollywood celebrities, starting in the 1970s, brought the Pilates program greater visibility, and today it is part of the fitness mainstream along with other once-esoteric practices like yoga. The biggest local Pilates operation is now on West 42nd Street, but you can still take classes in the original studio on Eighth Avenue, too.

Pizza

Yes, it comes from Southern Italy—Naples or thereabouts—as did hundreds of thousands of Italians who moved to New York at the end of the nineteenth century, bringing with them their tomato-intensive style of cooking. One of them, Gennaro Lombardi, in 1905 was running a restaurant on Spring Street in Little Italy that by most accounts was the first to serve pizza in the United States. (The pies made there were bigger than those in the old country because America usually does that.) Lombardi and his chef, Anthony "Totonno" Pero, began firing their oven with coal, which burns hotter than wood, and found that placing the raw dough on a 900-degree stone made it bubbly and crisp as never before in a mere two or three minutes. Because the neighborhood's residents were mostly short of cash and many worked in factories and needed lunch, Lombardi began to sell pizza by the piece (*see also* DOLLAR SLICE), another innovation unheard-of in the old country.

Joseph Pilates with a client in his
Eighth Avenue studio, October 4, 1961.
PHOTOGRAPH BY I. C. RAPOPORT

Within a generation, pizza was well established in America, though mostly limited to Italian enclaves. Totonno eventually went off and opened his eponymous place in Coney Island, and other U.S. cities got their pizzerias as well. (The notable Frank Pepe Pizzeria Napoletana in New Haven, Connecticut, opened in 1925 serving slightly charred pies that are still a huge draw today, particularly the white pizza with clams.) In 1944, the New York *Times* ran a story about this curious foodstuff, defining it for readers as "a pie popular in Southern Italy . . . filled with any number of different centers, each including tomatoes" and noting that a restaurant on West 48th Street offered it to go, "packed, piping hot, in special boxes for that purpose." After World War II, when American soldiers came back from Italy with a taste for pizza, it began to make its way around the country. The Pizza Hut chain, for example, was founded in Wichita in 1958 and now has about 19,000 outlets.

By the 1950s, seemingly every New York street corner had its own slice joint, and the average quality was shockingly high. Most offered an Americanized version of the Italian margherita: thin crust, a layer of sweet tomato sauce, and a layer of low-moisture processed mozzarella, cooked hot and fast. Chicago, meanwhile, cultivated its own bastardization of the form, first served at a restaurant called Pizzeria Uno around 1943. It's usually referred to as "deep-dish" pizza and is more or less a big focaccia with gobs of toppings on it, served in a frying pan. (It's edible, if you're hungry.) By contrast, the 1980s Los Angeles innovations of Wolfgang Puck, who introduced weird new toppings (smoked salmon, pears) to the canon, are not especially Italian but are often delicious.

In the twenty-first century, New York has seen a rush of obsessive fine-tuning of the classic margherita, as dozens of restaurants have tried to up the ante with better high-gluten (or gluten-free) crusts, superior tomatoes, buffalo mozzarella, basil snipped directly from a living plant for maximum freshness, and a hesitation to put the result into a takeout box lest it steam itself into cardboard mediocrity. (Lombardi's, shuttered in 1984 and reopened nearby ten years later, is still excellent and has lines out the door at dinnertime.) An approximation of New York–style pizza has become universal in the United States and beyond, from school cafeterias to tens of thousands of Domino's delivery-car warming ovens.

Poets, New York School of

After a generation of poets and critics consolidated modernism's innovations and retreated from its experimental tendencies, a second avant-garde revolution in American poetry commenced in three regional hot spots—San Francisco, Black Mountain College in North Carolina, and New York City—in the 1950s. The Beats (*see also* BEATS, THE), the San Francisco Renaissance, and the Black Mountain poets bloomed and faded, but the poets of the New York School had staying power, and successive generations have extended and reinvigorated their approach to verse.

The cohort was codified in Donald Allen's anthology *The New American Poetry, 1945–1960*, with selections from John Ashbery, Barbara Guest, Kenneth Koch, Frank O'Hara, and James Schuyler. The grouping was as much social as it was aesthetic, and the poets had strong ties with the Abstract Expressionist painters who roved the same art galleries and bars and made their way into their poems. They worked as art critics and at MoMA, where O'Hara wrote some of his most beloved poems on his lunch breaks. Some of them lived together, and some collaborated in their writing, as in *A Nest of Ninnies*, a novel Schuyler and Ashbery wrote in alternating passages. In contrast to most canonical poetry, their verses were witty, informal, conversational, and filled with pop-culture references. They never sounded "official."

Ashbery would emerge as the most famous, prolific, garlanded, and longest-lived of the group. His style was multifarious and in early books tended toward surrealism, but across his work there is a strain of romanticism, presented in the muffled modes of collage and elegy. All of them were poets of the city, who sought to capture a living response to urban life in their work, whether that life consisted of parties, headlines, radio signals, cavernous avenues, or canvases mounted on walls. Ashbery's poems involve a high degree of self-concealment; he is always there and not there. O'Hara conjured a pantheon that put celebrities on the same plane as his personal friends, and he is ever present in lines like "I have been to lots of parties / and acted perfectly disgraceful / but I never actually collapsed / oh Lana Turner we love you get up." He died young, struck by a jeep after a party on Fire Island in 1966, at the age of 40.

Another generation of bohemian poets swept

downtown in the 1970s, among them Anne Waldman, Ted Berrigan, Ron Padgett, Alice Notley, and Joe Brainard, whose book-length poem *I Remember* is a deadpan, profane, funny index of mid-twentieth-century experience from Brainard's youth in Oklahoma through his arrival in New York City, told in hundreds of stanzas of prose that begin with the words of the title. "I remember my first sexual experience in a subway. Some guy (I was afraid to look at him) got a hardon and was rubbing it back and forth against my arm. I got very excited and when my stop came I hurried out and home where I tried to do an oil painting using my dick as a brush."

The live performance of poetry also became a crucial part of the equation, and the Poetry Project at St. Mark's Church in the East Village became the hub of the New York School's activities, which later spread to radio and public-access cable. Meanwhile, Ashbery's influence was widening as his style, despite its obscurity, became the most difficult sort of poetry conventional poets would admit to admiring. A third wave, which is now an old guard, took over the Poetry Project in the 1980s, including Eileen Myles and Charles Bernstein, one of the founders of the Language Poetry movement. It's hard to point to a specific New York School these days, but it's also hard to find a poet in America or abroad whose poems aren't written at least a little under its spell.

Political Journal, American Conservative

In 1955, there was still such a thing as a liberal Republican, and one of them (arguably), Dwight D. Eisenhower, was in the White House. Pro-business patricians of the Northeast were locked in an uneasy alliance with the "Old Right" of the Midwest, while the South was dominated by racist Democrats committed to Jim Crow. In this climate, a young reactionary had an idea for a magazine that would synthesize what he saw as the three tenets of the true conservative: traditionalism, libertarianism, and anti-communism. These ideas survive in pieties mouthed on Capitol Hill today—God, free enterprise, and a strong defense—and the organ most responsible for delivering them to our time was *National Review*. Its founding editor, William F. Buckley Jr., was a Manhattan native who'd grown up in Mexico and Paris and at various boarding schools. He was a veteran of the CIA, and among the many books he wrote are *God and Man at Yale* and *McCarthy and His Enemies*. (Yes, the latter is a defense of McCarthyism.)

The magazine's project was to "stand athwart history, yelling *Stop!*" as Buckley so famously put it. Among his original stable of editors and writers in New York were the ex-Marxist James Burnham and the former communist spy Whittaker Chambers. An early, continuous project was to define conservatism by excluding its fringe elements: Ayn Rand, the racist and nativist John Birch Society, blatant anti-Semites. It featured an excellent literary section, bolstered by the New Critics Hugh Kenner and Guy Davenport. Several young lights who would later turn left did their early work in its pages, among them Garry Wills, John Leonard, and Joan Didion. To put it politely, Buckley and his journal were not exactly ahead of their time on civil rights, and the backlash against the movement bolstered their brand. By 1964, the magazine and its partisans had a nominee on the GOP ticket in Barry Goldwater, and by 1981, after a migration of intellectuals (*see also* NEOCONSERVATISM) from the left, they had one of their own in the White House. By then, Buckley had become a celebrity of political chat for his transatlantic drawl on *Firing Line*.

Today, *National Review* has many cousins: the formerly liberal *Commentary*, the neocon and recently deceased *Weekly Standard*, the culture-oriented *New Criterion*, and the paleocon *American Conservative* (whose writers believe they embody the true spirit of Buckley, who stepped down as editor of *National Review* in 1990 and died in 2008, aghast at his allies' worship of markets and the march into Iraq); two of its own, David Brooks and Ross Douthat, now write columns for the New York *Times*. *National Review*'s biggest existential problem came from its stepchild, the contemporary Republican Party, and the president (*see also* TRUMPISM) who proved the conservative movement and the GOP aren't the same thing. Sensing this in 2016, the magazine devoted an entire issue to the case against Donald Trump, rolling out many of its stalwarts, to no avail. Trump's ascent to the White House signaled the waning influence of *National Review* and respectable conservative opinion generally. Trump's stated preferences were for Fox News (on and off), Breitbart, InfoWars, OANN, and whatever cranks he saw on Twitter. It would be easy to mistake the nativists who marched in Charlottesville for the face of the new right. So much for excluding the fringe.

Political Journal, American Liberal

When the Civil War ended, the Boston abolitionist William Lloyd Garrison felt his work was done. He shut down his weekly magazine, *The Liberator*, and devoted himself to the cause of women's suffrage. But *The Liberator*'s backers were still interested in funding a radical publication "on broader grounds," so they linked up with journalist and Central Park landscape architect Frederick Law Olmsted, who was looking to start a magazine in Manhattan. The result was *The Nation*, first published in July 1865, a few months after the assassination of Abraham Lincoln; it is now America's oldest continuously published weekly. It took some time for the magazine's politics to find its footing, initially wobbling (along with its first editor, E. L. Godkin) on Black suffrage and Reconstruction. For decades, it was fused with the New York *Post*—then a lefty broadsheet (*see also* TABLOID NEWSPAPER)—in a weekly edition. By the turn of the century, its modern left-liberal sympathies had taken hold: It became the country's strongest voice for anti-imperialism, opposing U.S. entry into World War I and calling instead for "peace without victory," for women's rights, for civil liberties, and for organized labor. It also praised "those amazing men, Lenin and Trotsky" who accomplished a socialist revolution that withdrew Russia from the war.

Relations with the Soviet Union were perhaps the defining issue on the left for most of the twentieth century, and while other liberal journals arose to join *The Nation* in support of, say, the New Deal or entry into World War II, there were often intra-left disputes on foreign policy as the Cold War set in. Rivals to *The Nation* emerged. The progressive *New Republic* was launched by Herbert Croly, Walter Lippmann, and Walter Weyl in 1914; the initially socialist *New Leader* began in 1924. Liberalism split into anti-communist and dovish camps, with *The New Leader* launching a vendetta against *The Nation* and accusing it of Stalinist sympathies, rehashing feuds their contributors had famously conducted in the CUNY cafeteria. This foreshadowed the march of many *New Leader* writers into neoconservatism and the Republican Party, a path also taken by the editors of *Commentary*. During the upheavals of the 1960s, the liberal journals were staunch defenders of the civil-rights movement but split on Vietnam and the

New Left, depending on their degree of anti-communism. In the 1970s, *The New Republic* adopted, along with *Washington Monthly*, the pro-market outlook of neoliberalism. This would make it the essential magazine of Third Way Democrats, when, during the Clinton administration, it was known as "the in-flight magazine of Air Force One."

The 9/11 attacks and the war on terror were more occasions for feuds and schisms on the left, with *Nation* columnists like Christopher Hitchens turning hawkishly rightward and breaking with the magazine. Financial exhaustion doomed the likes of *The New Leader*, which burned out in 2010. Changes in ownership have also resulted in changes in politics, as in the case of *The New Republic*, which returned to New York in 2015 and shed its neoliberalism in favor of a soft "woke" centrism. *The Nation* still leads a vanguard of magazines on the left, including *Mother Jones* in San Francisco, *In These Times* in Chicago, and *Dissent* in New York. But the most influential magazine on the left in recent years defines itself as not liberal but socialist: *Jacobin*'s rise has paralleled the political fortunes of Bernie Sanders and the Democratic Socialists of America, and its reading groups have become grassroots incubators of electoral campaigns. Magazines still play a vital role on the American left; the only question is how long we'll be calling them liberal.

Political Machine

New York City was the nation's first, fractious capital, so naturally we invented "factions," or political clubs. The Democratic Republicans were led by Virginia's Thomas Jefferson, and the Federalists followed local hero and future Broadway sensation Alexander Hamilton. It made admirable civic sense, as the country took shape, to form these clubs supporting competing political ideologies. This being New York, though, things quickly became about money. The Spartan Club, for instance, drew its membership from newly arrived and miserably exploited Irish immigrants and was led by Mike Walsh, a brawling working-class radical. But the proto-Marxist Spartans were outmuscled by the rival, pseudo-populist Tammany Hall, whose "Boss" Tweed developed the exchange of jobs for votes into a corrupt art form and created the first American organization worthy of being called a political machine.

As the grand sachem of Tammany Hall in the years after the Civil War, Tweed inflated the prices of city contracts and invested kickbacks to accumulate a real-estate empire. He savvily pushed the weak city government to build orphanages, public baths, and hospitals, earning himself a populist sheen—for a while. Thomas Nast's editorial cartoons in the pages of *Harper's Weekly* eventually helped to expose Tweed's corruption, which had siphoned an estimated $200 million from city coffers. Tammany Hall's power lingered in Manhattan, however, all the way to Fiorello La Guardia's election as a "reform" mayor in 1933, and one of Tammany's protégés, James A. Farley, went on to run a massive federal New Deal jobs racket. Outer-borough political machines enjoyed greater longevity: Brooklyn's Meade Esposito ran a potent patronage operation for decades and was a pivotal player in the election of Ed Koch as New York's mayor over Mario Cuomo in 1977. The Queens machine proved even more durable, controlling judgeships and ballot access, with its leadership passing from Donald Manes to Tom Manton to Joe Crowley—who may go down as New York's last old-school political boss. The 20-year U.S. congressman was defeated in 2018 by Alexandria Ocasio-Cortez, whose power flows from a very different machine, the internet.

Pooper-Scooper Law

Seeing as New York's worst problems in the mid-1970s were enormous job and population losses twinned with a spiraling crime rate (*see also* MAYHEM), the incontrovertible fact that the streets were minefields of dog poop was perhaps not the most pressing issue. Nonetheless, nobody likes to step in it, and the laws of the day required dog owners merely to move off the curb when their animals relieved themselves. The statute said nothing about cleaning up, and it went unheeded and unenforced. By one estimate, 125 tons of dung landed on the city's streets and sidewalks daily. You might expect a law addressing this problem to be popular and uncontroversial.

Instead, when Jerome Kretchmer, head of New York City's Department of Environmental Protection, announced in July 1978 that new legislation would require residents to clean up after their dogs, people went bananas. Lawsuits were filed; bags of feces were hurled by and at activists; questions were raised regarding civil liberties, the social contract, and whether a millionaire resident of the mightiest city on earth should be expected to pick up steaming dog shit. (In that situation, who's really the pet owner and who's the owned?) Kretchmer, it was noted, did not own a dog; he had turtles.

He also had the backing of Mayor Ed Koch, and when the City Council declined to pass the bill, Koch managed to get the State of New York to do so. Taking effect on August 1, 1978, the Canine Waste Law, as it is officially known, applies to cities of 400,000 or more people—which numbered just two back then, New York City and Buffalo—and sets a fine of up to $100 for failing to eliminate what the law refers to as "a nuisance." Entrepreneurs jumped in, selling dustpan-like scoops and other gadgets to keep dog owners' hands unbesmirched, but most people just used a scrap of cardboard or a plastic bag.

Judging by the press coverage at the time, New York collectively expected the law to be ignored, but the social contract came into play: Although relatively few tickets were written for the new infraction, it soon became socially unacceptable to leave your dog's droppings on the sidewalk where someone might step in them. New Yorkers who did not want their shoes soiled would give the negligent a dirty look or even snap at them. It was an example of the accidental self-policing described by Jane Jacobs (*see also* "EYES ON THE STREET") and perhaps of the stopping-small-infractions-to-prevent-bigger-ones attitude the police would soon adopt on a larger scale (*see also* "BROKEN WINDOWS" POLICING).

Most American cities have since followed New York in this, without needing the statewide intervention that Koch sought. Today, you have to clean up after your dog in Los Angeles, in Ithaca, in San Antonio. The law can be seen as an early milepost in the taming—up to a point, anyway—of the purportedly ungovernable city of New York, one that perhaps has echoes in more recent attempts to regulate everyday behaviors like smoking (*see also* NANNY STATE).

Whether you find it acceptable or intrusive, it inarguably makes the summer months a little better for most of us, and a little worse if you happen to be the owner of a dog with a touchy stomach.

James Rosenquist's Campaign *(1965)*
ARTWORK BY JAMES ROSENQUIST

Pop Art

On January 20, 1958, in two small rooms on the fourth floor of a townhouse at 4 East 77th Street, art history turned on a dime. That day marked the opening of Jasper Johns's first solo exhibition at the new Leo Castelli Gallery, the first sharp art-world break from the enormous, angsty style (*see also* ABSTRACT EXPRESSIONISM) that had dominated American painting for a decade. Johns, a 27-year-old bisexual Southerner living in New York with his lover, the artist Robert Rauschenberg, exhibited small works made in encaustic—a nearly lost medium of paint embedded in wax that had once been used for mummies' burial portraits. They represented, as he put it, "things the mind already knows." Johns painted flags, targets, numbers, letters. By the time the show closed on February 8, it had sold out to prestigious collectors and museums. MoMA purchased four pieces—one of them a promised gift—for a total of $2,835, which would be about 30 grand today.

The most powerful art critic of the time, Clement Greenberg, dismissed Johns and Rauschenberg and much of the related work that followed as "novelty art," "far-out," and "not even up to Grant Wood." All the same, Johns made the cover of *ARTnews*, and what was initially called "neo-Dada" soon came to be known as Pop Art. The term was not, as many people believe, an Andy Warhol invention; it was coined by the British critic Lawrence Alloway, describing work made by artists like Richard Hamilton that similarly drew from popular culture and media.

Over the next five years, a new generation of artists working in this form came to dominate in America and beyond. The AbEx idiom—big, macho, slashy paintings made mostly by straight white men—gave way to work that was smaller, realistic, and based on comics, advertising, sign painting, pop culture, movies, and TV. Its successful artists were still nearly all white and male, although fewer were straight. That first class included (in addition to Johns) Andy Warhol, Roy Lichtenstein, Robert Indiana, James Rosenquist, Jim Dine, Tom Wesselmann, Claes Oldenburg, and a raft of others from all over the world. Their art was accessible yet strange, irreverent, brightly colored, fun, and visually wild: What was a precisely accurate painting of an American flag? A flag, a painting of one, both, either, what? Were paintings of romance-comics panels serious? Gigantic categories yawned before critics, collectors, museums, and the public. And the artists seemed to multiply overnight, most living in abandoned or cheap lofts downtown and all forming multiple overlapping social circles that spawned only more energy. Art was less of an exclusive club than ever. But it still felt resistant, underground, important, and, once again, fun!

After Johns and Rauschenberg stoked the long train of art history to an unprecedented speed, Warhol got it to jump the track, landing someplace totally new that felt like the first completely American art. (Only later did all recognize that this change was happening simultaneously worldwide.) But something else came into existence in New York at this time, and some call it a monster: The contemporary art market was born (*see also* MEGADEALER). Even with its wild ups and downs, it made New York City the undisputed center of the art world. It no longer is—because happily there isn't one—but New York is still art's trading floor.

Positive Thinking

Norman Vincent Peale, the pastor of a Reformed church in Chelsea, often told stories about how he was ashamed of being scrawny as a kid. "I longed to be hard-boiled and tough and fat," he once wrote. He didn't overcome his inferiority complex until young adulthood, when he discovered "positive thinking," which he claimed was a teaching from the Bible. He outlined the principles in his 1952 book, *The Power of Positive Thinking*: Picture yourself succeeding, cancel out negative thoughts with positive ones, repeat every day the mantra "I can do all things through Christ which strengtheneth me."

The scholarly community, from therapists to theologians, was appalled. Uptown at Union Theological Seminary, Reinhold Niebuhr accused Peale of "corrupting the Gospel" and doing readers a disservice. But the book was phenomenally popular; it ultimately sold more than 7 million copies and was translated into some 15 languages. Both Dwight D. Eisenhower and Richard Nixon declared themselves fans.

Some critics said that Peale was just repackaging New Thought, a spiritual movement developed in the U.S. in the nineteenth century, or that he was Christianizing Dale Carnegie's self-help advice. But Peale has a distinct

(2) **The Best Spots for a Power Lunch**

Chosen by Tina Brown, author and former editor of Vanity Fair, The New Yorker, Talk, *and* The Daily Beast

↠ **The Lambs Club**
132 W. 44th St.

↠ **Aretsky's Patroon**
160 E. 46th St.

↠ **Sant Ambroeus**
1000 Madison Ave.

↠ **The Grill**
99 E. 52nd St.

legacy. It's hard not to hear him in the sermons of the Houston megachurch pastor Joel Osteen or in the opportunistic faith pronouncements of Donald J. Trump (*see also* TRUMPISM), who grew up attending Peale's church. Peale officiated at the first of Trump's three weddings.

Postindustrial Park

In 1980, a decades-old elevated railway on the West Side of Manhattan, running from Gansevoort Street to 34th Street, carried its last boxcars of freight (frozen turkeys). Then it went dormant, rusting silently for the next two decades, principally because it wasn't worth the expense to tear it down. In 1999, two enthusiastic novice planner-architects, Robert Hammond and Joshua David, offered a startling proposal: that it be turned into an elevated park. A precedent for their idea lay in the nascent rails-to-trails movement, which was beginning to turn old transit rights-of-way into hiking paths and the like. The most notable among those projects is the Promenade Plantée in Paris. But constructing such a thing thirty feet above New York's streets seemed like one of those academic exercises that architecture students offer, not a real plan for the real city.

Except it was. Hammond and David pulled in an enormous amount of public and (mostly) private funding, in particular drawing on the interest of the residents and businesses around the elevated trestle in far-west Chelsea. The locals constituted the nexus of the American art world (and had little green space in the neighborhood), so they were perhaps unusually receptive to this relatively avant-garde scheme. By 2006, construction had begun, and by 2009 the first section (of three) was open to the public. The second and third were completed over the next eight years. The High Line was an immediate, resounding success, in part because of its superior design (by James Corner Field Operations, Diller Scofidio + Renfro, and Piet Oudolf) and in

part because the experience of walking it was uniquely lovely. The views through the low-rise buildings of Chelsea were excellent, and the rather severe, blackened remains of the formerly industrial area set off the park's lush, green plantings. In 2015, the Whitney Museum of American Art moved downtown to a giant new home on Gansevoort Street right next to the High Line's southern end. A relic not worth its own demolition cost had pulled America's largest cultural institutions off the Upper East Side and into its magnetic grip.

A lot of other cities have derelict infrastructure, and many of their mayors have eyed the High Line enviously. Chicago's Bloomingdale Trail, Atlanta's BeltLine, Miami's Underline, just to name a few, all have organizations clamoring for conversions into parkland. But the High Line is tricky to duplicate. The concentration of wealth around this particular structure meant public funding could be heavily supplemented—and it needs to be, because the park's maintenance is extremely costly. Despite its length, it's also pretty small in area, a boutique project rather than a sprawling one. And it does have a downside: The High Line today has been marred by its own success. On pleasant days, it is jammed to capacity. The tourists it draws have turned a relatively quiet neighborhood noisy and chattery. But most of all, access to the High Line has become a selling point for developers, and a great many new apartment towers have sprung up on either side of the park, which is increasingly being walled up in a glass canyon. The Chelsea community that helped make the High Line possible is feeling it may soon be pushed out of the neighborhood altogether.

Power Lunch [2]

Lee Eisenberg, writing in the October 1979 issue of *Esquire*, named it. "Good day, Philip Johnson, William Bernbach, Henry Grunwald. What are you doing for lunch?" is how his feature opened, and it focused on the hours between 12:30 and 3 p.m. at The Four Seasons, the restaurant in the Seagram Building on Park Avenue. Johnson himself had designed the rooms, Grunwald was running Time Inc., and Bernbach was the reigning genius of the ad business (*see also* MADISON AVENUE), all representing peak success in their respective creative fields.

It also represented a second life for The Four Seasons itself. Impossibly chic when it opened in 1959, it had lost some of its luster by the early 1970s. Its food had gained a reputation for mediocrity, and the midtown expense-account-lunch crowd had mostly scattered to traditional-French competitors like Lutèce and La Grenouille. After The Four Seasons was sold in 1973, its new owners introduced a lighter menu focused on grilled food that could be cooked and served quickly. It worked because of two trends that were converging in the 1970s: The powerful creative folk (editors, admen, fashion executives) the restaurant drew were increasingly trying to stay thin, and the workday was getting less leisurely, less boozy, and more packed. Wine was sold by the glass rather than the bottle, a rather new idea. The widely separated tables—a mark of luxury in New York, where every square inch costs money—allowed conversation on sensitive topics. As Simon & Schuster's Michael Korda told Eisenberg, "This place is a stroke of genius: You can have a simple, fine meal and be back at your desk in two hours." The Four Seasons was not the only place for power lunches—those French restaurants, for example, served their share as well. But if you wanted to spot S. I. Newhouse and nod at Henry Kissinger while on your way to your table, the Grill Room, the restaurant's slightly more exclusive southern end, was the place to be. That is, as long as you didn't get seated in the balcony, a.k.a. "Siberia."

The food, it should be noted, was not the point. The power lunch was mostly about touching antennae, a place where a CEO could be among his own kind, demonstrating that he (and, in this era, very occasionally

she) was a Bigfoot. It was a ritual, a demonstration of alphaness. At the same time, some business was transacted, in the form of loose handshake deals that would later see contracts, briefs, and commercial scripts produced by less glamorous employees—the ones eating chicken-salad sandwiches at their desks.

As the 1970s gave way to the '80s, the power lunch became an idea as much as a fact. Places like Le Cirque found midday followings. In the '90s, Le Bernardin introduced a two-course prix fixe menu that enabled 30-minute dining. The Four Seasons retained the power crowd right up until it lost its lease in 2016 and tried to reopen a few blocks away. (The new location failed and closed within a year.) The Grill, which replaced it in the Seagram Building, did manage to hang onto some of the old customers. And indeed the idea of the power lunch lingers, although in practice the meal rarely happens over linens and cocktails and grilled branzino. The younger generation's start-up conversations typically take place over coffee at Starbucks or its independent brethren. Somehow, though, "Power Frappuccino" does not have the same ring.

Prospect Park *see* CENTRAL PARK

Public Defender

On March 8, 1876, a group of German-Americans met on Wall Street with the lawyer and former Wisconsin governor Edward Salomon, aiming to form an organization that would provide legal assistance to German immigrants who could not afford a private attorney. Out of that group, the German Legal Aid Society was born with the purpose of defending immigrants from, as its chief attorney, Leonard McGee, put it, "unscrupulous people, who, on one pretext or another, would manage to rob them of the little they possessed."

The Society soon opened an office at 39 Nassau Street and handled 212 cases in its first year; in its fifth, it took on 2,832. The Congregational clergyman and abolitionist Henry Ward Beecher donated expansion space in the Plymouth Church in Brooklyn, allowing the group to serve residents of the borough who couldn't even afford the trip to Manhattan. In 1890, the group began offering assistance to non-Germans. The only qualifications necessary for help seekers were to "appear worthy and at the same time be unable to pay." The organization changed its name to the Legal Aid Society on June 1, 1896. By 1926, it had 35 staff members and six offices in New York City. Today, there is a similar society, if not more than one, in every state.

The historic *Gideon* v. *Wainwright* decision, handed down by the Supreme Court in 1963, ruled that states are required under the Sixth Amendment to provide representation to defendants in criminal cases who cannot afford their own attorneys. In response to this (along with the federal government's assumption of legal services for the poor in 1962), the Society has since prioritized criminal defense. The program accepts 48 public defenders from 300 to 400 applicants each year.

Public Relations

The problem with calling a single person the inventor of public relations is that everyone who's campaigned for the title has, almost definitionally, bent the truth to enhance his own story. But—assuming you don't count Moses bringing down his ten-bullet-point press release from Mount Sinai—the principal candidate is probably Ivy Ledbetter Lee. A Princeton graduate who worked for New York newspapers, he became the press representative for a better-government group called the Citizens Union in 1903 and from there began to represent other organizations, including the Pennsylvania Railroad as it fought off nationalization. His biggest triumph came with the Rockefeller family, whose reputation he helped change from vicious to generous, steely to kindly. (In 1933, a year before his death, he also advised the German Dye Trust during the early days of the Third Reich, for whom his strategic advice boiled down to "You have a PR problem in America because your policies are unacceptable.") Lee's great insight was that public relations depended not on closing ranks but

on opening them: He knew that reporters and public opinion were more easily swayed by information than by its absence and that flooding the public with one's preferred point of view displaced the opposition's.

Lee's principal rival for the crown is his contemporary Edward Bernays, whose name is more widely known today. Bernays is most famous for his campaign to promote Lucky Strike cigarettes in the 1920s by connecting smoking with women's rights, coaxing suffragettes to march with "Torches for Freedom." (In the process, he helped establish cigarette smoking as a weight-loss aid for the modern woman.) He was also the person who persuaded America of the purity of Ivory soap and the sanitariness of the Dixie disposable paper cup. Even by the standards of his profession, he was a fantastic self-promoter, and he lived for such a long time—he died in 1995, at 103, and worked nearly until the end—that the title he cultivated continues to attach itself to him. In the public-relations war for "Father of Public Relations," he won.

Puerto Rican Culture *see* NUYORICAN

Puffer Coat

NOTE: *Norma Kamali introduced the puffy down-filled jacket—her version is known as the "sleeping-bag coat"—in 1973 and continues to produce its descendants today. The designer and New York native talked about its origins and the design's enduring appeal.*

When did the idea for the sleeping-bag coat first come to you? In the early '70s, during a camping trip in Narrowsburg, New York. I went with friends of mine. Some of them worked in fashion, others in design or architecture. We all had our sleeping bags. In the middle of the night, I had to go to the bathroom. It was really cold, like that crisp, cold air. And, you know, we were in the woods ... so, that's where I had to go. I picked up my sleeping bag and wrapped it around me. I went running into this little area that was hidden. As I was running—and I'll never forget—I thought, *Jeez, this is really keeping me warm. This is a good idea for a coat.* The next day, I told a friend, and he said, "You've gotta do this."

So that's what I did when I got back home. I couldn't wait to wear it. Everyone started saying, "Can you make

André Leon Talley wears a puffer coat,
or possibly the other way around.
PHOTOGRAPH BY IKE EDEANI

me a coat like that?" I bought tons of sleeping bags from army-navy stores. Each one was different. The number we were making just kept increasing. Every season after that, I made sleeping-bag coats. Now technology has taken us so far that I can make a sleeping-bag coat that's as light as a feather.

Was there anything else like it on the market at the time? People were doing very crafty, one-of-a-kind things. I would cut up blankets and quilts to make coats. But in terms of this coat, no.

How did the bouncers at Studio 54 start wearing them? I was actually dating Ian Schrager at the time. Steve Rubell was freezing his little butt outside the Studio 54 door, and he said, "Can you make me a jacket?" And I did. Then the other doormen bought sleeping-bag coats. Talk about influencers!

There have been different times throughout the life of the sleeping-bag coat where either the trend was big shapes, or [it was] something like 9/11.

9/11? How? Two weeks after 9/11, I decided to come back to the office and regroup. At the time, there was no cell-phone [service], so I picked up my landline and saw all these messages. It was unbelievable: One after another, people asking for sleeping-bag coats. It was a very warm, muggy September, and we hadn't started production yet. I called everybody back to work, and we started going through the sample room and looking at fabric we had on hand. We put as many in the store as we could. The sleeping-bag coat literally kept us in business for at least five months where we would not have done any other business. I think it's the comforting, cocooning effect of the coat that made New Yorkers feel safe. I don't think it was a conscious decision. I think it was more like, *I need one of those.* I also remember thinking, *I'm not going to wear high heels ever again. If I have to run down 100 flights, I want to be in sneakers.* It's practical.

Why do you think it's still successful? The '70s and now have so many parallels and experiences. One thing is this gender-fluid movement. The sleeping-bag coat was born in an environment in the '70s of experimentation and disruption. It was about spending time with nature, like the flower-power thing: Let's get back to the earth. We looked at government with curiosity. The city was bankrupt. There's so much that's the same.

Are more people buying the coat today? We're seeing more men buy sleeping-bag coats, which is why I mentioned gender fluidity. I think it's such a natural fit for men. It's practical. It's comfortable. It rolls up in a little sack. You can store it when you travel. It's convenient. At the same time, depending on who you are, it can be fashion.

Punk³

Born from the same wave of restless New York City youth as the early hip-hop DJs and breakers and from the same sense of disillusionment with the promise of prosperity put forth in the old Sinatra standard—"If I can make it there, I'll make it anywhere"—punk pointed out the lie in plain terms. Progenitors like the Velvet Underground documented the city's seedy dark side in songs like 1967's "I'm Waiting for the Man," a heroin deal set to locomotive garage rock, and, the next year, "White Light/White Heat," which races luridly along the path of intravenous drugs through the bloodstream detailing bodily reactions along the way, à la *Fantastic Voyage*.

At its inception, punk was simultaneously a rejection of wholesome values and a purification of rock and roll in an era when the genre had begun to lose contact with the grit underfoot. The early '70s in rock saw odes to wizards and stars; high concepts, intricate instrumentation, and longer song lengths impacted the charts. Alongside the seriousness and formal musicality of the prog-rock movement was yacht rock, easy listening, and album-oriented rock, a glut of sometimes great, sometimes awful adult-contemporary party music that carried rock and roll away from the frantic sexual energy that had birthed it. Punk pressed RESET. The Ramones, from Forest Hills, Queens, weaned on '50s and '60s pop and guitar music, remade it in their own image, half as nice and twice as fast, starting with their 1976 self-titled debut album (fourteen songs in under thirty minutes, including "Blitzkrieg Bop," "Beat on the Brat," and "Now I Wanna Sniff Some Glue"). Meanwhile, the New York Dolls had broken the mold of what rockers were supposed to look like, playing raucous gems like 1973's "Personality Crisis" in drag.

Nothing cool and unique happens in New York City without reverberating around the world, so the story of punk rock in the mid-'70s is a tale of imports and exports. London boutique owner Malcolm McLaren encountered the Dolls in 1973 along with his girlfriend, the fashion designer Vivienne Westwood. They styled the band and brought a piece of downtown New York culture back home with them, giving their London shop, renamed SEX in 1974, a makeover spotlighting fetish gear and creating the darkly flamboyant, provocative foundation of punk style. The pair broadcast the scene's fashion to its constituency of edgy Brits—which included the founding members of the Sex Pistols, a band McLaren assembled out of the store's favorite regulars. The Clash soon formed after a corker of a Pistols show, and suddenly there was a movement on both sides of the Atlantic. The Sex Pistols would take the British media by siege; back in the States, the angsty new music from New York trickled westward. Spiky haircuts and equally spiky clothing, as well as the spiky attitudes they conveyed, trickled into mainstream style as well.

Punk rock metastasized through the late '70s, as scenes manifested in the Midwest and up and down the West Coast. Stiv Bators and the Dead Boys descended on New York from Cleveland, touting a younger, louder, and snottier brand of the music introduced to them by the Ramones. Greg Sage's Wipers made lean, nihilistic noise in Portland, Oregon, that would have a profound effect on a meek young latchkey kid from Aberdeen, Washington, named Kurt. Down the coast, Germs, the Angry Samoans, and Dead Kennedys played harder and faster than their Big Apple contemporaries, paving the way for the hardcore breakthroughs that would happen in the next decade. Back in the city, the creative outpouring from a network of geniuses, junkies, and artists was documented in landmark albums by Blondie, Talking Heads, Patti Smith, Television, and Richard Hell and the Voidoids.

In the Reagan '80s, hardcore did for punk what punk had done for hard rock, sanding down the edges and jettisoning all but the riff and the message. By then, the music had infiltrated every major city. D.C. pumped out legends from Minor Threat to the Bad Brains, whose music was a vehicle for their message of respect for the body and mind. Out in Minneapolis, Hüsker Dü and the Replacements partied hard and added a dash of melody. While hardcore raced for escape velocity, punk shattered into shards, spawning subgenres like postpunk, synth-punk, and no wave, which deviated from the original format and instrumentation. Back in New York, the experimentation continued as Suicide worked up a frenzy on keyboards and drum machines, James Chance and the Contortions spazzed on guitars and sax, and Sonic Youth made tense, tuneful noise.

No one was quite prepared for what happened in the early '90s, when, with fervor mounting from coast to coast, punk rock exploded out of the underground. Kurt from Aberdeen and his band, Nirvana, provided the spark, breaking through with 1991's *Nevermind*. Soon, long-simmering bands like Green Day and the Offspring would see their albums *Dookie* and *Smash* become multiplatinum-selling pop-punk hits. In the glow of nationwide attention, prominent punk acts either embraced recognition or shunned it. The question of what was lost in the trip to the top of the charts still lingers.

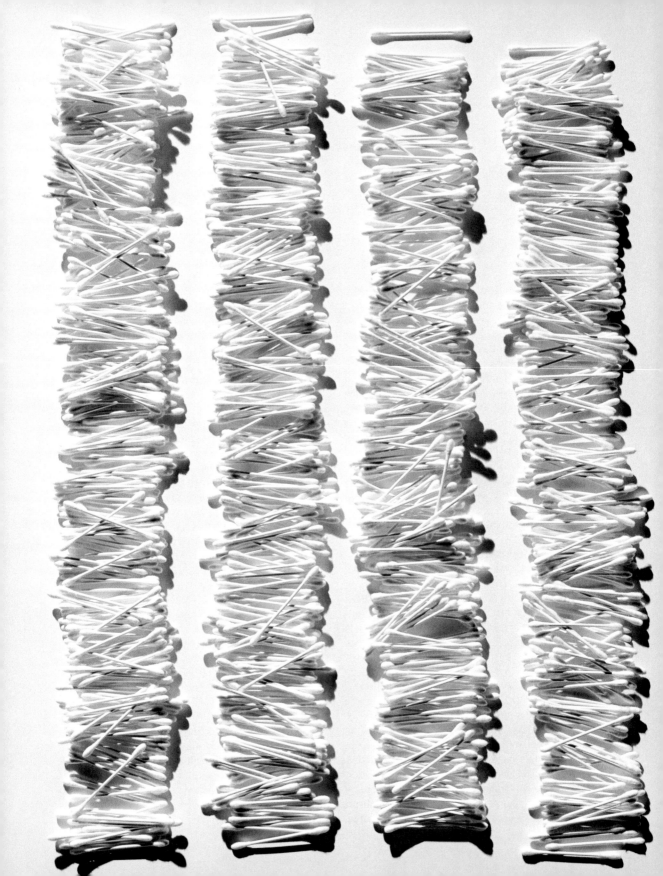

From
Q-TIPS
to
QUARANTINE

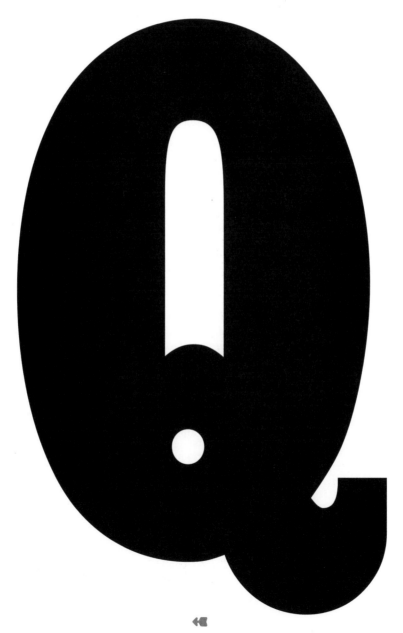

Q-tips: They were originally called "Baby Gays."
PHOTOGRAPH BY CRAIG CUTLER

① **How to Clean Your Ears the Right Way**

From Dr. Maura Cosetti of New York Eye and Ear Infirmary of Mount Sinai

"You do not need to clean your ear canal because it cleans itself: **Wax naturally migrates out** by chewing, jaw motion, and exfoliation of skin. Earwax is made in the outer part of the ear canal, and a Q-tip typically pushes the wax deeper into it (closer to the eardrum) and can be dangerous.

"If you are going to use a Q-tip, **use it only at the outermost opening of your ear canal** (do not stick it inside). Safe non-Q-tip options for cleaning your ear are a moist washcloth at the outer portion of your ear canal; putting a few drops of mineral oil or diluted room-temperature hydrogen peroxide, vinegar, or rubbing alcohol in your ear canal; an over-the-counter 'cerumenolytic' eardrop; and removal through direct visualization by a doctor. **Ear candling or aggressive irrigation with water can be dangerous.** If your hearing is affected or you are having pain, you should have a doctor look in your ear to confirm the problem is a wax buildup."

Q-tips [1]

As a young father in the early 1920s, a Polish immigrant named Leo Gerstenzang watched his wife, Ziuta, try to clean the crevices of their new baby's ear with a wad of cotton wound around a toothpick. In 1923 he took the idea commercial, making and selling swabs (assembled by hand in the early days) of cotton and wood. He called his products Baby Gays—"Gay" was a nickname for his daughter, Elizabeth, because of her giggly disposition when her ears were tickled—and set up a factory in Manhattan. By 1927, he'd made three innovations: He designed and patented a machine to manufacture the swabs, he started dipping the tips in boric acid as a sanitary measure, and he came up with a better name. The *Q* is said to stand for "quality," although Elizabeth's parents told her "Q-T" was also a reference to her, because she was … a cutie.

Within a few years, the company (headquartered on West 36th Street) was a national brand, and the Gerstenzangs had moved to Central Park West. As demand grew, the business relocated to Long Island City, where it remained until the company was sold to the makers of Vaseline in 1962. Elizabeth Gerstenzang Marcus, the baby whose ears started it all, became a Palm Beach socialite and died at 94 in 2017. Despite the product's origin story, Q-tips' packaging today blares that you're not supposed to use the swabs to clean your ear canal. Otologists everywhere tell you the same thing. You probably do it anyway.

Quant

The presence of math in finance would seemingly stretch back to day one, but its modern systematic application didn't begin until 1973, when the applied mathematician Fischer Black and the financial economist Myron Scholes developed a model at the University of Chicago that helped traders determine how to sell stock options in a way that minimized risk. Their work would ultimately win a Nobel Prize for its role in the "rapid growth of markets for derivatives" and would start the great migration of physics Ph.D.'s from the lab to Wall Street to become quantitative analysts, a.k.a. quants.

By 1984, Black was in New York at Goldman Sachs, where he developed a second equation with William Toy and Emanuel Derman. An in-house calculation for the bank, the Black-Derman-Toy model identified how the short rate would predict the evolution of all interest rates, helping the bank take the guesswork out of valuing bond options and fixed income securities. It would also blow Goldman's value sky-high: Between 1985 and 1994, the bank's partnership capital grew from $1.2 billion to $5.8 billion. Toy became a Goldman Sachs VP; Black died in 1995, well before Goldman got caught up in the subprime-mortgage crisis and had to be bailed out with $10 billion (*see also* MORTGAGE-BACKED SECURITIES); and Derman went on to become a Columbia professor, writing a memoir, *My Life as a Quant*, that popularized the term *outside finance*. Within the field, the quant, essential to mitigating risk, has become the ace in the hole for investment banks and is paid nicely for it—a Ph.D. quant's starting salary is often around $150,000, not including a bonus that often exceeds the base pay.

Quarantine

The term itself comes from medieval Italy, where potentially sick people were isolated for forty (*quaranta*) days. We have been sequestering ourselves to stay safe ever since: Think of Isaac Newton, holed up in the countryside outside London to avoid the plague, inventing calculus to pass the time. New York, though, has a unique history in the development of this practice, which was bound up with the city's status as a port of entry (*see also*

IMMIGRATION). As early as 1738, Bedloe's Island—known today as Liberty Island, renamed for the statue that rose there later—was designated as the spot where incoming ships had to stop if a passenger displayed symptoms of smallpox or cholera. At various later times, Staten Island, Governors Island, Swinburne Island, Hoffman Island, and Wards Island all served as places of isolation. In 1863 a new state law established a quarantine commissioner for New York City who was empowered to order a ship fumigated and detained as necessary. A million people poured through Ellis Island each year at its peak, and every one of them was (quickly and not especially thoroughly) checked for disease. Inspectors sometimes cleared a thousand immigrants per hour, setting aside about 1 to 2 percent to be examined further, isolated, or turned away altogether.

That surely helped, but it hardly stopped waves of infectious disease from crashing over the city, especially in its densest districts. One cluster of tenements on the Lower East Side was so full of tuberculosis it was nicknamed "the Lung Block." Patients sometimes ended up on the East River islands, including North Brother Island, where a hospital had been built initially to isolate smallpox patients. It was in a small building on those grounds that Mary Mallon, famous as "Typhoid Mary" for having worked as a cook all over town despite investigators naming her as a carrier, spent the last twenty-five years of her life.

The two most extensive citywide quarantines in New York's history occurred just over a century apart. Arriving aboard a ship in 1918, the Spanish flu moved rapidly through the city, its contagion aided by a decision—dodgy in hindsight—not to close public schools and theaters. (Germ theory was still relatively new, and the city fathers believed airy school buildings to be safer for kids than packed tenements were. As for the theaters, they were kept open so audiences could get public-health announcements before the curtain went up.) The sick, however, were efficiently and rigorously quarantined at home, and that worked pretty well. New York ended up with 20,000 dead, a formidable number that nonetheless indicates a lower death rate than that of other American cities.

In 2020 a new pandemic swept the country, this one more insidious. COVID-19, the novel coronavirus, found its twin footholds in Wuhan and then Italy and made its way from Europe to New York. From there, plus a few other small points of entry, it spread across the United States. Because it was passed from person to person by airborne droplets—and thus coughing, sneezing, or even talking—it was quickly understood to be an existential threat to densely populated places. Its presymptomatic period made it particularly difficult to control: You could walk around with it for a while without knowing you were spreading it silently among thousands of people, and you might never manifest symptoms at all. This meant that a city defined by its close quarters and crowds—whether in subway cars, at adjoining restaurant tables, or simply on the sidewalk at rush hour—had to stop doing virtually everything. Starting on March 12 of that year, New York City essentially froze, closing most of its retail stores, restricting restaurants to takeout and delivery, and eventually shutting down the subway system at night for the first extended time in its history (see also SUBWAY) so the trains could be disinfected. Hospitals were very nearly overwhelmed, kept going only by health-care workers' laboring to exhaustion and significant intervention by the State of New York (and, much less effectively, the Trump administration, whose efforts were late to start and poorly organized thereafter; see also TRUMPISM). New York maintained its quarantine rules for months, and social distancing and closures appear to have somewhat blunted the devastation. The economic toll was another matter: Nearly a million New Yorkers lost their jobs because of the pandemic.

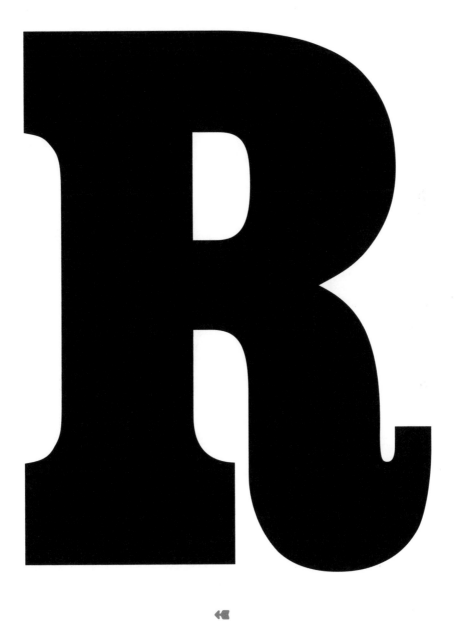

*Romantic comedy: You should, in fact,
have what she's having.*

FROM *WHEN HARRY MET SALLY...* (1989),
DIRECTED BY ROB REINER

① **How to Cultivate the Perfect Radio Voice**

From WNYC's Alison Stewart, host of "All of It"

"For me, a good public-radio voice is **the aural equivalent of an oat-milk mocha latte.** To get into the zone, think about what it would be like if your favorite teacher from childhood magically appeared and offered to read you a bedtime story after you've had a really crappy day. Your voice should be warm yet authoritative, smooth but engaging, and your tone should always let the listener know ... **even if the news is bad, it's all going to be okay."**

Rabbit Ears

Any piece of wire—of metal, really—can function as an antenna. In the era of over-the-air television broadcasting, you could, of course, install an aerial on your roof to boost reception, but that wasn't always easy or practical. Which brings us to Illinois's Ralph Leonard and New York's Milton Spirt, who in 1948 and 1949 each filed successful patent applications showing a pair of telescoping rods on a base that could be placed atop a TV. (Leonard got the form down on paper; Spirt, the technical details.) Because the rods could be extended to correspond to the wavelength of a given channel, functioning as what's called a dipole, they did indeed work, and nearly everyone with a TV bought a pair (and often tried to add some juju with bits of aluminum foil). A number of manufacturers jumped in, notably an inventor in Rego Park, Queens, Marvin Middlemark, who made further improvements on the design and grew very rich through his company, All Channel Products Corporation. Middlemark's other inventions—water-powered potato peeler, dead-tennis-ball repressurizer—didn't do as well.

Today's over-the-air digital signals require different antennas, but the rabbit-ears silhouette lingers as a durable symbol. (Graphic designers still make it the *V* in TV.) TiVo—a DVR service that has little to do with broadcast analog anything—still has a cartoony one in its logo.

Radio Broadcasting[1]

On February 25, 1909, a group of physics students crowded into a Barnard College classroom to listen to a voice from all the way across town. Radio technology was just a few years old—until fairly recently it had been a curiosity from Guglielmo Marconi's lab—and the students were interested in how it worked. On the transmitting end, in a building on Park Avenue, was Mrs. Stanton Blatch, the mother-in-law of Lee de Forest, the inventor of the vacuum tube that enabled the signal amplification. As soon as the students had assembled, Blatch said she would explain the science to them. Instead, she launched into a fiery speech in favor of women's right to vote. "Travel by stagecoach is out of date, kings are out of date ... an aristocracy is out of date, none more so than a male aristocracy," she told her audience. Some male Columbia College undergrads who had dropped in to learn about the new technology took offense at the one-way nature of radio communication. "That is a mean way to talk at a poor chap when he can't say anything," one said. And then, according to the *Times*, a group of listeners made "a bee line" for the transmitter.

De Forest had been struggling to develop a technology to enable live radio broadcasts for the past decade, much of it in a laboratory in the Parker Building at Fourth Avenue and 19th Street. His early attempts were made all the more difficult by his often shady business partners, who twice defrauded him. But by 1907, he had developed a device called the Audion tube, which could receive sensitive wireless signals much more reliably than any competing technology. That year, in one of de Forest's experiments, the opera star Eugenia Farrar became the first person to sing on the radio. From a studio in Manhattan, she said, "Here goes something into nothing," and began the opening lines of the song "I Love You Truly." By utter coincidence, the broadcast was heard by a civil engineer aboard the U.S.S. *Dolphin*, anchored in the Brooklyn Navy Yard, who happened to be testing his ship's new radio technology just as Farrar was singing. He had no context for hearing any words—rather than Morse code—being transmitted and assumed Farrar's voice was that of an angel.

Like that sailor, the public had no understanding of what radio was or could be. De Forest needed publicity to secure continued funding for his work, and fast, so he contrived a stunt: In 1910 he convinced the Metropolitan Opera to let him install microphones in the wings at a blockbuster performance. Receivers were set up around the city, their locations advertised in advance. Reporters were called in. Static and other noise made the music nearly unrecognizable, but de Forest's publicity tactic was the first-ever public-radio broadcast. Word of de Forest's radio device spread, and within the next decade, amateur radio fans were using the technology he'd developed to receive and transmit broadcasts from homes across the country.

Radio City Music Hall

When it opened in 1932, Rockefeller Center, that first aesthetically peerless Art Deco expression of the office-tower complex, had as its marquee tenant the Radio Corporation of America and its subsidiary National Broadcasting Company. The central building at 30 Rockefeller Plaza housed several NBC radio-broadcast studios, including one big enough for a symphony orchestra, and the whole group of buildings was, futuristically, known as Radio City. The complex included two movie theaters, one of which—the big one—was a 6,200-seat monster with a sunburst proscenium arch spanning 100 feet. It had been the crowning project of Samuel Rothafel, the impresario known as Roxy. He intended to revive the fading glory of vaudeville (see also VAUDEVILLE) with a super-vaudeville, built for the machine age, one with dancers and big theatrical entertainments and a kickline he called the Roxyettes. There would be none of the intimate and slightly homespun quality of plain old touring vaudeville shows: This was to be huge and sparkly, more like the Busby Berkeley films that were coming into vogue.

Radio City Music Hall opened during Christmas Week 1932, with a slate of seventeen acts in one night. The program went till 2 a.m.

It bombed. Nobody wanted Roxy's super-vaudeville. After a couple of weeks of increasingly desperate flop sweat, the programming at Radio City was scaled back sharply to a first-run movie preceded by a modest-length stage show featuring the Roxyettes, which were renamed the Rockettes. The movie-plus-a-stage-show was a not uncommon format in the 1930s, and it was moderately successful, saving the theater. What's amazing is that, although it disappeared from the rest of the country during the Depression, it lingered at Radio City until 1979.

By that time, Radio City Music Hall was an overscale, money-losing anachronism. Movie palaces were being cut up into multiplexes all over the country, and most audiences were in the suburbs anyway. A 6,000-seat city auditorium could not be filled even if it showed the very biggest hit films—and Radio City's management refused to show anything R-rated, ruling out many blockbusters. The theater's glitzy Christmas and Easter shows, to which a third generation of city tots were now being brought to see the Rockettes, seemed dated and doomed as well. Plans were offered to convert the auditorium into tennis courts or jam an office tower on top of it. The Center Theatre, its smaller sibling down the street, was already gone, demolished in 1954.

New Yorkers are notable for rallying behind only-for-tourists institutions that they themselves avoid, and "Save Radio City" became their cause. The Landmarks Preservation Commission (see also LANDMARKS LAW) stepped up, the management ditched the dated stage shows (apart from the Christmas and Easter pageants), and Radio City entered its second life. Since being saved from the wreckers, it has emerged as a fantasy empress of performance spaces. Its immensity is now an asset rather than a liability, one where the degree of fame and success required to fill its seats has become a mark of

having made it, a pop analog to Carnegie Hall. It has also become useful as a venue for the Tonys and Grammys and other televised awards shows. And, somehow, timelessly, the Rockettes continue to perform in their uncannily precise kicklines, year after year, now on their fifth generation of wide-eyed kids.

Rape, Modern View of

NOTE: *Before the 1970s, rape was seen primarily as just another form of assault, like a particularly violent robbery, and one in which women were often deemed halfway complicit. The publication of Susan Brownmiller's* Against Our Will: Men, Women, and Rape *by Simon & Schuster in 1975 changed that. It was the first broad piece of general scholarship on the subject, and it redefined rape for a mainstream audience as a crime of male power against the bodies of its (usually though not exclusively female) victims. Here, Brownmiller relates the evolution of her thinking and the book's origins in context.*

It came from my discovery that I had absorbed all these myths and misconceptions about rape from a variety of avenues. Liberals and leftists and psychoanalysts all had distorted what rape was all about. They didn't see it as a crime against a woman's body, or they didn't see that as political. I remember when this woman in my consciousness-raising group, New York Radical Feminists (*see also* CONSCIOUSNESS-RAISING), came in one evening late in 1970 with an alternate feminist newspaper from California called *It Ain't Me Babe*. It was a transcript of a woman's account of her hitchhike rape in California, and it was a very powerful piece. Diane Crothers, who had a subscription, brought it to us, threw it down on the table, and said, "This is our next issue. This is it."

I was slow to get it, because I had absorbed all these myths—that rape was political only when a white woman falsely accused a Black man, and that was it. But we did what we always did during consciousness-raising; we went around the room—there were maybe ten of us—and this woman named Sara Pines calmly talked about her rape when she was hitchhiking and how she'd called the cops, and the first thing they said was, "Who'd want to rape a nice girl like you?" Well, what I said to her, because I'd done some hitchhiking, was "You were alone and you got into a car with two guys?" And I soon figured out that Sara was a much more trusting person than I was, and that was a big difference, and that more women were like Sara than like me.

So we in NYRF organized the first speak-out on rape in the nation [in 1971 at St. Clement's Episcopal Church in midtown], and my friend Alix Kates Shulman [the feminist activist and writer whose best-selling *Memoirs of an Ex-Prom Queen* was published the next year] was one of the first to speak out. One woman had been raped by her therapist, and she said, "Therapist. The rapist!" I'll never forget that. Gail Sheehy wrote it up for *New York* Magazine—we had good media contacts in NYRF—and I saw it and thought, *What's my role in this movement? I'm helping to create events that other writers write about?*

So I spent four years writing my book at the New York Public Library, and it got to be a main selection of the Book-of-the-Month Club, which was important in those days. At Simon & Schuster, it was just one of many books they were hoping would catch fire, and in fact mine was not the one they expected. I got attacked by Alice Walker, who wrote a letter to the *Times Book Review* about my being oblivious to the false accusations. Angela Davis started an attack for the same thing, then wrote an essay that haunts me to this very day, saying [that my book] "borders on racism." The Me Too movement certainly has [dealt with the subject], but most of them are much younger and don't know the history and are discovering it. When I speak at colleges now, I can't say everyone agrees with me, even though

attraction, but he wasn't able to purchase it until he reached 'Believe It or Not!' fame. By that time, however, the statue had disappeared. Ripley spent twenty years hoping to locate it again, eventually finding it in a curio shop. **He bought the masterpiece for a mere ten dollars in 1934."**

the Me Too people are talking about every kind of thing that happened to them.

Remote Control

In September 1898, Nikola Tesla staged a demonstration at Madison Square Garden as part of the first annual Electrical Exhibition. His invention, covered under patent No. 613,809, was a radio-controlled torpedo boat, a battery-powered steel craft about four feet long. Examiners from the U.S. Patent Office were skeptical about the claims in Tesla's application for a "Method of and Apparatus for Controlling Mechanism of Moving Vessels or Vehicles" but changed their minds when they saw a functioning model. Switches controlled by radio signals adjusted the boat's rudder, propeller speed, and running lights without "intermediate wires, cables, or other form of electrical or mechanical connection with the object save the natural media in space," as Tesla put it. He later said his device caused "a sensation such as no other invention of mine has ever produced." Some viewers believed he was using mind control.

Tesla acknowledged the versatility of remote control, recognizing that it could be used with all sorts of vehicles. "The greatest value of my invention," he wrote, "will result from its effect upon warfare and armaments, for by reason of its certain and unlimited destructiveness it will tend to bring about and maintain permanent peace among nations." Indeed, Germany used an explosives-packed remote-controlled motorboat in the First World War. A generation later, during World War II, the technology was expanded to radio-controlled missiles, tanks, and bombers, after which electronics companies began experimenting with remote controls to make life easier for the average person. Soon enough, the hand-held remote was being used in countless applications, from household items (*see also* AIR-CONDITIONING; HOME SECURITY SYSTEM) to toys and cars.

"Ripley's Believe It or Not!"[2]

Robert L. Ripley was a young sports cartoonist, recently fired from the San Francisco *Chronicle*, when he decided to move to New York and shoot his shot. At the start of 1913, he got a job on an evening daily, the New York *Globe*, and gradually became one of the paper's marquee names. In 1916 his cartoons included a page of "Unusual Records," which featured (among other accomplishments) a man who'd skipped rope 11,810 times in a row without stopping. The idea stuck with Ripley and became a recurring one, and in the December 19, 1918, issue, he took it further, publishing a cartoon page devoted to eccentric world records, called "Champs and Chumps." It wasn't an instant smash but worked well enough to keep appearing, and a year later it carried the name "Believe It or Not." (The exclamation point came later.) By 1922, it was enough of a hit that Ripley could sustain an around-the-world research tour; by 1930 he had been hired by the Hearst newspapers, which syndicated his column globally and made him rich. A book collection of the comic strips was one of the very first successes for Simon & Schuster, putting the fledgling publishing house on the map. He received literally tons of mail each year, including many envelopes addressed in riddles to see if they'd get to him. Perhaps the ultimate was one showing nothing but a sketch of a wavy ("ripply") river. It was—believe it or not!—successfully delivered, although the U.S. post office eventually began asking people to lay off the stunts.

Next came the exhibition halls (called "Odditoriums"), radio, and finally, in March 1949, television. The TV success was brief: As Ripley finished filming the thirteenth episode of his series, nearly three months after the premiere, he collapsed on the set and died shortly thereafter at 58. "Believe It or Not!" did not die with him, however. The comic strip, which continues to run today, inspired a couple of successful TV series (notably, one hosted with unsettling intensity by Jack Palance), and there are Odditoriums in tourist centers all over the world, including Times Square.

Robber Baron [3]

Oligarchs have been around since people started buying and selling things, but the Gilded Age in Manhattan saw the craft taken to new levels of wealth and amorality. In the nineteenth century, industrialists and tycoons like John D. Rockefeller (oil), Andrew Carnegie (steel), and Cornelius Vanderbilt (railroads, shipping) assembled fortunes well into the hundreds of millions of dollars. (It is difficult to compare such vast figures across eras, because of differences in the size of the economy and in purchasing power, but $100 million then is something like $25 billion now.) They recklessly endangered the men who built their empires in the process: During the peak era of American industrialization in the last quarter of the century, 35,000 laborers died each year in violent workplace accidents. But back in the middle of the century, the press had begun to push back against the magnate class. In February 1859, a *Times* article compared Vanderbilt, who accepted payoffs from other shippers to keep him from doing business along their routes, to the medieval German *raubritters*, the land barons who extorted travelers on their demesne.

It would take another seventy-five years for the term *robber baron* to enter the lexicon, but in the meantime, the grift continued: When Vanderbilt died in his Greenwich Village brownstone in 1877, he possessed one-ninth of the American currency in circulation. Jay Gould, perhaps the most rapacious man in a rapacious crowd, tried to corner the gold market in 1869, eventually contributing to a national market crash. (He had hedged against it and came out ahead.)

Until the ratification of the Sixteenth Amendment in 1913, virtually none of their income was taxed.

Up and down Fifth Avenue, immense mansions rose to house these men, their families, and their vast domestic staffs. Most of the homes are gone now, demolished and replaced by apartment buildings, but some remain: the Cooper Hewitt design museum occupies Carnegie's immense house, and Henry Clay Frick's mansion and art collection are intact and on public display. The richest person of all was John D. Rockefeller, whose Standard Oil in 1880 controlled 90 percent of the American petroleum market. When asked why he'd been the one to get so rich, he replied, "God gave me the money." In an effort to soften his vulpine image, he (at the urging of the public-relations pioneer Ivy Lee; *see also* PUBLIC RELATIONS) began to hand out dimes to people—particularly children, but adults as well—on the street.

The robber-baron epithet finally came into its own in the U.S. when *The New Republic* editor and banker's son Matthew Josephson shifted his focus from the arts to inequality. In the 1920s, the Brooklyn-born writer worked at the lit mag *Broom*, which published work by Pablo Picasso, Man Ray, and William Carlos Williams. But by 1934, the Great Depression—and a stint working in Wall Street regulation—had inspired Josephson to write *The Robber Barons*, an account of the "aggressive," "lawless" class that reworked the nation's finances "without those established moral principles which fixed more or less the conduct of the common people of the community." Published in the gut of the Depression, the book took off, remaining on the *Times* best seller list for a year and a half, and New Deal reformers hurled its title as an insult. The term has stuck with us, perhaps because it's so flexible: It can describe both the *There Will Be Blood* oilman in a top hat or a shaven-headed tech executive in Chelsea dreaming of outer space.

The assets of today's oligarchs do not keep up with those of the originals. When he died in 1937, John D.

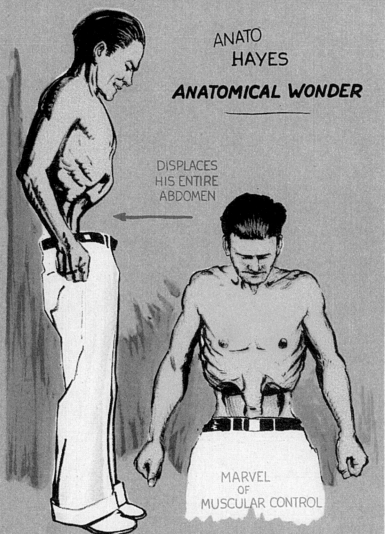

Anato Hayes, "Anatomical Wonder," did his thing in Ripley's Odditorium at the New York World's Fair, 1940.

Andrew Carnegie laundering his robber-baron reputation, 1903.

$100,000,000

GIVEN FOR THE PUBLIC GOOD

CANADA
N. DAKOTA
S. DAKOTA
NEB.
MINN.
IOWA
WIS.
ILLINOIS
INDIANA
OHIO
KENTUCKY
W. VIRGINIA
VIRGINIA
TENNESSEE
NORTH CAROLINA
PENN.
ALA
LIBRARY
LIBRARY

Dalrymple

(4) A Director's Favorite Rom-Coms

Chosen by Friends with Money *and* The Land of Steady Habits*'s Nicole Holofcener*

» **Harold and Maude** "Not just one of my favorite rom-coms, one of my favorite movies."
» **Say Anything...** "Lloyd Dobler was the most romantic movie hero ever, and I wanted someone to love me like that, so badly that it hurt."
» **Modern Romance** "Albert Brooks, genius."
» **The Heartbreak Kid (1972 version)** "Can't even explain."
» **Terms of Endearment** "Yes, it's a cancer movie, but the relationship between Jack Nicholson and Shirley MacLaine is so hilarious, and moving."
» **Broadcast News** "Albert Brooks, Jim Brooks, perfect movie."
» **Jerry Maguire** "Again, the hurt."
» **Working Girl** "Joan Cusack. Joan Cusack. Joan Cusack."
» **Annie Hall** "No words."
» **The 40-Year-Old Virgin** "So sweet, hilarious, and romantic."

AND FIVE MORE SHE COULDN'T LEAVE OUT: Eternal Sunshine of the Spotless Mind / Melvin and Howard / Roman Holiday / Notting Hill / Tootsie

---

Rockefeller's were equivalent to 1.5 percent of the nation's economic output. (Today, by comparison, Jeff Bezos's fortune of around $150 billion represents about .07 percent of GDP.) But the inequality continues: In 1897, the 4,000 richest families in the U.S. had as much wealth as the other 11.6 million. One hundred twenty years later, the three richest Americans had as much wealth as the bottom half of the nation, one of the reasons the term *robber baron* still hangs on Bernie Sanders's lips.

Rockefeller Center

see CHRISTMAS; RADIO CITY MUSIC HALL; SKYLINE

Romantic Comedy [4]

The first onscreen kiss—fifty feet of celluloid, running about twenty seconds—was shown in New York in 1896. Appropriately titled *The Kiss*, it was among the first motion pictures ever shown theatrically to a paying public, it was produced by Thomas Edison, and it starred May Irwin and John Rice, who reenacted their final, happy smooch from the stage musical comedy *The Widow Jones*. (It also caused a brief uproar over the depiction of such wanton sexuality.) In the early days of the medium, much of what passed for movies were extensions of Broadway plays and other shows (*see also* BROADWAY; MUSICAL THEATER; VAUDEVILLE), and over the ensuing years, New York was the hub for much of the industry (before producers and directors discovered Hollywood and the lucrative spoils of the Western). The city was also a cinematic laboratory where several notable genres were created (*see also* MOVIES).

The comedy-romance as a literary and theatrical idea dates back to the days of Shakespeare, but on film, it developed organically through situational and romantic vignettes produced by such New York–based studios as Vitagraph, Mutoscope (later Biograph), and Independent Moving Pictures. Films like 1910's *A Tin-Type Romance* and 1912's *Up Against It* were simple and charming, though not particularly New York–y. (The former is set on an empty beach, the latter mostly in drawing rooms.) Oddly enough, the city emerged as a popular setting only after the industry began to move west. Cecil B. DeMille, a New Yorker who had decamped for California (he directed Hollywood's first feature film), re-created New York locations in Los Angeles for 1914's *What's His Name* (a baker's daughter marries a soda jerk, then becomes a Broadway star) and 1915's *Chimmie Fadden* (set among the city's tenements and Long Island's mansions). DeMille would go on to make a series of successful remarriage comedies, including 1919's *Don't Change Your Husband* and 1920's *Why Change Your Wife?*, both starring Gloria Swanson. Also in 1920, the young vaudeville star Buster Keaton found his first leading role in *The Saphead* as the hapless scion of a wealthy New York family desperate to impress the girl of his dreams, who happens to be his adopted sister. (Keaton would hone the form over the next five years in *Seven Chances* and *Sherlock, Jr.*) Movies like these, mixtures of screwball comedy, farce, slapstick, and melodrama, weren't called "romantic comedies" back then, but they laid the groundwork for the genre as we know it, and New York was a significant part of its foundation.

Romantic comedies are driven by connection, and the city was an ideal cinematic setting for finding unlikely romance. Whether the characters were chorus girls, journalists, bankers, or office drones, New York was where you'd find them, and the ways the city regularly forced rich and poor and men and women together made it a land of romantic opportunity. Its complexity and difficulty of navigation enabled plot twists and missed connections; the anonymity of city life allowed screenwriters to incorporate mistaken identities and surprise revelations, where, say, someone you work with and loathe also turns out to be your pen-pal soul mate.

Broadway was a central setting for backstage musical rom-coms like *Gold Diggers of 1933* (the third cinematic iteration of Avery Hopwood's 1919 New York–set play *The Gold Diggers*). And New York became the backdrop for now-iconic examples of the genre like *My Man Godfrey* (1936), *You Can't Take It With You* (1938), and the Katharine Hepburn–Spencer Tracy classics *Woman of the Year* (1942), *Adam's Rib* (1949), and *Desk Set* (1957). Teeming streets and crowded offices and apartments stacked atop one another made ideal locations for the "meet-cute," whereby our soon-to-be-lovers chance upon each other in some unlikely circumstance. That applied even in movies that are only marginally comedies and questionably romantic: Think of *Breakfast at Tiffany's* (1961), in which the elegant Audrey Hepburn and the unemployed George Peppard play neighbors who meet thanks to a doorbell screwup; *The Apartment* (1960), in which insurance-company employee Jack Lemmon falls for elevator operator Shirley MacLaine; and *How to Marry a Millionaire* (1953), in which Marilyn Monroe, Betty Grable, and Lauren Bacall play three marriage-minded beauties who settle into the penthouse apartment of a rich businessman. Even the tragic *An Affair to Remember* (1957), in which Cary Grant and Deborah Kerr, who are involved with other people, attempt to reunite at the Empire State Building, was reimagined as *Sleepless in Seattle*, which, despite its title, is still an iconic New York rom-com.

In the 1970s and '80s, New York's status as an ideal milieu for comic-romantic shenanigans would become even more pronounced—perhaps ironically, since much about the city itself was, at this time, decidedly unromantic in any traditional sense (*see also* MAYHEM)—through the work of Woody Allen, Neil Simon, Paul Mazursky, and Nora Ephron and other directors' films such as *Moonstruck* (1987), *Crossing Delancey* (1988), and *Working Girl* (1988). These set the stage for a slew of New York rom-coms that would explode in popularity as the city recovered from its disarray and decay: everything from *You've Got Mail* (1998) and *Serendipity* (2001) to *Maid in Manhattan* (2002), *Two Weeks Notice* (2002), and *13 Going on 30* (2004). If there's any common thread to this sprawling century's worth of films, it's this: A remarkable number of them incorporate a walk in Central Park, and even though it's a cliché, it usually works.

Rube Goldberg Machine

Reuben Garret Lucius Goldberg, born in San Francisco in 1883, came to New York as a young man to stake out a career as an editorial cartoonist. His early work, for papers like the New York *Evening Mail*, was mostly sports related and was followed by a successful comic-strip series called "I'm the Guy." Goldberg found the emerging high-tech New York City of the teens (Electricity! Automobiles! Telephones!) bewitching, perhaps slightly alarming, and a number of his cartoons involved the odd effects of the new devices.

With a cartoon published in the *Evening Mail* on July 12, 1912, he expanded on that theme, creating the first of the mechanical contrivances for which he became known. "The Simple Mosquito Exterminator," it was labeled, and the image showed a mirror, a telescope, globs of rare beef, and a chloroform-soaked sponge, all acting in concert in a sequence of absurd ways to achieve the stated goal. For the next twenty years, he drew one every two weeks, and for thirty years after that, about one a month.

"Rube Goldberg device"—a moniker used to describe any such ridiculous, roundabout way of getting something done—was first recognized by dictionaries in 1966. Goldberg himself died in December 1970, two weeks after attending the opening of an enormous retrospective of his work at the Smithsonian. The National Cartoonists Society's annual award for outstanding work is, in his honor, called the Reuben.

Rush Tickets

The insoluble core problem of Broadway theater for the past generation has been its high ticket prices. A variety of forces—the inherent costs of mounting a show in New York City, union contracts, the irreducible fact that most productions fail—have conspired to drive the cost of a single good seat well into three figures, turning theatergoing from a frequent habit to a rare splurge. High prices disproportionately shut out young people, and in the 1970s the Broadway audience simultaneously started to age and to shrink as it began failing to replenish itself.

The first good solution came in 1972 with the Theatre Development Fund's TKTS booth in Times Square, where unsold same-day tickets were offered at half-price to buyers who waited in line, winter and summer.

A real-life Rube Goldberg machine, doing more and also less than meets the eye.

It was (and is) an effective, successful way to address part of the problem—these cheaper seats were typically available for straight plays and for musicals on the downslope of their popularity—but hit shows had no unsold tickets and thus remained expensive.

Then came *Rent*. Written by a young composer-songwriter named Jonathan Larson, it was a loose adaptation of *La Bohème*, reset in the East Village world of squatters, drugs, AIDS, and defiant, enthusiastic bohemianism, and it was the buzziest and youngest musical to have come along in years. It opened in 1996 at New York Theatre Workshop, and the word of mouth grew and grew—carried along in part by a ghost, as Larson died unexpectedly from an aortic dissection the morning after the show's first preview. When *Rent* transferred to Broadway a few months later, it arrived with a built-in difficulty: The very people it celebrated were too broke to see it. The best seats were $67.50 each, about ten times the cost of a movie ticket.

The solution that producer Jeffrey Seller and his team devised was to reserve a couple of dozen seats in the front rows—good but slightly less desirable to full-price-orchestra-ticket-buyers—and sell them for $20 apiece on the day of the show. It was an extremely clever idea because it catered to students, young actors, and actual bohemian types (at least some of whom, lacking day jobs, could wait in line all afternoon). It also put young people up front, where they were visible, and injected energy into the richer, older orchestra-seat cohort. Like the TKTS booth, the *Rent* rush line was a success, with lines of hopeful, camped-out people at the box office each day. Many Broadway shows do the same today, though the queues now form in digital lotteries as well as at the box office. When in 2015 *Hamilton* became a white-hot Broadway phenomenon, rush seats were sold for ten bucks, in homage to the central character's presence on the $10 bill. On some days, the drawing for those 24 spots received more than a thousand entrants.

From
SAFETY PIN
to
SYNTHESIZER

The archetypal socialite: Nan Kempner.
PHOTOGRAPH BY THOMAS HOEPKER

Safety Pin

Walter Hunt was the type of nineteenth-century inventor we don't really have anymore. First of all, he genuinely was, by profession, an *inventor*, one who came up with and patented all sorts of unrelated mechanical gizmos. He made improvements on long guns and shirt collars; he designed an ice-breaking boat, artificial stone, a better inkwell and then a writing instrument to replace it (*see also* FOUNTAIN PEN); and he patented an early sewing machine, leading to a long, drawn-out intellectual-property battle with Elias Howe. Most notably, though, in 1849 he devised an object that is both nearly invisible and completely ubiquitous. The story goes that he was in debt, on both his house on West 17th Street and his shop on Gold Street—he owed $15—and, out of anxiety, he began anxiously twisting a piece of wire around his fingers. The nervous tic gradually gained direction and focus, and a few minutes later he'd created a "dress pin," as he called it, with a spring and a catch that encased the sharp point. That same day, he took it to a nearby shop owner and sold the rights for $400—more than enough to pay off his debt, but hardly enough to make him the rich man he should have become.

St. Patrick's Day Parade[1]

In the eighteenth century, the army defending the British colony of New York included Irishmen as well as Englishmen. On the annual feast day of Patrick, patron saint of Ireland, in 1762, those homesick Irish soldiers assembled for a little march through lower Manhattan. A small-scale tradition followed, and over the following years the Ancient Order of Hibernians and other groups would hold regular parades on March 17. With the mass migration of Irish citizens to the United States after the famines of the 1840s and their coalescence into a political bloc over the subsequent decades, the parade

expanded from a social event into a strategic, unskippable one for politicians as well. (Only Boston's parade rivals it in size and scope, owing to the immense Irish-American presence there.) Since then, every ethnic bloc has claimed an avenue and an afternoon, and the warmer months in New York now constitute a unique parade of parades, from the Greeks in March to the Persians in April to the Ecuadorans in August to the Italians in October.

But the St. Patrick's Day Parade in particular has also become a controversial event, because Irish New York is overwhelmingly Irish Catholic and church teachings infuse the decisions made around this ostensibly secular celebration. The requests of pro-life and pro-choice groups to march have been consistently denied over the years. In 1990, during the first wave of the AIDS crisis, a group called the Irish Lesbian and Gay Organization applied for permission to march in the parade and was rejected. Mayor David Dinkins was booed when he marched with a gay group the following year, and the annual cycle of dissent and dissatisfaction continued for three decades. Bill de Blasio, elected mayor in 2013, refused to march in the parade until gay and lesbian groups were also permitted. In 2016, they (and he) did so for the first time. There is, however, one political statement the parade has allowed for decades: the banner reading ENGLAND GET OUT OF IRELAND. Even twenty-plus years after the Good Friday Accord of 1998 quieted the simmering war between Northern Irish nationalists and loyalists, the slogan still draws cheers.

Salsa Music[2]

As a musical genre and dance style, salsa has so many ancestors, varieties, and dueling definitions it's difficult to nail down a birth date or even a consensus on whether it was born at all. But the where is easy: in the barrios of New York.

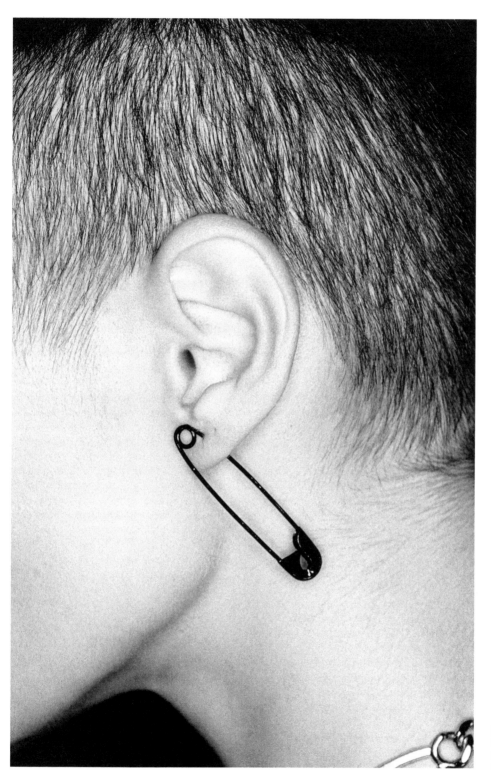

The safety pin
(see also PUNK*).*
PHOTOGRAPH BY
ALEX CAYLEY

② **The Three Basic New York Salsa Moves**

From salsa dancer Ahtoy Juliana

» **New York–Style "On 2" Basic** "The basic is the most essential step in New York–style salsa. It shares the characteristic rhythm of salsa styles danced in Cuba and Latin America, but it highlights other complex percussion elements by emphasizing the upbeat, the second beat of the music. This is why it's often referred to as 'On 2' salsa."

» **Stationary Turn** "New York *salseros* are famous for their dizzying spins. A basic turn usually rotates clockwise in place, continuing into the basic step. Both the lead and the follow can turn separately or simultaneously. To avoid getting dizzy, keep your eyes on your partner as you turn."

» **Cross-Body Lead** "This is a variation of the basic step with a traveling half-turn, creating a lot of freedom to move around the dance floor. The lead guides the follow from one side to the other while staying connected. One important rule is that the follow always dances in a straight line—so leads, get out of the way!"

Its prehistory is long. Throughout the 1940s and '50s, many Americans, notably hedonists, gamblers, and con artists, shuttled back and forth to Havana, and Cuban musicians followed the money trail north. They brought the *son*, a traditional song-and-dance form based on a syncopated rhythm called the clave: *one*-and *two*-*and three*-and *four*, one-and *two*-and *three*-and four. That was just the backbone; as percussion sections grew, they added multiple layers of syncopation and infill rhythms, creating a complex structure of pulsations.

In 1948, the Palladium dance hall on Broadway at 53rd Street, riding Havana's glamour and the cool of a new immigrant wave, recast itself as the headquarters of Latin dance in the city. Puerto Ricans like the percussionist Tito Puente and the singer Tito Rodríguez (a.k.a. the Big Three with the Cuban singer Machito) were regular performers and helped launch the mambo craze that would sweep the United States. By the end of the 1950s, the Cuban revolution cut ties to the island, and its musical emissaries developed their styles in exile. As ballroom bands gave way to rock and roll, a new, more raucous type of music emerged in the city's Latino neighborhoods, replacing the high-gloss spectacles of the Palladium with street parties farther uptown.

The word *salsa*, used to describe the brassy, rhythmic sound or the exuberant, hip-rolling movement that goes with it, didn't catch on until long after the phenomenon already existed. But it was undoubtedly Izzy Sanabria who popularized it: The Puerto Rican–born, Bronx-bred graphic artist and tireless partyer drew posters and album covers for the legendary New York Latin label Fania Records, and his hypercharged, amiably surrealistic style fused with the idea of music that was spicy and rich in flavor. He also published *Latin N.Y.* magazine, where he pushed the term every chance he got. Still, musicians rejected salsa as a marketing gimmick that had nothing to do with the intricate relationships of mambo, cha-cha, danzón, and other genres. Puente loathed the term—salsa is something you put on food, he said—but he found that it paid the rent. By 1975, it finally percolated to the *Times*.

Saturday Night Live *see* SKETCH COMEDY

Schist, Manhattan

About 450 million years ago, as the tectonic plates around what is now the northeastern United States were moving, the edge of what's now called North America began to plow under a volcanic island in the Atlantic. The Taconic Orogeny, as this collision is known, placed the shale in that area under immense heat and pressure, and it began to metamorphose and fold together. Over subsequent millions of years, the shale turned into a much harder stone called schist. Subsequent continental collisions squashed and rippled and turned up that layer, bringing portions of it to the surface, including an outcrop next to which the Hudson River began to flow. We call that outcrop Manhattan Island.

Schist exposed in Central Park.

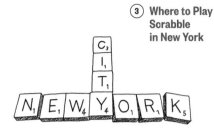

③ **Where to Play Scrabble in New York**

➥ **The Uncommons,** 230 Thompson St.
➥ **The Brooklyn Strategist,** 333 Court St., Carroll Gardens
➥ **Hex & Company,** 1462 First Ave.
➥ **Chess Forum,** 219 Thompson St.

➥ **The birthplace of Scrabble,** 35th Ave. at 81st St., Jackson Heights, Queens (You can't technically play a game here, but you can spot a one-of-a-kind street sign not far from the church basement where Scrabble was born. Each letter on the sign has its point value underneath.)

Manhattan schist is extremely hard, and this particular knob of it is seismically stable. It comes close to the surface downtown, dips down into the earth a mile to the north, and then returns to the surface in midtown. That variation in turn governed the city's real-estate development. Tall buildings rose on the firm bedrock of downtown first, and as the city's center gradually moved northward, builders skipped over the area with softer soil and proceeded to midtown, where they could build upward. Geology begot sociology because, over the next century, that soft spot in the ground remained less desirable and less expensive. To the east, it became the tenement blocks of the Lower East Side; in the center and to the west, the bohemian enclave known as Greenwich Village. Although the technology now exists to put up skyscrapers there, and both the Lower East Side and the Village are indeed punctuated by the odd high-rise, sections of both neighborhoods have been permanently declared off-limits to development, not by tectonics but mostly because the residents like them the way they are.

Scrabble [3]

An architect named Alfred Mosher Butts invented the game he first called Lexiko in 1933 while he was unemployed. In his fifth-floor walk-up in Jackson Heights, Queens, he inked gridded boards with a blueprint machine and cut sets of 100 wooden tiles. He and his friends began playing at his apartment and at the nearby Community United Methodist Church on 35th Avenue. (His wife was much better at it than he.) The game went through a couple of names in its early years, including Criss Cross Words, and Butts made small refinements to the board; still, he was selling just a few sets a month. He pitched it to Parker Brothers and Milton Bradley, but both turned him down.

After a not especially lucrative decade, Butts sold the manufacturing rights to a Connecticut fan of the game,

James Brunot, in 1948. Brunot changed the name to Scrabble, tweaked the design very slightly, and made a few thousand sets, but for several years sales were extremely modest. That is, until one set ended up in front of Jack Straus, the president of Macy's, who soon asked to carry it in the store. There, in the mysterious alchemy that governs fads, it abruptly caught on. Within a year, demand jumped from about 200 games per week to several thousand, and to keep up, Brunot sold his rights to the game company Selchow & Righter. In 1954, nearly 3.8 million Scrabble sets were sold, and even after the craze leveled off, it was moving more than a million sets a year.

Selchow & Righter was eventually merged out of existence, and Scrabble today is owned by Hasbro (*see also* MR. POTATO HEAD) in the U.S. and Mattel overseas. It has become a game show (twice), the subject of multiple books and documentaries, and the source of more rainy-day vacation arguments than anything except perhaps Monopoly.

Seinfeld *see* SITCOM

Seltzer

An Englishman, Joseph Priestley, invented artificial carbonation in 1767, infusing water with carbon dioxide that he'd collected in a pig's bladder. (Extremely *trayf*.) A Scotsman, John Nooth, followed with a glass lab apparatus, eliminating the porcine aftertaste. The Swiss Johann Jacob Schweppe figured out how to mass-produce it. The French were first to the seltzer craze, during the cholera epidemic of the 1830s. But it was John Matthews, a British immigrant to New York, arriving in 1832 and opening a shop on Gold Street, who became the soda-fountain king of the city, putting fizz into a thousand candy stores and a million phosphates

④ **How to Attend Shakespeare in the Park**

From Laurie Woolery, director of public works at the Public Theater

» **Get your free ticket.** "Each performance day, tickets are offered through an in-person lottery downtown at the Public, a digital lottery through the TodayTix app, and distribution at partner organizations."

» **Don't let the weather be a deterrent.** "We never cancel a show before 8 p.m. So if it's cloudy or drizzling, don't let that stop you. Weather is part of the Shakespeare in the Park experience, and it is a New York rite of passage to witness a play with Mother Nature making a cameo appearance. It's also a great time to grab a last-minute ticket. Bring a poncho, because no umbrellas are allowed to be open during the show."

and rickeys and Moxies and ice-cream sodas and other local specialties (*see also* EGG CREAM). And it was New York's immigrants, especially its Jews, who embraced seltzer as their *vin ordinaire.* The "2¢ plain," they called it, the most basic drink at the counter and the one that (everyone learned much later) was pretty good for you. It certainly settled your stomach.

They also got it delivered at home in wooden crates, each holding ten freshly refilled siphon bottles made of thick glass in Bohemia—not the Greenwich Village simulacrum but the actual capital-*B* Bohemia, in Czechoslovakia. The bottles' heft and sturdiness gave siphon seltzer an extra tang and kick because the pressure was so high. (A Brooklyn expression: "Good seltzer should hurt.") Many bottles were etched with the words GOOD HEALTH, simultaneously a motto, an affectionate wish, and a toast. They also made good comedy props, and the image of the clown getting spritzed has long outlasted the spritzer bottles themselves.

The business went into decline after World War II with suburbanization and no-deposit-no-return glass bottles and the final, crushing indignity of plastic one-liter screwtops. Besides, by the 1990s, barely anyone was drinking seltzer outside New York City and its environs. You could get club soda—seltzer's cocktail-mixer sibling, which contains some mineral salts—in any bar in America, but if you asked for a seltzer, they'd look at you funny. With the millennial generation, though, came a new awareness of the bad outcomes that go with consuming a lot of sugary soda, and there arose a new appreciation for this ancient zero-calorie, zero-sweetener, zero-sodium refreshment. In the mid-2010s, an array of new, lightly flavored seltzers became actively trendy. (The voguish brand La Croix led the way, particularly with its *pamplemousse*—that is, grapefruit—flavor, but every bottling company immediately piled on.) And finally, perhaps inevitably, they were joined by canned, flavored "hard seltzer," a newly invented booze containing about as much alcohol as a Budweiser.

Meanwhile, the final half-dozen or so seltzer men in New York, schlepping those 70-pound crates of now-antique siphon bottles up and down stairs and in and out of trucks, became minor celebrities, relentlessly exalted in nostalgia features even as their knees went bad. The last working plant that fills up their bottles, the Gomberg Seltzer Works in Canarsie, Brooklyn, is now being run by the third- and fourth-generation Gombergs, who have no intention of closing it down. Good health!

Seventh Avenue

American fashion has an address, and it is Seventh Avenue. Just about every giant of the industry has kept an office or a showroom there: the one-namers (Ralph, Calvin, Donna), the gala-circuit kings (Oscar de la Renta, Bill Blass), and other icons like Halston, Stephen Burrows, and Norman Norell. "For many designers," the New York *Times* wrote in the late '70s, "a showroom at 530 Seventh Avenue is something to work toward and a 550 Seventh Avenue address may be a sign of arrival." But the association of the rag trade with "Fashion Avenue," as the street signs now read (with a Fashion Walk of Fame embedded into the pavement between 35th and 41st Streets), goes back much further. Since the early twentieth century, *Seventh Avenue* has been a metonym for the industry itself as well as a site of design and production. When Paris trends had to be reproduced and Americanized, Seventh Avenue, literally and figuratively, was up to the challenge. "Seventh Avenue is getting quite expert at this job," a Miss Shanna Simon, the "fashion counselor for dress departments" at Macy's, told the *Times* in 1964. "Nobody has called me to say, 'It can't be copied!'"

Seventh Avenue has not always been celebrated for its efforts. The garmentos, their factories, warehouses, and workers—many of them recent immigrants—got to Seventh in the first place only because the undesir-

SHAKESPEARE IN THE PARK

» Eat. "I highly recommend visiting our concessions for hot dogs, popcorn, and adult frosé. Seriously, our snacks are bomb, and you can bring food and drink into the theater as long as it's not in glass containers."

» Look out for wildlife. "Raccoons are a big part of the Delacorte experience. Every summer, they make their home under the stage waiting for their moment to steal focus from Richard II or join a dance number."

» Bring the three essentials. "Bug spray, sunscreen, and hydration. Our actors, crew, and artistic teams make it a point to spray, apply, and consume, all day and night."

able odor of trade had begun to sully the expensive real estate of Fifth Avenue, where the grand department stores stood. A landmark zoning resolution in 1916 "protected" Fifth Avenue from the loft-style factories that were mushrooming up to support the growing garment industry and sent manufacturers toward a new neighborhood they'd claim as their own: what we now know as the Garment District, bordered by Ninth Avenue, Broadway, 34th Street, and 42nd Street. The first such designated buildings were developed there in 1920, and by 1926, the neighborhood was seeing more construction than anywhere else in the city. By the World War II era, the fashion industry was the city's largest employer.

These days, you're as likely to find American designers off Seventh as on it, with studios scattered throughout lower Manhattan, mid-gentrified Brooklyn, and wherever anyone can set up a sewing machine in a rent-stabilized garret. When the Ralph Lauren Corporation finally gave up its space at 550 Seventh Avenue in 2018, *Women's Wear Daily* called it the end of an era. But the halo remains. It's the street that helped scrappy, self-starting New York yank the focus of international fashion from the tony boulevards of Paris, allowing American designers, no longer mere copyists, to thrive creatively. Some of Seventh's original innovators are now billion-dollar businesses with outposts all over the globe—witness Calvin or Ralph. And for those who can, it is still a spot to hang a spangled shingle. Just ask Carolina Herrera, at No. 501.

Sex and the City *see* SITCOM

Shakespeare in the Park[4]

Joseph Papirofsky grew up poor in a tough part of Williamsburg, Brooklyn, and became absorbed by theater when he began discovering plays to read at the public library. While serving in World War II, he produced shows on the decks of aircraft carriers in the Pacific. By 1954, he was working as a stage manager for CBS—which snipped his name to Joseph Papp for the credits—and organizing Shakespeare workshops on the side. From there, he proceeded to church-basement productions, then to a mobile stage built out of a truck bed to make anywhere in the city his theater. In 1956 he began mounting free productions in East River Park on the Lower East Side, moving them to a lawn in Central Park the following year. The New York *Herald Tribune* critic Walter Kerr called the 1957 staging of *Romeo and Juliet* one of the best he'd ever seen. Lines began to form hours before the tickets went on offer.

From there—after a battle with Parks Commissioner Robert Moses's aides, who disliked Papp's leftist politics—the series became an annual event. Moses soon decided it was not only a good thing but deserving of its own outdoor theater, and in 1962 the city completed construction on the Delacorte, which is still the festival's principal home. That June, *The Merchant of Venice* inaugurated the building with George C. Scott starring as Shylock.

To produce plays year-round, Papp went on to found the Public Theater, establishing it downtown on Lafayette Street in the old Astor Library building. Free Shakespeare in the Park has become a much-beloved institution with two shows per summer, and even waiting in line all day for free tickets has become a communal tradition. The series is also a prestige job for actors both emerging and established: Martin Sheen and James Earl Jones in the 1960s, Meryl Streep and Morgan Freeman in the 1970s (and beyond), Liev Schreiber, Al Pacino, and Anne Hathaway more recently. Although a number of tickets are now set aside for patrons who make large donations to the Public, most of the seats remain free.

Singles Bar [5]

As long as there have been bars, there have been assignations, trysts, and pickups. Yet unaccompanied women at a dockworkers' saloon or hotel bar were, until a generation ago, marginally welcome at best. More often, they were turned away on the assumption that they were prostitutes. (Places like McSorley's Old Ale House banned women altogether until 1970.) The cleverness of T.G.I. Friday's founder Alan Stillman, who opened the original bar by that name at 415 East 63rd Street in 1965, was to frame it as a place completely open to young New York singles—in particular, single women—shortly after the birth-control pill came on the market. Moreover, he did so in a neighborhood full of unmarried young adults, since Upper East Siders of the era tended to leave for the suburbs once they married and began to consider having children.

Friday's, unlike its predecessors, was a place where secretaries and copywriters and stewardesses (as they were called then) could go in groups or alone and mingle, chat, maybe go home with someone, maybe just have a fun evening out. Whereas your average New York saloon was dark, with perhaps a steam table full of corned beef and cabbage, this place was playful with good burgers and fries. It felt young. As Stillman said in a 2010 interview, "All I really did was throw sawdust on the floor and hang up fake Tiffany lamps. I painted the building blue, and I put the waiters in red-and-white-striped soccer shirts. If you think that I knew what I was doing, you are dead wrong. I had no training in the restaurant business or interior design or architecture—I just have a feel for how to use all those things to create an experience." Equally important: "Apparently, I invented the idea of serving burgers on a toasted English muffin—but the principle involved was to make people feel that they were going to someone's apartment for a cocktail party."

Soon enough, there were other bars catering to singles, most prominently Maxwell's Plum, opened in April 1966 by Warner LeRoy (later of Tavern on the Green fame) across First Avenue from Friday's. It too was extremely successful and within a few years had expanded and added a more elaborate menu, once receiving a four-star review from the *Times*. It became *the* place to spot celebrities under the Art Nouveau murals (*Is that Bill Blass? Hey, look, there's Barbra*

At T.G.I. Friday's, the original singles bar, 1967.
PHOTOGRAPH BY
RALPH MORSE

Streisand!), drink brandy Alexanders or vodka stingers, and maybe make a love match—exactly as it was intended. LeRoy himself met his second wife, Kay O'Reilly, there, and she was indeed a flight attendant.

Lots of knockoffs of T.G.I. Friday's opened over the next decade (one was called Somebody Tuesday's). Many were successful, to the point where the term *fern bar*, referring to watering holes gussied up to appeal to single women, became something you'd say with a roll of the eyes. Even Maxwell's Plum eventually lost its luster: The quality of the food started to slip, downtown superseded the Upper East Side as the place to be, a long twilight followed, and the restaurant closed in 1988. Friday's, by contrast, became an enormous national chain with nearly 900 franchise locations supplying English-muffin-cradled burgers to happy hours in practically every American city. (The East 63rd Street original closed in 1994.) In 1977, Stillman moved on to open the Smith & Wollensky steakhouse on Third Avenue, and even after he sold that chain, he continued (and continues, as of 2020) to own and operate the first location. And even in the era of the dating app, the 4 a.m. closing-time hookup endures, and is sometimes even preferred.

Sitcom [6]

In November 1947, the DuMont television network aired the fifteen-minute premiere of a show called *Mary Kay and Johnny*. It was the first American television sitcom, appearing several months before the first officially programmed season of network television, and it was unlike anything viewers had seen before. Most early experimental shows were either adaptations of radio programming, coverage of sporting events, variety shows, or stand-alone fictional stories like those on *Kraft Television Theatre*. But *Mary Kay and Johnny* returned every night to the same two characters (played by real-life couple Mary Kay and Johnny Stearns) in the same tiny New York apartment. It was an ongoing comedy about an American family at home and featured short, funny stories about domestic life and minor marital squabbles. In the show's one surviving episode, Johnny chides Mary Kay for buying a small brush from a door-to-door salesman, only to get suckered into buying a much more expensive vacuum when the salesman returns.

Like the best sitcoms, *Mary Kay and Johnny* balanced small, easily resolved conflicts with a longer-term fondness for its lead characters, and cramped New York apartments like theirs would become a familiar, stage-like setting for dozens of sitcoms over the next several decades. Mary Kay and Johnny were supposed to live in Greenwich Village, but the show was broadcast live from a small set in the Wanamaker's department store at 770 Broadway. (The set had only one room, which had to be redecorated depending on whether the day's episode called for the living room or the bedroom.)

That idea, the small residential space serving as a regular backdrop for mundane but meaningful, humorous stories about everyday life, became a foundational piece of sitcom DNA. It's there in *The Goldbergs*, the long-running radio sitcom that transitioned to television in 1949, and in *The Honeymooners*, the 1955 Jackie Gleason sitcom about a New York bus driver. And the city continued as a go-to setting even after most TV production moved to Los Angeles and sitcoms branched out into workplace backdrops and single-cam setups. *I Love Lucy*, set on the Upper East Side through most of its run, was shot entirely in California.

In its seven-plus decades, the sitcom has uncannily mirrored, and shaped, public perceptions of New York City. Lucy and Ricky Ricardo, in later seasons, moved from Manhattan to the suburbs like hundreds of thousands of New Yorkers did. During the urban-decay years, angry white conservatism in Queens made itself known on *All in the Family*, and as Black Americans made their way into the upper-middle class, so too did

George and Louise Jefferson, movin' on up from Queens to Manhattan. The 1970s impulse toward social conscience, told through two generations at a Brooklyn high school, made itself seen on *Welcome Back, Kotter*.

Since then, sitcoms have helped America reconceive New York not as somewhere to get stabbed but as a place where you could live your best life. Starting in 1989, *Seinfeld* began to promulgate the idea that New York City existence was principally about having wacky, if venal, neighbors, and it conveyed local references—H&H bagels, black-and-white cookies, subway seat-stealers, George Steinbrenner as perpetual white noise—to a national audience. Jerry Seinfeld once described the premise of the show like this: "In New York, you can do nothing, and it's very entertaining."

Starting in 1994, the six friends of *Friends* took that premise further, conveying merely by their existence that New York was *the* place you ought to live if you wanted to enjoy your young adulthood. Never mind that the characters live in apartments their careers could not possibly pay for; never mind that they seem to work half as much as any actual New Yorker with a job does. The world's teenagers saw their lifestyle—and still do in reruns—and liked it, and upon graduation, they and their futons began to descend upon Murray Hill and Boerum Hill and Carnegie Hill in droves.

As those young people reach thirty or so, another show in endless syndication often starts to resonate with them: *Sex and the City*, about another tight-knit group, this time four single women seeking love. They too live beyond their ostensible means; their New York is principally built on commerce and glitz, a fantasy of pink cocktails, over-the-top fashion, and the social whirl, somehow undergirded by a mysteriously substantial income. Yet it again (like its millennial successor, *Girls*) is attuned to certain aspects of real-life urban existence: Your closest friends become a family of choice, and New York can, against all evidence, be conquered into livability.

Sketch Comedy

The origin of sketch comedy, defined roughly as "a group of people get on a stage and do funny bits," is as amorphous and widespread as modern theater itself. Its roots are in vaudeville acts and variety shows from the early twentieth century, which can be traced back even further to nineteenth-century British music halls. Sketch comedy as we think of it today, though—a troupe that puts on an entirely comedic show (no interstitial jugglers allowed)—was born on TV.

Variety shows were, at the start of television broadcasting, one of its first staples. *You're Invited* (1948) and *Texaco Star Theater* (which premiered the same year, and was later renamed *The Milton Berle Show*), among others, featured comedians and ventriloquists as part of their lineups. But modern TV sketch comedy was really invented when *Your Show of Shows* premiered on NBC in 1950. Starring Sid Caesar, Imogene Coca, and Carl Reiner, with a writing staff that included Mel Brooks and Neil Simon, *Your Show of Shows* dropped the vaudeville presumption of lots of different kinds of entertainment and instead focused solely on comedy. It was 90 minutes of new material every week, filmed at the International Theatre on Columbus Circle. Though it ran for only four years (succeeded for another three by the similar *Caesar's Hour*), *Your Show of Shows* defined the form that would later be adopted by *SCTV* and *Saturday Night Live*: a mix of one-off sketches and returning conceits, a cast that played dozens of characters, and mountains of original material that ranged from the satirical to the transcendently silly.

At its 1975 premiere, Lorne Michaels's *SNL* was the first show to not only internalize those conventions but wink at them onscreen. From the beginning, it incorporated backstage goings-on and in-jokes about television itself (that it was broadcast "live from New York!" inherently referred to an earlier TV era), and over its nearly five

The Jeffersons *(1975–1985)*

How I Met Your Mother *(2005–2014)*

Will & Grace *(1998–2006; 2017–2020)*

The Honeymooners *(1955–1956)*

The Goldbergs *(1949–1956)*

30 Rock *(2006–2013)*

Taxi *(1978–1983)*

Friends *(1994–2004)*

I Love Lucy *(1951–1957)*

Seinfeld *(1989–1998)*

Sex and the City *(1998–2004)*

All in the Family *(1971–1979)*

decades, *SNL* has attained outsize weight in this idiom as the only large-scale outlet for sketch comedy on network TV, and it remains highly popular and widely discussed on Sunday morning. Although its casting draws from all over North America—Chicago, Toronto, and Los Angeles in particular—the New York improv scene is dominated by its alumni, its aspirants, its washouts, its success stories, and its lore. The Upright Citizens Brigade, the venue and school where many of the city's comics have honed their skills, was co-founded by Amy Poehler, who went on to become one of *SNL*'s (and comedy's) biggest stars.

Skully

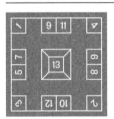

The street game of skully, also known as "skelly" and "skellzies," requires only bottle caps, chalk, a sidewalk, and one or more friends. Its roots are obscure, but it seems to have developed out of the game of marbles, adapted to urban play surfaces such as concrete and asphalt rather than bare dirt. It was well-established by the early twentieth century, and widely played into the 1980s. Although it has faded from view since then, it is not, like some old street games, entirely extinct (*see also* STICKBALL). You can still find the odd skully match on the streets of Brooklyn.

To play, draw the board pictured at left on the pavement, about six feet square. There are many local variations in the rules, but generally, each participant has a bottle cap, usually weighted with clay or melted wax or crayons. The first player attempts to flick his cap into Box 1. (It can't touch the lines.) If successful, or if he or she hits another person's cap, the player gets to take a turn at the next box and then the next. If not, it's the following player's turn. (You can sabotage others through a technique called "blasting," which involves hitting someone else's cap so hard that it's knocked way down the block.) Players advance from Box 1 to Box 13 and back, then through the four central trapezoids in succession, declaring in turn, on each one, "I'm," "a," "killer," and "diller." Get through that sentence and you're a killer; you can then knock other players out of the game by hitting their pieces. Last player on the board wins.

Skyline [7]

Until the end of the nineteenth century, the word *skyline* referred to a mountain ridge, while American cities were almost uniformly low slung, their flat silhouettes punctuated by the occasional church spire. By the 1890s, two innovations—steel-frame construction and the passenger elevator—allowed buildings to shoot up to thin-air altitudes of fifteen to eighteen stories. In 1897, the *Times* speculated that "it may very well be that the limit is already reached, and that lower New York may continue for many years to present the ragged skyline … which a recent foreign visitor found 'hideous and magnificent.'" Two years later, the twenty-nine-story Park Row Building opened amid a rush of new towers, and Manhattan began to be visible from a ship far off in the harbor. Neither the skyscraper nor the skyline was a New York invention—Chicago led the way on height—but nowhere else did they become so lastingly embedded in the city's identity and iconography.

In 1904, the writer Henry James returned to New York after spending twenty years in Europe and was shocked to see commercial buildings looming above the spire of Trinity Church, a development he found unbearably crass. Five years later, the New York *Sun* published an illustration showing one view of lower Manhattan evolving in four stages from a huddle of mostly wooden structures to a high wall of neo-Gothic, neoclassical, and Italianate palaces. From then on, the race to build taller was never just about one building, but the certainty that

the city's collective future lay in the clouds. Even at the start of the Depression, skyscrapers continued to surge with glamour. In 1929, 40 Wall Street was reaching for the title of the world's tallest tower when, in a stealth move, the Chrysler Building acquired a spire. That achievement lasted only eleven months until the Empire State Building topped them both.

The towers' Art Deco energy emerged from the interaction of aesthetics and legislation. In 1916, as Manhattan threatened to turn into a granite-and-limestone forest, the city began regulating the skyline (*see also* ZONING). Hugh Ferriss, the architect whose brooding renderings made him the Piranesi of New York, understood the romance embedded in the new codes, which allowed greater heights on wider streets. "We are not contemplating the new architecture of a city—we are contemplating the new architecture of a civilization," he wrote. In 1929, he published his graphic manifesto, *The Metropolis of Tomorrow*, a book that shaped the dreams of architects, planners, comic-book illustrators, and Hollywood set designers. In a long essay with one hundred and eight drawings, he described a city of fantastical drama in which pedestrians would move around by skyway and towers would have rooftop landing pads.

But the ongoing Depression and World War II eventually stifled that urban exuberance, and the city's skyline remained relatively stable until the late 1940s, when it acquired a new appearance that was less EKG and more bar graph. Like so many New York triumphs, the postwar office building, a glass skin clipped to a steel frame over a concrete backbone, had an out-of-town tryout (the first was Pietro Belluschi's Equitable Building in Portland, Oregon), but within a few years, New York had adopted the trend as its own invention. In place of heavy stone behemoths and stepped-back Art Deco skyscrapers, architects designed towers that aspired to be light, lean, and transparent. Among the pioneers was the architecture firm Skidmore, Owings & Merrill,

which was founded in Chicago and opened a New York office in 1937. Led by Gordon Bunshaft, SOM produced some of the movement's early masterpieces, including, in 1952, Lever House: a merger of flamboyant showmanship and austere modernism in a bottle-green glass tower with an enclosed plaza, like a corporate version of a medieval bell tower and cloister. Showmanship also featured in the 1952 U.N. Secretariat Building, designed by Le Corbusier and Oscar Niemeyer. One great glass wall, threaded with glittering aluminum mullions and framed by pale concrete sides, faced east toward Europe, a signal that American-style corporate efficiency could manage the problems the Old World's wars had botched.

The sleekness and precision of New York's modernist office buildings also helped create the look of 1960s America, a cocktail of luxe and simplicity. Amplifying the power of straightforward geometries, their taut planes, gridded frames, and straight lines beguiled architects (but exposed every imperfection). The new style thrilled the critic Ada Louise Huxtable; in 1957, she hoped it would "deliver us from the present anarchy and return us to this perennial ideal" of "serenity, harmony, and repose." Architectural historian Vincent Scully, however, couldn't abide such slate wiping. Glass buildings, he wrote, derived their meaning from juxtaposition with their chunkier predecessors in the pleasing contrast of crystal and stone. For Scully, the new towers and plazas, lined up in a parade of quasi-military uniformity, destroyed the street. And anyone inclined to see architecture as a metaphor for the stultifying control of large corporations had only to come to Park Avenue.

The popularity of these office skyscrapers would not only transform New York but turn the central business district of virtually every American city into a midtown Manhattan knockoff. Transparent boxes proliferated, and good buildings generated fleets of shoddy imitations. The construction of the original World Trade Center in the early 1970s seemed like the apotheosis of the modernist tower: two immense, identical steel frames curtained in glass and aluminum, square and sheer and utterly divorced from the messy city at their feet. Their destruction, thirty years later (*see also* 9/11 ERA), seemed at first like the end of an architectural age, but it wasn't. The glass-box era goes on.

Happily, the constantly changing skyline didn't just preen for photographs from below; it offered a selection of imperial views from above. On the afternoon of December 20, 1932, the photographer Berenice Abbott took the elevator to one of the highest manmade points in the world to chronicle a completely new sight. The Empire State Building was just nineteen months old, and from the eighty-sixth-floor observation terrace, Abbott beheld the city of towers from above. She left her shutter open for fifteen minutes during that fleeting stretch between sunset and 5 p.m., when she knew office workers would start to click off their lights. Her wait in the cold, windless air yielded the famous *Nightview*—and celebrated the era of the skyscraper observation deck.

Putting a lookout destination atop a skyscraper is yet another almost entirely New York innovation. The Singer Tower, opened in 1908 on lower Broadway, appears to have been the first, with a small balcony for a few dozen observers. When the Woolworth Building—at sixty stories, vastly taller than anything else around—opened in 1913, the floors within its pyramidion cap were given over to paying gawkers, who disembarked from an elevator a few floors below the top, then stepped into another (a cylinder of glass and steel) that carried them all the way to the highest balcony outdoors. As the race for height accelerated, the city gained other observatories: the Cities Service Building at 70 Pine Street, the Chrysler Building, 30 Rockefeller Plaza, and the Empire State, supreme above all; a generation later, the World Trade Center joined them. Today every Asian megacity's signature building has one, as do the giant towers in the Middle East, like the Burj Dubai. The latest addition to New York's crop of crow's nests (competing with the high-tech aerial entertainment centers now in place at 30 Rock, the Empire State Building, and One World Trade) is The Edge, a triangular platform jutting from the top of 30 Hudson Yards, 1,100 feet up. These views are astounding moneymakers. During the Depression, the half-empty Empire State Building was able to pay its real-estate taxes only because of income from observatory admissions. A standard adult ticket to its two observatories now costs $72; nearly 4 million people pay the price each year.

In this century's teens, ever-higher-priced residential views had a dramatic effect on the New York skyline. Developers discovered they could multiply the value of tight, expensive lots by threading slender apartment towers through the strictures of the zoning code (*see also* SLIVER BUILDING). Super-tall residences like One57, 432 Park Avenue, and Central Park Tower added a modest number of glass-walled, mostly unused gajillion-dollar units, co-opting the public goods of light, air, and visibility for the benefit of a handful of billionaires. Instead of acting like signs of America's capitalist vigor, the new skyscrapers treated New York real estate like a compartment under the floorboards: a place to park money until it's time to run.

Sliver Building

In districts where land is expensive, real-estate developers traditionally attempt to assemble big parcels for big buildings, buying up groups of small buildings in secret, one by one, over many years. Inevitably, though, some lots, especially mid-block, are considered too small for building—they're essentially leftovers. As the early-1980s real-estate boom began in New York, improved construction and rising prices made it possible to put up tall towers on many of those narrow lots, some the width of just two brownstones. Owing to their slenderness, the resulting structures came to be known as "sliver buildings"—perhaps fifteen to thirty stories with one or two apartments per floor, each selling or renting for top dollar. Because they're expensive to build relative to the number of apartments they contain, they tend to appear only in highly desirable neighborhoods. Most of the early examples surfaced on the Upper East Side, including 350 East 86th Street, 344 East 63rd Street, and 266 East 78th Street. Another one on the site of (and behind the preserved gate of) J. P. Morgan's carriage house at 211 Madison Avenue came to be known as Morgan Court.

As a rule, the neighbors hated them and complained that they wrecked the scale of the area and loomed over otherwise pleasant streets. In 1983, as developers rushed to get a final few foundations poured, the City Planning Commission banned the construction of slivers in residential areas. Perhaps owing to the buildings' reputation for chilly aesthetics, *Sliver*, a 1991 novel by Ira Levin (who began his exploration of sinister New York real estate with *Rosemary's Baby* in 1967), used one such (fictional) building as the setting for a story of sexual obsession and murder. When the book became a film, starring Sharon Stone and William Baldwin, Morgan Court was used for the exterior shots.

The ban on sliver buildings doesn't extend outside those low-scale residential blocks, so (given today's outlandish real-estate values) it's no surprise that they are occasionally still worth building. But nowadays, they're significantly taller. In 2009, a condominium tower was finished at 785 Eighth Avenue that is 24 feet wide at the street façade and 517 feet—that's 42 stories—high. Arguably, the newest super-tall apartment buildings on 57th Street, twenty times as tall as they are wide, are their descendants on an immense scale.

Socialite

The term *socialite* was coined in 1928 by Briton Hadden, who was, with Henry Luce, a founder of *Time* magazine. (Hadden died just a year later, at 31, which explains why you've only heard of the other guy. *See also* NEWSWEEKLY.) The term wasn't a serious one—a socialite was simply someone prominent, or seeking prominence, in fashionable society. Her predecessors in England and France had been the wives and mistresses of court, where a woman could wield power or influence. A good socialite was a great diplomat, a repository of gleaned information, an expert in the many forms power can take. But in twentieth-century New York, at least according to Hadden, a great socialite was both *R*'s—rich and racy. She was an often fun character connected to a great fortune, a man, or a legacy going back generations. Newport was often involved, or Southampton.

And she treated the role as a job. The purpose of the New York socialite was for many years to give away the piles of money earned by her husband or her genes and to do so at a series of annual galas, where she would often wear a dress costing more than her contribution to said cause. Heiresses in the years between the wars, like Doris Duke, Barbara Hutton, Brenda Frazier, and Gloria Vanderbilt (*see also* JEANS, DESIGNER), were sometimes called "poor little rich girls" in the press, feeding an insatiable public appetite for gossip items about their lavish debutante balls, wardrobes, world travels, and many marriages, stories that masked a variety of family tragedies and battles with eating disorders and addiction.

By the early 1970s, the socialite was often known, in the pithy phrase coined by Stephen Sondheim, as a "lady who lunches," one regularly seen in party pictures and the "Suzy" column (confusingly, written for more than fifty years by a woman named Aileen Mehle; *see also* KNICKERBOCKER). And she was entertaining, certainly in Tom Wolfe's telling: He called the party girls of the '80s Upper East Side "social X-rays" for their emaciated frames and the piles of satin and tulle they carried, particularly when fashioned by Christian Lacroix. Gayfryd Steinberg was a socialite. So were Nan Kempner—whom Valentino praised because she had a "body like a hanger"—and Pat Buckley and Babe Paley. Truman Capote befriended many of them, then wrote a vicious roman à clef and was cast out. The socialite was as ornamental as she was urbane, but you didn't cross her.

Paris Hilton turned it all around in the early aughts. As an heiress, she had the well-born part down, but that was about it. The rest was tight tracksuits, spray tans, and reality TV—and, of course, a night-vision sex tape in which she fellates poker player Rick Salomon. Hilton turned her socialite status into a business; there was no shame in her game, no charity attached. There were handbag lines and pop singles and lucrative "DJ" gigs, and then the doors were open. Go out in a dress, get your picture on Patrick McMullan's or BFA's site, or even on Instagram, then leverage the hell out of it. Nowadays, every socialite has a side hustle—vegan snacks, silly stationery, stripy tops, Egyptian sheets—and instead of socializing in vague and distant service to a tragic cause, the New York socialite now exists openly in service to something else: herself.

Spaghetti and Meatballs

Spaghetti is Italian, and meatballs are Italian, but spaghetti and meatballs is not. Until Italians immigrated en masse to the United States, meatballs and pasta were,

Jay Wilson squeegees a car window on Twelfth Avenue, 1993.

separately, considered first courses—*primi*, in small portions—rather than the combined main event. The cuisines of Southern Italy and particularly Sicily, where most New York Italians originated, tended toward thick tomato sauces, dried pasta rather than fresh, and as much meat as one could afford (which, in the old country, hadn't been much). In their new city, with access to less expensive beef as well as bread crumbs and spaghetti, they put them on one plate, using marinara ("sailor sauce," probably named for the galley cooks who made it) to tie the dish together.

Though no one person or restaurant claims credit for it, spaghetti and meatballs was by the 1930s a staple of the red-checkered-tablecloth restaurants of Greenwich Village, as well as the North End in Boston and other Italian-American enclaves. During World War II, a former Plaza Hotel chef named Ettore Boiardi, who had been selling canned tomato sauce and Italian meal kits, got into the business of canning food for soldiers, and at the end of the war, he began to put cooked spaghetti in cans with the

sauce; he soon added a version with mini-meatballs. For American tongues that found "Boiardi" difficult to pronounce, he rendered his name as "Chef Boy-ar-dee" and put on the requisite puffy white hat for his television commercials. A billion heat-and-eat meals followed.

Spaldeen *see* STICKBALL

Sports Talk Radio

The signature, foundational idea of sports radio is that every conversation about sports can go on endlessly, sprouting in an infinite number of directions and covering literally centuries. But if you don't follow sports and happen to be listening in, it may as well be in some sort of alien code. It's for obsessives who can spend their entire lives poring over one ultimately insignificant topic that is impenetrable to anyone outside their enclosed orbit, an insular pastime for insular people. Is it any wonder that sports radio was invented in New York? Insular obsession is in the civic charter.

Sports talk actually originated in northern New Jersey in 1965, with a postgame call-in show for Seton Hall basketball on the school's student-run station, but the notion of talking about sports on the radio was solely a New York City innovation, pioneered mostly by Bill Mazer on 660 WNBC Radio in the mid-1960s. He ended up with his own show, broadcast out of Mickey Mantle's restaurant, when WFAN launched in 1987; it was the selling point for a new station that would eventually give us Mike Francesa and Chris "Mad Dog" Russo, along with the billion-dollar industry that sports talk has become. It was all based on this idea: *Youse gotta listen to me.* When the Patton Oswalt film *Big Fan* came out in 2009, about a man so dangerously obsessed with his teams that he goes violently insane … he's of course a Giants fan from Staten Island, and of course he spends the entire movie calling in to radio shows. They're for the lunatic sports fan in all of us.

Even as terrestrial broadcasting has lost influence, the structure and thrust of sports radio—*You're wrong, no you're wrong, here's my hot take!*—is basically the way all of media works now. It's about strong, bite-size, easy-to-understand opinions that can be digested in time for the traffic and weather. You can hear Mazer in every Alex Jones rant and every Rachel Maddow monologue. Sports talk radio has never lent itself to nuance. There's no time for that.

Squeegee Men

It is very strange to consider the massive ramifications produced by the combination of a few dozen ragged men and one skilled demagogue. In the mid-1980s, men started appearing at major intersections where traffic reliably congealed—along Canal Street near the entrance to the Holland Tunnel, on Eighth Avenue as it approached the Lincoln Tunnel. They would squirt water onto the windshield of a stopped car, squeegee the surface, then shake a cup at the driver's window, looking for payment. Sometimes the windshield was cleaner, sometimes it wasn't; occasionally, when drivers declined to pay, the squeegee men reacted violently. The city was a fragile place at the time, economically and racially, with the number of annual murders on the way to setting a record in 1990 (*see also* MAYHEM).

When New York's first Black mayor, David Dinkins, ran for reelection in 1993, his opponent, Republican Rudy Giuliani, made crime the main issue, seizing on the squeegee men as a potent symbol of the city's declining quality of life. Giuliani won narrowly and, with Police Commissioner Bill Bratton, began implementing policies (*see also* "BROKEN WINDOWS" POLICING) based on the belief that the key to preventing major crimes is enforcing the laws against smaller ones, like turnstile-jumping and the unbidden squeegeeing of windshields. New York got much safer, the cops became more efficient, and the crack plague ebbed, but the number of arrests for minor offenses, particularly of young nonwhite men, grew and grew until 2012, when the attendant lawsuits against the city were working their way through the courts.

The ironies piled up nearly as thick: Giuliani got media and political credit for vanquishing the squeegee men, but it was Dinkins's police commissioner, Ray Kelly, who really cracked down after he was reinstalled at One Police Plaza in 2002 by Giuliani's successor, Michael Bloomberg. Kelly presided over an explosion of quality-of-life arrests, then dialed them down, but *his* longtime rival, Bratton—the police boss who'd originally set the stop-and-frisk machine in motion—got the credit for returning the NYPD to a more enlightened approach under Bloomberg's successor, Bill de Blasio. And that marauding, pervasive horde of squeegee men, the menace that helped elect a mayor and enshrine a crime-fighting theory that swept police departments worldwide? At their peak in 1993, according to an NYPD report, there were 75 squeegee men in the entire city.

Stand-Up Comedy *see* COMEDY CLUB

Statue of Liberty *see* IMMIGRATION

Steamboat

Every schoolkid learns that the first practical steam-powered boat was called the *Clermont*, but it didn't get that name until ten years after its debut. In its time, it was simply called the *North River Steamboat*, the North River

Vacant-lot stickball, 1947.
PHOTOGRAPH BY RALPH MORSE

in question being the old name for the lower Hudson where it meets New York Harbor. The inventor Robert Fulton constructed the boat with a Watt steam engine built in Britain, and the New York politician and American Founding Father Robert Livingston financed it. On August 17, 1807, it set out from its West Side pier; thirty-two hours of travel later, including a stop at Livingston's family estate, Clermont Manor, it reached Albany. It was no faster than a sailing ship in the right conditions—but it made much of its trip *into* the wind rather than with it.

It also may have been a ripoff. In the late 1780s and 1790s, a Revolutionary War veteran named Robert Fitch had been conducting tests of small steamers he'd built, including a run in 1796 on the Collect Pond, the small lake in lower Manhattan that later became the site of a notorious slum (*see also* MAYHEM). Fitch never found backing and, depressed, took his own life in 1798. But several decades thereafter, a group of people who'd been there all testified that they'd seen Fulton and Livingston walking around the pond, watching him, and that they'd lifted the idea that made them famous.

The technology took off almost immediately. Within 15 years, a ship crossed the Atlantic partly under steam power, and by 1838 the steamship *Great Western* was in regular operation between the U.K. and New York. For a half-century, such vessels dominated trade on American rivers. Even as railroads, then trucks, cut into that business, steam-turbine-driven ocean liners began ferrying thousands of people and hundreds of tons of cargo across oceans at a clip. That remained true until a generation ago, when diesel-electric and nuclear systems finally superseded steam power.

Stickball

A baseball field requires three or four acres of land. The few such open spaces in Brooklyn or the Bronx a century ago didn't lend themselves to pickup games, and anyway, tenement kids of that era were unlikely to be able to travel outside of their neighborhoods to play ball, or to have bats, gloves, and baseballs if they did. By the 1920s, those street kids had figured out their own substitute: a baseball variant called stickball. (There are earlier games by that name, notably one played by members of the Cherokee Nation that's a little like lacrosse. Brooklyn didn't know from lacrosse.)

The bat was a cut-down broom handle, sometimes friction-taped for a better grip; the ball was a pink rubber Spalding product, essentially a tennis ball without its fuzz, colloquially known as a "spaldeen." On the asphalt field of play, home plate and second base were usually manhole covers. First base and third could be anything that was in more or less the right spot: the corner of a parked car, a bus-stop sign, a parking meter, a hydrant. The "pitcher's mound" was often a chalk mark. Most great stickball hurlers threw half-underhand, essentially sidearm, from behind that line.

There are many variants of stickball, differentiated from standard baseball practice to correct for the liveliness of the spaldeen. Two strikes are usually an out, and there are two outs per side. In the old days, any ball that went over a fence into a hostile neighbor's enclosed yard was an automatic out, because spaldeens were scarce in poor communities and a lost ball could end the day's play. If a worn spaldeen split in two across the seam, it could be used in yet another version of the game called "egg ball" or "half ball" to produce irregular, floppy hits of little range.

The best measure of a hitter was distance, which was measured by how many curbside sewer grates the spaldeen passed while airborne. A two-sewer hitter was considered a strong player. Willie Mays, in his early years with the New York baseball Giants, would not infrequently join a game of Harlem neighborhood kids and claimed he learned how to hit breaking pitches that way. He was a consistent three- and even four-sewer hitter.

Stickball's golden era ran through the Depression and the war years, when baseball dominated New York's sports culture and Brooklyn in particular took pride in the Dodgers. The game's slow fade thereafter can be ascribed to all the usual reasons: suburbanization, air-conditioning, TV watching, and, worst of all, car traffic, which made most street fields unplayable.

Today, it's basically extinct among the young, although a not dissimilar game called *vitilla* is played in the Dominican Republic with a broomstick and a big plastic bottle cap. Stickball now exists principally among nostalgists in places with high concentrations of elderly men from Brooklyn and the Bronx. Since 2002, there has been a league in Wellington, Florida, on a paved stretch of park that the city has designated Stickball Boulevard. The players are virtually all retired

New Yorkers, many now over 90, some of whom have been playing stickball for 85 years. They lay down replica manhole covers for bases.

Stork Club *see* CAFÉ SOCIETY; NIGHTCLUB

Streetwear As Luxury Fashion

Long before Fendi happily collaborated with Fila, or Louis Vuitton with Supreme, or Prada with Adidas, or Versace with Kith, luxury and streetwear—high-end, high-fashion clothes and their lower-cost, less rarefied street-friendly cousins—lived separate lives. That is, until Dapper Dan's Boutique opened on 125th Street in Harlem in 1982. Daniel Day, a Harlem native and former gambler turned furrier, operated the shop as a bespoke atelier offering custom furs (and leather jackets, car interiors, and more) to an African-American clientele whose patronage was neither sought nor particularly desired at the designer-label stores downtown. Day combined luxury logos from the likes of Gucci, Fendi, and Louis Vuitton with urban styling and sizes. For a flush customer looking to telegraph his (more often his, but sometimes her) net worth—Dapper Dan's coincided with both the rise of hip-hop and the burgeoning crack epidemic, and Day served an ascending class of rappers, gangsters, and drug dealers with equal enthusiasm—a Dapper Dan piece was a status object, a bragging right, and a confirmation of clout.

At first, Day bought up items like Gucci garment bags and deconstructed them to kit out the pieces he and a team of on-site tailors were making. But eventually, he started supplanting the luxury brands by simply screening their logos onto leather himself. He'd been impressed by a customer who came into the shop with a logo-printed Louis Vuitton pouch. "I had already been studying religion," Day has said. "I knew the significance, the power behind symbols. I'm going to unleash this power like it's never been before." Soon he was turning out reversible Louis Vuitton–logo furs and mink jackets with enormous Gucci-logo-printed puffed sleeves, creations the luxury brands would never have dared. His boutique became, in essence, the crucible of logomania. Clients like Mike Tyson, LL Cool J, and Salt-N-Pepa ate it up. The store sometimes stayed open 24 hours a day.

It wasn't hard for the brands getting bootlegged to figure out where these pieces were coming from, and counterfeiting raids and lawsuits from the European luxury houses finally brought about Dapper Dan's closure in 1992. (A young attorney named Sonia Sotomayor represented Fendi in its pursuit of Day.) But the legend of Dapper Dan's lived on, as did its influence. Hip-hop never abated, and designers began mining looks like Day's for an increasingly hybridized luxury streetwear and displaying an increasingly unabashed, over-the-top freedom with logos. Now they openly court and collaborate with street and sports brands, and the stores that sell a mix of Air Jordans and runway fashion (like Ronnie Fieg's Kith empire) have lines down the block. All came full circle in 2017, when Gucci sent a puffed-sleeve, Gucci-logo-printed jacket down the runway in Florence, one that commentators quickly recognized as a takeoff on a classic Dapper Dan piece. The bootlegger had become the bootlegged, and accusations of appropriation flew until Gucci, acknowledging Day's influence, went into business with him. The house now sells a Dapper Dan collection and has funded and supported the reopening of Dapper Dan's bespoke shop, twenty-six years after the closure of the original, in his beloved Harlem.

Submarine Attack

Some European prototypes notwithstanding, the first military use of a submarine took place in New York Harbor. During the American Revolution, a Yale student, David Bushnell, was developing underwater mines and created a submersible ship to deliver them to their targets. It was basically a wooden ovoid just big enough for one occupant, powered by his pedaling feet, and it was called the *Turtle*. On September 6, 1776, it set off to attack the British flagship HMS *Eagle*, anchored just offshore. The idea was that the pilot would drill into the ship's wooden hull, attaching an explosive mine. But the *Turtle*'s operator, Ezra Lee, found the sub extremely difficult to maneuver, and it took him a couple of hours to get settled beneath the *Eagle*'s hull—after which he discovered the target ship had copper sheathing that his tools couldn't penetrate. He backed off and just released the mine in the open water, where it exploded without doing much. Over the next several weeks, the *Turtle* made a few more stabs at stealth combat, none of them successful. The sub was lost for good in November, during the battle of Fort Lee, when a larger ship transporting it was itself sunk.

Subway

The Tube and the T and the Métro all preceded the IRT, yet none of those earlier systems quite became an avatar for London or Boston or Paris. The New York City subway system, however, utterly defines our way of life. It is a metaphor for virtually everything good and bad about New York. It is bigger than all those other rail systems, with more stations, and it very rarely shuts down. On its trains, billionaires can (theoretically) ride next to homeless people. For three generations, it has seemed ready to fall apart any day now, yet it works considerably better than it looks, at least most of the time. It's simultaneously underfunded and an endlessly draining money pit, an efficient amenity and a bureaucratic nightmare to run. It moves a mere five and a half million people each workday.

Our subway's origins lie in the consolidation of New York City in 1898, which accelerated the desire for all the boroughs to be connected by rapid transit. (An earlier, experimental system built by Alfred Ely Beach, driven by an enormous fan that pushed a train through a tunnel with air pressure, didn't make it past the proof-of-concept stage.) Financed by August Belmont II, the Interborough Rapid Transit Company began digging in 1900. Four and a half years later, on October 27, 1904, the first train ran from City Hall to Grand Central and then across to Times Square and up to 145th Street. It was driven by the mayor.

Within minutes, the first of the New York system's great innovations was on display. It was the first subway to run paired tracks, for express and local trains, on one line, a fitting idea for a city that is always in a hurry and for a system that included the word *rapid* in its very name. Within hours, its second great innovation became evident: The trains didn't stop that night. New York's subway was the first to run 24 hours a day, seven days a week. Apart from the odd and very brief weather-related closure, nothing—not wartime austerity, not fiscal crises, not terrorist attacks, not pandemics—has stopped it for any substantial stretch since.

Surprisingly, the system was not mainly a municipal project. It was built by three entities, one owned by the city (known as the IND) and two private (the IRT and

BMT), with free transfers among the systems. The fare was fixed by law at five cents for decades, and raising it was considered political suicide. That fact led to generally poor subway maintenance and financial distress, especially during the Depression. In 1940, the IRT went bankrupt, whereupon all three systems were merged under city control. That agency was the forebear of the New York City Transit Authority, now administered not by the city but by the state of New York.

A handful of other cities today maintain 24/7 schedules, but all of them save one (Copenhagen) have extremely limited nighttime service or none at all. It has been argued that New York should do that as well, because a system that never closes is difficult to maintain in good repair. Late-night subways are so ingrained in the city's identity that a 2017 think-tank proposal to curtail their numbers was immediately dismissed by just about everybody, citing graveyard-shift workers and Tinder hookups alike. Only during the COVID-19 crisis of 2020 did overnight closures become a frustrating necessity, allowing train cars to be disinfected (*see also* QUARANTINE).

Subway Series[8]

For there to be a subway series—that is, a baseball championship (*see also* BASEBALL) played between two teams whose stadiums can be reached by the same underground transit system—you need two basic things: (1) a city with subways and (2) a city with more than one baseball team.

In the 1920s, three places met those qualifications: Boston (which had the Braves and the Red Sox), Philadelphia (the Phillies and the A's), and New York. Both Boston teams and the Phillies were lousy. Thus the only place a subway series could unfold was New York, and in 1921 the Giants and Yankees faced off at their shared hometown park, the Polo Grounds, in upper Manhattan. The Giants won in eight games. It happened again the next year, and the next—by which time the Yankees had moved to their own Yankee Stadium in the Bronx, a short subway ride away—and then three more times in the next three decades. The Yankees took four championships, the Giants two.

The term itself came into use during the same era. Its first known published appearance, per the independent historian Barry Popik, was in the New York *Herald*

(8) **The Best New York Sports Bars, Team by Team**

» GIANTS
East End Bar & Grill
1664 First Ave.

» JETS
Whiskey Rebel
129 Lexington Ave.

» METS
**The Playwright
Irish Pub**
27 W. 35th St.

» YANKEES
Yankee Tavern
72 E. 161st St.,
Concourse Village, Bronx

» RANGERS / ISLANDERS
Warren 77
77 Warren St.

» KNICKS
The Beekman Pub
15 Beekman St.

» NYC FC
Smithfield Hall
138 W. 25th St.

» HARLEM GLOBETROTTERS
Harlem Tavern
2153 Frederick Douglass Blvd.

» BROOKLYN NETS
Brooklyn Tap House
590 Myrtle Ave.,
Clinton Hill, Brooklyn

in 1921, referring to a regular-season Giants-Dodgers game, and it showed up as a reference to the World Series in several papers, including the New York *Daily News*, in the fall of 1928. The phrase *nickel series*, referring to the transit fare, also pops up here and there.

In the 1940s, as the Brooklyn Dodgers crept out of their seemingly permanent cellar-dwelling position, they began to challenge the Yankees more regularly than the Giants did. These subway series, conducted on the BMT rather than the IRT, played out seven times between 1941 and 1956. Only once, in 1955, did the Dodgers win. And then—*poof*—the term appeared headed for extinction as the Dodgers and Giants both moved to California for the 1958 season. Any subsequent meeting of the Yankees and their old rivals would be conducted not by subway but by jet.

Even after the Mets made New York a two-team town again in 1962, the subway series seemed unlikely to return because the new team was breathtakingly, historically terrible. Uncannily, over the next forty years, the Mets and Yankees had a knack for seesawing across the standings. When one was playing well, the other was not. They came close to a shared World Series a few times in the late 1980s, when the Mets led their division and the Yankees fell just short, but it didn't happen until the new century. (Nonetheless, the arrival of interleague play in 1997 brought the term back to New Yorkers' lips, ultimately denoting the annual dozen games between the city's two teams.) In 2000, the baseball planets finally aligned, sending the Yankees and the Mets to the Series, where the Yankees won in five. It hasn't happened since.

Superhero [9]

To find the first superhero, do you go back to John Henry? Maybe all the way to Gilgamesh? And what are superheroes anyway? Are they defined by the costume, the powers, the secret identity? Ultimately, you know a

superhero when you see one. And no one would have seen the world's most famous superheroes without the fly-by-night business that was New York City publishing in the early part of the twentieth century (*see also* COMIC BOOK).

The earliest universally agreed-upon superhero character was, of course, Superman, who first repelled a bullet in the summer of 1938. But he (and his name) was not without precedent. Nietzsche had written of the Übermensch in 1883, George Bernard Shaw published *Man and Superman* in 1903, and the oldest extant use of the word *super hero* dates back to 1917. Popular characters like the Scarlet Pimpernel and Zorro introduced audiences to the notion of masked adventurers with dual identities, and Philip Wylie's 1930 novel *Gladiator* featured a physically and mentally perfect man who defied social conventions. When New York publishers started cranking out pulp-fiction and comic-book heroes like the Shadow, the Phantom, and Mandrake the Magician in the 1930s, the pump was primed for something big.

That something had been conceived years earlier and a thousand miles away in the vicinity of Cleveland, Ohio. Two Jewish teenagers, writer Jerry Siegel and artist Joe Shuster, concocted something they called "the Superman" in fits and starts over the course of the decade. Initially, their Superman was a sinister figure, but they gradually began to think of him as an unnaturally strong good guy. They tried to get his adventures published but continually ran up against walls of rejection. In a not-so-far-away parallel universe, the world has never heard about the Man of Steel.

In our universe, he saw the light of day thanks to a slightly shady Manhattan publishing house. In the late 1930s, a gangster-friendly loudmouth named Harry Donenfeld; his buttoned-down business manager, Jack Liebowitz; and an eccentric former soldier named Malcolm Wheeler-Nicholson were running a company called National Allied Publications. Donenfeld and

Liebowitz had previously been in the pornography trade but were trying to clean up their act during a swell of interest in the newly invented kids' medium of comic books. They hired Siegel and Shuster to do work for them—mostly crime stories—and in November 1937, desperate for content to pay some massive debts, National picked up Superman from the slush pile. Siegel and Shuster's previously unseen work was tossed into *Action Comics* No. 1, the comic sold 900,000 copies, and a gold rush began.

Within months, every publisher in New York was scrambling to come up with the next big superhero. A cavalcade of young, artistically inclined, almost solely Jewish New Yorkers were happy to help. Three of the biggest minds in the nascent genre were from the Bronx and had all attended DeWitt Clinton High School: Batman co-creators Bob Kane and Bill Finger, and the Spirit's creator, Will Eisner. Lower East Side street tough Jack Kirby (né Jacob Kurtzberg) joined up with Rochester boychik Joe Simon to concoct Captain America for National's rival, Timely (a company that had just hired another DeWitt Clinton alumnus, young writer Stanley Lieber, who preferred to sign his work "Stan Lee"). A rare exception to the New York Yiddishkeit pedigree of the early superheroes was the Wasp-created Captain Marvel, who briefly outshone Superman in sales but was eventually clobbered by a lawsuit from National's successor, DC Comics. Men like the publishers Victor Fox and Jerry Iger established artistic assembly lines (some even called them sweatshops) to crank out superhero content. The characters conquered radio, film serials, and cartoons, becoming the vanguard of contemporary entertainment, their good-and-evil worldviews suited to the wartime national mind-set.

It didn't last forever—superheroes fell out of favor after World War II, and a moral panic about comic books led to an industry collapse in the 1950s. But in the 1960s, Kirby, Lee, and writer-artist Steve Ditko took the helm of Timely's successor, the Madison Avenue–based Marvel Comics, and revitalized the superhero genre with now-legendary characters like Spider-Man, the Avengers, and the X-Men. Superheroes have waxed and waned since then, but they remain a staple of modern storytelling and iconography, as evidenced by the explosion of their Hollywood adaptations. But New York City remains the environment in which the characters most often thrive: Spidey swings from the Empire State Building, and though Batman may patrol Gotham City and Superman soars above Metropolis, everyone knows what burg the two stand for.

Supermarket

When the Smithsonian Institution tried a few years back to decide what the first supermarket was, it came up with a set of criteria: It had to be big, probably part of a chain; it had to put all its specialties (butchery, baked goods, produce) under one roof; it had to aim for low prices and high volume; and, unlike the typical retail experience of a hundred years ago, it had to let you shop by yourself, without a clerk who took things down from the shelves at your request. A number of businesses—A&P, Piggly Wiggly—deployed one or another of these methods, but the first store that hit every one of those benchmarks opened in a former garage on Jamaica Avenue in Queens on August 4, 1930, and it was called King Kullen. (The founder, Michael Cullen, took the new spelling from a drawing his little boy had made.) The store was petite by today's standards but significantly larger than its competitors. The Cullens had a fast-moving success on their hands, opening seventeen stores in six years, and when Michael died in 1936, his wife, Nan, took over. Although today it's far smaller than the national chains, King Kullen is still going, with 32 stores scattered around Long Island. Its ownership stayed in the family until 2019, when the Cullens sold it to Stop & Shop.

Superpremium Ice Cream

Standard-issue ice cream, the kind sold in supermarkets by the half-gallon, is about 10 percent butterfat, and more than half its volume is legally allowed to be air (which is incorporated during churning to lighten and bulk up the product by as much as 120 percent). "Premium" ice cream, per FDA rules, has 12 to 14 percent butterfat and not as much air. In 1961, however, a Brooklyn couple, Reuben and Rose Mattus, began marketing a product classified as superpremium: 15 to 16 percent butterfat and only about 20 percent overrun (the industry term for the quantity of air). They made up a fake Scandinavian name, Häagen-Dazs, and even put a map of Denmark on the carton, citing its clean reputation and its history as a haven for refugees during the Holocaust. (The Mattuses were enthusiastic Zionists.) The brand went national in the early 1970s, and its niche soon grew and attracted competitors, notably the Vermonters Ben Cohen and Jerry Greenfield, another excellent fake-Scandinavian brand called Frusen Glädjé, and various folksy labels like Steve's Ice Cream. The Mattuses sold their company to Pillsbury in 1983, and today it's part of General Mills.

Suspension Bridge

You can go only so far with stone, wood, bronze, and iron. To span a river more than a quarter-mile wide, you need steel, with its high tensile strength relative to its weight and the ductility that allows it to be stretched and spun into cables. The man who brought that principle to the East River was John Roebling, an engineer whose family wireworks in Trenton, New Jersey, had built iron-cable bridges in Niagara Falls, Pittsburgh, and Cincinnati. In 1867 he began work on his final, greatest project, designed to join the then-separate cities of Brooklyn and Manhattan. This would be the first steel-cable bridge, and it was immense—1,600 feet between the two towers. Before building began, while Roebling was surveying the site, his foot was crushed by a ferryboat that had bumped into a Brooklyn dock. The consequent infection killed him. He never saw a single bit of his bridge built.

His son Washington picked up the job, and construction began on the bridge's tower footings, called caissons, in 1870. As they were burrowed down into the riverbed, Washington too was almost fatally sickened on the job with "caisson disease," a.k.a. the bends, caused by the high air pressure within them. His wife, Emily, took over as the bridge's ad hoc chief engineer, relaying his instructions and doing significant parts of the work herself as he watched the stonework rise and the steel spread across the river from his sickroom window. The Brooklyn Bridge went wildly over its cost estimates, bankrupted its parent company, was engulfed in scandals over substandard steel, and had been called a giant boondoggle and swindle by the time it opened in May 1883.

The memory of its difficult birth has long since faded. Brooklyn grudgingly merged with the other four boroughs in 1898, and those big steel main cables (the same ones Roebling's workers put up by hand in the 1870s) still bear New Yorkers across the water on foot or in a taxi. So do their technological descendants on the Williamsburg, Manhattan, George Washington, Bronx-Whitestone, Throgs Neck, Robert F. Kennedy Triborough, and Verrazzano-Narrows bridges.

Sweet'n Low

Ben Eisenstadt, a Brooklyn cafeteria operator who founded the Cumberland Packing Company to make tea bags in 1945, did not discover saccharin. That had been the work of the Johns Hopkins University chemistry professor (and, later, president) Ira Remsen and his assistant Constantin Fahlberg in 1879. Nor was saccharin the only artificial sweetener around: There's a whole class of chemicals called cyclamates, among others, that taste like sugar. What was invented in Brooklyn was the packaging, manufacturing, distribution, and branding that turned these lab curiosities into a globally available, easy-to-use consumer product.

In the late 1940s, Eisenstadt had expanded his company into the business of producing little packets of various things, including sugar, and realized in 1957 that there was a demand for a calorie-free sweetener. He and his son Marvin, who had studied chemistry, combined cyclamates with a few other ingredients, figured out how to make the result granular and non-clumping, and, in a masterstroke of product identity, made its packets a distinctive pink, instantly recognizable on a coffee-shop table. A dozen years later, when cyclamate consumption was connected to cancer in lab tests and banned in the U.S., he reformulated Sweet'N Low to use saccharin. Five hundred billion of those pink packets have since come out of Cumberland-affiliated factories, including the original one near the Brooklyn Navy Yard, which kept running its ancient machinery until 2016. Since then, the packing has moved to other locations, although Cumberland's headquarters remains across from the Navy Yard, on the site of Ben Eisenstadt's long-gone restaurant. His family still owns the company.

Synthesizer

One day in 1958, a truck drove from Princeton, New Jersey, to a converted milk-bottling plant on West 125th Street and unloaded a dozen refrigerator-size metal boxes crammed with circuits, oscillators, and vacuum tubes: RCA Mark II synthesizers. The story of electronic music stretches back to the nineteenth century, but that special delivery and the establishment of the Columbia-Princeton Electronic Music Center mark the moment when composers had the tools to generate new sounds, even entire works, from scratch, rather than manipulating notes and noises that exist only in physical space.

In a spasm of utopian inventiveness, RCA had developed a machine that, the *Times* breathlessly reported in 1955, "can synthesize musical sounds which a trained ear cannot differentiate from records made by a good pianist." That was hogwash: Even an untrained ear could tell that the engineers' best efforts produced a limited range of tinny bleeps. But just as the company was writing off the effort as an unprofitable experiment, avant-garde musicians saw a new frontier. RCA provided the technology, Columbia the real estate. Soon, a corps of patient and enthusiastic composers, including Milton Babbitt, Vladimir Ussachevsky, and Mario Davidovsky began translating their musical thoughts into holes punched in a roll of paper.

The Mark II was the first fully programmable music synthesizer, which meant a composer could control all of a sound's qualities. Frequency, volume, duration, timbre, attack, decay—each parameter required a different turn of a knob. Though the process was laborious, the machine could perform music of infinite complexity. Rhythm no longer depended on the speed of a musician's fingers or the ability to divide a beat into seven, thirteen, or nineteen pulses. The synthesizer could slide between distant notes, add reverb, play multiple tones at different volumes, and perform whatever other variations its control-freak musical masters could think up.

Among the arty engineering types who gravitated to Columbia's windowless room was Robert Moog, who in 1964 would go on to invent a synthesizer that a musician could fit into the back of a station wagon and operate with a piano keyboard. The system depended on two elements: the transistor and the standardized module, which allowed players to make music in real time without being forced to make decisions about every facet of every sound. Moog was the first to adapt the esoteric experiments of the Mark II's high priests for the commercial and popular world. He was not the last—a direct line of influence and experimentation runs from the room-size behemoth on 125th Street to the GarageBand app on an iPhone.

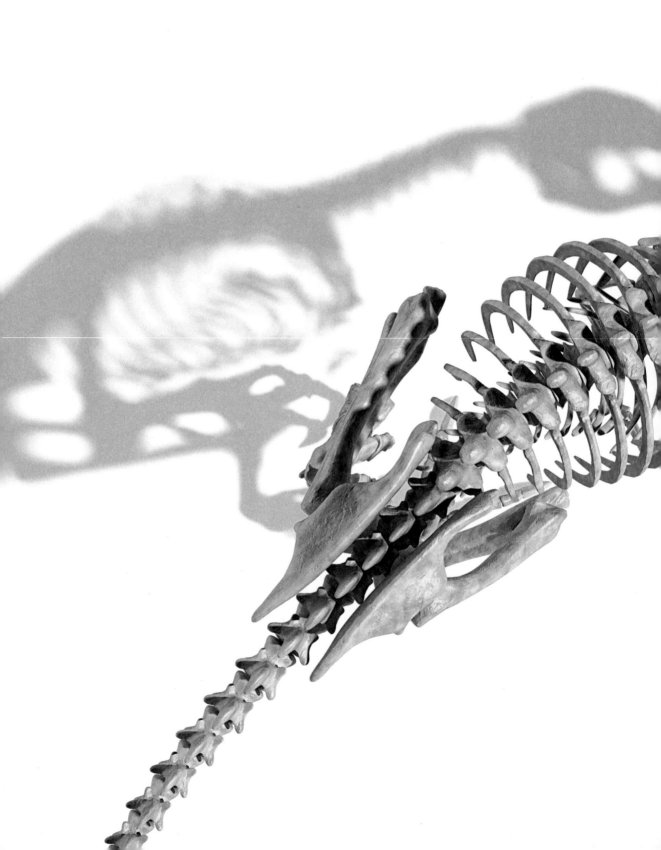

From
TABLOID NEWSPAPER
to
TYRANNOSAURUS REX

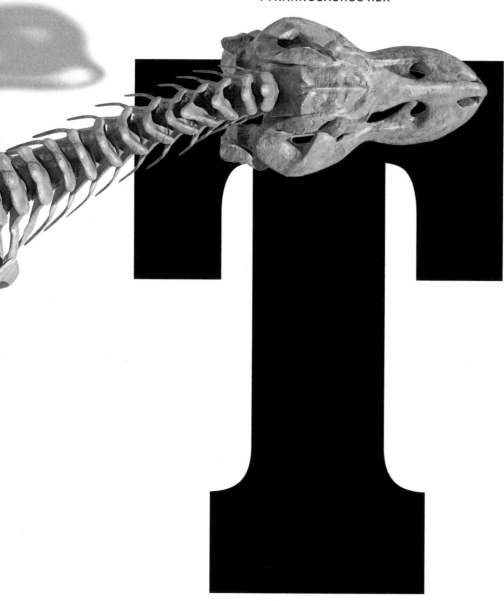

Tyrannosaurus rex: It got its name
on the Upper West Side.

Tabloid Newspaper

The tabloid newspaper—half the size of a broadsheet and (usually) without the horizontal fold across the middle—was born with the twentieth century. In 1900, the New York *World* was arguably the most inventive paper in America, featuring elaborate color illustrations and a sensational approach to the news (*see also* YELLOW JOURNALISM). When its publisher, Joseph Pulitzer, found himself in an experimental mood, he imported Alfred Harmsworth, the publisher of London's broadsheet *Daily Mail*, to guest-edit an edition of the *World*; the resulting January 1, 1901, paper carried an opening editorial offering "all the news in sixty seconds." Billed as "the newspaper of the future," it was printed in that new, smaller layout. "I claim that by my system of condensed or tabloid journalism," Harmsworth wrote, "hundreds of working hours can be saved each year." (The word *tabloid* was apparently meant to evoke pharmaceuticals, suggesting a tightly compressed and easily swallowed tablet.) He also implied that the twentieth century would eventually be covered by national newspapers, their contents transmitted between cities by wire and printed from coast to coast. Harmsworth soon went back to Britain, where in 1903 he founded the extremely successful national *Daily Mirror*, the world's first daily in the new format.

The tabloid didn't return to America until 1919, after a conversation atop a pile of manure. Or at least that's the story, and (as a news editor might say) it's too good to check. In the waning days of World War I, two American servicemen sat on a dung heap near a tiny French village. They were wealthy cousins; Colonel Robert McCormick was the publisher of the Chicago *Tribune*, and Joseph Medill Patterson was his Sunday editor. They saw an opportunity for a populist paper in New York, admired London's *Daily Mirror* (which had reached 800,000 in circulation and was still climbing), and saw in the new field of photojournalism a way of telling stories vividly to an audience that didn't read at length. The first issue of their New York *Daily News* rolled out on June 26, 1919, and within a few months they added the slogan *New York's Picture Newspaper*. It was not an instant success, but its readership soon grew, and in 1924 William Randolph Hearst started publishing an editorially similar competitor, New York's own

Daily Mirror. A third tabloid, the *Evening Graphic*, followed, capturing the bottom of the market with exceptionally lurid scandal coverage (*see also* GOSSIP COLUMN). They were well suited to the city in one particular way: Being less broad than a broadsheet, they could be read on a packed subway without spreading one's arms wide.

The *Graphic* was eventually sued out of business, but over the next decade the *News* and the *Mirror* became the two largest papers in the United States. Before 1939, they focused mostly on local stories—one longtime writer for the *News* said it contained "no foreign news at all except for an occasional story about the Prince of Wales falling off his horse"—but World War II made both papers more worldly, and although they were never in quite the same game as, say, the New York *Times*, by 1945 they were giant news organizations with hundreds of reporters. In 1947, the *Daily News* printed 2.3 million copies on weekdays and 4.7 million on Sundays, a figure no American paper will ever come close to matching again. Because it was so ubiquitous, New York paperboys who delivered the *News* used to note which houses did *not* subscribe rather than those that did.

In 1942, the New York *Post*—then a liberal, pro-union, moderately intellectual paper owned by Dorothy Schiff—switched from broadsheet format to tabloid. Before long every major American city had one: the Los Angeles *Daily News*, the Boston *American*, the Chicago *Daily Times*. In the 1950s, the wildly downscale *National Enquirer* joined the pack, and before long it and its imitators were selling millions of copies a week on usually well-sourced but often wildly exaggerated scandals. As television began to edge in on this business, the word *tabloid* was increasingly used to describe a type of news rather than a physical paper size, and the U.S. clearly had an endless appetite for it. We were, and are, a tabloid nation—and not the only one, either.

In 1976, the tabloid landscape was transformed when Schiff sold the *Post* to Rupert Murdoch. Its leftism and upper-middlebrow qualities had somewhat eroded by then, but none of that had prepared readers for the transgressive paper that soon appeared. Its coverage of urban chaos (*see also* MAYHEM)—the Son of Sam killings, the rising crime rates, a sense that the city was spinning out of control—was reflected in its headlines, most famously the one about a murder in a Queens

Mayor Abe Beame with the quintessential Daily News *front page, October 1975.*

PHOTOGRAPH BY
BILL STAHL JR.

saloon that read HEADLESS BODY IN TOPLESS BAR. *Post* lore holds that after the story came in, editor V. A. Musetto wrote the headline and dispatched a reporter to make sure the bar was indeed a topless joint; when the call came back that she'd seen a sign there promoting "Topless Dancing Tonight," the newsroom erupted in cheers. Even after Murdoch sold the paper in 1988, its Murdochian vibe remained intact.

By then, both tabloids had jumped into the gossip business in a big way, covering the likes of Leona Helmsley and Donald and Ivana Trump (*see also* TRUMPISM). Conventional wisdom held that the *News* was serious if loudmouthed and the *Post* was the wild-eyed maniac in the room. In truth, both were facing headwinds—largely from TV news, which had also gotten into the if-it-bleeds-it-leads game—and both became shakier as businesses. In the early 1990s, each went through a near-death experience and ended up with a wildly inappropriate owner. The *Daily News* went to a British billionaire named Robert Maxwell, who turned out to be a con man; the *Post*, after a bankruptcy, went to the financier Steven Hoffenberg and a parking-garage magnate named Abe Hirschfeld, who turned out to be, respectively, a crook and a nut. Relative sanity returned after Mortimer Zuckerman bought the *News* and the *Post* went back to Murdoch.

Their editors spent the next two decades trying to beat one another, keeping the race going. But as the internet arrived, neither paper was great at digital news for way too long. Layoffs came, followed by losses and more layoffs as circulation eroded dramatically. In July 2019, as the *News* staggered to its 100th birthday, its reporting staff was down to about 40 people (perhaps 10 percent of what it once had been) and its daily print run to around 200,000 copies (ditto). Each paper's survival plan seemed to be waiting for the other to die. Most American cities are now down to a single newspaper, often a Gannett broadsheet that shares a lot of its content with other Gannett broadsheets. Only in London do the "red-top" print tabloids—so called for the color behind their logos—seem to be a sound business.

Although the tabloid-newspaper era is pretty clearly coming to a close, the tabloid-news era is not nearly ending, because that ethos absolutely dominates the public discourse. We read about celebrities everywhere, and there's an entire paparazzi-industrial complex built on semi-invasive pictures of them. The *National Enquirer* itself may be dying, but TMZ has picked up its irresistible formula and run with it. When a New York gossip-column fixture turned reality-TV-show host gets elected to the presidency of the United States, we are unmistakably living in the world the tabloids created. We're all sitting on that manure pile now.

Tap Dancing

What makes tap dancing tap dancing? Depending on your answer to that—the isolation of the feet and lower legs, syncopated patterns, bravura steps, the clattering metal-bottomed shoes—you'll come up with a different family tree for the art. The truth is that tap has tangled roots, many of which dive down into American plantation earth. That's where enslaved people performed African dances (including Igbo percussive dancing and the *gioube*), sometimes in celebration or resistance, sometimes at the command of white masters who staged "breakdown" competitions for their own entertainment. Taproots also reach back to Ireland, land of rat-a-tat step dancing, and still others stretch to Northern England, where clog dancing emerged in Lancashire's mining towns. As long ago as the sixteenth century, indentured servants and enslaved people were exchanging moves, rhythms, and forms.

But it was in New York that the techniques cohered into tap. In the nineteenth century, in the Lower East Side slum known as the Five Points, poor Irish and free Black solo performers were able to swap knowledge: Anglo-Irish jigs melded with West African styles in halls where the two groups danced together. Both Black and white minstrel performers had long been doing what were called "Ethiopian" buck-and-wing dances. Yet the artist whom academics credit with fusing loose upper-body tempos to precision footwork was African-American—the Five Points dancer William Henry Lane, known as Master Juba and as King of All Dancers (after he defeated a white minstrel dancer in competition). He was globally famous: Charles Dickens wrote a delirious description of a performance he witnessed in New York ("dancing with two left legs, two right legs, two wooden legs, two wire legs, two spring legs—all sorts of legs and no legs—what is this to him?"), and Lane toured internationally throughout the 1840s with white minstrel groups. His prestige and virtuosity elevated the form, and his innovations—the way he used different parts of the foot, for instance—laid the groundwork for tap today.

Even the name of the style may have originated in New York. In the 1890s, the white comedian, dance director, and pianist Ned Wayburn—billed as "the Man Who Invented Ragtime"—came to the city from Chicago. In 1902 he produced Ned Wayburn's Minstrel Misses, an all-girl act that used blackface and split-sole clogs; he advertised them as performing "tap and step dancing." (So many documents have been lost it's uncertain who first used the word *tap*, but many credited Wayburn for coining it—and he accepted that credit unhesitatingly.) Wayburn went on to choreograph for the Ziegfeld Follies, and indeed, Ziegfeld occasionally bought (and then recast) entire all-Black musical revues, as he did in 1913 with J. Leubrie Hill's *Darktown Follies*. By this point, metal-plated shoes were de rigueur for Broadway hoofers, and tap dance was also firmly ensconced on the vaudeville circuits. When stars like Bill "Bojangles" Robinson, Fred Astaire, and the Nicholas Brothers appeared in films in the 1930s and '40s, tap cemented its keystone place in the culture.

Teddy Bear

The teddy in question was the president of the United States, and the original bear was very much alive. On November 14, 1902, Theodore Roosevelt was on a hunting trip in Mississippi that had yielded no success. His local assistants eventually turned up a black bear, tied it to a tree, and marched their guest in to shoot it. Roosevelt refused, thinking it unsportsmanlike; newspaper reporters picked up the story and ran with it all over the country, as did Clifford Berryman, a cartoonist who drew the scene for the Washington *Post*.

That cartoon eventually made its way to a Brooklyn couple named Morris and Rose Michtom, who (in addition to owning a candy shop) made stuffed animals. They created a bear to sell and got permission from the White House to call it "Teddy's bear." The Michtoms'

immediately successful product was the first smash hit for what eventually became the Ideal Toy Company, whose later successes included the game Mouse Trap, the Betsy Wetsy doll, and Rubik's Cube.

Telephone

Alexander Graham Bell, right? Not really. In 1870, six years before Bell submitted his patent declaration, Antonio Meucci, an Italian immigrant in the Rosebank area of Staten Island, reportedly transmitted a voice signal a full mile via copper wire. He'd already been successful as an inventor (medical devices, smokeless candles), and a year later, he filed a "patent caveat"—not a full application but essentially a declaration of intent to do so—for his *telettrofono* and set up a company.

It soon collapsed, as two of his partners departed and another died. The patent caveat expired after a year, and Meucci was too broke to renew it. He built a demonstration of his system for an oceangoing diver in 1873, after which his project stalled again. Three years later, after Bell put in his own patent application, Meucci tried and failed to challenge it, and that was that.

Curiously, Meucci is remembered in New York less for his claim to telephonic fame than for one of his friendships: Before he came to America, he'd been associated with Giuseppe Garibaldi, the politician who established modern unified Italy. In the 1850s, Garibaldi spent a few years in the United States and lived in Meucci's house in Rosebank. That house still exists—Meucci is interred on the grounds, in fact—and it's known as the Garibaldi-Meucci Museum. Its telephone number is 718-442-1608.

Television Commercial

Appropriately enough, the first images broadcast in the first official moments of commercial television were an advertisement. On July 1, 1941, at 2:29 p.m., just before a cut to a live game at Ebbets Field (Brooklyn vs. Philadelphia), an image of a Bulova clock appeared in the lower quadrant of the WNBT test pattern. The watchmaker's branded time checks were already well established on radio, and its ad agency, the Blow Company, was ready to adapt these for the new medium. Bulova paid $9 to place the nine-second ad, which was broadcast from the network's studio in Manhattan. Although Bulova has the honor of being first, that day featured several other sponsors as well, including Sun Oil Co. and Lever Brothers' Spry shortening, who paid up to $100 for more involved spots.

The Bulova ad was simple to display. Much of the rehearsal time the day before had been spent on an advertisement for Ivory soap, scheduled to run with the game show *Truth or Consequences*. That soap commercial, which featured WNBT announcer Ed Herlihy, included the first televised images of dishpan hands, and an actress informing viewers how to prevent them.

Television Network

Early network television was the product of many fits and starts. Broadcast images were being tested as far back as 1927, when then–Secretary of Commerce Herbert Hoover gave a speech in the laboratory of the American Telephone and Telegraph Company in Washington, D.C. "Today, we have, in a sense, the transmission of sight for the first time in the world's history," he declared. The next day's New York *Times* noted that "at times the face of the Secretary could not be clearly distinguished."

Experiments with long-distance broadcasting became more regular in 1941, when the proto-NBC TV station WNBT started relaying broadcasts from its Manhattan studio to the General Electric–owned station in Schenectady, New York, and later to the Philco station in Philadelphia. The picture quality on those was also pretty poor; the Schenectady station picked up the Manhattan signal from the air and rebroadcast it, significantly degrading the images. In 1945, the DuMont network linked its New York studio with its second studio in D.C. via coaxial cable, creating more robust, reliable long-distance programming.

As television grew profitable in the late '40s, CBS and ABC joined DuMont and NBC, each building networks of television affiliates operating from a central New York transmitter. As a result, national TV had a local New York bias from the start. The event largely considered to have proved the long-term use value and popularity of network television was the 1947 World Series, in which the New York Yankees played the Brooklyn Dodgers. Nearly 4 million people watched the NBC broadcast in New York, Schenectady, D.C., and Philadelphia.

Tenement [1]

In parts of the U.K., *tenement* just means "apartment building." In the U.S., however, it refers to a certain kind of apartment building constructed to house poor, often immigrant residents and having a narrow street frontage, a deep profile, and very little natural light. When tenements started to appear, around the 1830s, they were New York's first purpose-built multiple dwellings and were considered horrible even at the time—crowded from the start, overcrowded soon after. A 150-family complex called Gotham Court, built as a speculative venture at 36–38 Cherry Street in 1851, was regarded as a particularly awful example, filthy and riddled with smallpox.

Over the next couple of decades, thousands of tenement buildings were raised, the preponderance of them up and down the edges of Manhattan and all over the Lower East Side. Many were filled with windowless bedrooms that were often linked in a "railroad flat" arrangement, one after the other, in such a way that virtually no resident had any privacy. In many cases, a second, similar tenement was put up in the backyard of the first, reachable only by going through the street-facing building and out its back door. "Backhouses," these were called. They were not nice places to live, but they capably squeezed even more monthly rents out of one small plot of land.

Eventually, reformers got involved, and laws were passed in 1867 and 1871 mandating fire escapes, minimal backyards, and ceilings at least eight feet high. Subsequent proposals offered the so-called dumbbell tenement, designed with narrow courtyards acting as air shafts between buildings; these further reforms were enshrined in the New Law, enacted in 1901. Many hundreds of buildings taking that form went up in Manhattan, Brooklyn, the Bronx, and Queens over the next couple of decades, and by 1905, the Lower East Side's Seventeenth Ward housed 648 people to the acre—roughly four times its population density today—making for the most intensely crowded living conditions in the history of the United States. Only when immigration was cut off by the federal government in 1924 did the construction of tenements peter out. After World War II, New York began demolishing blocks of them to construct high-rise housing projects, which, though airier and more spacious, sometimes cemented those neighborhoods as islands of poverty.

Tenements on Mott Street in Chinatown, 1941.

PHOTOGRAPHY BY CHARLES W. CUSHMAN
COLLECTION: INDIANA UNIVERSITY ARCHIVES

① **The Most Interesting Object at the Lower East Side Tenement Museum**

Chosen by the museum's curators

"A can of **Durkee's Curry Powder,** sold between 1918 and 1935, was discovered during the 2008 restoration and conservation work to create the Tenement Museum's 'Irish Outsiders' tour. The preliminary assumption had been that curry powder was primarily a North African, South Asian, or Asian spice. Why was it found in an apartment at **97 Orchard Street,** which, during this period, was home to immigrants primarily from Eastern and Southern Europe?

"Through subsequent research, we learned that curry powder has a long history in the United States, with popularity as far back as the

---

The tenement nonetheless endures as housing in the preponderance of New York neighborhoods, its ancient gaslights long since electrified and its globby corridor walls given yet another coat of paint. One example from the 1860s has been impeccably preserved on Orchard Street as the Tenement Museum, which exhibits the chipped and worn rooms as residents lived in them, down to the washtubs and teakettles. Others have been remade, some of them to an absurd degree of luxury. On Minetta Street in Greenwich Village, an Old Law tenement dating to 1883 that once held twenty families has been gut-renovated into a single-family home. After a protracted legal battle with nine tenants who did not want to be evicted, another tenement building on East 3rd Street recently became a mansion of 11,600 square feet. The family dining room seats twenty-six.

Theater *see* BROADWAY; MUSICAL THEATER

3-D Movie

You can create the illusion of three dimensions onscreen in several ways, but all of them, broadly speaking, involve two images taken from slightly different angles, mimicking the binocular images sent to the brain by a person's two eyes. Superimpose them, figure out how to get one of them to go to one eye and one to the other, and the cerebral cortex handles the rest.

The most straightforward 3-D moviemaking method is known as the anaglyph system. It involves a pair of red and green (or sometimes blue) filters, worn as glasses, and matching red-and-green-filtered onscreen images, and it was first demonstrated at the Astor Theatre in Times Square in June 1915 by Edwin S. Porter and William E. Waddell, who ran a little film of some dancing girls and footage of Niagara Falls.

New York can also take partial credit for the better

3-D glasses that are still used for some Hollywood blockbusters. They depend on a thin plastic filter known as a sheet polarizer, patented by Dr. Edwin Land in 1929 and commercialized a few years later under the name Polaroid. (Yes, that Polaroid. The instant cameras came along a few years later.) The company's laboratories were in Cambridge, Massachusetts—Land was a Harvard dropout—but a number of his technical breakthroughs took place while he was working in a lab at Columbia and living on the Upper West Side. Moreover,

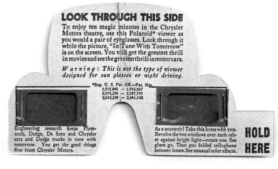

3-D glasses issued to watch a film at the Chrysler Pavilion, New York World's Fair, 1939.

mid-nineteenth century. As early as 1876, recipes featuring it started to appear in the New York *Times*, indicating at least some common knowledge of the dishes as well as its general availability.

"What does this all mean? The discovery suggests that some recently arrived immigrants engaged with American mass-consumer food culture during the early twentieth century. Despite their limited discretionary income, **the purchase of seemingly 'exotic' spices was not beyond the reach of the immigrants who lived at 97 Orchard.** They were aware of and participated in culinary trends, adapting to their new home by both maintaining their own traditions and incorporating new ones. It also suggests the early-twentieth-century immigrants were finding a sort of common ground with neighbors of differing origins by participating in food trends that crossed boundaries of class and culture."

---

the first big application of his invention to moviemaking was demonstrated at the Chrysler Corporation pavilion of the 1939 New York World's Fair in Flushing, Queens. There, moviegoers could sit through a promotional film showing Plymouths and Dodges coming together, in three dimensions, on the assembly line. In the early 1950s, when 3-D films became a huge fad for a year or two, Polaroid supplied most of the glasses to movie theaters, giving its bottom line a huge bump before the craze cooled down.

Ticker

The stock ticker was created by a damp and irritated man. In 1867 Edward A. Calahan, while working as a telegraph operator at New York's Western Union offices, ducked into a doorway during a rainstorm only to be continually shoved back out into the rain by the endless flow of messenger boys bearing stock-price updates. He passed the soggy time thinking a telegraph signal would do the job better, and he went on to render those messenger boys obsolete by inventing a machine that supplied a printout of continuously updated stock and gold prices on a ribbon of paper tape. He soon sold his patent to a manufacturer for the enormous sum of $100,000, bought himself a nice house on Cumberland Street in Brooklyn, and subsequently patented and developed further improvements to his invention, including multiplex systems of ganged stock tickers. The paper-tape stock ticker has long since gone obsolete, of course, but its digital descendant continues to run on computer screens and across the bottom of cable-financial-news television shows throughout the workday.

Ticker-Tape Parade

The stock ticker (*see above*) printed its output on paper tape, half an inch wide, supplied on big rolls. At the end of a workday, offices on Wall Street (*see also* WALL STREET) were piled high with discarded tangles of it. On October 28, 1886, following the dedication of the Statue of Liberty, a parade made its way down Fifth Avenue and Broadway to the Battery, and on Wall Street, some young finance bros took action. "All this display was an inspiration to so many imps of office boys," wrote the *Times*, "who, from a hundred windows began to unreel the spools of tape that record the fateful messages of the 'ticker.' In a moment the air was white with curling streamers … This was altogether too much fun, and the office boys had to give way to their elders. More and more of the tape went skimming through the air. It was dangled in the faces of solemn horsemen; it was jiggled tantalizingly just out of the reach of the college youth, and the pretty country cousins were tickled under the chin with carefully directed points until they screamed in feminine alarm. There was seemingly no end to it. Every window appeared to be a paper mill spouting out squirming lines of tape. Such was Wallstreet's novel celebration."

Ten years later, the *Times* reported that people did the same to mark the election of the pro-business president William McKinley. Within a few years, the ticker-tape parade up Broadway—through the "Canyon of Heroes"—became a regular celebration, held to mark the return of a pioneering pilot or a sports champion or a visiting dignitary. In 1928 alone there were seven parades. Arguably the biggest marked V-J Day, the end of World War II, after which the city's Sanitation department swept up 5,438 tons of paper.

The parades happen less frequently than they used to, and Wall Street's tickers have long since gone electronic, using no paper tape. (In the 1980s, finance

A ticker-tape blizzard welcomes John Glenn back from orbit, March 1, 1962.
PHOTOGRAPH BY
TED RUSSELL

297

workers were known to tear up old phone books and throw those out the windows, but those are gone now, too.) Also, most of the postwar office buildings in the financial district have sealed windows, so you have to go up on the roof to throw confetti. Still, despite the impediments, whenever a hero's safe return is celebrated, the Yankees win the World Series, or the U.S. women's soccer team wins the World Cup, a scattering of paper still rains down, made from streamers bought for the occasion or documents put through the shredder.

Times Square

In 1811 a state commission drew up the numbered Manhattan street grid as we know it, specifying rows that marched in orderly succession uptown from the untidy tangle of Greenwich Village (*see also* GRID, STREET). Because it sliced diagonally across the rectilinear blocks of the plan, Broadway created bow tie–shaped intersections at several street-and-avenue crossings, including 42nd and Seventh. A number of carriage-makers set up shop there as the nineteenth century progressed, and the area became known as Longacre Square, after a similar district in London. Other businesses began to spring up nearby too, notably brothels but also theaters and other live entertainment. In 1904, after the New York *Times* (*see also* NEW YORK *TIMES*, THE) built its new headquarters at the south end of the bow tie, the IRT subway opened with a Times Square stop and the crossroads received its new name. On New Year's Eve 1907, a crew marked the stroke of midnight by lowering an illuminated ball on the Times Tower's rooftop flagpole, and apart from a wartime pause, it has happened every year since.

By the 1920s, Times Square had established itself as the hub of the city, where theatergoers (*see also* BROADWAY; MUSICAL THEATER), transit lines, and immense numbers of pedestrians and businesses crossed paths. A continuously lit sign known as "the zipper," wrapped around One Times Square starting in 1928, became a gathering spot where people watched and waited for the latest bulletins during breaking-news events. The area was simultaneously glamorous and seedy, with movie palaces and grind houses on the same blocks, a place where Damon Runyon's raffish *Guys and Dolls* characters were drawn from real life. The theaters (both

live and cinema) already had large display marquees, and they were increasingly joined by billboards and other illuminated signs (*see also* ILLUMINATED ADVERTISING SIGN). Most were built by a company called Artkraft Strauss, and the biggest were called "spectaculars," some not merely lighted but animated: A Camel cigarette billboard blew actual smoke rings, Planters' Mr. Peanut waggled his neon cane, and an enormous Pepsi ad incorporated a waterfall. Piccadilly Circus and Ginza and the Las Vegas Strip had some neon extravagance, but nothing had quite the gorgeous, commercial, breathtakingly vulgar ebullience of Times Square. It was tacky and truly beautiful all at once, a global symbol of all that was good and bad about American capitalism.

Which made it doubly poignant when it started to go downhill. The 1960s and '70s saw the district's old seediness descend into something else. Broadway theaters closed and were converted into TV studios and nightclubs. First-run movie houses became second-run theaters, and some of them began to run porn films. The sex trade came out of the shadows, as hustlers male and female worked openly on 42nd Street. So did drug sellers and muggers. Times Square was flat-out dangerous, and filthy to boot (*see also* MAYHEM). A couple of hotels and office towers were built in hopes of revitalization, but they had a modest effect at best and cost the city some great old buildings in the process. Plans came and went to redevelop the area, at least one of which would have wiped out most of its signage in favor of gray office towers.

After significant intervention by the city and state, several new skyscrapers did indeed rise along Broadway and nearby but under new ordinances—specific to Times Square—requiring them to bear many square feet of illuminated signage. In the 1990s, most of the theaters along 42nd Street were restored, and others were selectively rebuilt with their architectural elements combined. National retailers proliferated, opening stores (including, later, one devoted entirely to M&M's) that served essentially as walk-in billboards, advertising their contents to tourists. One of the oldest Broadway theaters in the neighborhood, the New Amsterdam, erected in 1903, had been a ruin, its roof open to the sky; after massive restoration efforts by the Walt Disney Company, it reopened in 1997 and soon became home to the musical *The Lion King*. In fact, "the new Times Square," as it came to be known, was suddenly faced with a fresh criticism: It had been, people said, deracinated, delocalized, "Disneyfied." Never mind that the glitz in Times Square's (first) heyday was considered just as tacky then, and that there isn't a substantive difference between flashy twentieth-century ads for Admiral televisions and even flashier twenty-first-century ads for Samsung televisions. It was a place where jaded New Yorkers could roll their eyes and complain about the tawdriness of it all while fighting to keep it that way. That was never more evident than when, during the COVID-19 crisis of 2020, photographs of a deserted Times Square drove home the drama of a shut-down city (*see also* QUARANTINE).

Tin Pan Alley

Many of the composers and lyricists behind the Great American Songbook got their start banging on out-of-tune pianos on one block of West 28th Street, between Sixth Avenue and Broadway. From the 1880s up to the Great Depression, this stretch, known as Tin Pan Alley, was home to the city's thriving sheet-music business. Dozens of music publishers packed the block, with three or four companies sometimes dividing up a single brownstone. (Nobody quite knows where the name Tin Pan Alley originated, but it was likely connected to the din coming from the buildings' open windows on warm afternoons.) This was a time before phonographs or home radios, and Tin Pan Alley churned out hundreds of songs not only for the city's nightlife performers but also for the amateur musicians who entertained their families in living rooms across the country.

Each publisher employed a staff of songwriters to produce music and lyrics in a range of styles, from ragtime to operetta to ballad. Musicians called "song pluggers" would then play the new tunes in those Tin Pan Alley shops, hoping to sell them to performers looking for new material. In 1914, when George Gershwin dropped out of high school, he landed a job as a song plugger at the Jerome H. Remick music company, at 45 West 28th Street; there, he sold an early composition to Fred Astaire. Irving Berlin, Oscar Hammerstein II, and Cole Porter were all Tin Pan Alley mainstays. As the industry took off, demand for new music was fierce, but not everybody could write like Gershwin. "I want some radishes and olives, speckled trout and cantaloupe and

cauliflower," went the lyrics to a song recorded by Stella Mayhew. "Some mutton broth and deviled crabs and clams and Irish stew."

Tin Pan Alley–style songwriting went out of style at mid-century, with the rise of rock and roll and then the all-in-one singer-songwriter. But its factory approach to music continued into the early rock and R&B era (*see also* BRILL BUILDING), and today drives Nashville's country-music production lines as well as pop hit-making.

Toilet Paper

"Gayetty's Medicated Paper. For the Water Closet," read the ad in the New York *Times*, published in 1858. "Cures and Prevents Piles." Until Joseph Gayetty came around, one might have used that very newspaper on a trip to the outhouse, or a page from a mail-order catalogue or perhaps the tissue sheets that had cushioned oranges in their crates. (Though there is evidence of luxury toilet-paper production in China as early as the sixth century A.D.) Starting in 1857, Gayetty began selling his soothing, scented wipes—he said they were dosed with "four grand medicines"—at his drugstore at 41 Ann Street. They were premium-priced, at $1 for a 1,000-sheet pack; their medical utility was ridiculed by doctors in print; and, as a commercial product, they soon disappeared down the pipes. The Scott brothers of Philadelphia, a couple of decades later, added the key innovation that began to turn TP into a middle-class household product: They put perforated sheets on a roll.

Tootsie Roll

Not chocolate, not chewing gum, not quite taffy, but in a fourth place approximately equidistant from those three, Tootsie Rolls were ostensibly invented in 1896 by Leo Hirschfeld, a Brooklyn candy-store operator who had arrived from Austria a dozen years earlier. In 1908 he got a patent for the process of boiling and stretching sugar that gives the candy its distinctive chewiness and ability to hold up in the heat. He gave it his daughter Clara's nickname, Tootsie. Around that time, he merged his business with a partnership called Stern & Saalberg on far West 45th Street. (Some research suggests that the Brooklyn-candy-store origin story may have been cooked up after the fact, to disguise the Tootsie Roll's corporate

origins.) All three men grew wealthy. But according to the persuasive detective work of the historian Samira Kawash, Hirschfeld made the breakthrough while already working for Stern & Saalberg, to whom he'd sold another patented invention, Bromangelon (*see also* JELL-O).

Hirschfeld eventually cashed out and started another candy company, which did not take off. But his signature product rolls on. S&S changed its name to the Sweets Company of America and then to Tootsie Roll Industries. Because Tootsie Rolls held up well in warm weather, they were included in field rations during World War II, and soldiers came back with a taste for them, cementing the brand's status as a bit of Americana. It is today headquartered in Chicago, still independently owned by a family that acquired it in 1935, and does about a half-billion dollars of business per year, making not only its namesake product but also Andes mints, Dubble Bubble gum, Dots, Charms, Charleston Chew, various other movie-theater treats, and (of course) Tootsie Pops.

Traffic Regulations[2]

If you've ever driven counterclockwise around a traffic circle, obeyed a speed limit, or crossed a street at the corner where the white stripes are, you've paid unwitting homage to William Phelps Eno. The scion of a wealthy real-estate family who didn't drive because he had a chauffeur to do it for him (he also preferred horseback riding), Eno came to be known as the Father of Traffic Safety. Alarmed at the motorized free-for-all that was taking over New York's streets, he issued a call to sanity in a 1900 article for *Rider and Driver* magazine headlined "Reforming Our Street Traffic Urgently Needed." One proposal seemed especially promising, though no one adopted it for another 15 years: putting a sign at intersections with the curt instruction to STOP. In 1903 Eno published *Rules for Driving*, in which he laid out

② **Three Traffic Rules Specific to New York**

1. There are no right turns on red. Unless there is a sign indicating you can do so, you must wait until the traffic light is green before making the turn.
2. In an attempt to halt traffic congestion, New York has cracked down on **"blocking the box."** In other words, if the light is about to change, don't drive into the middle of the intersection. You might be fined. And you're definitely in the way.
3. You may not be able to tell by the sound of things, but **"unnecessary honking"** is technically illegal and can carry a hefty fine.

directives that seem obvious now but were novelties then—signal before turning (with your hand stuck out the driver's-side window), drive on the right, engage the brake before leaving your vehicle unattended.

Eno, who was born before the Civil War and died after World War II, claimed that the course of his life had been shaped on a Manhattan street well before automobiles even existed. In 1867, when he was nine, he and his mother got caught in a snarl of horse-drawn carriages that took a dozen shouting drivers no less than half an hour to untangle. A few simple rules of the road would have prevented the problem and sped up its resolution, but they didn't exist. And a cop would have been just another hollering participant.

Once motorized vehicles arrived on the scene, bringing fresh dangers and new levels of congestion, Eno dedicated himself to the idea of imposing order on the streets, mostly so cars could speed along unimpeded. The police weren't always enthusiastic, because they believed a moderate amount of chaos prevented excessive speeds that would cause even greater chaos. (Cops did like one of his ideas: giving police the power to write tickets.) But resistance was futile. Automobiles took over the streets, and cities bent to their needs. Safety was redefined as the goal of getting a motor vehicle from point A to point B as quickly as possible with a minimum number of casualties (*see also* JAYWALKING; "WALK" SIGN).

In New York, that meant giving cars more space. Fifth Avenue was widened in 1910. In the 1920s, Park Avenue, a verdant pedestrian esplanade flanked by a single lane of roadway on either side, was turned into the multilane monster it is today. By then, Eno was a traffic sage, having created the Eno Foundation for Highway Traffic Regulation, based at his Connecticut estate, to carry on his work, while he branched out to transportation issues at sea and in the air. (In 1945 he warned that noise from low-flying planes would inflame the traumatized nerves of returning GIs.) He needn't have worried about his legacy: By the time he died, the job of reorganizing the landscape to benefit drivers had passed to far more powerful public figures.

Transistor

Bell Laboratories, the technology-research arm of AT&T, was created in 1925 in a building at 463 West Street (*see also* WESTBETH ARTISTS COMMUNITY). Over the next 60 years, it became a peerless institution from which the future was imagined in countless ways, its very large budget coming from the Bell System's monopolistic profit margins. By the 1930s, operations began to shift to New Jersey, where Bell's physicists could conduct delicate experiments in clean, silent environments, but the work moved back and forth between city and suburbs. And it was in those labs that perhaps the most significant invention of the twentieth century was born: the transistor.

Before 1948, virtually all electronic devices—anything that needed to amplify an electrical signal, whether audio, data, or some other type—required vacuum tubes. They were bulky, they were usually encased in glass and thus breakable, they required a lot of current (because they had to get warm to work), and they failed regularly. What came out of Bell Labs in 1948 was the first amplifier that required not a big glass bulb but a little chip of germanium, within the crystal structure of which the signal was amplified. "Solid state" was the term used for these devices, in opposition to the "hollow state" of a vacuum tube. The transistor was tiny—the size of a pea—and ran cool on very little power. Although multiple hands were involved in its invention and development, and various interstitial leaps were made by individual members of the team, the device was mainly the work of three scientists: John Bardeen, Walter Brattain, and the irascible William Shockley.

When Bell presented the new technology to the press on June 30, 1948, at the West Street building, its significance was seismic among scientists and engineers and largely lost on most everyone else. The New York *Times* buried a short note about it in the "News of the Radio" column, tenth among ten items, beneath such announcements as a schedule change for the "Waltz Time" program on NBC. The nontechnical world began to wise up only a few years later, when the first hearing aids and transistor radios came to market and big digital computers started to appear on the scene.

Shockley eventually left Bell Labs and went out to Palo Alto to found his own company, Shockley Semiconductor, a pioneering presence in Silicon Valley. His difficult personality—later revealed to manifest itself in rank racism—drove away his lead scientists, who started their own firm, Fairchild Semiconductor. Fairchild executives in turn created several other companies, the most successful of which is the global giant Intel Corporation. But the transistor—through its descendant, the silicon-based microprocessor—remains one of the most far-reaching, versatile, life-altering inventions of humanity. It ranks with the harnessing of fire and the domestication of agriculture. Virtually everything that is made today and powered up (see also RADIO BROADCASTING; TELEPHONE), from supercomputers to cars to coffeepots, is run through solid-state circuits. Without it, life as we know it would not exist.

Trotskyism

After participating in the failed 1905 Russian revolution, Leon Trotsky went into exile, hopping across Europe and eventually the Atlantic. Two months before the czar's overthrow in 1917, Trotsky had settled in the Bronx, paying $18 a month for an apartment on Vyse Avenue. He eked out a living writing for *Novyi Mir*, a Russian-emigré daily, and lecturing on all the newfangled methods American capitalism had for oppressing workers, singling out "disgusting candied gum," which workers chewed "like some silent prayer to God-Capital." The city at the time was teeming with radicals fresh off the boat from Europe working in sweatshops, and Trotsky helped spread antiwar propaganda, huddling with fellow exiles and soon-to-be Russian revolutionaries like Nikolai Bukharin, a Bolshevik who would die by Stalin's orders, and Alexandra Kollontai, who would help establish the Bolsheviks' socialist feminism.

Trotsky's relationship with New York was very much love-hate ("city of prose and fantasy, of capitalist automatism, its streets a triumph of cubism, its moral philosophy that of the dollar," he wrote in his autobiography), and he griped about the shocking poverty and "jammed" subway cars. Aside from Eugene Debs ("a sincere revolutionary"), he wasn't much impressed by American socialists, whom he saw as smug dilettantes. But in the city's capitalism he saw modernity's future, saying it had given him "a peep into the foundry in which the fate of man is to be forged." After three months, he headed back to Europe, where he went on to lead the Red Army to victory in the Russian Civil War. After Lenin's death, he was outmaneuvered by Stalin, and in 1940, Stalin's henchmen tracked Trotsky down in Mexico and sunk an ice ax into his skull.

First in his persecution and then after his death, Trotsky's ideas grew in prominence as "Trotskyism" gave a voice to progressive Americans who cheered the legacy of the October Revolution but were horrified by Stalin's butchery. For New York intellectuals, he was a romantic figure: a revolutionary and an aesthete. Max Eastman helped translate and publish Trotsky's exposé *The Real Situation in Russia* in 1928 and formed the first Trotskyist group in the U.S., which led to Eastman's denunciation by the Communist-aligned *Daily Worker* as a "British agent" and even by Stalin himself, who called him a "Gangster of the Pen." As reports of the heinous Moscow Trials and the deadly Great Purges began to trickle into the country in 1936, Trotskyism as an intellectual force in the U.S. was truly born.

The next year, *Partisan Review* relaunched as an anti-Stalinist socialist publication with modernist poetry (discouraged under Stalin's socialist realism) from Wallace Stevens and even a review of Kafka's decidedly non–socialist realist work. In 1938, while Trotsky was living in Mexico with Diego Rivera and Frida Kahlo, *Partisan Review* even ran a letter from Trotsky himself on the miserable state of art under Stalin: "Do you wish to know what revolutionary art is like? Look at the frescoes of Rivera."

The love affair proved to be more of a political way station than a destination. As professional-class men and women, the New York intellectuals had few or no ties to any workers' organizations. Add the vast power and omnipotence of the Cold War in American life and you have a gravitational field that increasingly pulled them toward mainstream anti-communism soon after the war's end. As early as 1945, *Partisan Review* editorial-board member James Burnham repudiated the Trotsky-ist critique of the USSR: "Under Stalin the communist revolution has been, not betrayed, but fulfilled." (Three years later, Burnham would testify before the House Committee on Un-American Activities.) Irving Kristol, who started out as an enthusiastic Trotskyist, became one of the founders of the neoconservative movement; for Kristol and thinkers like him, the "permanent revolution" of Trotskyism's imagination found its greatest instrument in American military conquest (*see also* NEOCONSERVATISM). Today, the Soviet Union long gone, only the faintest echo of Trotskyism exists in American politics, in the much milder democratic-socialist politics of Bernie Sanders and Alexandria Ocasio-Cortez.

Trumpism

Hucksterism will get you far in life, doubly so in a city stocked with image-makers, quadruply so in one where being a big public character is valued, loudness is not only acceptable but encouraged, and aggression itself is venture capital. It is an old game, going back at least to P. T. "There's a sucker born every minute" Barnum (see also FREAK SHOW), and today, with electronic and digital media available to the shyster, it works faster and better than ever. By the time he took the presidential oath of office in 2017, Donald John Trump—New York City's eighth resident to move into the White House—had honed that particular set of skills to its ultimate degree. He began as a rich man's outer-borough son with financial capital but no social capital. He soon learned that working the press, relentlessly and utterly without shame, would turn image into reality: If you told everyone often enough that you were a wildly successful real-estate developer, people would buy your apartments and turn you into the person you'd said you were.

(He was absolutely correct about that.) You could then leverage that success out the window, financing the next project and then the next. The fame could also get you a hot wife, then a hotter wife when the first one showed signs of aging or independent thought, and then still another trade-in after the new wife became tiresome. Trump Tower begat Trump Parc begat Trump International Hotel & Tower begat Trump World Tower as well as a big Atlantic City casino that went bust.

Bankruptcies, in fact, characterized Trump's career, much of which was constructed on the principles that you can ignore long-term strategy, deal with problems when they're ten minutes in front of you, and just muddle through, take your payday, and leave the wreckage behind no matter how much distress it causes others. If you did business with him, you'd probably get paid only if he needed something else out of you, and if you tried to collect on an invoice, you'd face a bottomless well of expensive lawyering. He kept his circle small and put as little as possible on paper, hiring old cronies and his own kids, forgoing expertise in favor of unquestioning loyalty in the manner of the contractors who poured his buildings' concrete (*see also* MOB, THE). Nothing mattered but the final public image of success, measured principally by newspaper clips and TV ratings. Trumpism might well be summed up as bullshitting your way through anything, a cynical mix of modest actual achievement and enormous hype. A lot of people have deployed these techniques to get somewhere in life, but many of them inadvertently or semi-consciously limit themselves. Trump does not.

By the early 2000s, Trump had failed enough times that he was finding it difficult to get projects financed. The Trump Organization had become largely a successful licensing game, one in which its name served as a façade for projects built with other people's money (as well as Trump University, purportedly teaching people how to make money in real estate, and products like Trump Steaks, Trump Vodka, and *Trump* magazine). So what better role for him to perform, then, than hosting what was essentially a game show (see also GAME SHOW)? *The Apprentice* allowed him to play a rich and successful businessman on TV. New Yorkers knew how ridiculous that was—we'd watched him flop around on the dock, trying to save himself, for years. Yet when he took that show on the road via NBC, the rest of the country, which knew him only vaguely as a businessman whose name adorned a tower on Fifth Avenue, ate it up.

He had dangled the idea of running for president now and then, probably as a lark to get some press, and in 2015 he sometimes seemed half surprised that he was going through with it. He was perhaps motivated by revenge: Barack Obama had tossed a few barbs at him during the White House Correspondents' Dinner, inflaming every bit of Trump's I'll-show-'em arriviste insecurity. Mostly, he saw a weak primary field that he could defeat by bullying and taunting. He'd picked up something shrewd—that American politics, while seemingly ruthless, was surprisingly constrained by norms. You weren't supposed to appeal openly rather than tacitly to racism, or make fun of your opponent's height, or call reporters names and mock their disabilities when you disliked their coverage. If it took activating the fringes of the American electorate to get those last couple of percentage points and pull ahead at the finish, well, you were supposed to stop at nothing, right? *If they like me, I like them.* And again, it worked: He became the person he had said he was. In every sense.

There was talk at the start of his presidency that Trump might be changed by the office. Instead, he applied to it exactly the same veneer of thin-sliced baloney, ignoring most traditional aspects of operating the government and instead running the world the way he had the Trump Organization. He kept everything close, made giant decisions on the fly with minimal information or research, and hired mostly relatives, friends, and donors known to be loyal. Many staff jobs and ambassadorships remained unfilled for years, in large part out of indifference to the expertise their occupants had previously supplied. He displayed a tiny attention span and a minimal capacity for strategic thinking. What he did do was watch cable news for hours a day, hiring his chief economic adviser off the air and believing *Fox & Friends* gab over the world's best intelligence briefings. He continued to bully reporters, to whine about his treatment, and to claim success even as a pandemic (*see also* QUARANTINE), national protests and ruthless crackdowns, and a stock-market crash (*see also* WALL STREET) all showed his incompetence. And as of mid-2020, after three and a half years spent mostly shoring up his voter base, appointing conservative judges, and telling everyone he was the greatest president ever, he still had more than a third of all voters backing him.

Tunnel, Automobile

Building a tunnel was a well-understood technology by the early twentieth century. In London, a tube was being burrowed under the Thames in the 1830s; it was meant for horses and carriages, eventually used by pedestrians, and still later adapted for rail. Various borings through mountains and mesas in Switzerland and the American West followed. Much of Park Avenue is itself the top of a rail tunnel several miles long, its tracks knitted into the infrastructure of Grand Central Terminal. But those tunnels were all for pedestrians, canalboats, and (especially) trains, and most were not particularly long. Those that were extensive, by the twentieth century, carried trains powered by electricity, which produced no smoke.

A tunnel for automobiles required far more engineering because the buildup of their exhaust fumes would cause misery at best and asphyxiation at worst. In the years after World War I, Clifford Milburn Holland, a civil engineer who'd worked on the construction of the New York subways, figured out how to make it all work by adding four mechanical ventilation stacks that pumped fresh air through the length of the tube. His Hudson River Vehicular Tunnel (as it was first called) was not an easy project to build, and the stress of construction, combined with the degradation of his health after working in the compressed-air caissons beneath the riverbed, was hard on Holland. He had a nervous breakdown in 1924 and died soon after at 41. When the finished tunnel opened on November 13, 1927, it was named the Holland Tunnel in his memory. Nearly a century later, it is absolutely vital to New York City's functioning, and it carries 90,000 cars and trucks every day.

Tuxedo

Tuxedo Park, New York, a small village about an hour from the city, was founded as a private retreat for the wealthy by the tobacco heir Pierre Lorillard IV. There, in 1886, his son Griswold Lorillard embraced the idea—previously floated by the Prince of Wales, Queen Victoria's son and the future Edward VII—of wearing a shorter, tailless suit in the evenings rather than the full white-tie getup. Griswold soon began wearing this

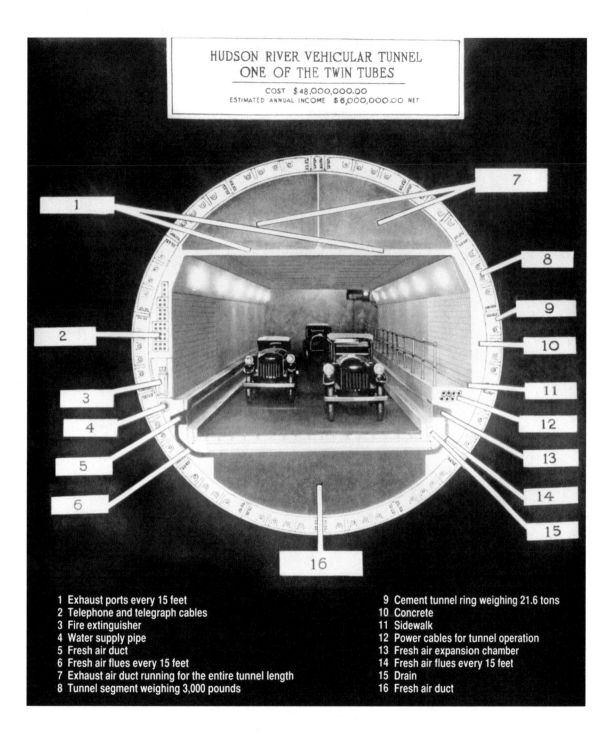

HUDSON RIVER VEHICULAR TUNNEL
ONE OF THE TWIN TUBES

COST $48,000,000.00
ESTIMATED ANNUAL INCOME $6,000,000.00 NET

1 Exhaust ports every 15 feet
2 Telephone and telegraph cables
3 Fire extinguisher
4 Water supply pipe
5 Fresh air duct
6 Fresh air flues every 15 feet
7 Exhaust air duct running for the entire tunnel length
8 Tunnel segment weighing 3,000 pounds

9 Cement tunnel ring weighing 21.6 tons
10 Concrete
11 Sidewalk
12 Power cables for tunnel operation
13 Fresh air expansion chamber
14 Fresh air flues every 15 feet
15 Drain
16 Fresh air duct

*Why you don't suffocate
in the Holland Tunnel:
a 1920s explainer.*

Semi-formal tuxedos mingle with full-on white tie at the Montauk Club in Brooklyn, ca. 1900.

③ **Why T. rex Is the Dinosaur Everyone Knows**

From Dr. Mark Norell, chair and Macaulay curator of the American Museum of Natural History's Division of Paleontology

"**T. rex was arguably the largest terrestrial predator of all time** and had the largest bite force ever calculated for a land-based predator—**so strong that bones would have exploded when prey** was bitten by its eleven-inch teeth, half the length of which was hidden in the jaw. These animals could grow to adult size (about forty feet long) in eighteen years, at times adding about five pounds a day."

"dinner suit" when he was down in the city, where it became popular with a younger set of sartorial rule-breakers. A century ago, the tuxedo was considered only semi-formal, inappropriate for an event where ladies were present. Nowadays, white tie is extinct for all but the rarest, most ceremonial occasions (e.g., a state dinner with the British monarch), and the tux is the peak sartorial experience of most men, worn only at proms and weddings.

Tyrannosaurus Rex[3]

Sixty-six million years after its extinction, the giant North American dinosaur with the tiny little hands reappeared in 1900. Its bones were first uncovered and identified by Barnum Brown, the swashbuckling fossil hunter who was also assistant curator at the American Museum of Natural History in New York. He found his first partial skeleton in Wyoming, the second in Montana, and within a few years, his colleague Henry Fairfield Osborn, president of the AMNH, gave this immense creature its name, adapting the Greek words *tyrannos* ("tyrant") and *sauros* ("lizard") and the Latin *rex* ("king"). Those first discoveries were exhibited elsewhere, but in 1915, the museum got its first (nearly) complete *T. rex* skeleton and set it up in the Hall of Man because that was the only room big enough. It was mounted standing more or less upright, its tail dragging behind it, in a stance familiar to everyone who has ever seen the poster for *Jurassic Park*—and one that, research has revealed, was almost surely incorrect. By the 1990s, when the dinosaur halls at the American Museum of Natural History were renovated, the mount was rebuilt to adopt a more accurate pose: nearly horizontal, somewhat birdlike, the giant skull close to the ground, leaning forward in a way that dramatically and terrifyingly evokes the last thing its prey would ever see.

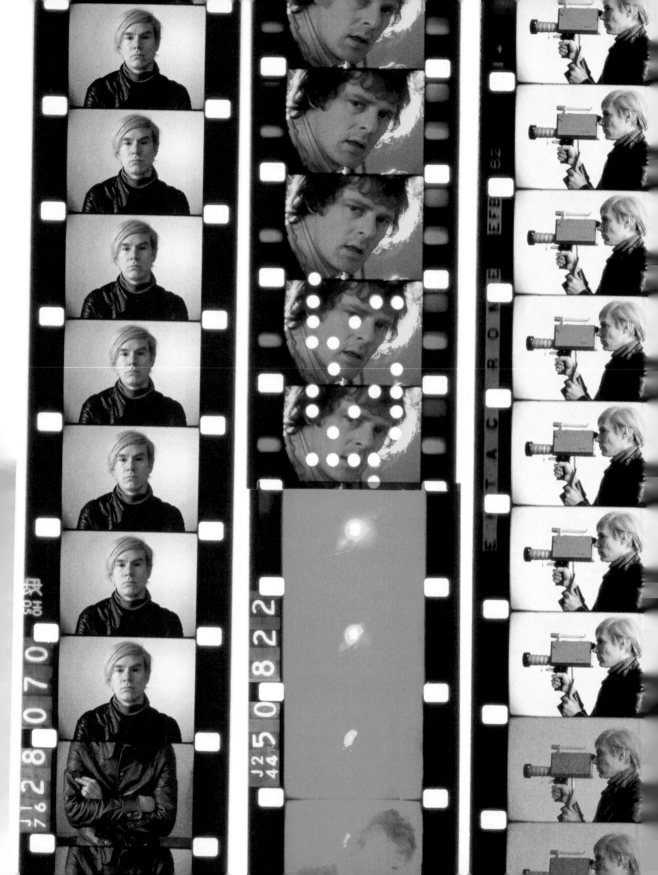

From
UNDERGROUND CINEMA
to
URINAL

Trash *(1970), by Andy Warhol (producer) and Paul Morrissey
(writer-director), starred Joe Dallesandro and Holly Woodlawn.*
PHOTOGRAPH BY DOUGLAS KIRKLAND

① **The Essential Underground Movies**

Chosen by New York *film critic Bilge Ebiri*

» **Flaming Creatures,** by Jack Smith
» **Walden,** by Jonas Mekas
» **Chelsea Girls,** by Andy Warhol
» **The Queen of Sheba Meets the Atom Man,** by Ron Rice
» **Shadows,** by John Cassavetes
» **The Very Eye of Night,** by Maya Deren

» **Visual Variations on Noguchi,** by Marie Menken
» **Tom, Tom, the Piper's Son,** by Ken Jacobs
» **Scorpio Rising,** by Kenneth Anger
» **Twice a Man,** by Gregory Markopoulos

Underground Cinema [1]

Experimental films have been around since the earliest days of cinema—indeed, we could say that all early films were experimental and the narrative ones came later (*see also* MOVIES). But it took a unique set of circumstances to turn experimental, avant-garde, or (as later advocates would call it) "poetic" cinema into an alternative movement, a true underground in opposition to the mainstream. And New York would become the center of that crusade.

Ironically enough, however, the city was initially one of its key obstacles. On Christmas Eve 1908, Mayor George B. McClellan closed all of New York's nickelodeons, some 550 of them, ostensibly in the interest of "public health" but really under the influence of Christian groups, many of whom were bothered that these motion-picture establishments were often owned and/or frequented by Jews and recently arrived immigrants from Southern and Eastern Europe. These actions soon led to the creation of the state's Motion Picture Commission, a board of censors that would oversee any films shown in New York. (The many disparate efforts to censor movies across the United States would eventually coalesce into the MPAA's ratings system, but state censor boards remained active for much of the twentieth century.)

In 1946, a 24-year-old film buff and Austrian immigrant named Amos Vogel saw an evening of works by the experimental filmmaker Maya Deren at Greenwich Village's Provincetown Playhouse. Impressed by the professionalism with which Deren had planned the evening, as well as the audience turnout, Vogel and his wife, Marcia, decided to start programming a regular series at the venue to showcase art films and other works outside the mainstream.

"The two-hundred-seat auditorium was filled for sixteen evenings, two shows an evening," Vogel later recalled. Thus was born the Cinema 16 society and, with it, true American underground cinema. To get around the problem of the censors, who still requested that all films screened in the state be submitted to them beforehand (along with their scripts), the Vogels opted to turn Cinema 16 into a private club. Under that arrangement, the authorities could still close them down for showing obscene films, but the Vogels no longer had to submit anything beforehand.

As a result, they regularly programmed avant-garde and experimental movies from the likes of Kenneth Anger, whose openly homoerotic works often caused controversy; over the course of its sixteen-year existence, the society also screened the work of such seminal avant-garde figures as Stan Brakhage, Hans Richter, and James Broughton. Programs came with written notes designed to place each work in context. At its height, Cinema 16 had about 7,000 members, each paying a $15.50 annual subscription. It changed locations often—from the Fifth Avenue Playhouse to the Central Needle Trades Auditorium (which seated 1,600!) to the Paris Theater and others. Members included downtown artistes, revolutionaries, suburbanites, and celebrities such as Marlon Brando and Elia Kazan.

Cinema 16's success demonstrated audiences' desire for films that challenged the status quo formally and narratively. As film historian Scott MacDonald put it, "Instead of accepting moviegoing as an entertaining escape from real life, Vogel and his colleagues saw themselves as a special breed of educator, using an exploration of cinema history and current practice not only to develop a more complete sense of the myriad experiences cinema makes possible, but also to invigorate the potential citizenship in a democracy and to cultivate a sense of global responsibility."

The baton would eventually be passed to Dan and Toby Talbot, who opened the New Yorker Theater, the city's premier art house, in 1960, and the Lithuanian critic, programmer, and filmmaker Jonas Mekas, who the same year started what would become the Film-Makers' Cooperative (and, later, the research and preservation center Anthology Film Archives, which still exists), initially as a response to Cinema 16, which he found too bourgeois. Andy Warhol, then an up-and-coming artist, regularly visited Mekas's loft to watch films and was inspired to start making his own movies; in turn, Mekas served as cinematographer on Warhol's 1964 magnum opus *Empire*. Over the following decades, avant-garde cinema worldwide would be fed by this downtown nexus of loft screenings, theaters, productions, and artists' collectives, traditions that continue today via microcinemas and pop-up screening spaces scattered across the city.

Unions

The labor union is primarily a British invention, and New Yorkers have been railing against the power of bosses since before New York was a state or *boss* was even an English word. In 1768, the city's journeyman tailors launched the first recorded strike in U.S. history in order to secure a greater share of their employers' profits. Two decades later, in a Federalist paper addressed to his fellow "people of New York," Alexander Hamilton declared, "A power over man's subsistence amounts to a power over his will."

Granted, Hamilton himself was more of a boss than a labor radical. But his simple observation—that personal and political freedom require (at least some) economic autonomy—was among the most radical of the nation's founding principles. In the early years of the republic, (white male) Americans believed they could achieve such autonomy by securing control of a small plot of arable land or becoming self-employed skilled craftsmen. But the industrial revolution had other plans. The rise of factory production and mechanized

agriculture spared some artisans and small farmers, but eventually those forces would turn the vast majority of Americans into employees.

As New York's working class was quick to recognize, employees can secure economic autonomy not through rugged individualism but only through collective solidarity. The individual garment worker on the Lower East Side was helpless in the face of a boss whose capital ensured her sustenance, but if that garment worker organized with her workmates around their shared interests—and formed an organization that could leverage their collective resources—they could shut down production until the bosses agreed to provide higher wages, better working conditions, and shorter hours. And that is precisely what New York's garment workers once did.

Samuel Gompers, the father of craft unionism in the United States, once called New York City "the cradle of the American labor movement" and for good reason. Where modern Manhattan's glassed-in condos and ubiquitous bank branches now stand, many of the most important labor struggles in history once raged. In 1834, stonemasons protested NYU's use of prison labor in Washington Square; in 1882, in the nation's first Labor Day parade, 25,000 allies of the Knights of Labor marched down the Bowery to demand an eight-hour day; in 1909, the Uprising of the 20,000 saw seamstresses and members of the International Ladies' Garment Workers' Union stage a three-month walkout with picket lines in Greenwich Village; and in 1930, 35,000 men and women pauperized by the Great Depression clashed with police while demanding some kind of new deal in Union Square.

In New York today, bosses still have power over plenty of people's subsistence. But thanks to labor unions, modern New Yorkers (and most workers nationwide) also have the weekend, the minimum wage, unemployment benefits, disability insurance, Social Security, and workplace safety protections—as well as, admittedly, dauntingly high costs for public projects like subways and services like garbage collection. Taken together, though, that seems like a pretty solid collective bargain.

United Nations

 Kids were still dying and cities were still being pulverized during World War II when the Allied nations started hammering out a postwar order governed by a federation of sovereign states. No sooner did the United Nations write itself into being in 1945 than it faced the challenge of turning idealism into real estate and deciding where to set up camp. The choice of the U.S. was relatively straightforward, since it was the one part of the world to have resisted foreign invasion. Detroit, San Francisco, Boston, and Philadelphia made bids; the Black Hills of South Dakota and Niagara Falls were also in the running. Robert Moses talked up Flushing. Greenwich, Connecticut, emerged as a favorite, but the town signaled that world government would be unwelcome there.

Eventually it became clear that diplomats wanted plenty to do and places to eat after their long days of meetings, which could only mean Manhattan. With the deadline for a selection bearing down, John D. Rockefeller Jr. dispatched his court architect, Wallace Harrison, to buy a 17-acre stretch of slaughterhouses and tenement buildings along the East River. The land belonged to Rockefeller's rival and fellow developer William Zeckendorf, who had planned to turn the site into X City, an enclave of apartment towers with a domed opera house at its heart. Harrison grabbed a site map, crashed Zeckendorf's anniversary party at the Club Monte Carlo at Madison Avenue and East 54th Street, and offered him $8.5 million of Rockefeller's money for the land. The developer scribbled his assent on Harrison's map and went back to celebrating. Rockefeller donated the land to the United Nations—and made sure Harrison got the job of designing its headquarters.

Harrison actually wound up trying to herd an international team of architects, including the intransigent geniuses Le Corbusier and Oscar Niemeyer, into cooperation. The process was chaotic—Le Corbusier complained of the "apparent kidnapping of [his] UN project by USA gangster Harrison"—but it produced the first monument of postwar architectural modernism.

New York in the late 1940s was already a world city in finance, pop music, television, advertising, and modern art. Rockefeller's real-estate deal made it a global political capital as well. It's an achievement regularly rued by anyone who has tried to move around midtown Manhattan when the General Assembly is in session. But when you see a tyrant rant, a revolutionary rouse, or a celebrity pitch peace to a worldwide audience, it usually happens in front of the same green marble wall—uniquely located in stateless international territory while also being on East 42nd Street.

Uptown *see* DOWNTOWN

Urinal

If you accept the fact that anything in New York (tree, wall, MetroCard machine) may eventually become an ad hoc urinal, the innovation really was creating the urinal's flushing system. And credit for that generally goes to Andrew Rankin, a smith whose business was located at 248 East 11th Street. In 1866 he patented an improvement that incorporated an upright flushing valve packed with deodorizing material. He arguably, therefore, simultaneously invented the urinal cake.

Although Rankin's name usually comes up first in a U.S. patent search, at least one inventor preceded him in line for the men's room: Two years earlier, another New Yorker, William S. Carr, patented a nifty swing-away pissoir that looks mighty urinal-like. His invention was filed as an "improvement in Urinals," implying at least one earlier American water-closet hero. And prior patents in the U.K. also mention designs for urinals, suggesting that London was shoulder-to-shoulder with New York in this particular creative realm.

One thing is sure. None of these people ever expected that a later pissoir—mass-produced by the New York firm J. L. Mott Iron Works, rechristened *Fountain* by Marcel Duchamp, signed with the name "R. Mutt," and exhibited at midtown's Grand Central Palace in 1917—would become the definitive piece of Dada provocation and, perhaps, the most significant artwork of the twentieth century.

At CBGB, it was best to avoid touching the urinals.
PHOTOGRAPH BY
SCOTT GRIES

VERMONT.

SCALE.

10   20   30   40 Miles.

From
VAUDEVILLE
to
VOGUING

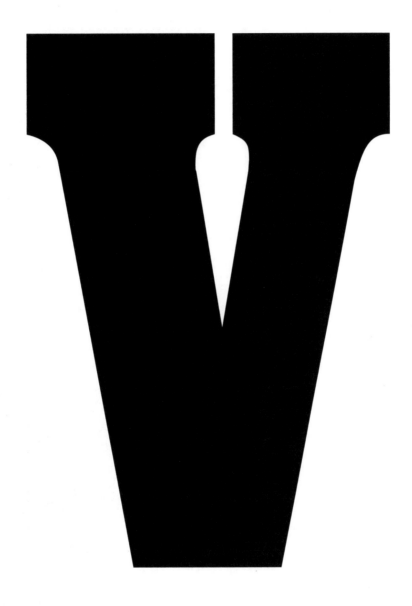

*Vermont: the state formerly known
as upstate New York.*

Vaudeville

Once everywhere, now effectively extinct, the light-entertainment genre known as vaudeville—staged variety shows with popular song-and-dance numbers, comedy, and bits of drama, shot through with minstrelsy—has many roots. It is variously traced to France (the word attributed to the phrase *voix de ville*, "voice of the city," or to the town of Vau de Vire in Normandy, known for its bawdy songs), London (where *variety* was the preferred term), Boston, and San Francisco. Its first permanent venue, though, is generally recorded as the "concert saloon" called the Bowery, which opened on the Bowery itself around 1848. Within a few years, similar performances had popped up at a variety of theaters, notably the Melodeon Concert Hall at 539 Broadway, from which performers took their shows on the road.

The form matured when a New York impresario named Tony Pastor got his hands on it. After a couple of decades in the business, he had the idea of turning this salty style into family entertainment, and in October 1881, he began performances at his Fourteenth Street Theatre (a thousand-seat venue that happened to be located inside Tammany Hall, the city's center of Democratic political power), at which no alcohol was sold. Despite the ban, the house stayed full, and Pastor was briefly at the top of the vaudeville heap.

But it was a big, rollicking field, and he had a lot of competitors with thousands of seats of their own to fill. Over the next few years, the business began to be dominated by several chains known as "circuits"—companies that operated a theater in every midsize city and could therefore book tours efficiently. Their executives were almost celebrities themselves, akin to the studio heads of the next century. Edward Albee II (grandfather of the playwright) ran the Albee circuit; B. F. Keith, the Keith circuit; the West Coast's Alexander Pantages, the Pantages circuit; Gustav Walter and later Martin Beck, the Orpheum circuit. They booked everything imaginable, including jugglers and ventriloquists. Reflecting the standards of the day, blackface performances were common, as were broad ethnic-immigrant stereotypes, from the drunken Irishman on down.

Harry Houdini's escape act, signed to Orpheum, was a major draw (*see also* ESCAPE ARTIST). Lillian Russell, the actress and soprano, performed musical comedy, and W. C. Fields cultivated a world-class juggling act. An entire generation's showbiz performers, from Ethel Merman to the Marx Brothers, learned their craft in the vaudeville houses. At their peak in the 1910s, the business involved 1,800 theaters around the country, and its biggest stars earned thousands of dollars a week. Vaudeville's New York presence had begun to coalesce around Times Square after the turn of the century, and in 1913, shortly after the Keith and Albee circuits merged, Martin Beck opened the enormous Palace Theatre, which almost immediately became Keith-Albee's crown jewel.

Then came a triple whammy. Silent film took a big bite out of the vaudeville business (even though short films were sometimes screened between the live acts); movies required no touring expenses and could run in any neighborhood at any time, and talkies, launched in 1927, were an even harder blow. Radio too was an existential threat, allowing people to hear pop songs and comedy without leaving their homes. And then came the Depression, when those cheap-to-consume entertainments were often the only option. Around the country, many circuit theaters converted to showing films, while movie studios offered big money to vaudeville stars to perform their acts before the cameras, exhausting their repertoires and effectively ending their touring careers. (To see a lot of the Marx Brothers' vaudeville act, watch their first few films; in each one, a couple of set pieces are clearly repurposed from the stage.) The Radio Corporation of America (RCA) bought out the Keith-Albee and Orpheum circuits and

① **The Dip, Explained**

From Pose *star Jason Rodriguez*

"If you know vogue, you know what a dip is. **It's a moment when a voguer hits a particular pose on the floor,** gracefully and fearlessly finding the ground with their arms, with an arched back and an extended leg. **A dip is the period to our sentence, a seal of our expression.**

A moment when the crowd extend their hands toward the voguer to embrace a moment in time that they've slayed the ballroom floor."

became a movie studio, RKO Pictures, whose initials retain a ghostly trace of the old names. In 1932, the Palace's live acts gave way to full-time cinema, marking the end of vaudeville as a major genre. The impresario Samuel Rothafel, known as Roxy, tried to give it a final boost by supersizing the venue, but that too flopped (*see also* RADIO CITY MUSIC HALL). Whatever was left of vaudeville after that was finished off by wartime austerity and then TV.

Which is not to say you couldn't still see it: Because performers trained in vaudeville created many of the early radio and then television shows, their styles came to define the new formats. The comedy-variety hours that dominated TV in the 1950s, '60s, and '70s were basically vaudeville slates translated to the small screen, starring many middle-aged performers—Sammy Davis Jr., Judy Garland, Pearl Bailey, George Burns, Jack Benny—who'd lived out of a trunk on the circuit when young. When Garland performed nineteen weeks of comeback shows at the Palace Theatre in 1951, she wistfully sang, "So I hope you understand my wondrous thrill, / 'Cause vaudeville's back at the Palace, and I'm on the bill!" And you can draw a pretty straight line from the Jewish-inflected wisecracker voices of the Marx Brothers and Milton Berle all the way up through, say, *Seinfeld* and *Curb Your Enthusiasm*.

Vermont

In the 1750s, the British colony of New York—whose capital was then New York City—began granting white Europeans land in the rough triangular region to its northeast. But so did the colony of New Hampshire, disputing New York's authority. Eventually, the British Privy Council had to adjudicate, and on July 20, 1764, New Hampshire's claims were invalidated by a declaration from King George III, one that officially designated the area a part of New York. The New Hampshirite

settlers didn't like this and pursued challenges, but New York retained ownership.

After the Revolution began and the territory of not-yet-Vermont sent soldiers to the Continental Army, the question of whose land it was continued to simmer. Residents of the territory didn't want any part of this internecine squabble and in 1777 declared full independence from both Britain and New York. The new nation called itself the Republic of Vermont and drafted its own constitution. Only in 1791, several years after the war's end, did it give up on its self-governing dreams and join the new USA as the fourteenth state—after sending a big payment to New York to resolve any lingering land claims.

Since then, a couple of Vermonters have become president and a third has come very close, and, by coincidence, New York can lay claim to two of them. In 1881, Chester Alan Arthur, born in Vermont but a New York City resident for most of his adult life, won the vice-presidency and then, upon the death of President James A. Garfield, took the oath of office in his townhouse on lower Lexington Avenue. And in 2020, the democratic socialist Bernie Sanders—child of Brooklyn, onetime mayor of Burlington, and three-term senator from Vermont—came within shouting distance of the White House as well.

Voguing[1]

Channeling the glamorous hauteur of fashion models on the runway, the acrobatic competitive dancing known as voguing is the signature invention of the ballroom subculture that got its start in New York in the 1960s, when queer people of color, many of them transgender, created a parallel world to the one that usually excluded them. Its fierce theatricality and jargon were later adopted by white gay culture and eventually the pop mainstream.

Drag balls in Harlem (*see also* HARLEM) are documented as early as 1869, when the Hamilton Lodge hosted its first gay masquerade (*see also* GAY-RIGHTS

MOVEMENT). By the 1920s, the poet Langston Hughes, after seeing a few white celebrities mix with a large gay, Black audience at one of them, could signal that Harlem was "in vogue," but the drag scene continued to develop along racial lines. The 1968 documentary *The Queen* shows a confident Black contestant, Crystal LaBeija, who seems set to win a predominantly Caucasian midtown drag pageant until the judges, including the artists Andy Warhol and Larry Rivers, pass her over in favor of a young white upstart. LaBeija storms off, accusing the event of being rigged against people of color. In 1972 she and her close friend Lottie founded the first of New York's "houses," now the standard term for a team of drag performers, and held its inaugural ball at the Up the Downstairs Case club on West 115th Street in Harlem. Houses often function as surrogate families for people who have been rejected by their biological ones, some even attracting kids who are uninterested in drag.

Most competitions evolved to include categories of identities that contestants try to perfect: butch queen, "town and country," and so on. They're judged on "realness," i.e., the performers' ability to pass. The best-known convention, voguing, is (despite other roots) customarily credited to a performance by Paris Dupree in the early 1980s. According to the DJ David DePino, "At an after-hours [club] called Footsteps, on Second Avenue and 14th Street ... Paris had a *Vogue* magazine in her bag, and while she was dancing she took it out, opened it up to a page where a model was posing, and then stopped in that pose on the beat. Then she turned to the next page and stopped in the new pose, again on the beat." Another drag queen tried to one-up her with a different pose, but Paris returned the move. In 1981, at the first House of Dupree ball, voguing became a competitive category, the goal being to outshine your opponents—to put them in the shade, as participants began to say.

The 1990 documentary *Paris Is Burning* (titled after Dupree's balls) revealed this scene to a wider world, as did Malcolm McLaren's 1989 dance single "Deep in the Vogue" and Madonna's 1990 hit "Vogue." Proving that this tiny subculture has achieved maximum realness, RuPaul has since become a ubiquitous celebrity, House of LaBeija member Kia has been celebrated with a cover story in *Artforum*, and Billy Porter, starring in Ryan Murphy's soapy ballroom drama *Pose*, won an Emmy award in 2019.

Striking a pose in Brooklyn, 1986.
PHOTOGRAPH BY
JENNIE LIVINGSTON

From
WALDORF SALAD
to
WRECKING BALL

The ubiquitous water tank: site-specific,
assembled by hand.
NEW YORK CITY, CROSBY ST./HOUSTON ST., USA (1978)
PHOTOGRAPH BY BERND & HILLA BECHER

Waldorf Salad

Apple and celery tossed in mayonnaise over a bed of lettuce. Those are the components of the beloved Waldorf salad, which definitively dates back to March 14, 1893. It was on that day that Oscar Tschirky, the Swiss-born maître d' at the Waldorf Hotel (and a recent alumnus of the pioneering restaurant Delmonico's) introduced his creation to the world, serving it to dukes, viceroys, and a president at a charity ball benefiting St. Mary's Hospital for Children. The salad may have been invented to satisfy the very rich, but it would become a classic American diner dish. As Tschirky warned in his 1896 recipe book, cooks should just "be careful not to let any seeds of the apples be mixed with it."

"Walk" Sign

By the beginning of the 1930s, horse-and-buggy pedestrian deaths had fallen off, but vehicular pedestrian deaths were a rising problem. Determined to address a combination of egregious jaywalking, ineffectual traffic cops, and essentially futile red lights, Dr. John A. Harriss, a former special deputy police commissioner for traffic and a millionaire (he had designed and donated the city's first permanent traffic light in 1920), created an experimental pedestrian-traffic system. Installed on Fifth Avenue between 40th and 45th Streets, it was similar to the now-familiar three-color traffic light, but an added symbolic hand, palm facing out, lit up with the yellow lens to alert oncoming motorists that it was time to allow passengers to cross. According to a February 1934 issue of *Public Safety* magazine, "Dr. Harriss hopes the new signal will eliminate a source of irritation and danger when drivers fail to see, or claim they have failed to see, the traffic officer's uplifted hand. The lighted hand should also, he thinks, curb the practice of passing a red light, which he believes to be one of the most dangerous and serious violations of the traffic rules."

In 1952 the New York Department of Transportation began to install separate dedicated signs bearing two words: WALK (always lit) and DONT (switched on and off with the traffic cycle; note that it lacked an apostrophe). Twenty years after that, the lights gained a third word, displaying DON'T WALK, illuminated en banc, alternating with WALK. And as the new century arrived, the globalized city replaced those with symbols: a walking figure illuminated in white and a raised don't-walk hand in red. By coincidence or design, it's nearly a return to Harriss's glowing safety hand from the prototype.

Wall Street

There was a wall there once, built of wood by the Dutch. It stretched the width of Manhattan Island and was intended as a fortification to keep out both the natives and the British. (It was torn down in 1699.) Until well into the nineteenth century, the street that ran along the wall was as much residential as mercantile, although one particular trading market—in enslaved human beings—is documented there as early as 1711. At the end of the Revolution, City Hall, at No. 26 Wall Street, became Federal Hall, and George Washington took the oath of office on its balcony in 1789 (*see also* CAPITAL OF THE UNITED STATES). The metonym for the financial sector came later, after the New York Stock Exchange moved to Broad and Wall Streets in 1865.

By then, the centrality of lower Manhattan to American finance was well established. Most historians accept the (perhaps overtidy) story that the exchange itself was founded on May 17, 1792, as an agreement among twenty-four stockbrokers signed under the buttonwood tree in front of 68 Wall Street. These men did a lot of their trading out of two local hangouts, the Merchants' Coffee House and, especially, the Tontine Coffee House at the corner of Wall and Water Streets (which would remain a political center for several decades). The earliest securities were insurance and banking stocks, but trading at the Tontine also involved cargoes of imports, including enslaved people, coming through the nearby port. By the 1830s, most of the country's bank holdings were based in Manhattan, a position that was consolidated after 1836, when the Second Bank of the United States, in Philadelphia, was privatized and later closed. After the building of the Erie Canal and the changes of the Industrial Revolution came stock trading in textiles, iron, oil and coal, and—above

On the floor of the New York Stock Exchange, ca. 1900.

all—railroads, by far the dominant investments of the late nineteenth century, making up 81 percent of the New York Stock Exchange's companies by 1885. Multiple exchanges competed with the NYSE, and only around 1880 or so did it achieve primacy.

Yet for all its importance, New York was still not the world's financial center. At the turn of the twentieth century, Britain's exchanges made up 25 percent of the global market, while New York had 15 percent and Germany 13 percent. But the rising flood of immigrants into New York fed the factories, the markets they drove,

and the city's talent pool. Many new arrivals had little to lose and a lot to gain—the very definition of self-selecting risk-takers, well suited to the speculation the stock market demanded. Although the traditional financial firms of the time did business almost exclusively within the Wasp Establishment, a few others (notably Lehman Brothers; Kuhn, Loeb & Company; and the future titan Goldman Sachs) were owned by, and backed businesses started by, Jewish Americans. The relative openness of the U.S. market further fueled its growth, as did the protections (modest at first,

The choreographer and filmmaker Edith Stephen moved to Westbeth in 1970, the year it opened. She turned 101 there in 2020.

substantial later on) for smaller shareholders and the market's appetite to encompass new technologies, like telephone and electrical companies.

Most of all, World War I and the subsequent boom in investment banking did the trick: From 1915 to 1920, the number of listed stocks on the NYSE more than doubled, and by 1925 they had doubled again, as had trading volume. Their prices zoomed upward as well (*see also* DOW JONES INDUSTRIAL AVERAGE), giving the Roaring Twenties their nickname and leading to the Dow's peak at 381 in September 1929. After the imminent crash, it eventually fell to 41, and images of bankers leaping out of Wall Street windows to their death became symbolic of the era. It took until 1954 for the Dow to return to 1929 levels, although that downturn looks longer than it could have been, owing to deflation, war, and other factors affecting the U.S. financial markets.

By then, the U.S. had become the richest country in the history of the planet, and New York was far and away its financial capital. Stock ownership, which, apart from a brief vogue in the 1920s, had been a relatively rare kind of investment, except among institutions and the wealthy, became more widespread in the 1950s. As volume increased, the NYSE's paper-based trading methods grew inadequate, and in 1969 the exchange switched to electronic trading (*see also* TICKER TAPE). The NASDAQ exchange was founded two years later, and various new financial products—the individual retirement account, the index fund, the 401(k) plan—fueled the growth of the financial-services industry, the lion's share of which operated here (*see also* HEDGE FUND). As the city's manufacturing base drained away, Wall Street increasingly became the core of New York's taxpaying population. It largely

(1) **Where to Visit Working Artists' Studios**

Chosen by James Cohan, founder of James Cohan Gallery

» **International Studio & Curatorial Program**
1040 Metropolitan Ave., Williamsburg

» **The Elizabeth Foundation for the Arts' EFA Studio Program**
323 W. 39th St.

» **The NARS Foundation**
201 46th St., Sunset Park

» **Smack Mellon**
92 Plymouth Street, Dumbo

» **Residency Unlimited**
360 Court Street, Carroll Gardens

---

drove the city's financial recovery in the 1980s, particularly during the boom years that ended, abruptly, in 1987 (*see also* YUPPIE). Since then, it has constituted an ever-larger sector of the city's economy, and although it is hardly recession-proof, an increasing proliferation of complex financial instruments allow its investors to sometimes make money on bear markets almost as well as they do during flush times. (The defining characteristic of the hedge fund is its hedging.) Today, the financial-services sector pays nearly a quarter of New York City's total wages and many more indirectly. The average Wall Street employee in 2017 took home $422,500. It remains to be seen whether the financial collapse of 2020 (*see also* QUARANTINE) will have a long-term effect on those incomes or on the city they in large part support.

Water Tank, Rooftop

Water flows down but not up. This obvious point is the basic science on which New York's water system is constructed. The various reservoirs that deliver fresh water to 8 million residents are a couple of hundred feet above sea level, and their contents run downhill to the five boroughs through aqueducts and pipes. Once in the city, however, there's a complication: The pressure this system supplies at street level is enough to drive water up only six stories. It's no accident that nearly all New York buildings dating from before the widespread use of electricity—every brownstone, every tenement—are five or six stories high.

Occupants above the seventh floor need a pump that fills a tank on the roof, which gravity-feeds water to the taps and toilets below. And for a hundred-plus years, since tall buildings began to rise in New York, those tanks have been made of cedar and redwood planks in the style of giant barrels: shaved into wedge-shaped staves, held together with steel bands, and assembled in the wind by people with safety harnesses and nerves of steel. There are buildings with steel tanks as well, but wooden ones predominate; they're cheaper, they last a comparable amount of time, and (if well kept) they keep the water smelling and tasting good.

Although necessary in any tall building, rooftop tanks are uniquely associated with New York. For one thing, the city's architects and developers have tended to leave them exposed, leading to their exaggerated presence on the skyline. They also seem to suit the gritty postindustrial look—exposed-brick walls, rough lumber, weathered steel—that dominates much of New York. Virtually all of the city's wooden water tanks are custom-built, mostly by hand, by three companies with roots in the ancient craft of barrel-making. American Pipe and Tank, Isseks Brothers, and Rosenwach Tank are multigenerational businesses, each over a century old, and—unless New York improbably stops building and renovating tall buildings—are likely to stick around for much longer.

Westbeth Artists Community[1]

In the mid-1960s, AT&T moved its research laboratories out of their longtime home at West and Bethune Streets, and the huge, empty industrial building was, with a combination of private-foundation funds and grants from the predecessor of the National Endowment for the Arts, converted into housing and studio space for artists. The Westbeth project, designed by the young and not yet famous architect Richard Meier, was an early, successful example of a now commonplace idea: "adaptive reuse," wherein factories become condos and department stores become floors of tiny, shared offices. (Five decades after the renovation, the Westbeth building is once again beginning to show its age.) Among the early residents were Merce Cunningham, whose studio was here for decades, and Diane Arbus, who lived there for a couple of years before taking her own life in 1971.

Diane von Fürstenberg with her most durable invention, the wrap dress, 1976.

PHOTOGRAPH BY BURT GLINN

② **Tips for Reading a Wine List**

From Brendan Kimball, sommelier at Le Bernardin

"I like to cut out a lot of the noise right away by deciding how much money I want to spend. **Get comfortable with your budget!** Once you've trimmed out what isn't in your price range, start thinking about what you like versus what fits the situation. I tend to like wines with age, so I further narrow it down to the best price for the oldest vintage out of those choices. In the end, **asking for help is key.** Questions like these are a great start: What's new and hip? What goes best with these dishes? How can I impress my date without blowing up my bank account?"

Because few New Yorkers ever want to give up a real-estate bargain, the texture of Westbeth has changed over the years. The majority of residents are now elderly. Since the famous have usually left Westbeth for somewhere more luxe, those who have stayed tend not to be as commercially successful. Some observers have seen this as an inherent flaw in the system of subsidized artist housing, while others consider Westbeth a success for precisely that reason: These working artists of no particular prominence would long ago have been driven out of New York, but instead they provide diversity of viewpoint and outlook to an increasingly monocultural neighborhood, sustaining the disappearing bohemian legacy of Greenwich Village.

Wine List [2]

The first wine list in the U.S. appeared at a Manhattan restaurant that was opened, unsurprisingly, by a wine importer: John Delmonico, who with his brother Peter started the country's first fine-dining establishment. Historians can't swear that no one ever stuck a wine list on a menu before 1838 (at Delmonico's or elsewhere), but this one—with sixty-three bottles, several from vintners still world-renowned today, like Château Margaux and Château Latour—is the earliest example on record.

Before becoming restaurateurs, the brothers made a fortune selling European wines and Cuban cigars to New Yorkers. The original Delmonico's was a storefront on William Street in the Financial District that sold French pastries and coffee alongside a plethora of imported alcohol. In 1837 the brothers upgraded to an imposing three-story edifice a block away, which they converted into a full-service French restaurant. Its prized possession: a 17,000-bottle wine cellar.

The 1838 wine list closes out an epic menu that makes the Cheesecake Factory's look like a haiku: forty-seven veal entrées alone, plus more than a page of sides and, on the final page, eighty-eight liquors, wines, and beer. A snifter of brandy could be yours for a penny, but swallowing the heftier prices might require an antacid. The Latour (an 1825 vintage) cost twenty shillings, roughly $280 today, while a bottle of Madeira, then considered among the world's finest wines, would have come to almost $675.

This price range was less a stab at democracy than a public display of the riches down in the cellar. The New York *Times* was even intimidated by the selection. In 1959, its first-ever restaurant review claimed, "We are made nervous by the sneerful smirk of the waiter, if we order the wrong wine in the wrong place; the Delmonican creed ... being 'the right wine in the right place.'" The critic witnessed a fellow diner "call for beer with his soup," which allegedly caused the server to faint. "An atrocity," he wrote, "never before committed in those classic halls."

Woolworth Building *see* SKYLINE

World Trade Center *see* 9/11 ERA

Wrap Dress [3]

When the Belgian-born designer (and new European princess by marriage) Diane von Fürstenberg immigrated to New York in the 1970s, she arrived with a suitcase full of Italian-made prototypes and visions of the American Dream. With long legs, lustrous hair, and unrivaled cheekbones, von Fürstenberg, in her early twenties at the time, quickly found her way to the office of *Vogue* editor-in-chief Diana Vreeland, who thought her ballet-inspired garments were "absolutely smashing"—not only for their look and feel but for the idea they embodied. For working women at the time,

③ How (Not) to Wear a Wrap Dress

By the Cut's Kelly Conaboy

"In 2016, I purchased a wrap dress in black velvet with long sleeves. I wore it never. Every time I attempted to put it on, I couldn't figure out how to make it function as a dress. Instead, it was sort of a sloppy, open robe, a misaligned disaster.

"Not until Tuesday, December 18, 2018, in my thirty-*cough* year of living, did I decide I'd had enough and typed 'How to put on a wrap dress' into YouTube, where I realized **every dress wearer held a secret and was guarding it** (from me). Wrap dresses have a little hole in them under the right arm. Incredible! I found the hole, put the string in, and it worked."

von Fürstenberg's dresses were nothing short of life altering. You could throw them on in ten seconds; they were comfortable, conforming to any body type; and with a cinch at the waist, they were flattering on virtually all those bodies. They were the equivalent of a turtleneck and jeans for men, only more versatile and available in an array of eye-catching prints.

By 1976, von Fürstenberg had sold more than 5 million wrap dresses to everyone from Bensonhurst secretaries to ladies who lunched. After so much success, she essentially took the 1980s off and relaunched her brand in 1997, finding that the daughters of her original customers were equally enthusiastic about her designs. "I had no idea that it would pay all my bills, all my life," von Fürstenberg later said of her most famous creation. She likes to point out that *wrap dress* in French, *robe portefeuille*, translates to "wallet dress." She's still cashing in.

Wrecking Ball

Instead of succeeding his deli-owner father, Sussman Volk (*see also* PASTRAMI SANDWICH), in the construction of edible high-rises, Jacob Volk went into high-rise destruction, becoming New York's foremost expert in the demolition of tall buildings. In his early days in the business, these were painstakingly taken down by hand, mostly by men with crowbars. But in the 1930s, seeking speed and greater destructive power, Jacob and his brother Albert began knocking down walls and columns with a hanging slab of scrap iron suspended from a crane. By 1936 (according to Jeff Byles, author of the definitive *Rubble: Unearthing the History of Demolition*), the Volks were using a 3,000-pound "iron cannonball" swung from a 90-foot-tall arm.

By mid-century, the wrecking ball had become ubiquitous, as the low-rise nineteenth-century city gave way to the high-rise twentieth and thousands of brownstones and tenements were replaced with hundreds of towers. When the Brooklyn Dodgers' Ebbets Field came down in 1960, the wrecking ball that smashed it to bits—wielded by Volk's company—was showily painted white with red stitches to look like an enormous baseball.

In recent decades, the use of the wrecking ball has declined. For big buildings—stadiums, outmoded hotels—implosion is faster and more efficient. For smaller ones, a backhoe or similar tool is more controllable, allowing the building to be clawed and pried into bits rather than banged to pieces willy-nilly. Although it hasn't vanished from the demolition trade altogether, it is used today less as a physical tool than as a convenient metaphor, notably by Miley Cyrus, whose 2013 single "Wrecking Ball" was accompanied by a video of her riding one as it swung from a chain. A smash hit.

From

XEROGRAPHY

to

X-RATED FILM, GOLDEN AGE OF

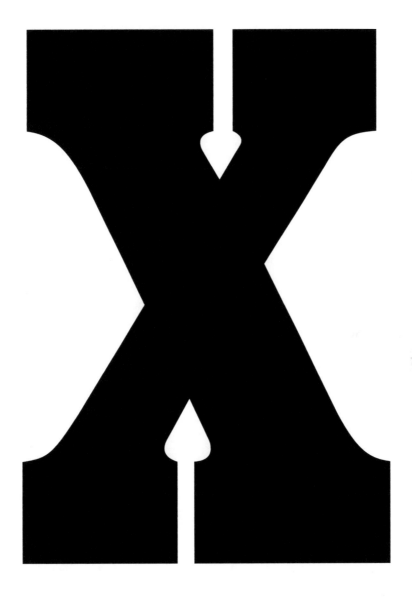

Xerography: A technology that sold
one machine after another after another.

Xerography[1]

Before the middle of the twentieth century, if you wanted to duplicate a document, you retyped it or rewrote it, perhaps with carbon paper if you needed a spare. There were techniques for making mass numbers of copies—mimeographs, Photostats, Ditto machines, and the like—but most of those required specialized equipment and involved wet chemistry. Often, the most straightforward way to record a document for posterity was simply to photograph it and print the pictures in a darkroom.

In the 1930s, Chester Carlson worked at Bell Laboratories (*see also* TRANSISTOR) as a patent clerk. He recognized that a simple copying technology would be world-changing, and, in a rented apartment at 32-05 37th Street in Astoria, Queens, he and a colleague set to solving the problem. Their system depended on a photoreceptor—broadly speaking, a light-sensitive material that would pick up and retain an electrical charge when light hit it. Since a document is variously light and dark, its reflection on the photoreceptor would be similarly varied. The static charge would in turn attract a powdered ink, which could then be affixed to a fresh sheet of paper. "Dry copying," this was called, since there were no trays of processing chemicals, no tanks of solvent. Carlson's biggest breakthrough came on October 22, 1938, and, knowing the patent game as he did, his first photocopy read "10.-22.-38 ASTORIA."

In 1946, a few years after his patent had been granted and Carlson had begun developing the process, his invention was picked up by a photographic-paper company in Rochester called Haloid. The first Haloid copier was announced ten years later to the day, on October 22, 1948, and the company began using a new word for it: *xerography*, from *xeros*, Greek for "dry," and *graphein*, for "writing." That early machine and its immediate descendants were slow and ungainly to use,

and their commercial success was modest; they remained specialty tools, like mimeographs. That changed in 1959, with the introduction of the Xerox 914 copier. It was the first that looked and ran like the copiers we know today—glass pane, facedown paper, seven copies a minute, regular paper jams. Every big office wanted one. Haloid changed its name to Xerox a short time thereafter and produced hundreds of thousands of Model 914 machines—duplicating the duplicator, if you will.

For fifty years thereafter, no modern office existed without thousands and then millions and billions of photocopies. And although a certain amount of that paper flow has abated—first with email, then with the widespread digital sharing of documents—the copier room still stands at the core of every office, and every laser printer does its work, again and again, using a highly refined version of Chester Carlson's technology.

X-Rated Film, Golden Age of

Pornography is invariably one of the first applications attempted with any media innovation, and indeed some of the first experimental films featured dancing women who—*gasp!*—showed their legs. As Hollywood's censorial Hays Code broke down through the 1950s and '60s, mainstream movies (like the culture at large) grew more explicit, showing slivers of nudity. (The MPAA's letter-grade system that rated films from G to X was established in 1968.) But blue movies stayed in the shadows, in dedicated theaters and back rooms, until 1969, when Andy Warhol released his *Blue Movie*, which contained explicit, unsimulated intercourse, as an art film (*see also* UNDERGROUND CINEMA). It was screened first at his Factory workspace on Union Square and then at the Elgin Theater in Chelsea, and it was almost certainly the first porno to be covered in the New York *Times*; Vincent Canby's review was mixed.

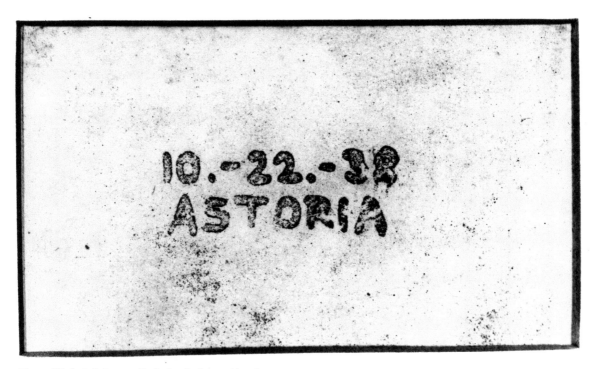

The world's first photocopy, displaying its date and location.

Within a year, the mainstreaming of non-artist-endorsed actual porn had ensued. Producer Bill Osco's *Mona* got a full-on national release, and films like *Behind the Green Door* and *The Devil in Miss Jones* followed. But above all, there was *Deep Throat*, starring Linda Lovelace and directed by Gerard Damiano. It had an absurd and, as we'd say today, extremely problematic plot (a young woman's clitoris is somehow located in her throat; she can reach orgasm only by performing vigorous oral sex on men), and it became not just a cultural talking point but an honest-to-God hit. People brought dates to it; people bragged about having seen and appreciated it; the Washington *Post*'s Howard Simons even applied its title, jokingly, to Bob Woodward's deep-background source in the Watergate case. When it premiered at the World Theater in New York in 1972, *Deep Throat* provoked a legal challenge (won, then overturned), which fed a complicated chain of similar cases in other jurisdictions. Ultimately, the U.S. Supreme Court ruled on one of those, *Miller* v. *California*, deciding that "community standards" were a major factor—that is, a film was pornographic rather than artistic if the local culture declared it to be.

Needless to say, New York's community standards were pretty broad, and over the next decade, porn theaters appeared across the city. (Many were old neighborhood movie houses that could no longer make it economically by showing regular films.) Their biggest concentration was around 42nd Street (*see also* TIMES SQUARE), where a lot of older movie theaters had already given over their screens to low-rent, violent grind-house films; now it was almost all sex.

In the 1980s, several forces convened to end porn's purportedly golden age (which was only a precursor to the triple-platinum age that followed once the internet arrived). One was, of course, the videocassette player. (Why go to a gross old theater full of gross old guys when you could watch a dirty movie from the comfort of your own bed?) The AIDS crisis, which threw a wet blanket on the culture of casual sex, didn't help either. And in New York, at least, it finally came down (as it so often does) to real estate: Rising rents in many neighborhoods, as well as the government-funded cleanup of Times Square, pushed the porn theaters and video-rental shops out in favor of squeaky-clean family entertainment and retail.

From

YELLOW JOURNALISM

to

YUPPIE

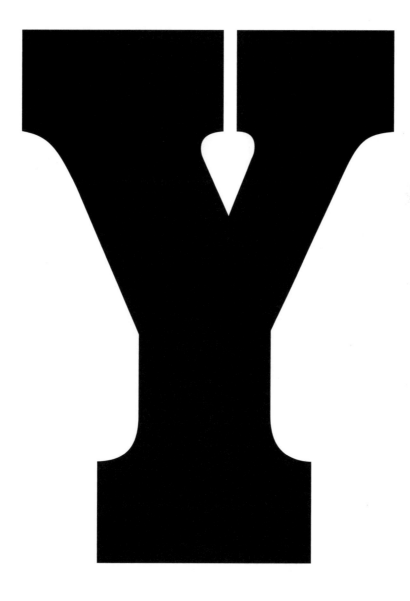

◀◧

*The Yuppie in his natural habitat
(note crocodile on shirt, insouciant pose).*
PHOTOGRAPH BY CHARLES H. TRAUB

Yellow Journalism

Joseph Pulitzer did an excellent job of reshaping his legacy when he endowed the highbrow awards given each year in his name. During his career as a publisher, he worked at a far less lofty level. In 1883, Pulitzer took over the New York *World* and immediately set out to build its business by any means necessary. There wasn't much photography in the paper yet—it was technologically almost impossible to turn a photo into a printing plate on deadline—but illustration was another matter and the *World* was soon filled with it. By 1893, it had become the biggest-circulation newspaper in New York City, and that May it introduced the industry's first Sunday comics section. Pulitzer soon hired a young cartoonist named Richard Outcault, and on January 13, 1895, he published a cartoon featuring a bald-headed, gap-toothed, slum-dwelling boy wearing a dresslike nightshirt. His was an image familiar to any tenement denizen; the dress was a hand-me-down, and the shaved head was the standard treatment for lice. Over the next couple of years, as the Sunday supplement went from black-and-white to blazing color, his tunic turned a brilliant gold, and he got a nickname: the Yellow Kid.

In these same years, Pulitzer's paper was locked in a circulation war with William Randolph Hearst's New York *Journal*. At one point, Hearst hired Pulitzer's entire editorial staff en masse. Pulitzer struck back by cutting his cover price in a bid for bargain-hunting readers. Hearst retaliated by scooping up Outcault and his Yellow Kid. And both papers—particularly the *Journal*—began making questionable quasi-journalistic moves, overselling trivial events with sensational headlines and sponsoring promotional stunts mainly to report them as news. After one such event, a cross-country bicycle trek paid for by Hearst and then covered by his papers, a writer at the New York *Press* named Ervin Wardman noted that the bicyclists wore yellow. He gave this practice of news-manufacturing a sneering name: "yellow journalism."

Despite the thinnest connection between the two, the yellow jerseys and the Yellow Kid melded in the popular imagination, and most histories today link the character with the term *yellow journalism*. (Wardman did once refer to "yellow kid journalism," suggesting that

Hearst's ad for the New York Journal *touting the Yellow Kid, 1897.*

MAURICE SCHWARTZ. director of the
YIDDISH ART THEATRE.. making up
for opening night...

The Yiddish Art Theatre's
Maurice Schwartz backstage on
opening night, October 1, 1945.
PHOTOGRAPH BY WEEGEE

he also associated the two.) That is most likely true because the circulation war—in which Outcault's cartoons figured prominently, at least at the beginning—continued for years thereafter. In 1898, Hearst's papers all but created the Spanish-American War out of thin air. (It's said Hearst told his illustrators, "You furnish the pictures, and I'll furnish the war"; a lightly altered version of that moment appears in *Citizen Kane*.) By then, the Yellow Kid's regular strip had been shelved, and the character was making cameo appearances in Outcault's other work. There he lingered well into the twentieth century, fading out for good around 1910. Pulitzer eventually wearied of the downscale turn and put the *World* back on sounder journalistic footing, where it stayed until it was merged out of existence in 1931. The term *yellow journalism*, however, outlasted it all. Today it gets thrown around constantly, used by political figures to describe genuinely sleazy stories (*see also* TABLOID) as well as anything they dislike seeing aired or written.

Yiddish Rialto

In the last quarter of the nineteenth century, hundreds of thousands of Jews from Eastern and Central Europe began to flow into America through Ellis Island. A large percentage of them settled on the Lower East Side, especially in the tenements east of the Bowery. (West of the Bowery was populated mostly by Italians, and a young man of either tribe crossed the street at his own risk.) They came from all over—Germany and Russia, the Baltics and the Balkans—and although their national languages differed, most had their spoken Yiddish in common. This community was simultaneously clinging for dear life to its familiar traditions and looking to assimilate, and in very short order, it began to create its own pop culture. On August 12, 1882, inside Turn Hall, at 66–68 East 4th Street, a small troupe performed an operetta called *The Witch* in Yiddish, and an Old World–New World hybrid genre was born: the American Yiddish theater.

Within the next couple of years, a small cluster of Yiddish-language venues opened around the corner on the Bowery. They specialized in melodramas and operettas in a wide variety of styles. Some shows were dramatizations of contemporary news events; others were heavily fictionalized biblical or historical tales. Many more were stories of everyday immigrant life: family, striving, betrayal, separated lovers, multigenerational strife. By and large, these productions were popular entertainments, broad and sentimental rather than cerebral, although there were Yiddish-language productions of Shakespeare and other highbrow fare. With more immigration came more theaters and more success, and in 1900 the Yiddish theaters of the Lower East Side sold 2 million tickets.

They had, to an extent, also moved (slightly) uptown. Around 1900, Second Avenue below 14th Street began to supplant the Bowery as the center of Yiddish entertainment. While uptown, first in the Union Square theater district known as the Rialto and later around Times Square, was home to John and Ethel Barrymore and George M. Cohan, downtown on the Yiddish Rialto, Boris Thomashevsky, Jacob Adler, and Molly Picon had their names in lights. The big theaters on Second Avenue were large and opulent, similar to their equivalents on Broadway (*see also* BROADWAY; MUSICAL THEATER; TIMES SQUARE), and large Jewish communities in the Bronx and Brooklyn eventually got their own venues to match. By the 1920s, the Yiddish theater was an immense business in New York, not nearly as big as its English-language sibling but in the same league.

The first great era of immigration ended with restrictive new laws in 1924, and—*mene, mene, tekel upharsin*—the writing was on the wall. Assimilation was, of course, the proximate cause of the genre's decline. The children and grandchildren of immigrants stopped speaking Yiddish, went to college, moved to the suburbs, and generally made their way into the mainstream. The Depression badly dinged all forms of live theater, as did radio, movies, and then television. And Gentile artists began to dip into the Yiddish-theater well, de-ethnicizing it for wide consumption. The song "Bei Mir Bist du Schön" became a huge radio hit—after the extremely goyish Andrews Sisters recorded it in English in 1937.

As the Yiddish-speaking world of Second Avenue faded, some performers took their acts to Jewish summer resorts in the Catskills. The Café Royal, the social center of the strip, closed in 1952. Picon, probably the biggest female star in the Yiddish theater, resettled on the radio

① **Yuppie Signifiers That Have Stood the Test of Time**

Chosen by New York *design editor* Wendy Goodman

➻ **Brooks Brothers pastel shirts and pants** "They are always there for the adult yupster."

➻ *Seinfeld* "It'll be in reruns until the earth blows up."

➻ **Designer jeans** "Gloria Vanderbilt jeans are still hot on eBay."

➻ **Dorrian's Red Hand** "Poor Jennifer Levin was at the bar there before the preppy psycho murdered her."

➻ **Top-Sider boat shoes** "A certain collegiate look of people who never grow out of their tribe. Worn sockless."

---

and in films and had a big hit with *Milk and Honey* on Broadway in 1961. And the definitive tribute to the Yiddish theater came along in 1964, when Jerry Bock, Sheldon Harnick, Joseph Stein, and Jerome Robbins joined forces to adapt a principal text of Yiddish-speaking America—the stories of Sholem Aleichem—into the Broadway musical *Fiddler on the Roof.* (Robbins himself had been a child performer in the Yiddish theater; the show's set designer, the great Boris Aronson, had started there as well.) *Fiddler*'s story of Anatevka was an elevated, somewhat more sophisticated rendering of the immigrant stories familiar to those audiences, and it spoke to the Americanized children of those Second Avenue theatergoers as few shows ever had.

Very little physical presence remains of the Yiddish Rialto. Probably the last of its major stars, Fyvush Finkel, had a late-in-life rebirth on the CBS drama *Picket Fences* and won an Emmy for it in 1994. The Yiddish Art Theatre's home, on the corner of East 12th Street, is a mainstream movie theater now. The great film director Sidney Lumet, who had been a child actor with the company, died in 2011. In the 1990s, Abe Lebewohl, proprietor of the Second Avenue Deli, embedded in the sidewalk at Second Avenue and Tenth Street a Yiddish Theater Walk of Fame, a Jewish echo of the one on Hollywood Boulevard, with Finkel and Picon in place of Jack Nicholson and Faye Dunaway. Beginning in the 1990s, a new generation of young advocates, attempting to keep the flickering flame of their grandparents' language alive, mounted small-scale stagings of some old Yiddish-theater productions, notably through a troupe called the National Yiddish Theatre Folksbiene. In 2018 the Folksbiene closed the assimilative loop with a staging of *Fiddler on the Roof*—translated into Yiddish.

Your Show of Shows *see* SKETCH COMEDY

Yuppie [1]

The baby-boom generation born after World War II, the first raised on a television diet, was generally far more aware of consumer culture and its sociological significance than its predecessors had been. Their parents might have been reliable Ford or Chevrolet buyers, but boomer kids would make much finer distinctions—between, say, a Chevy Camaro (not bad) and a Camaro SS (much cooler). Although many relatively affluent kids influenced by the 1960s counterculture flirted with anti-consumer attitudes, in young adulthood they too began to fall back into comfortable materialism. A frustration with the era's economic malaise contributed to the rise of a dominant neoconservatism, its first defining peak coming with Ronald Reagan's election in 1980. In New York City in particular, the Reagan-era recovery took place primarily in the finance industry, which tended to hire young, aggressive, educated people (including for the first time quite a few women), many of whom lived in Manhattan and drew solid junior-executive salaries. The other glamour industries—law, publishing, advertising—were similarly staffing up, in many cases giving employees solid expense accounts and even the occasional signing bonus. The upshot of all this was the accidental creation of a new archetype: the young urban professional, a.k.a. the yuppie.

The yuppie was not necessarily flat-out rich but lived well. (One subset of yuppiedom was the DINK, or "dual income, no kids," household. DINKs were notable for their high levels of disposable income.) The distinguishing characteristic of the type was bourgeois taste justified on the grounds of craftsmanship, worthiness, and authenticity. Buying a Mercedes-Benz was good materialism because it was sturdy and smooth on the road and might last for decades; buying a Cadillac, less so, because it was too plush and had fake wood grain and might break down. The same went for fancy European plumbing fixtures and non-iceberg salad greens, Nakamichi stereo equipment and Prince carbon-fiber tennis racquets, Lacoste polo shirts and Michael Graves for Alessi teakettles. Not to mention a name-brand college education.

Yuppies could be found among book editors, ad executives, academics, and lawyers—especially lawyers. Every city in America had them (Michael and Hope Steadman, the quintessential yuppie couple from television's *thirtysomething*, lived in the inner-ring suburbs of Philadelphia), but New York probably had more than any other because of its concentration of professional jobs.

Nobody liked to be called a yuppie; virtually no one accepted the label. And people hated yuppies. *Hated* them! Issues of class, issues of race, issues of privilege—yuppies by their mere presence evoked them all. A commonplace graffito in these years read DIE YUPPIE SCUM. You'd see it most often in neighborhoods like the East Village, which remained relatively inexpensive because it was too grungy for your average yuppie, a risky place to park a BMW. Yet even as the media reported on the yuppie phenomenon with cocked brow and jaundiced eye, they catered to yuppies, carrying Rolex ads and reviewing restaurants that used truffle oil, because that was where the spending lay. Jay McInerney and Bret Easton Ellis wrote novels disdaining yuppie culture and its signifiers, but both of them lived, and continue to live, a solid approximation of that life.

Needless to say: The yuppies won. New Yorkers live in Yuppietown now, a place where in quite a few neighborhoods, a Starbucks is easier to find than a hardware store. Even in the ostensibly anti-yuppie enclaves of artisanal enthusiasts (*see also* HIPSTER), much the same obsession with material culture and quality applies, albeit with different aesthetics and emphases. In fact, the yuppie has been superseded in the battle of privilege. Your typical mid-level book editor or ad copywriter or marketing associate can barely afford New York these days, and the competition for resources is between the solidly rich and the absolutely super-rich. To sustain a genuinely comfortable New York lifestyle today requires quite a bit more than two average professional incomes. You have to compete with hedge-funders to get a nice apartment, and you probably can't do that. The yuppie has been out-yupped.

From

ZIPLESS FUCK

to

ZONING

Zoning: It's why our city is shaped like this.
PHOTOGRAPH BY BERENICE ABBOTT

Zipless Fuck

"The zipless fuck was more than a fuck. It was a platonic ideal," Erica Jong wrote in 1973 in *Fear of Flying*, a sexual and spiritual bildungsroman that follows 29-year-old Isadora Wing as she flees her uptight psychiatrist husband at a conference in Vienna and travels across Europe with a bawdier, dirtier (in all senses of the word) shrink in an effort to answer Freud's question for herself: *What do women want?*

Jong wrote the novel in her grandfather's spacious apartment (which he'd eventually bequeath to her) on West 77th Street, opposite the American Museum of Natural History. The book's reviews alternated between raves (John Updike said it extends "the tradition of *Catcher in the Rye* and *Portnoy's Complaint*—that of the New York voice on the couch") and misogynist attacks (Paul Theroux called Isadora a "mammoth

Fear of Flying's *first edition: the original zipless fuck.*

pudenda"). But even the plaudits reeked with the casual sexism of the time, as shown in the persistent refrain, *Wow, who knew chicks were so into sex?*

In nearly five decades, *Fear of Flying* has sold more than 20 million copies worldwide and translated *zipless fuck* into languages from Japanese to Arabic to Croatian. So just what is it? It's the "purest thing there is," Jong writes in the book. "It is free of ulterior motives. There is no power game." Also, "for the true, ultimate zipless A-1 fuck," the two people involved must be near-strangers.

The zipless fuck became emblematic of the sexual revolution of the 1970s and the new freedom of women to pursue casual sex with hedonistic abandon. But Jong, now 78, says she offered it only as a fantasy, not to advocate for it. Indeed, the only zipless fuck detailed in *Fear of Flying* is one Isadora imagines (featuring a pretty Sicilian widow and the scruffily handsome soldier who sits down next to her on a train). Alas, Jong has said, she never had an orgasm sleeping with someone she didn't know. "Any zipless fuck I've ever had was a terrible disappointment. Which is why it's kind of funny that the zipless fuck is more famous than I am."

Zoning

When startled by the sudden appearance of a whole new neighborhood like Hudson Yards or another super-tall tower poking past the Empire State Building, New Yorkers routinely ask, "Who let them build that?" The answer often involves zoning.

Urbanites have long argued over how to use their scant acreage, but Manhattan has been turning such rulemaking into an art as far back as its New Amsterdam days. Peter Stuyvesant, the settlement's iron-fisted governor, issued what you might call the first zoning code in 1647, limiting the number of taverns, designating certain areas off-limits to pigs and goats, preventing property owners from letting their shacks and fences spill over onto public streets, and encouraging residents to live closer together for security reasons. (Most of his rules, though, had to do with drinking.)

By the end of the nineteenth century, crowding had rendered New York nigh unlivable. New technologies like steel and elevators permitted ever more massive structures (*see also* SKYLINE), factories spewed noxious pollution, and reformers complained about the scarcity of light and air. When the forty-story Equitable Building at 120 Broadway went up in 1913, eating up a whole block and looming over lower Manhattan's old, narrow streets, New Yorkers clamored for more regulation.

It was already on the way. Two well-connected reformers, the newspaperman George McAneny and the lawyer Edward Bassett, wrote the nation's first zoning resolution, a revolutionary document enacted in 1916, which shaped growth for decades and provided a model for cities everywhere. The law limited building heights in residential districts and required tall office buildings to step back as they rose, funneling sunlight to the sidewalk and creating the characteristic profile of the Art Deco skyscraper. Hugh Ferriss, the architect who rendered the future metropolis in a brooding style that made him the godfather of Batman's Gotham City, saw the law in epic terms. "Our future buildings, with their superimposed, receding stages, will produce as definite a sense of strength and unity as did the medieval cathedrals," he wrote, correctly.

But by the late 1950s, the rapidly expanding metropolis chafed under these dated regulations. A global financial center demanded modern towers with sheer glass cliffs instead of gradual setbacks. The 1961 update to the zoning resolution was a vastly more flexible and complex document than the one it modified. Instead of imposing maximum heights, it regulated the number of usable square feet each site could accommodate and left it to developers and architects to figure out how to distribute them. It traded extra height for open space and segmented the city into industrial, commercial, and residential areas. It also adapted the metropolitan geography to the era's dominant vehicle, the car, favoring highways and requiring most new buildings to include sizable amounts of parking.

Zoning regulations can get detailed and arcane, but they express the way each place and period sees the challenges of living in close proximity. In much of the country, that legalistic urban invention enshrined suburban sprawl, devoting each residential lot to a freestanding, single-family house. In New York, the code has continued to evolve into an ever more unwieldy, picayune rule book covering every block in three dimensions. Its very complexity sometimes defeats its purpose. When developers started building super-tall apartment buildings along 57th Street, monetizing aerial views of Central Park, many New Yorkers were surprised to discover that was legal. But the zoning code is as remarkable for what it *doesn't* govern as for its arcane prescriptions. It has little sway over the skyline, does nothing to protect legendary views (of the Chrysler Building, say), and doesn't limit the shadows cast on Central Park.

Ideally, planners use zoning to anticipate the next phase of urban development, but changing the code is a political process and inherently controversial. In 2016 the de Blasio administration pushed through a centerpiece of the mayor's agenda: Mandatory Inclusionary Housing, an amendment aimed at creating more affordable apartments. At the same time, the city overhauled the rules for East Midtown, allowing a whole new generation of gargantuan skyscrapers to spring up around Grand Central Terminal. One of the principal tools local government has to create new wealth is to upzone (that is, loosen the restrictions on) a desirable part of the city, because it multiplies the value of the land.

But zoning also protects the entrenched interests of New Yorkers who aren't interested in change. Despite Manhattan's verticality and extra-high density (and Brooklyn's newly spiky downtown), the other boroughs are mostly a low-rise expanse of stumpy buildings and single-family houses; the political cost of trying to change that is formidable. In fact, rezoning any single patch of New York is almost always a ferocious battle because the code isn't just a technocrat's tool: Zoning is an urban frontier, where battles over gentrification, equality, and justice are waged and the future of the city is defined.

Contributors

Laurie Abraham: *Zipless Fuck*
Josef Adalian: *Game Show*
Kevin Baker: *Baseball*
Katherine Barner: *Public Defender; Remote Control*
Rafe Bartholomew: *Hoops*
Josh Barro: *Credit Default Swap*
Brian Boucher: *Graffiti As Art; Megadealer*
Michael Bullock: *Electroclash; Voguing*
Jonathan Chait: *Neoconservatism*
Brock Colyar: *Consciousness-Raising*
Melissa Dahl: *Bystander Effect*
Justin Davidson: *Brownstone Rowhouse; Gentrification; Grid, Street; Landmarks Law; Microphone; Minimalist Music; Salsa; Skyline; Synthesizer; Traffic Code; United Nations; Zoning Law*
Bilge Ebiri: *Romantic Comedy; Underground Cinema*
Jesse David Fox: *Comedy Club*
Rhonda Garelick: *Jeans, Designer; Leotard As Fashion*
Mark Greif: *Hipster*
Mark Jacobson: *Folkie*
Craig Jenkins: *Break-Dancing; Hip-Hop; New Wave; Punk*
Sarah Jones: *Labor Laws*
Boris Kachka: *Blockbuster Museum Show*
Connor Kilpatrick: *Trotskyism*
Simone Kitchens: *Walk Sign*
Edward Kosner: *Newsweekly*
Priya Krishna: *Halal Cart*
Jane Larkworthy: *Makeover*
Amy Larocca: *Socialite*
Will Leitch: *Sports Talk Radio*
Eric Levitz: *Federalism; Unions, Labor*
Hugo Lindgren: *Hedge Fund*
Christian Lorentzen: *Feud,*

Literary; Free Verse; Little Magazine; Obscenity Trial, American Literary; Poetry, New York School of; Political Journal, American Conservative; Political Journal, American Liberal
Noreen Malone: *Period Underpants*
Tim Murphy: *ACT UP; Hare Krishna*
Rob Patronite and Robin Raisfeld: *"Brooklyn"*
Emilia Petrarca: *Puffer Jacket; Wrap Dress*
Claire Bond Potter: *Gay-Rights Movement*
Clint Rainey: *Club Sandwich; Flagel; Hot Dog; Wine List*
Max Read: *Digital Ad Exchange*
Frank Rich: *Anchorman*
Nikita Richardson: *Burlesque, American Style; Cronut; Eggs Benedict; Harlem Shake; Lap Dance; Lindy Hop; Pickleback; Pilates; Pizza; Spaghetti and Meatballs; Waldorf Salad*
Abraham Riesman: *Chabad Judaism; Comic Book; Fandom; Superhero*
Jerry Saltz: *Abstract Expressionism; Conceptual Art; Modern Art; Pop Art*
Matthew Schneier: *Seventh Avenue; Streetwear, Luxury*
Katy Schneider: *Ibogaine*
Amelia Schonbek: *Disco; Freak Show; Frozen Hot Chocolate; Gin Rummy; Long-Playing Record; Radio Broadcasting; Tin Pan Alley*
Helen Shaw: *Ballet; Broadway; Modern Dance; Musical Theater; Tap Dancing*
Chris Smith: *CompStat; Political Machine; Squeegee Men*

Genevieve Smith: *Skully*
Elizabeth Spiers: *News Blog*
Matt Stieb: *Bearer Bonds; Credit Report; Junk Bonds; Mortgage-Backed Securities; Quant; Robber Baron*
Nick Tabor: *Auteur Theory; Bebop; Christian Realism; Consensus Theory of History; Positive Thinking*
Rebecca Traister: *Birth-Control Clinic*
Kathryn VanArendonk: *Children's Television; Cooking Show; Late-Night Talk Show; Sitcom; Sketch Comedy; Television Commercial; Television Network*
James Walsh: *Barbicide; Getaway Car; Hall of Fame; National Rifle Association; Subway System*
Matt Zeitlin: *Federal Reserve System*

"121 Milestones in the Life of a City" timeline by Greg Young.

Sidebars and lists by Brock Colyar.

All other entries by Christopher Bonanos.

Image Credits

Original illustrations by Peter Arkle.

Introduction
p. vi, courtesy of Milton Glaser.

Timeline
p. x, Classic Image/Alamy Stock Photo (the *Halve Maen*); Lanmas/Alamy Stock Photo (Stuyvesant); Patrick Guenette/Alamy Stock Vector (Washington's house); Album/Alamy Stock Photo ("The Raven"); p. xi, North Wind Picture Archives/Alamy Stock Photo (King's College); Bettmann/Contributor (Arsdale); The Reading Room/Alamy Stock Photo (velocipedes); incamerastock/Alamy Stock Photo (Douglass); p. xii, Science History Images/Alamy Stock Photo (Brooklyn Bridge); Everett Collection, Inc./Alamy Stock Photo (the union label, Empire State Building); Glasshouse Images/Alamy Stock Photo (Chrysler Building); p. xiii, The History Collection/Alamy Stock Photo (Griffo); Matteo Omied/Alamy Stock Photo (car crash); George Karger/The LIFE Images Collection via Getty Images (Savoy Ballroom); p. xiv, Life on White/Alamy Stock Photo (alligator); Bettmann/Contributor/Getty Images (Roosevelt); Alan Welner/AP Images (Petit); p. xv, Science History Images/Alamy Stock Photo (Robinson); Richard Levine/Alamy Stock Photo (Fresh Kills Landfill); Rose Hartman/Getty Images (Jagger); Spencer Platt/Getty Images (mask).

Chapter A
p. xvi, © 1998 Kate Rothko Prizel & Christopher Rothko/Artists Rights Society (ARS), New York, The Solomon R. Guggenheim Foundation/Art Resource, NY; p. 2, © 2020 The Pollock-Krasner Foundation/Artists Rights Society (ARS), New York, The Metropolitan Museum of Art/Art Resource, NY (Pollock); © 2020 The Pollock-Krasner Foundation/Artists Rights Society (ARS), New York, Whitney Museum of American Art/Licensed by Scala/Art Resource, NY (Krasner); p. 3, © 2020 The Willem de

Kooning Foundation/Artists Rights Society (ARS), New York, Whitney Museum of American Art/Licensed by Scala/Art Resource, NY (de Kooning); © 2020 Barnett Newman Foundation/Artists Rights Society (ARS), New York, The Museum of Modern Art/ Licensed by SCALA/Art Resource, NY (Newman); L A Heusinkveld/Alamy Stock Photo (acrylic paint); p. 5, J. Scott Applewhite/AP; p. 7, courtesy of *The Village Voice*; p. 8, illustration by Gary Hallgren; p. 9, Giorgos Georgiou/NurPhoto via Getty Images; pp. 10–11, Associated Press; pp. 14–15, Berenice Abbott (1898–1991) for Federal Art Project, Museum of the City of New York, 43.131.2.45.

Chapter B
p. 16, Hulton Archive/Getty Images; p. 19, courtesy of Delmonico's; p. 21, Tom Schierlitz/Trunk Archive; p. 22, Wildlife Conservation Society, reproduced by permission of the WCS Archives; p. 25, Dennis Stock/Magnum Photos; pp. 26–27, Bruce Davidson/Magnum Photos; p. 29, Diomedia/Fine Art Images; p. 30, Tony Cenicola/The New York *Times*/Redux; pp. 34–35, Janette Beckman/Getty Images; p. 38, Ted Hardin; p. 41, Dick Richards.

Chapter C
p. 44, Hulton Archive/Getty Images; pp. 46–47, Stanley Kubrick for *Look* magazine, Museum of the City of New York, X2011.4.11834.1, used with permission of Museum of the City of New York and SK Film Archives; pp. 50–51, Bruce Davidson/Magnum Photos; p. 53, Anastasiia Skorobogatova/Alamy Stock Photo; p. 57, D. Hurst/Alamy Stock Photo (Christmas lights); p. 62, © 2020 Marina Abramovic, courtesy of Sean Kelly Gallery/(ARS), New York; p. 65, Allan Tannenbaum/Getty Images; pp. 66–67, National Museum of American History & Smithsonian Institution Archives; p. 68, Hugh Talman, National Museum of American History, Smithsonian; p. 70, Thomas Schauer/courtesy Dominique Ansel Bakery; p. 71, Granger.

Chapter D
p. 75, painting by James McMullan; p. 77, Hannah Whitaker; pp. 78–79, Bruce Davidson/Magnum Photos; p. 80, Ted Hardin.

Chapter E
p. 82, FPG/Getty Images; p. 85, Ruth Sondak/FPG/Getty Images; pp. 86–87, Holger Talinski/Redux Pictures; p. 89, Bettmann/Contributor/Getty Images; p. 90, National Museum of American History, Smithsonian Institution; p. 91, courtesy of Christopher Bonanos.

Chapter F
p. 92, Nathan Bajar/The New York *Times*/Redux; pp. 100–101, © Barry Feinstein Photography, Inc. All rights reserved; p. 102, Sarah Rogers/The Daily Beast; p. 103, Alfio Scisetti/Alamy Stock Photo; p. 104, John Van Decker/Alamy Stock Photo.

Chapter G
p. 106, Pari Dukovic/Trunk Archive; p. 109, courtesy Everett Collection; p. 110, Diana Davies/NYPL; p. 114, Charlene Bayerle/Shutterstock; p. 115, Mannie Garcia/AP Images (Obama image), courtesy of Shepard Fairey/obeygiant.com (poster); p. 121, Madlen/Shutterstock.

Chapter H
pp. 124–125, E. Westmacott/Alamy Stock Photo; p. 126, Herb Goro; p. 130, illustration by Chas B. Slackman; p. 139, Michael Flippo/Alamy Stock Photo.

Chapter I
p. 140, Jamie Chung/Trunk Archive; p. 142, Suwannee Suwanchwee/Alamy Stock Photo; p. 145, Edwin Levick/Getty Images; pp. 146–147, Pete McArthur/Alamy Stock Photo; p. 148, Juris Kraulis/Alamy Stock Photo.

Chapter J
p. 152, United Artists/Kobal/Shutterstock; pp. 154–155, Chan Yuen-man/South China *Morning Post* via Getty Images.

Chapter K
p. 158, Michel Friang/Alamy Stock Photo; p. 160, Foodcollection RF/Getty Images; p. 161, Print Collection, Miriam and Ira D. Wallach Collection of Art, Prints and Photographs, The New York Public Library.

Chapter L

p. 162, Gjon Mili/The LIFE Picture Collection; p. 165, Eddie Hausner/The New York *Times*/Redux; p. 167, Carl Fischer; pp. 168–169, Fairchild Archive/Penske Media/Shutterstock; pp. 172–173, photograph by Wayne Hollingworth © Chuck Close courtesy Pace Gallery; p. 174, illustration by Haruo Miyauchi; p. 175, Kaspri/Shutterstock.

Chapter M

p. 176, Charles Frattini/New York *Daily News* Archive via Getty Images; p. 179, © The Advertising Archives/Bridgeman Images; p. 182, Gabe Palmer/Alamy Stock Photo; p. 185, Alan Ward/Alamy Stock Photo; pp. 186–187, Christopher Sturman/Trunk Archive; p. 189, Jonathan Hordle/Shutterstock (Mr. Potato Head); painting by Harvey Dinnerstein (Mob, the); p. 192, © 2020 Succession H. Matisse/Artists Rights Society/Art Resource, NY (Matisse); Image copyright © The Metropolitan Museum of Art. Image source: Art Resource, NY (Chanler); Image copyright © The Metropolitan Museum of Art. Image source: Art Resource, NY (Ryder); p. 193, Image copyright © The Metropolitan Museum of Art. Image source: Art Resource, NY (Weir); Image copyright © The Metropolitan Museum of Art. Image source: Art Resource, NY (Young); p. 197, Keith Homan/Shutterstock; p. 198, Hank Walker/The LIFE Picture Collection via Getty Images.

Chapter N

p. 200, Martyn Goddard/Corbis via Getty Images; p. 202, GK Images/Alamy Stock Photo; p. 205, photograph by Rollie McKenna.

Chapter O

p. 216, photograph by Christopher Anderson/Magnum Photos.

Chapter P

p. 224, Oksana Mizina/Shutterstock; p. 227, I. C. Rapoport/Getty Images; p. 231, courtesy of Thomas Alberty; p. 232, © 2020 Estate of James Rosenquist / Licensed by VAGA at Artists Rights Society (ARS), NY. Used by permission. All rights reserved p. 237, Ike Edeani/The New York *Times*/Redux.

Chapter Q

p. 240, Craig Cutler/Trunk Archive.

Chapter R

p. 244, Columbia Pictures/Everett Collection; p. 246, Red Rocket Stock/Alamy Stock Photo; p. 251, Mary Evans/Grenville Collins Postcard Collection/DIOMEDIA; p. 252, Photo 12/Universal Images Group via Getty Images; p. 255, Jeffrey Coolidge/Getty Images.

Chapter S

p. 256, Thomas Hoepker/Magnum Photos; p. 259, Alex Cayley/Trunk Archive; p. 260, John Kaprielian/Getty Images; pp. 264–265, Ralph Morse/The LIFE Picture Collection; p. 268, Columbia TriStar Television/Everett Collection (*The Jeffersons*); Monty Brinton/CBS via Getty Images (*How I Met Your Mother*); Chris Haston/NBC/Everett Collection (*Will & Grace*); courtesy Everett Collection (*The Honeymooners*); Moviestore Collection Ltd./Alamy Stock Photo (*The Goldbergs*); Collection Christophel/NBC Universal/Alamy Stock Photo (*30 Rock*); p. 269, Walt Disney Television/ABC Photo Archives/Getty Images (*Taxi*); Getty Images (*Friends*); FPG/Archive Photos/Getty Images (*I Love Lucy*); Castle Rock Entertainment/Everett Collection (*Seinfeld*); HBO/courtesy: Everett Collection (*Sex and the City*); Bettmann/Contributor (*All in the Family*); p. 274, Richard Drew/AP Photo; p. 276, Ralph Morse/The LIFE Picture Collection; pp. 282–283, Bruce Davidson/Magnum Photos; p. 284, Carolyn Jenkins/Alamy Stock Photo.

Chapter T

pp. 286–287, Leonello Calvetti/Alamy Stock Photo; p. 289, Bill Stahl Jr./New York *Daily News* via Getty Images; p. 291, Division of Political and Military History, National Museum of American History, Smithsonian Institution; p. 293, Charles W. Cushman Collection: Indiana University Archives; p. 294, courtesy of Christopher Bonanos; p. 295, James Steidi/Alamy Stock Photo; pp. 296–297, Ted Russell/The LIFE Picture Collection; p. 300, Kristin Lee/Alamy Stock Photo; p. 303, illustration by Tim O'Brien; p. 305, Underwood &

Underwood/Getty Images; pp. 306–307, Museum of the City of New York/Byron Collection/Getty Images.

Chapter U

p. 308, Douglas Kirkland/Corbis via Getty Images; p. 313, Scott Gries/Getty Images.

Chapter V

p. 314, Buyenlarge/Contributor/Getty Images.

Chapter W

p. 320, © Estate Bernd & Hilla Becher, represented by Max Becher, courtesy of Die Photographische Sammlung/SK Stiftung Kultur—Bernd and Hilla Becher Archive, Cologne, 2019; p. 322, MSPhotographic/Shutterstock; p. 323, Bettmann/Getty Images; p. 324, Frankie Alduino; pp. 326–327, Burt Glinn/Magnum Photos.

Chapter X

p. 330, Getty Images; p. 333, courtesy of Xerox Corporation.

Chapter Y

pp. 336–337, Collection of the New-York Historical Society, USA/Bridgeman Images; p. 338, Weegee (Arthur Fellig)/International Center of Photography/Getty Images; p. 340, Brian Hagiwara.

Chapter Z

p. 342, Berenice Abbott (1898–1991) for Federal Art Project. Museum of the City of New York 51.16.11; p. 344, courtesy of Christopher Bonanos.

Puzzle Solution

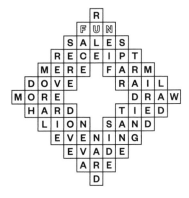

NEW YORK MAGAZINE

EDITOR-IN-CHIEF
David Haskell

WRITER-EDITOR
Christopher Bonanos

DESIGN DIRECTOR
Thomas Alberty

DESIGNERS
Aaron Garza, Hitomi Sato

PHOTOGRAPHY DIRECTOR
Jody Quon

PHOTOGRAPHY EDITORS
Graylen Gatewood, Kristen Geisler,
Ivan Guzman

CONSULTING EDITOR
Adam Moss

SENIOR EDITORS
Genevieve Smith, Camille Cauti

RESEARCH DIRECTOR
Katherine Barner

COPY MANAGER
Carl Rosen

RIGHTS MANAGERS
Elle Tilden, David Bressler

PREPRESS DIRECTOR
Kevin Kanach

IMAGING SPECIALISTS
Gary Hagen, Matt Kersh

SENIOR RIGHTS SPECIALIST
Lindley Sico

SPECIAL THANKS
Ann Clarke, David Kuhn, Pam Wasserstein,
Jim Bankoff, Edward Hart, Carl Swanson,
Brock Colyar

AVID READER PRESS

PUBLISHER
Jofie Ferrari-Adler

EDITOR
Julianna Haubner

MANAGING EDITOR
Amanda Mulholland

PRODUCTION MANAGER
Brigid Black

PRODUCTION EDITOR
Kayley Hoffman

ART DIRECTOR
Alison Forner